YOUNG LONGFELLOW

HENRY WADSWORTH LONGFELLOW, *aet.* 33
From the painting (1840) by C. G. Thompson in the Craigie House.

YOUNG

LONGFELLOW

(1807–1843)

BY

LAWRANCE THOMPSON

1969

OCTAGON BOOKS

New York

Reprinted 1969
by special arrangement with Lawrance Thompson

OCTAGON BOOKS
A Division of Farrar, Straus & Giroux, Inc.
19 Union Square West
New York, N. Y. 10003

Library of Congress Catalog Card Number: 78-76011

Printed in U.S.A. by
NOBLE OFFSET PRINTERS, INC.
NEW YORK 3, N. Y.

To
My Mother
and
My Father

TO THE READER

DURING THE SIX YEARS in which *Young Longfellow* has been written, I have received hearty assistance from many longsuffering friends. If I were to list all their names here, each would lose deserved significance. I have preferred telling each, individually, my strong sense of indebtedness and gratitude. As I thank them here again, collectively, I take pleasure in remembering that this book is built on the foundation of their warm and coöperative friendliness.

I must be content to mention briefly only the four cornerstones of this foundation. Professor Ralph Leslie Rusk of Columbia University first called my attention to unpublished material in the Craigie House, and when my cursory survey of that splendid collection caused me to return to him without open vision, he played Eli and sent me back again. Since that beginning, he has been of continual assistance with his scholarly suggestions.

One authority on Longfellow—Mr. Carroll Atwood Wilson—has worked so unselfishly with me that his name deserves to appear on the title page as that of my collaborator. He has made pleasant much of the hardest research by placing at my disposal not only his collection of Longfellow books and manuscripts but also his unexcelled bibliographical knowledge. Furthermore, his incisive criticism of my work and his painstaking assistance in correcting proof have saved me from many pitfalls and errors.

The Longfellow family, represented by Miss Anne Thorp and Dr. Henry Wadsworth Longfellow Dana, have given generous aid and advice which have been of peculiar value. They granted me the unrestricted privilege of examining manuscripts in the

Craigie House and have given me permission to quote, generally, from unpublished papers of Longfellow there and elsewhere. They have also permitted me to paraphrase several important passages which I am not allowed to quote directly.

The fourth cornerstone of this book-foundation is the patient encouragement and wise guidance of my mother and father. They know all that I leave unsaid.

For permission to use unpublished manuscripts in private collections and in public libraries, I am happy to express my gratitude to the following—to Mr. W. T. H. Howe, to Mr. Carroll Atwood Wilson, to the Boston Public Library, to the Bowdoin College Library, to the Henry E. Huntington Library, to the Massachusetts Historical Society Library, and to the Williams College Library.

For permission to reproduce as illustrations certain original paintings and manuscripts (the location of which is indicated in the list of illustrations) I am indebted to the Longfellow family.

Houghton Mifflin and Company have very generously given me permission to quote from the editions of the *Life* and the *Complete Writings* of Longfellow which are described in the introduction to the notes and have also allowed me to reproduce the picture of Frances Appleton which appeared in *New Light on Longfellow*, by James Taft Hatfield, Boston, Houghton Mifflin, 1933.

As for the mis-spellings and faulty punctuation, I have tried to preserve them faithfully—without apology except when the sense of a passage was obscured.

The reader will observe that I have constantly concerned myself with a strictly biographical study of Longfellow's development and that, because of my conviction that this fundamental reinterpretation was of initial importance, I have resisted the tempting bypath of literary criticism. Although I have written a

detailed study of each poem or prose work published by Longfellow from 1821 to 1843 and had originally intended to include
it in an appendix, I have reserved it for subsequent use in my
projected critical bibliography of Longfellow.

L<small>AWRANCE</small> T<small>HOMPSON</small>.

Princeton University

INTRODUCTION

THE WHITE LONGFELLOW with the flowing beard—patting little children on their heads as he moved slowly about the shaded walks of Cambridge—has symbolized the poet too long. During the last few decades, curious notions have grown up concerning the personality and accomplishment of this most popular figure in the panorama of New England's Golden Age. Perhaps these notions are rooted in our failure to know and understand the true character behind the familiar and misleading portrait of the elderly gentleman with the halo of snowy hair.

Ever since William Dean Howells tagged him with Björnson's mildly deprecatory words as "the White Mr. Longfellow," the phrase has taken on significance not intended. Accurate as this summary may have been for the later years, it was unfortunate because it ignored the colorful and impetuous personality of the poet in the vigor of his youth and early manhood. And too many of us have perpetuated this error by taking the part for the whole.

Before Howells came to Boston, Longfellow had become firmly established. To a comparative stranger, the poet gave the appearance of having passed triumphantly—and with little effort—over an easy road to fame. By the time Howells grew to know him well, Longfellow had already published his most popular poems. Serene and peaceful in his later years, the poet entertained his friends, old and new, with the gracious charm and lettered hospitality of a retired aristocrat. This dignity was beautifully becoming to one who ruled as a favorite in Boston literary circles— even if his colored wine glasses, fine coats, and many servants did bother Emerson, who called occasionally. But neither the comparatively ascetic philosopher from Concord nor the enviously ambitious young man from Ohio had known the poet during his years of struggle; had watched the Portland boy who, having set his heart on becoming famous as a poet, had been diverted and delayed by a curious variety of obstacles.

Were there, then, shaping hindrances in his development, severe trials, and difficulties? Surely. To be fully aware of them, we must look closely at the long road which stretched between the simple Congress Street home in Portland and the ornately furnished Brattle Street mansion in Cambridge, where he lived out his last years. In those latter days, his old friends who had helped him along the weary road had died—or had forgotten. And Longfellow, calm now and reticent, took pleasure in recalling only the happy associations of the past. It was better that way. As the best loved poet of his time, he knew how to conform very gracefully to the ideal of his admirers.

With the coming of new generations after Longfellow's death, the patterns of Victorianism were rejected before the impress of those patterns had time to wear off. Many are the discrepancies and misunderstandings which have caught us napping because we have been prone to accept Victorian records and estimates of public figures even after we have lost our understanding of the Victorian point of view. In the present instance, we tend still to accept the characterization Howells gave us, without bothering to challenge the validity of it—even though we don't like parts of it. Here is a curious Victorian hangover, compounded partly of intellectual astigmatism and laziness. For instance, the last full-length biography of Longfellow—*Victorian American* by Herbert Gorman—was written entirely from secondary sources which had been garbled, in almost every case, by the technique of Victorian biography. Quite naturally, Mr. Gorman's attempt to interpret the poet's character was at times as blind, biased, and unfair as was his tendency to make fun of Longfellow's poetry.

It is high time to make a reinterpretation of Longfellow in the light of original sources. It is high time to attempt to visualize him as his early friends saw him, in the formative, vigorous years. For I am convinced that the present inaccurate notions concerning him are caused very largely by a failure to appreciate the man as he really was, in his own time. The task has its pitfalls and its rewards. It is difficult for us to approach him in the spirit of his contemporaries while at the same time we make proper use of the valuable perspective which distance in time has given us. Yet there is satisfaction always in looking back over the past to see whence we came. Perhaps we may yet add a new chapter to the study of the American mind—the spirit and character of a national and cultural adolescence—as it is so well reflected in the spirit and character of Longfellow, poet of the people. There can be no doubt that his songs, stories, and felicitous translations found warm welcome in the hearts of a culture-hungry America, just when the people were beginning to reach out after the scarce-tasted fruits of hard-earned accomplishment and leisure. To understand Longfellow, then, is to appreciate the temper and intent of those countless thousands who heard him so eagerly. And therein grow the roots of our own heritage and tradition.

In returning to original sources, I have concentrated on the conflicting problems which confronted Longfellow as a young man, and have described their effect on his growth. I have set out with no pet theories to prove. Yet I have slowly come to believe that the essential traits in his character were moulded by the repeated inner struggle between his inherent Yankee opportunism and his dominantly romantic attitude toward life. In other words, his shrewd, calculating desire to get ahead as an independent man of letters was complicated by his reluctance to face the risks and dangers involved in striking out on such a course. It seems probable that his keen longing for the leisure of the unhampered scholar was prompted in part by his very distaste for the drudgery necessary to the achievement of success through any of the accepted professional channels open to a young man in the 1820's and 1830's.

Although he could, and did, work hard to secure recognition through scholarly work and teaching, his heart was never in those tasks for long. He was attracted not by the present but by the past—the past of poetry, chivalry, and romance. He longed to turn his face away from all the coarse reality of a work-a-day world. A mist of sentiment always prevented him from looking at the painful and the unpleasant—or if he looked, the outlines were blurred and softened until they were not what they seemed.

There is no simple answer to any problem of growth. Longfellow's development, if studied at another angle, may be found to have been hampered by the very materialism and earthy struggle for existence which surrounded and annoyed him. When he left college, the time was out of joint for one who wished to make writing a profession. He felt that strongly. In his youth, he and his elders believed that to justify existence one must serve one's fellow man in some obvious fashion. The idea was a Puritan keepsake—and a good one—handed down from generation to generation. In colonial New England, the ministry had offered the best chance to teach and preach. After the Revolution, the law had grown increasingly dignified and popular. But could one teach and preach if he were merely a poet? Longfellow's father, serving his State as a lawyer and as a representative in Congress, quietly decided that the ambitious boy should follow this good example. Writing could be kept for a pastime.

Dreading this dreary prospect, and seeking ways of escape from it, Longfellow impulsively welcomed the pleasant alternative of teaching modern languages at Bowdoin, and of going to Europe for two years of preparation. Would he enjoy the classroom routine? Sufficient unto the day. The strong romantic longings for distant story-book lands silvered the prospect of travel in Europe and blinded him from looking beyond.

Impetuously he had set out for Europe on a quest which enriched his entire life—and which diverted him farther than he dreamed from the realization of the coveted literary ideal. If he had returned to devote himself solely to writing, all might have been well. Instead, he came back to teach. The trouble started as soon as the shackles of academic routine began to chafe. Imprisoned and unhappy in a narrow-minded backwoods Maine college, after roaming through France, Spain, and Italy, he comforted himself by remembering those fair lands beyond the sea.

Slowly he lost faith in his destiny as a poet during the busy years of teaching at Bowdoin. Trying a substitute for a time, he sought eminence by writing quaint travel-essays and articles on European languages. To lead the gentle reader through picturesque byways of strange literatures, much as Irving had led the way through strange lands, was a part of his newly devised scheme. That was what the American reader wanted, he was sure: a picture of Europe as a store-house of antiquity, legend, and romance. Although he wrote very little original poetry from

1826 to 1838, the early college practice which had produced hundreds and hundreds of smooth lines enabled him to make graceful translations of poems which fitted well into his essays and sketches.

The ardent fire in him had burned first for eminence as an author, but it burned fiercest for eminence. And yet, the scholarly road proved too steep, arduous, and dull. Furthermore, the early longing persisted; the gleam, the poetic ideal, still led him back from his byway excursions, even though it flickered only vaguely at times through the confusion of his desires.

An important turning in the long road of experience came while he was in Heidelberg in 1836, preparing for a new position at Harvard. In Rotterdam, his young wife had died—and for a brief moment the blurred vision became clear. Then, impelled by stark grief and loneliness, he plunged into the literature of German romanticism, the diluted mysticism of Matthisson and Novalis, the high-soaring extravagances of Jean Paul. With intense persistence he drank his fill. He could not have come to these authors better prepared, for their spiritual affinity made them particularly satisfying. And Longfellow, slowly beginning to write poetry again, after this winter in Heidelberg, made the true beginning of his career as a poet, because he had learned to write from the heart.

At this time and also in the months immediately following, he found the accidents of life too much for him. Through them all, he kept groping vaguely toward a happiness beyond his reach. At times his search for inner peace (so closely linked with his yearning for literary success) was a wishful quest after some miraculous philosopher's stone which might accomplish what his own powers were too weak to achieve.

Another episode which profoundly stimulated his growth as man and author came while Longfellow was still dominated by the style and ideas of the German romantics. When his sorrow over the death of Mary Potter Longfellow was followed in less than three years by his utter desolation over Frances Appleton's refusal of his love, he turned back to Novalis and Jean Paul in search of comfort. His passion for the auburn-haired beauty of Beacon Street and his failure, during seven long years, to win her love, was a maturing experience which, coupled so closely to the tragedy of his wife's death, brought him from youth to manhood. This double sorrow drove him constantly in on himself; taught him more completely to look into his own heart for poetic inspiration. Thus, for a brief time, he wrote his "Psalms" which were so largely autobiographical. Projected against this personal background, even the smooth-worn "Psalm of Life" takes on new vitality.

The same subjective yearnings after a new creed are found echoing from page after page of *Hyperion,* for that book was fashioned out of the identical heartbreak which produced the "Psalms." In the light of previous biographies, the love story in *Hyperion* never seemed to touch either the author or the reader very deeply. Yet Longfellow's unpublished letters reveal the close relationship between that book and the self-torturing passion from which he tried to write himself free. During no other period in his life did he link personal experience so closely to his writings, or reveal himself more completely in his letters and journals. Drawn off his guard, temporarily, by his fondness for German *Sturm und Drang* writers, he indiscreetly dared to assume the rôle of a pale American Byron, bearing "the pageant of his bleeding heart" across Europe, in the pages of *Hyperion.* Not long after the book was published, he came to his Yankee senses—and never again did he step from behind his ingrained reticences.

Under the weight of the new sorrow and the old loss, his brave but simple action-philosophy demanded more courage and persistent will-power than he could muster—and finally he was forced to abandon it. To see Longfellow fumbling through the pages of Goethe and Jean Paul in search of ideas which might raise him from despondency is to recognize his need for liberation. The struggle to follow Goethe, then the surrender and return to the voices of twilight and the night—here indeed was a new kind of escape, a new twist to romanticism, and a human weakness which arouses our sympathy.

Finally, when the battle seemed completely lost, he gave up writing "Psalms." Few as these subjective lyrics were, however, his publication of them clarified once and for all his confused search for the true literary road. That these poems, most of them written out of a sheer desire for self-expression—a rare situation in his life—should prove so popular throughout the land was a surprising revelation to him. With the success of his first volume of original poems, *Voices of the Night*—43,000 copies were sold —his faith in himself grew strong. What was true for him, he found, was true for others. And his growing fame rested primarily on his ability to reflect so perfectly the romantic sentiment and popular moralizing which he shared with his contemporaries. Furthermore, he chose the best language and rhythms for saying what the people wanted most to hear. Even in his use of the now unfashionable lesson-tags, he was justifying himself in the traditional sense as one who served as teacher and preacher.

Nevertheless, new confidence did not bring satisfaction. In his own heart, he was still troubled by the wasted years and by the meagreness of his accomplishment, measured against his intention. No matter how much others praised, he could not shake off the feeling that he was constantly falling short of his goal. In Germany for the third time, he looked back over his literary journey with genuine discontent:

Mezzo Cammin

Boppard on the Rhine. August 25, 1842

Half of my life is gone, and I have let
    The years slip from me and have not fulfilled
    The aspiration of my youth, to build
    Some tower of song with lofty parapet.
Not indolence, nor pleasure, nor the fret
    Of restless passions that would not be stilled,
    But sorrow, and a care that almost killed,
    Kept me from what I may accomplish yet;
Though, half-way up the hill, I see the Past
    Lying beneath me with its sounds and sights,—
    A city in the twilight dim and vast,
With smoking roofs, soft bells, and gleaming lights,—
    And hear above me on the autumnal blast
    The cataract of Death far thundering from the
        heights.

This was his own summary of the struggle and the hindrances. Although the "sorrow, and a care that almost killed" may be interpreted liberally, they are not enough. They do not take into account the major hindrances: the lack of penetrating insight and the vague, romantic vision of the actual world in which he lived.

His unhappiness seemed to disappear when he finally married Frances Appleton in the summer of 1843, for she gave him a center to build his life around. Of primary importance was the richness of her nature, the spiritual depth and the mental stimulus she brought him. He had been right when he had written Greene that her love was as important to him as the air he breathed.

Then, too, although his love for Frances Appleton was far too intense to leave room for material considerations, her wealth and social position subsequently played an important part in removing many of the early difficulties. At the time of the marriage, her annual income was several times the size of the Smith Professor's salary. In addition, the prosperous Nathan Appleton gave his daughter full title to the spacious Craigie House and grounds in Cambridge. Thus the stage was set for Longfellow's later development as a poet and a gentleman of leisure, living in aristocratic semi-seclusion, protected from the unpleasant side of life.

No wonder, then, that a new life began for Longfellow in 1843, for that year brought to an end those vague longings so inextricably a part of youth. He had already won a liberal share of that recognition, esteem, and popularity which grew to such unbounded size both in America and in England before the end of his life. There still remained the millstone: the weekly routine at Harvard. Eleven years later he was to break entirely free, to achieve complete fulfilment of the orginal ideal. But the Portland boy had come a long way. The goal was in sight—the peaceful years when he would give new richness to a growing literature with his *Evangeline, Hiawatha, Courtship of Miles Standish, Tales of a Wayside Inn,* and the later, splendid sonnets.

Such a delineation, based on the essentials of original sources, gives added vitality to Longfellow. In the past, however, he has been concealed not only by the beard but also by another relic of Victorianism: the official, three-volume biography, written by the poet's brother and published in 1886–87. Samuel

Longfellow could have revealed the nature and extent of these early trials, if he had wished. But being a member of the family, he quite naturally preferred to leave the later picture of serenity and peace intact, so far as that was possible. His account of Longfellow's growth was a pretty, idyllic story which counted only the sunny hours. The turbulent days of storm and stress were neatly minimized or glossed over. Such a policy demanded much editorial manipulation of passages quoted from the original letters and journals. When the most convenient process of deletion was not entirely satisfactory, Samuel Longfellow was not averse to emendation.

Because I have no desire to write a controversial book, I have not once mentioned the name of Samuel Longfellow in the text of *Young Longfellow*. But the official *Life* has stood alone for over fifty years as the most important source of biographical information concerning Longfellow. From it the general reader, the student, and the literary historian alike have been too prone to construct their view of the poet's character. And this *Life* gives an inaccurate, distorted picture which can no longer be used as a fair basis for interpretation.

Samuel Longfellow's motives for omissions and modifications are obviously unimportant. The result is, however, unintentionally vicious. For when passages are left out which would have revealed ambitions, prejudices, desires, projects, and influences, the remaining context which is quoted is frequently invalidated. For this reason, the poet as he is revealed in his own words in the *Life* is at times hidden behind a hedge of details concerning daily activities. One may finish the book without getting past the hedge to the man himself. To be blunt, the total effect is a misleading, emasculated, late-Victorian version of the truth; a scissor-silhouette, without color.

What did Samuel Longfellow conceal which was so necessary to our understanding? Specific answers will become apparent after a thorough reading of my notes. I should like, however, to give certain general indications here. First, he concealed almost all the details of struggle and conflict. These details are essential if we are to explain Longfellow's many excursions down side roads of literary activity during the very years when he should have been turning out his best poetic work. Samuel Longfellow seemed to think that nothing in his brother's life was important unless it produced obvious results; none of his aspirations needed to be considered unless they were finally consummated. In another sense, he seemed to think that whatever was, was for the best; therefore there would be no value in printing any accounts of unpleasant trials and disappointments.

Furthermore, Samuel Longfellow could not bring himself to mention certain perfectly innocent details of his brother's private life—even though these had direct bearing on his literary work. He refrained from giving more than a superficial account of the poet's courtship of, and marriage to, Mary Potter, the porcelain-frail girl who died when she was but twenty-three years old. Even more important, he carefully avoided presenting even the slightest basis for our understanding of the most crucial years in Longfellow's life—the years when he was so nearly distracted by his seemingly hopeless love for the vibrant and fascinating Frances Appleton. Curious that the biographer should have ignored this gloomy courtship, when the one most intimately involved had been bold enough to write a book about it!

These concealments were often made clumsily. For instance, Longfellow frequently wrote about his protracted broodings over Frances Appleton in his journals and letters. And Samuel Longfellow, consistently removing these references, occasionally left clues as to the kind of material omitted. One is expecting something more than an offhand reference to college routine, after reading such a sentence as this, in the *Life* (I, 300): "And now open your heart and hold it open by the four corners while I pour into it 'all thoughts, all passions, all delights' which fill my own. . ." Because the romantic story had to be chopped out, the editor made the necessary operation and then continued directly with this sentence: "I labor and work right on with what heart and courage I may."

Since the *Life* contains many inconsistent sequences of this sort, one is surprised that it has stood without serious challenge—and has even been praised—for more than fifty years. Charles Eliot Norton commended it highly, not long after it was published. Since then, many authors have accepted it in good faith and have compiled articles, even books, from it without bothering to verify the printed quotations against the original letters and journals. Only recently one scholar, carried away, apparently, by an excessive feeling of gratitude, referred to it as "one of the best of biographies" and as an "admirable work, characterized by objectivity, fulness, accuracy, and urbanity."

We need not explore the matter further here. I do not mean to imply that Samuel Longfellow's method was new. Such conduct on the part of a Victorian biographer was not considered too improper, for those were the days before the picayune methods of scientific scholarship had taught us to endow with sacredness every mis-spelled word and misplaced comma. Sophia Hawthorne had taken well-intended liberties with her husband's journals, as Dr. Randall Stewart has painstakingly pointed out. And long before her, Jared Sparks had set the style in his editing of the Washington letters. True, Sparks had been criticized severely, but had defended himself in a way which seemed to please later nineteenth-century editors—even though it failed to satisfy Lord Mahon. Obviously, such editorial zeal was always calculated to help and improve, not to injure. In the present instance, however, it accidentally stripped the poet's early life of too much color and vigor. Longfellow's original letters and journals, as they are quoted from the originals in the following pages, give an entirely different impression.

We shall never be able to get at the entire personality of Longfellow until his most important letters and journals are printed in full from the originals. Restrictions of purpose and space have hindered me from making more than a start in *Young Longfellow*. I hope, however, to have a share in the larger undertaking, because I am convinced that such a thorough treatment is deserved, in the light of Longfellow's literary reputation and significance.

CONTENTS

ILLUSTRATIONS

YOUNG LONGFELLOW

I

FROM THESE ROOTS

I remember the black wharves and the slips,
  And the sea-tides tossing free;
And Spanish sailors with bearded lips,
And the beauty and mystery of the ships,
  And the magic of the sea.
    And the voice of that wayward song
    Is singing and saying still:
  "A boy's will is the wind's will,
And the thoughts of youth are long, long thoughts." [1]

ALTHOUGH Captain Samuel Stephenson was a young man in
1806, he was already respected as one of the leading merchants
in Portland. From the windows of his white wooden house on
Fore Street he could look down across his bright green lawn to
the great harbor; could watch his own proud schooners getting
under way across the dark green waters of Casco Bay, as sailors
in the riggings shook out clean new sails. Or he could train his
sea-glass on distant ships putting into port, weather-beaten and
tired after long voyages to and from the West Indies and more
distant foreign ports. If he opened his door he could hear the
lusty bellowings of teamsters and stevedores at work on the
wharves below, busy with continual loading and unloading.
Heavy drays shuttled between the ships and the town from
morning to night. And nowhere along that bustling Portland
water front was there greater activity than at the Stephenson
docks.

The Captain's ancestors had grown up with the town of Falmouth, as it had been called in colonial times, and had shared
its vicissitudes. The notorious visit of the British in 1775, the
spiteful retaliations of Mowatt, the bombardment of Falmouth
Neck, and the burning of four hundred houses—these were also
a part of the Stephenson tradition, for the flames had consumed
their home and wharf. Undismayed, old Captain John Stephenson (grandfather of our young Captain Samuel) had rebuilt the
wharf and had continued as a successful merchant during the

Revolution. But he had not rebuilt the house on Fore Street. His nearest neighbor, the schoolmaster Longfellow, had also lost his house in the conflagration. Sea captain and schoolmaster had agreed that there was no sense in raising another home within gunshot of British ships—and had moved their families off the peninsula to the little village of Gorham, a few miles inland.

Schoolmaster Longfellow's son, who grew up to be a judge in the Portland Court of Common Pleas, drove back and forth daily from Gorham in his square-topped chaise for many, many years. When Jefferson's nonintercourse acts stirred bitter resentment among the Federalist citizens in Portland and caused talk of another war with England, Judge Longfellow, now grown old, could look back with approbation at his father's cautious decision to move away from the harbor. Apparently the Stephenson family was willing to risk having a second house burned over its head, for young Samuel Stephenson had recently moved into a sturdy, square house on Fore Street—and had audaciously taken with him from Gorham one of Judge Longfellow's own daughters as his wife. The merchant profession was remunerative and respectable, but precarious. The old Judge had preferred sending his son to Harvard, in the hope that he might achieve a higher distinction than that which came to most Portland boys, educated before the mast. This son, named Stephen, had been graduated from Harvard in the class of 1798 with such promising young men as William Ellery Channing (already a successful pastor of the Federal Street Church in Boston) and Joseph Story, soon to be appointed to the Supreme Court. Young Stephen Longfellow had pleased his father by studying law with Salmon Chase in Portland and, in 1801, opening his own office there—while young Stephenson was learning to take over the family shipping business on Fore Street, and gradually remembering to respond to the still unfamiliar salutation of "Captain."

These two brothers-in-law, one certain to become a prosperous merchant, the other just beginning to practice law, represented the two types of leaders who dominated civic affairs in the growing town of Portland at the beginning of the nineteenth century. To the merchants and the professional men was entrusted the duty of guiding both the commercial and the cultural growth of the town. And each of these young men had strengthened his position as a leading citizen by fortunate marriage. Stephen Longfellow had succeeded in winning one of the most desirable girls in Portland, when he had married the daughter of General Peleg Wadsworth, distinguished citizen and hero of the Revolution. Zilpah Wadsworth, tall and attractive, with dark hair and lively blue eyes, was a favorite in the social circles of the town. Some Portland gossips whispered that she was not nearly so beautiful as her younger sister Betsy, to whom Stephen was said to have been betrothed at the time of her death. But Zilpah's firmness of character blended with her genuine love of social diversion, music, and dancing, to make her extremely popular with all. Quite appropriately, this daughter of the General had been chosen, when twenty-one years old, to present the colors to the Federal Volunteers, the first uniformed military company in the District of Maine. This honor had come to her in 1799. Five years later, Zilpah Wadsworth had been married to Stephen Longfellow, with no little ceremony, in the parlor of the large brick Wadsworth house on Back, or Congress, Street.

For a year the young couple lived with the General and his family. Here their first child was born and, in pursuance of a Longfellow tradition, was named Stephen. A few months later, Zilpah and her husband moved to a home of their own on the corner of Congress and Temple Streets. And here Captain Stephenson called, one fall day in 1806, to invite the Longfellows to spend the coming winter with the Captain's wife on Fore Street. Young Stephenson, troubled by business difficulties arising from the detested nonintercourse acts, was obliged to make a voyage to the West Indies. He was unwilling to leave his wife alone. Would the Longfellows keep her company? The invitation was particularly welcome to Zilpah, soon to be confined again. With little trouble she closed the house on Temple Street and went to live with her sister-in-law. Thus, away from home, Zilpah gave birth to her second son, on February 27, 1807. In memory of her younger brother, who had died heroically on the fireship *Intrepid*, before Tripoli, three years earlier, she named the boy Henry Wadsworth.

When Captain Stephenson returned to Portland in the spring, the Longfellow family moved back to their Temple Street home. Again their stay there was brief. In the fall of 1807, General Wadsworth turned over to Stephen and Zilpah the entire Wadsworth mansion on Congress Street at the head of Middle, or Federal, Street. The General's surrender of this house was one step in a carefully prepared plan. He was working out a dream of years. Shortly after the Revolution he had purchased from the State of Massachusetts nearly ten thousand acres of wild land near the boundary of New Hampshire and Maine. With the help of his two unmarried sons he had cleared a large part of the territory for farm land. Later he had built a great frame house on an eminence overlooking his domain in the Saco River valley. And finally, in 1807, this sixty-year-old hero of many skirmishes, battles, and prison escapes revealed fresh joy in adventure by moving to his wilderness home with his wife and two sons.

General Wadsworth's adventure in opening up this new and undeveloped region was a tiny symbol of the vast pioneering movement already well begun in the fertile valleys beyond the Appalachian Mountains. No longer did the great opportunity centre only in the farm lands along the Atlantic seaboard, and in vessels such as those which Captain Stephenson kept sending out. Even while the ineffective Orders and Decrees of King George III and Emperor Napoleon, at war with each other, had increased the risks and profits of maritime shipping out of Portland, Boston, New York, and Baltimore, a new enterprise had begun to loom temptingly behind the flourishing seacoast states.

Backwoodsmen, fur traders, and adventurers had proved that the Atlantic ports were not the only outlet for produce. The rich bottom lands of the Ohio River and its northern tributaries were already settled with thousands of families who were raising increasingly large crops of corn and tobacco, and shipping them down the Ohio to the Mississippi, out on the great river and down, over hundreds of miles to New Orleans. In Tennessee and Kentucky, the old buffalo paths and Indian trails had been beaten into ever widening pack roads by the steady trek of farmers, lured with this prospect of easy fortunes.

But this was just the beginning. New England Federalists

shook their heads and were frightened (and even Jefferson himself was embarrassed) when Robert Livingston bought from Napoleon all of the Louisiana Territory, which seemed so extensive that it might one day develop into another nation large enough to dwarf the original thirteen states. Yet such land for farming! Limitless acres of fertile soil and virgin forest, stretching north from New Orleans up the Mississippi valley nearly two thousand miles, to the head waters of the Missouri—and from St. Louis west almost a thousand miles to the Rocky Mountains.

Only recently fresh news had come, that two clever fellows, Lewis and Clarke, had added amazing chapters to the story of what lay in the West—even beyond the Rockies. It was a glorious day to be alive, when one could march out and seize this land of boundless promise. Success and riches were there for the mere taking. Federalist though he was, old General Wadsworth would have liked having a hand in opening up a part of that new country. But his roots were sunk too deep in New England. And why not, when there were limitless acres of wilderness still to be subdued, near the Great Falls of the Saco, in the province of Maine?

The inhabitants of Portland were sorry to see him go. Some could remember just how he had looked when he had come to Portland as a war hero, to open a general store. They could recall the excitement caused by the news that he was building a large brick house—the first brick house in Falmouth. To express their pride in such a notable, they had elected him to serve as their senator in the Massachusetts General Court—and later, to represent the Cumberland District in the Federal Congress at Philadelphia. He might have remained a congressman to the end of his life if he had not refused further nomination, in order to have freedom for farm work.

In Portland he had always made a picturesque appearance, for he defied the changes of custom, along with old Judge Longfellow. Year after year, the General strode the streets of the town in the garments of an outmoded era: a three-cornered hat over his clubbed and powdered wig, knee breeches, long waistcoat, and lace kerchief at his throat. Although he tried not to reveal his annoyance in public, Peleg Wadsworth did not conceal from his family an added cause for his longing to escape into the wilderness. The boys of Portland were developing a habit of following him down the street—at a respectably safe distance from his cane —with shouts and laughter at his odd appearance. His frontier home would permit him greater freedom to wear to the last his favorite garb and to conduct himself as a country squire who ruled the region about his estate with all the dignity befitting a landed aristocrat.

Stephen Longfellow soon found that the front room of the Wadsworth house in Portland was advantageously situated for a law office. The thick walls of brick, the shuttered windows, and the broad pitched roof still preserved the appearance of solidity and permanence which had given prestige to the mansion many years earlier. Stephen had never known such tasteful luxury, for he was descended from generations of public servants who had learned only recently to make a living with the head instead of the hands. His great-grandfather, for instance, had earned his bread by hammering out horseshoes, to the end of his days, in his black-smith shop. On the other hand, Stephen's father-in-law, the General, had won prominence in Portland without abandoning sweaty labor; had gone from storekeeping to Congress, from Congress to farming. Portland customs were still influenced by the frontier. Accomplishment, and not clothes, determined the value of a man.

But the Maine frontier had already acquired the refinement of a genuine, simple culture, such as that symbolized by the Wadsworth house. The best families sent sons to Harvard and stocked library shelves with sound literature—the works of Pope, the essays of Addison, and the speeches of Burke. The devout members of the First Parish Church, encouraging good learning and high moral purpose, were kept in frequent touch with Boston and Cambridge by their ministers of God, who had received training at Harvard. In nearly one hundred years, but two men had been needed to fill the position of pastor. Parson Thomas Smith, a witty, learned man, had preached there from 1727 to 1790. His assistant, Rev. Samuel Deane, who had come from Boston in 1764, was still continuing the work alone when Stephen Long-fellow's second son was born. These faithful shepherds, devoted to principles that reached beyond the confining tenets of their religious belief, had helped transform into a cultured and enter-

GENERAL PELEG WADSWORTH'S HOUSE

*From a sketch of the house and store which Longfellow's grandfather built on
the outskirt of Falmouth after the Revolution.*

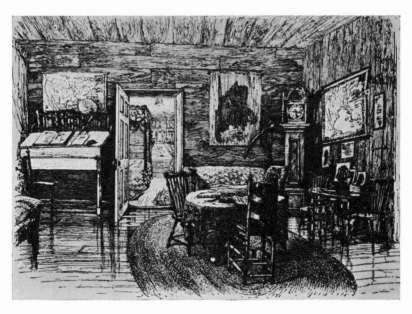

DRILL ROOM IN THE WADSWORTH HOUSE AT HIRAM

From an old drawing.

prising seaport the colonial fishing village of a few dozen families
—whom Parson Smith had described, on his arrival, as very poor
people including "some that were soldiers, who had found wives
in the place, and were mean animals." [2]

The very isolation of the community had been advantageous in
the early days. In Parson Smith's time, each annual town meeting
passed votes to exclude certain undesirable residents and approved
new citizens only on payment of ten pounds as proof of industrious purpose. Thus the town had expanded under the watchful
vision of the merchants who built their fine houses along the shore
on Front Street and the professional men who planted orchards
and flower gardens behind their Georgian mansions along the
high land of Congress Street. Quite naturally the gentry were
Federalists all, who looked with no little suspicion on the Jeffer-
sonian doctrines of democracy, while they clung hopelessly to a
narrow dogma intending to keep government in the hands of the
rich, the well born, and the able.

Perhaps the most impressive of all Portland residences was the
elegant home of the late Commodore Edward Preble, who had
given the United States Navy new standing in the world by dis-
posing of the Tripolitan pirates, only two years earlier. He had
been called into service before the house was completed; and had
returned to die before he could move into the new dwelling, now
occupied by his widow and young son. Yet the size of the Preble
house did not detract from the charm and dignity of the Wadsworth house next door, with its exceptional view of Portland and
the environs. The front door of Stephen Longfellow's new home
opened into a wainscoted hall, from which a broad stairway led
in easy progression to the upper floor. There one might look
out of the small-paned windows, across the roofs of low houses,
to the full sweep of Casco Bay, stretching from the ledges of Cape
Elizabeth on the south, around many clusters of green islands,
northward and eastward to the mainland. From windows in the
rear of the house, there was an unobstructed view over fruit orchards and fields, down the slope to Back Cove, less than a mile
away, and across the Cove to a distant panorama of foothills
stretching west to the often snow-capped summit of Mount
Washington.

But legal prestige was to be established neither on scenic advantages nor because Peleg Wadsworth had built in a region which attracted the Portland gentry. More important to the practical Stephen Longfellow was his knowledge that the business centre of the town was pushing up the hill of Middle, or Federal, Street toward the ridge which had been on the outskirts when Peleg had built his store there. The open space formed by the junction of Congress and Federal streets was losing its rural aspect and becoming a trading centre known as Market Square. Near the covered hay scales, a market house had been erected recently. And the small row of wooden shops kept growing steadily up both sides of Federal Street toward the Square. In the General's time, his house and store had faced Casco Bay across open fields. Stephen saw the nearest field transformed into a wood market. Enterprising teamsters brought loads of cordwood there from the country, tied their horses to convenient trees, and swapped endless stories with loud guffaws while waiting for the surveyors. In winter, bright red pungs loaded with butter and cheese, from remote farms in Vermont or New Hampshire, passed in front of the house and on down Federal Street to the wharves. Steaming horses dragged heavier loads of lumber, hoop poles, and shooks from the inland towns of Fryeburg and Baldwin to the docks on Fore Street.

With the revival of commerce after the War of 1812 and the renewal of trade with the West Indies, there was constant activity on Long Wharf and Portland Pier, with bearded Spanish sailors in water-front taverns, negro stevedores hoisting cargoes of molasses out of the ship holds to the decks, carts again rumbling over cobblestone streets, teamsters shouting, screaming, swearing. The town had lost the peaceful atmosphere which Stephen's grandfather had found when he came as a schoolmaster to live in Parson Smith's home. And Peleg Wadsworth could have discovered few of those rural attractions which had led him to set up a general store on the edge of the town. The schoolmaster had lived out his last days in Gorham. The General remained in Portland long enough to help the town come of age, to see his daughter Zilpah happily married, and to express a grandfather's delight over her two boys. Then he also turned his back on Portland. He was fond of his grandsons, but they must come to him, in Hiram.

II

A BOY'S WILL

*Out of my childhood rises in my memory the recollection of
many things rather as poetic impressions than as prosaic facts. Such
are the damp mornings of early spring, with the loud crowing of
cocks and the cooing of pigeons on roofs of barns. Very distinct
in connection with these are the indefinite longings incident to
childhood; feelings of wonder and loneliness which I could not
interpret and scarcely then took cognizance of. But they have
remained in my mind.*[1]

ZILPAH WADSWORTH LONGFELLOW surprised her father. She had
in her the same fortitude that had made the old General's life adventuresome. In the fall of 1807, when Henry was little more
than six months old, she wrapped her two babies warmly, tucked
them into the carryall, and drove with her husband over the forty
miles of rutted roads to the new Wadsworth home in the foothills
of the White Mountains. The great wooden house which Peleg
Wadsworth had built in Hiram was an amazing structure for any
traveler to discover in this section of the almost uninhabited woods
of Maine. With characteristic foresight, he had anticipated possible trouble with the Indians and, in expectation of a sufficient
number of neighbors to form a company of militia, had built the
central room on the first floor as a drill room, where they might
train on winter days, when drifting snow made outdoor practice
impossible. Some rooms had been made with carefully plastered
walls. But the drill room, high-posted to allow for long flintlocks
and fixed bayonets, was finished plainly, with wide, unpainted
pine boards on four walls and ceiling. Neighbors did congregate
there for drill, in later years. And as the General shouted his
orders, the little band of men tramped around and around the
boxlike room with serious mien and shouldered arms. But the
French and Indians were no longer a menace. They never came
to disturb the peaceful monotony of plowing and harvesting carried on by the Wadsworth men behind the ungainly plodding of
Peleg's oxen.

9

In such an atmosphere of frontier life, Henry Wadsworth Longfellow spent the summers of his childhood. Zilpah grew fond of taking frequent flights to the mountains, as she called these escapes from the tedious routine of household duties in Portland. And within a few summers her son grew to be a lively youngster, with chestnut hair and blue eyes, who liked nothing better than to follow his grandfather about the farm or help him bring in the cows at night. In many of his actions the boy seemed to have inherited old Peleg's ways, for he was adventuresome, impetuous, eager, affectionate, and cheerful. Zilpah knew that they were not characteristics of the Longfellow family, for her husband had been taught a shrewd caution, a calculating hardheadedness. She might have some difficulty in teaching Henry to understand his father.

Summers spent at Hiram were soon interrupted by early returns to Portland, for Henry was only three years old when he began learning his letters with his brother at Ma'am Fellows' small brick schoolhouse on Spring Street. The best families sent their children to private schools and thus abandoned the public schools to the rowdy and less favored urchins. But when Henry was five years old he was subjected to the harsher seasonings of such a town school on Love Lane, conveniently near his home. Unfitted by gentle home training, and by his tender age, for combating the inevitable cruelties of his boisterous schoolmates, he found the experience so unpleasant that he soon returned to the refinement of a private school.

In spite of this indication of suffering from over-protection, there was nothing soft about either of the Longfellow boys. They learned to mingle easily and naturally with their playmates, to join in their games and take sides in their quarrels. They could grow excited anew, whenever their grandfather, the old General, fed their imagination with tales of his military exploits. Rumors of another war with England in 1812 were enough to arouse Henry to action. At that time, his Aunt Lucia described the boys' interest, in a letter:

"A prophet tells us that a part of this country is to be laid waste by a hurricane the tenth of this month. Another says that two thirds of the world will be destroyed on the fourth of July. Canada must be subdued before that time or the opportunity will be lost. Our little Henry is ready to march; he had his tin gun prepared and his head powdered a week ago." [2]

The tin gun and powdered head were soon forgotten. But one significant event of the war was fixed indelibly in his memory. On the afternoon of September 5, 1813, the American brig *Enterprise* engaged the British brig *Boxer* off Penguin Point, to the east and north of Portland harbor. Although out of sight of the many inhabitants who gathered to stare seaward from the top of Munjoy's Hill, the grim struggle which reached them only as sounds of hammering explosions and hollow cannonading, caused great excitement and speculation. The six-year-old boy shared in the general hubbub, strained to catch each new pounding reverberation across the water, and stood fascinated, later, as he watched the victorious American brig bring the mastless *Boxer* into harbor. The funeral for the two dead commanders was carried out with all the honors that Portland authorities could bestow. The tolling of bells, the firing of minute guns, and the two graves side by side under the brow of Munjoy's Hill filled the boy's mind with details that were woven permanently into the long, long thoughts of his youth.

The martial spirit of the time was too intense to be overshadowed by ordinary games. One of Henry's first letters, fashioned with painful care, was written in January, 1814, to his father, then attending the General Court in Boston:

"PORTLAND
"Dear Papa
"Ann wants a little bible like little Betsy's. Will you please to buy her one if you can find any in Boston. I have been to school all the week, and got only seven marks. I shall have a billet on monday. I wish you to buy me a drum.
"HENRY W. LONGFELLOW." [3]

Zilpah, sitting beside her son as his clenched fist slowly pushed the pencil across the sheet, was also writing to Stephen, whose law practice carried him away from home many weeks during the year. She could not have supported the burden of family cares without the aid of her sister Lucia, whom she had acquired, fortunately, with the Wadsworth house. Zilpah had never been strong, and the constant strain of childbirth had increased her tendency toward invalidism. In less than five years she had borne four children—Stephen, Henry, Elizabeth, Anne—and was expecting a fifth before spring. But the courage and unselfishness, the cheerful spirit and love which crowded her letters to her husband, revealed the atmosphere of her home:

"I think my dear husband you will be able to pass a month from home very pleasantly, provided we should all continue pretty well. The Theatre will occupy many of your evenings, and attention to your friends and mine will I hope agreeably beguile the remainder. It is good for us all, especially for Gentlemen, occasionally to step beyond our own narrow sphere and enlarge our affections & ideas by an intercourse with polished society. Now as I am so entirely shut out from the world, you must be my representative, and enjoy the pleasures, and fulfil the duties of life for me as well as for yourself . . . I have written in the midst of the children; writing, chatting, laughing, crying. Amid the confusion of sounds who could write with much connection. Such as it is, receive it as a proof of the unalterable affection of

"Yours

"Z. W. L." [4]

With patient devotion Zilpah tended her growing family while she encouraged her modest though capable husband toward wider horizons with her shrewd understanding. "Enclosed is Henry's letter," she added as a postscript, "the product of some hours of attentive employment. I mention this that you may appreciate it not by its appearance but by its intrinsic value." Stephen took time, in spite of Boston duties and diversions, to answer his son's letter:

"I have found a very pretty drum, with an eagle painted on it but the man asks two Dollars for it. And they do not let any vessels go from Boston to Portland now. But if I can find any opportunity to send it down I shall buy the drum. . . . If I can get time I shall write you and Stephen an other letter & tell you about the State House the Theatre and other things that there are in Boston." [5]

In less than a week, Zilpah sent her husband further glimpses of his sons:

"Here is Stephen reading Shakespeare, and Henry engaged with Gays fable of the Hare & many friends, he is quite interested, it little accords with his generous feelings, and he comforts himself by saying he 'does not believe it is true.' They are my only companions this evening. Even now they have changed their amusement. Stephen is giving his brother a lesson in hieroglyphics, and laughing at his mistakes. . . . Henry was delighted with the description of the drum, he desires I would tell Papa that he does not think he can do without it, it is *so pretty*, and if you cannot send it home in a vessel, why you can get a string and hang it around your neck when you come in the stage. Well says Stephen and he can fasten on my sword with a belt and shoulder arms with the gun, but then, a wooden sword! folks will think he is a coward from Canada . . . Excuse this chit-chat. You will conclude I am not sick, if I can trifle thus. A mother must often be engaged in trifling plays, and conversation if she would be the companion of her children of seven & eight years and were you here I am sure you would join us." [6]

Zilpah's delight in her children, her liking for literature and music, her interest in the theatre, and her desire that her husband should share her interests, are all indications of the liberal and cultural spirit which surrounded Henry during his childhood. In religious inclination, Zilpah's faith and practice were earnest and devout without cramping her intellectual and social outlook. Her husband, on the other hand, had been exposed more constantly to the Harvard liberalism which had broken down faith in Calvinistic dogma without offering him a satisfactory substitute. While in Boston during the winter of 1814, he attended Channing's church and renewed his friendship with his former classmate. On February 6 he wrote to his wife:

"About Channing: I attended his Friday evening lecture, and I went again this morning, and I assure you my dear that after all, I find no minister whose preaching suits me so well as his. There is so much love & charity & benevolence, and goodness exhibited in the gospel as he preaches it that I am 'almost persuaded to be a Christian.'" [7]

A week later he wrote to her again:

"You ask me if I do not visit Mr. Channing? I passed Friday evening with him very pleasantly indeed. I found him the same kind, affectionate, intelligent friend that I expected to meet. The warmth of his heart has not abated in any degree, and he received me with the same open arms and glowing affection which he used to exhibit when we were intimate friends at College." [8]

Zilpah's comment in answer showed her continual solicitude for Stephen's spiritual growth:

"I thank you for your account of Mr. Channing. I wish that you may hear him again and again, and that his eloquence may be a means of persuading you to be not only 'almost' but 'altogether' a christian. . . . How amiable he appears as you describe him. Such an evening as you passed with him is worth a thousand ceremonial parties where 'not the heart is found.' I presume I love him better as he entertains so sincere an affection for my husband." [9]

The same strength of moral purpose was never absent in Zilpah's training of her children. She taught them the Bible story of the talents and showed them that they must be able to give a good account of themselves at all times and in all places. On Sunday she gathered them about her and encouraged them to take their turn in reading aloud from the large family Bible. For further spiritual edification on the Sabbath she gave them the moralizings of Hannah Moore. Although the day was set apart for worship, there was nothing cold or unpleasant about its observance. The entire family acquired the habit of going to the First Parish Church in the morning and again in the afternoon, walking together the short distance down Congress Street to the old Meetinghouse. Under the influence of Ichabod Nichols, a Harvard graduate who had come to assist the aging Parson Deane in 1809, the narrow Congregationalism of an earlier period gave way to moderately liberal Unitarian teaching. Zilpah had been a member of the church for many years, but her husband was not led to join until the fall of 1814, after the renewal of intimacy with William Ellery Channing.[10]

Henry was sent to a new private school after the unfortunate experiment in Love Lane. He was placed under the guidance of Nathaniel H. Carter, recently graduated from Dartmouth Col-

lege, who had opened a school in a small, one-story wooden building on the west side of Preble Street, just around the corner from
the Longfellow home. The people on Congress Street liked this
young teacher and gave him their cordial support. With Carter's
stimulus, Henry soon distinguished himself as an exceptionally
bright pupil. By the close of the spring term of 1814, Master
Carter reported that Henry had "gone half through his Latin
Grammar" and stood "above several boys twice as old as he." [11]
In the fall of that year, Carter was chosen headmaster of the celebrated Portland Academy and proudly took the Longfellow
brothers there with him. In spite of childhood ailments, Henry
continued to enjoy his studies. On the day before Christmas his
mother wrote to Stephen:

"We are all as well as when you left us, excepting the cough
of the children. Henry begins to cough hard, and though at first
he seemed pleased with the idea of having the whooping cough I
believe he would now be glad to be excused.

"Today the boys have an examination at the Academy. I conclude they were pretty well prepared; they were up before the
sun, and went with more cheerfulness than usual." [12]

Although Stephen Longfellow's legal duties were taking him
away from home with increasing frequency, he never lacked information concerning his family during these absences. Impatient with all protracted stays, he returned to his family as soon
as work permitted. Accepted as one of the leading citizens in the
town, he was constantly invited to accept new civic offices and
responsibilities. His neighbors had even honored him by electing
him Chief Fire Warden of Portland. Unfortunately, one of his
earliest services in this capacity was required on his own house,
one day in July, 1815, when he discovered a large area of roofing
about one chimney burning briskly. All his commands, shouted
through a brass trumpet at the frantic bucket brigade, were of
little avail. Before the fire was brought under control it had
destroyed almost all of the roof. And his assiduous firemen had
very thoroughly drenched with water all the walls, bedding, and
furniture which had escaped the flames.

With Yankee wisdom, Stephen turned the accident to good
account: he decided to build another floor on his two-story house

before putting up a new roof. With a family of five children and with the probability of more (there were three more) he expected to need the extra room gained by adding a third story and capping it with a hipped roof, in place of the old gable roof. Because the house could not be used until work was completed, Stephen arranged for his family to be distributed among relatives in Gorham and Hiram.[13]

Henry's visit to Hiram at this time was extremely unhappy. Through some mishap, he suffered an infection in his foot. And the consequent blood-poisoning nearly resulted in a decision to amputate his leg. Under date of July 30, 1815, Zilpah wrote to her husband from Hiram. After expressing her fear that the rain might again soak the furniture in their unroofed home she revealed the cause of her new worry:

"I have been much concerned about Henry. . . . It appeared to me that he must have taken a bad cold. He has been very unwell, and feverish & at times has cold chills. Do you recollect he was out the Saturday before we left home with only his gown, and in the evening complained of being sick. Nothing but cold I think could have affected his foot so suddenly. It was swollen so that he could not move his toes, and as far up as the calf of the leg, and much inflamed, around the ankle, with a large protuberance of proud flesh on the joint. The swelling has been reduced by allum curd, and Grandpapa who dresses it says it is in a very good way, and he can cure it. The little boy lies on the bed in the hall, and has all the house to wait on him. He has no inclination to sit up at all, and is carried from room to room. I thought best to let you know Henry's situation, that you may not be surprised should he not get well very soon." [14]

The condition of the leg did not improve. Nor could anyone believe that it had been changed, unless for the worse, by an unpleasant "green salve, prepared with verdigris" which the family doctor had prescribed. As the infection grew worse Zilpah reluctantly revealed to her husband the possible necessity for amputation. But after two weeks, Henry's wound began to heal. "I know," his mother wrote, "that nothing but inability to move could keep him on the bed and on one side for a fortnight, and I feel quite relieved now that he can turn himself and move without pain." [15] Soon he was about the house on crutches, despite a stiff ankle. On August 17, Zilpah wrote with great relief that Henry was improving steadily. She added, "You perceive there is now no kind of danger of the loss of the leg, and I believe there is none of a stiff ankle." [16] Not long after, he was well enough to return with his mother to the enlarged home in Portland.

When the boy went back to the Portland Academy in the fall of 1815 he found a new headmaster, Bezaleel Cushman, who had come to take Mr. Carter's place. Under this older gentleman's stern but capable tutelage Henry continued for the remaining six years of his Academy course. The simple fundamentals of reading, writing, and arithmetic were superseded by Algebra, Latin, and Greek. He had already begun to explore the books in his father's library. Guided by his mother he read stories carefully selected from the *Arabian Nights*, followed Robinson Crusoe [17] through his devious misfortunes, and made the acquaintance of the *Vicar of Wakefield* and *Don Quixote*. Accepting the normal prejudices of his day in poetry, he advanced quickly from the cold couplets of Pope and Dryden to the more exciting cadences and melodies of Scott, Campbell, and Moore.[18] Passages of *Ossian* pleased him so much that he committed them to memory and delighted his younger brother by sounding the melancholy and sonorous lines about the house. Many of his favorite poems, such as "Bonnie Doon" and "Oft in the Stilly Night," were popular songs of that time and were often sung by the children, gathered about the piano in the Longfellow parlor while Zilpah played the accompaniment. Prompted by her own fondness for music, Zilpah urged her boys and girls to take particular interest in their singing and dancing lessons. Henry responded eagerly. Before he was graduated from the Academy he had learned to play the piano and flute and had been a faithful attendant at the singing school. As the Longfellow children grew older they were encouraged to invite their neighborhood companions for informal gatherings that made the house ring with gay music and laughter. These were occasions to be remembered by the guests, for the Longfellows owned the first piano which was brought to Portland. The girls knew and played all the favorite dance tunes—"The Haymakers," "Money Musk," and "The Fisher's Hornpipe." [19]

Among the friends thus welcomed were Edward Preble, who lived with his widowed mother in the great house near by, and William Browne, a boy who had but recently moved to Portland from Boston. Ned Preble, bold and adventuresome, grew up with the Longfellow brothers. Together the three ranged the fields and woods of Munjoy's Hill, explored the large grove known as Deering's Woods, and swam in the protected waters of Back Cove. Browne, an entirely different lad, was two years ahead of Henry in the Academy. He seemed drawn to Longfellow because of mutual interest in reading and writing.

Possibly Browne was the first to stimulate Longfellow's earliest experiments in versification. In the fall of 1819 Henry began a copy book at school and wrote into it favorite passages from Scott, Campbell, and Rogers. Occasionally he added to this collection some lines and verses of his own contriving: epitaphs, acrostics, riddles, and elegies. The longest was a twenty-line elegy "On the Death of the Rev. Jesse Appleton Late President of Bowdoin College." [20] Less serious compositions, probably smuggled cautiously from hand to hand in the schoolroom, for the amusement of Browne and his best friends, were also preserved in this copy book.[21]

Quite naturally, these attempts at verse writing stimulated a more critical attitude toward the work of others—and increased the boy's curiosity in searching out new poems by contemporary authors. One of Henry's earliest book possessions was a thin volume of poems entitled *American Sketches*. The author was a young Dartmouth graduate named Thomas Cogswell Upham. Having culled a variety of anecdotes and legends from histories of New England, this native of New Hampshire used them as suitable material for narrative poems and lyrics. One poem in *American Sketches* held particular interest for Longfellow. It was entitled, "Lovells pond: The Scene in 1725 of a desperate encounter with the savages." Anyone who had spent summers in Hiram had been told all about the little lake near by, where Captain John Lovewell and his men had fought their day-long battle with the Indians. Peleg Wadsworth, so skilled in telling stories, must have been asked by his grandson to recount the particulars of this narrative many times. The old General was able to add a special touch of vividness by pointing out the path near his house which was said to have been used by the little band of Lovewell's men who escaped from that terrible fight.

Longfellow found references to this important struggle in a second poem by Upham, and read them with a critical eye which quickly detected errors in facts given or surmised.[22] Most annoying of all was Upham's conclusion that the heroism of these long-dead soldiers was forgotten and that the name of Captain Lovewell had almost faded into oblivion. As though in defense, the thirteen-year-old boy sat down to fashion verses in answer and refutation. No matter that he borrowed Upham's metre; that he even found certain of Upham's rhymes convenient.[23] The immediate need was to contradict the claim that only the owl and the raven chanted loudly and drear over the bier of these heroes. The young defender of Maine's traditions admitted that the dead had bled and gone to a last rest. But he definitely controverted Upham's assertion that they were forgotten, by concluding his answer thus:

> "They are dead; but they live in each Patriot's breast,
> And their names are engraven on honor's bright crest." [24]

There could be no satisfactory refutation so long as these lines remained unseen. One evening in November, 1820, the boy carried his precious manuscript down Exchange Street to the printing office opposite Milk Street, where Mr. Shirley, the editor and printer, prepared the weekly *Portland Gazette* for appearance on each Friday morning. With trembling hands he entrusted the sheet to Mr. Shirley's mail box and returned home. Because the secret was too big for him to keep he told it to his ten-year-old sister Anne, who frequently shared his confidences. Little wonder that the author, impatient for Friday to come, returned to the printing office the night before the paper was published and stood shivering for some time in the fall darkness as he peered hopefully up at the lighted windows behind which the printers worked.

The following morning he watched his father turning the pages of the *Gazette*. Surely, if the poem were there the title could not escape his father's eye. Or if he took no notice of that, there was

the simple but revealing name "Henry" at the end of the lines.
But Stephen Longfellow read slowly through the folded sheet
without making any comment. As soon as Henry had the paper
to himself, the boy opened it to the "Poet's Corner." The poem
was there! Slowly and proudly he read through the printed lines.
Many times during that day he went over them again, tasting each
word and finding it good.

That evening he visited Frederic Mellen, a friend whose father
was also a lawyer. The entire family was seated about the fireplace talking, when Henry Longfellow entered. After desultory
conversation, someone mentioned the subject of poetry. With a
grunt, Judge Mellen reached for the *Gazette*, saying: "Did you
see the piece in today's paper? Very stiff piece—remarkably stiff;
moreover, it is all borrowed, every word of it." The quiet guest
was terrified. Would somebody next ask who wrote it? Or did
everybody know? Henry quickly made his excuses and hurried
home. That night he cried himself to sleep.[25]

These harsh words of his first critic did not discourage the
boy from making plans for further publication. His friendship
with William Browne gave him constant stimulus and eventually
resulted in plans for collaboration. In the fall of 1820, Browne
entered Bowdoin College as a sophomore but continued to carry
on literary discussions with his friend by letter. The hindrance to
frequent meetings seemed to heighten the amount, if not the
quality, of their output. Acrostics, anagrams, epigrams, and occasional lyrics were exchanged. Longfellow even began a tragedy
in blank verse. It was abandoned, however, when he and Browne
decided to write a series of essays under the title *"De Tractatibus"*
for the Portland newspaper. The plan was not carried out. But
Browne's enthusiasm over his younger friend's poetry may account for the appearance of a sonnet by Longfellow in the *Portland Gazette* for January 22, 1821. It appeared with a note pre-
fixed, thus:

"WINTER

"Mr. Shirley—
    "The following effusion was handed to me by a friend, and I
now offer it to you for an insertion in your Gazette. It has some

faults, but is the production of a youthful muse and therefore I hope its imperfections will be overlooked.

"Yours, &c.

"AMICUS."

Autumn has fled; and hoary Winter now
   O'er hill and dale has spread his drear domain,
   Covering with fleecy snow the fertile plain.
With piercing storms the winds tempestuous blow
And block the way. The streams refuse to flow—
   Ev'n Nature's self, close bound with icy chain,
   With meek submission, owns stern Winter's reign.
Congeal'd before the frown of his dark threat'ning brow—
And ah! how hard the helpless wanderer's lot
   Who roams alone upon some hostile strand,
   And sighs to tread once more his native land,
To meet those friends by memory ne'er forgot,
And hail, yet once again, that fertile spot,
   Where Friendship binds him with her strongest bands.[26]

H.

Although critical Judge Mellen may not have exclaimed, "All borrowed!" when he found these lines in the "Poet's Corner" he might have found no difficulty in surmising correctly that the "youthful muse" had been reading enthusiastically in Thomson's *Seasons*, Cowper's *Task*, Goldsmith's *Traveller*, and Scott's *Lay of the Last Minstrel*.

A necessary increase in serious study crowded out much scribbling during Longfellow's last two years at the Academy. He was preparing for the Bowdoin College entrance examinations. Each candidate for the freshman class was required, according to official announcements published in the *Portland Gazette*, "to write Latin grammatically, to understand the fundamental rules of Arithmetic, and to be well acquainted with Cummings' Geography, Cicero's Select Orations, the Bucolics, Georgics, and Aeneid of Virgil, Sallust, the Greek Testament, and the Collectanea Graeca Minora." [27] Such demands required faithful application under the supervision of Preceptor Cushman and his assistant, Jacob

Abbott (later the author of the popular "Rollo" books). Always fond of studies, Henry completed all these requirements with no difficulty—except the precise and troublesome laws of arithmetic.

When the last class had been held and Longfellow was about to leave the Academy where he had spent so many years, he walked up to Cushman's desk. He had grown to like the nervous and irascible old schoolmaster, who was to be associated forever in his mind with the memory of a curiously blended odor of tobacco, india-rubber, and lead pencils. Failing to recognize the genuine affection which prompted Longfellow's farewell, Cushman launched sternly into a lecture on the trials of a teacher's life and the disgrace of a student's poor behavior.[28] As the young man stood watching the tired lines in the schoolmaster's face and listening to his firm words of reproach he may have taken his first dislike to the thought of teaching school—to a monotony such as that which had worn down Bezaleel Cushman until he could not even understand the sincerity of pupils who came to take leave of him with friendly words.[29]

III

BOWDOIN FRESHMAN

*Stephen and Henry must give us some account of themselves,
as how many evenings in a week they devote to study; whether they
are regular at meals; if they rise early; and let us know in particular
how they proceed with their mathematical studies.*[1]

STEPHEN LONGFELLOW was dissuaded by state loyalty from sending his sons to Harvard College. The dearly won independence
of Maine from Massachusetts, achieved amid great excitement in
1820, had created a great wave of regional pride. Furthermore,
the Longfellow family was influenced by a more personal interest
in the history of Bowdoin. Old Judge Longfellow of Gorham
had been one of the dignitaries who met at John Dunning's Inn in
Brunswick one midsummer day in 1796, to consider a site for the
college. Surely the quiet and sedate procession of gentlemen who
walked out Twelve Rod Road that day, clad in broad-skirted
coats and black cocked hats, cared little for scenic beauty when
they nodded their heads in agreement over the location. The
waste land along the Brunswick plain was a sandy, barren region.
But it was well isolated from the evils and distractions of large
towns, such as Portland—and that was very important.[2]

Braving inevitable delays, the committee had persisted until one
building had been erected at Brunswick, a president chosen, and
in the fall of 1802 a class of eight young men admitted as fresh-
men. From this humble beginning Bowdoin College had grown
rapidly. Old Judge Longfellow's son carried on the family tradition of service when he was elected with Ichabod Nichols to represent Portland on the board of trustees. So it was quite natural
that he should decide against sending his boys to Harvard. There
was really no need for it, since Bowdoin had been modelled after
Harvard in government, curriculum, departments—even in architecture and the choice of textbooks.

Henry and Stephen Longfellow were not permitted to pursue

23

their college studies at Brunswick during their freshman year.
Undoubtedly the immaturity of the boys had much to do with
their parents' decision, for Henry was but fourteen, and Stephen
only two years older, in the fall of 1821. Mrs. Preble had agreed
with her neighbors that such a course was prudent and had made
arrangement for her son Edward to join them in studying freshman assignments under the tutelage of Bezaleel Cushman at the
Portland Academy. But the boys were eager to visit their college,
even if they were not to live there immediately. In May, 1821, a
public "Exhibition" at Bowdoin furnished an excuse for asking
permission to make the trip. Letters were exchanged with friends
there, and all plans completed long before the day of departure arrived. Writing to her husband on May 20, Zilpah mentioned the excitement: "Henry & Edward Preble have engaged
their seats in tomorrow's stage for Brunswick. They thought it
best to be in season. Stephen concludes not to go, he says he
should like it very well, but shall not go. I do not know what
determines him." [3]

The stagecoach ride from Portland to Brunswick was an adventure. The thirty miles of country road through the small towns of
Falmouth, Cumberland, Yarmouth, and Freeport could be traversed in five hours, although such haste on the part of the driver
was considered dangerous by those who bumped about inside, or
clung to the pitching and swaying seats on top. As the coach
finally brought the young travelers to the outskirts of Brunswick,
the boys caught sight of the college buildings across the open plain.

The village, a compact assemblage of neat white houses grouped
along the main thoroughfare, had grown beside the head-tide falls
of the Androscoggin. But the college was beyond the immediate
limits of the little settlement. On the brow of the low hill at the
end of the main street three solid-looking buildings, grouped to
form three sides of a quadrangle, were backed by the dark green
foliage of tall pines. Two of the buildings, Georgian in design,
were built of brick and bore some resemblance to the Harvard
College buildings of colonial times. But the wooden chapel, bare
and unpainted except for the apologetic trimmings along the eaves,
was a fitting symbol of the austere, backwoods spirit of religious
conservatism which had conceived and fostered Bowdoin. The

same spirit continued to dominate the policy of the institution, through the control of the overseers.

Beside the chapel, and somewhat to the rear, was the frame house of President William Allen, a Congregational minister who had served as head of the short-lived Dartmouth "University" before coming to Bowdoin. The overseers, most of whom were also Congregational ministers, believed in holding a tight grip on the college government by keeping a trustworthy colleague in the president's chair. Protected from the new currents of liberal thinking which had emanated from Harvard since their graduation, the older clergymen in Maine, isolated in rural communities, clung to their birthright of Calvinistic severity. Dissenters like Ichabod Nichols were restricted in their academic service to the board of trustees while the overseers continued to enlist new members from the orthodox ministers. Thus the austere governing board had hoped to nurture seeds of enlightenment speedily just as it had thought to relieve the bareness of the college yard by setting out fast-growing balm of Gilead trees. But in both quarters the soil was poor and unpromising.

Such thoughts might concern Stephen Longfellow but would have been of little interest to his son or to Ned Preble, catching a first glimpse of Bowdoin. Probably the young men were met by their former Academy mate, William Browne, and guided about the dormitories and recitation rooms until their curiosity was satisfied. Massachusetts Hall, with its white wooden belfry (similar to that on the second Harvard Hall at Cambridge), already contained the beginnings of Parker Cleaveland's mineral collection. This professor was known to Henry, for he had visited occasionally in the Longfellow home. The extent of Cleaveland's interests was amazing. The curious chemical apparatus in another room of Massachusetts Hall indicated a second field which Cleaveland explored before the wide eyes of his students. He had taught nearly every subject in the curriculum at one time or another during his fifteen years of service. One year earlier, the college had established a medical school which had further taxed Cleaveland's energies by asking him to serve as professor of anatomy. He had quietly accepted. As secretary of the college he also shouldered much of President Allen's responsibility. Still, he found time for pottering about the flower gardens beside his pleasant home on Federal Street and pruning the grapevines back of his house in the spring.

The students admired and respected this shy, big-boned man, with his friendly manners. He offered a pleasant contrast to the pompous severity of stout President Allen. To Allen, rules were inflexible and must be enforced without mercy, even though such a code forced him to punish the most trivial infringements. If students did not like him, that did not affect his sense of duty. Morning and evening he took his place in the pulpit of the unheated chapel, just as the bell stopped sounding, and began the stiff service of worship. If any young man failed to appear or was late he was fined. But Allen could only frown at Professor Cleaveland, whose home was so far from the chapel that he frequently arrived during the reading of the Scripture and hurriedly tiptoed to his seat, hopeful that he might be quick enough to be seated before the students acknowledged his entrance by rising.

The chapel building housed four thousand volumes in the college library on the second floor. The shelves were well fortified with theological and sacred treatises, histories, and classical works. Although there were four times as many books of theology as of literature, James Bowdoin had bequeathed to the college the writings of his favorite eighteenth century authors: Addison, Swift, Burke, and Dr. Johnson. Only a few American authors, including Jeremy Belknap and Benjamin Franklin, were represented. It mattered little to the students whether there were few or many books, for the library was open only one hour each day and only one book could be taken out every three weeks.

Browne must have shown his friends his dormitory room, redeemed from the dreariness of bare floors and uncurtained windows by the fireplace blaze, essential to comfort in a building otherwise unheated. Other details of college life made known to the novices included the well established customs of taking occasional walks through the shadowy paths of the pine forest behind the campus, or longer excursions by the shortest road to Maquoit Bay. There the hardy ones who were fond of swimming braved the frightfully cold ocean water as soon as warm spring days came. In a shack, a mile down the Maquoit road, lived a town character known to everyone: old Uncle Trench, who baked gingerbread and brewed an innocuous root beer. The stoop-shouldered old fellow could be seen any pleasant day, trundling his wheelbarrow of food along the college fence to tempt customers from the dormitories to purchase his concoctions.

Pleased with all they saw and heard, Preble and Longfellow returned to Portland impatient of the restriction which kept them at home. But Stephen Longfellow had impressed his sons with a thorough understanding of an obedience which did not permit them to question his judgments. When the fall term began they returned to the Academy for instruction in freshman subjects which included Greek grammar, translations from Xenophon, weekly translations into Greek and Latin, readings in Livy, arithmetic, and English rhetoric. Henry kept in close communication with some of his classmates in Brunswick. George Pierce, a bright, witty lad who had recently moved to Portland, and John Kinsman, a former classmate at the Academy, wrote letters concerning activities in the Bowdoin halls. Whenever these correspondents lagged in their duties Longfellow chid them. In February he wrote to Pierce:

"Some of my acquaintances at Brunswick seem to have forgotten me—however do not mention it to them—for if they cannot remember me without having some one to 'drive it into 'em' I should choose rather to be forgotten than to be remembered.

"As to my classical studies—I am still going on in Xenophon—and have proceeded about 17 sections in the 2nd Book of Livy—if your course of studies are different from this—or if you have proceeded farther—please to let me know it." [4]

As the year continued, his interest in his studies was sharpened by a desire to equal, if not to surpass, the accomplishments of his friends at Bowdoin. Among the best students there was keen rivalry, intensified by regional pride. Faculty and students wished to demonstrate that the Maine college was the equal of Harvard in every way except size. To a lesser degree, the competition existed between students from various towns in Maine. Longfellow's letters reflected his sharp eagerness to see his Portland friends excel. In a later letter to Pierce he wrote:

"You must naturally suppose that I am desirous to know what

standing Kinsman holds in the Class—and whether he gets many
'screwings.' If you have had sufficient opportunity to form an
opinion upon this subject I wish you would tell me *exactly* what
you think about it and not disguise your opinion from any private
notions of friendship. . . . What do you think of Greenleaf?
and what is the opinion that the Schollars in general entertain of
him? Is he not considered as a fellow of excellent natural abilities? That is my opinion and I think he only needs application to
give him a high standing in his class. What I have heard of him
since he has resided at Brunswick, rather inclines me to believe
that he is not a very close applicant to his studies, and I am sorry
for it, because I wish that the 'Representatives from *our* Western
towns' should hold high rank in the Class. . . .

"I shall want to know when you commence reviewing—&c—and
how far the Class will probably proceed in Majora—and whether
we shall be examined in Algebra at Commencement . . ." [5]

In the spring Longfellow's father suffered from illness which
forced him to seek rest. His law practice had grown steadily and
had increased his prominence as a leading citizen so much that he
could not expect to rest in Portland. Mr. Longfellow's distinction was not confined to Portland, for while serving his district in
the Massachusetts legislature he had been sent from there to the
Hartford Convention.

He planned a trip with his wife to Saratoga Springs—a favorite
and fashionable resort for New Englanders—and arranged to
travel in leisurely stages by way of Boston and New York. The
eight Longfellow children were left in the care of Aunt Lucia, a
stern disciplinarian. Her competent eye watched with equal care
the work of the servants, the feeding of the three-year-old baby,
the play of the young children, and the study of the two college
students. Knowing the strict supervision which Aunt Lucia
would give, Zilpah wrote letters calculated to give moral support
to her sister's wise but possibly harsh rule.[6] She also wrote a separate letter to Henry:

"It is of the utmost importance that young people should well
employ their time. Their happiness in this world and the next
depends on a proper use and improvement of their time & talents.
God has given them to you, and to him you must account for the

use of them. . . . I write thus, my dear son, not because I think that you in particular require these cautions; they are for you all, and I write thus because I feel so deep an interest in the welfare of my dear children." [7]

Zilpah's persistent solicitations and her years of thoughtful direction had their desired effect. By the time Henry went down to Brunswick to take his examinations at the close of his first year, his grace of manner, his courteous expressions of friendliness and keen scholastic interests were tributes to the simple culture of the Longfellow home. Throughout his entire college years his mother remained a close friend and confidante. Although his father was a well bred son of Harvard, the duties of his profession afforded him little time for sharing with his son many of his new interests and discoveries. Henry, in turn, respected his father but continued throughout his college course to address him with a somewhat formal "Sir." To his mother, not to his father, he took his poem of New Year greeting, for he knew that she would praise his efforts even as she had encouraged him to discuss his reading with her. Zilpah's deep religious belief and her quiet ingrafting of lofty precepts and ideals so completely pervaded the impressionable mind of her son that she was able to send him away from home at the beginning of his sophomore year, reliable and self-dependent, although but a boy of fifteen years.

IV

COLLEGE LIFE

. . . the long succession of cold days & colder nights—frozen ears—cold feet & a thousand other "ills the flesh is heir to"—all these make it dull living in this dreary region of the East. Heigh-ho for the vacation.[1]

WHEN the Longfellow brothers arrived in Brunswick in the fall of 1822, they could not take rooms in the dormitory. Maine Hall, which had been gutted by fire the previous March, was completely repaired, yet even in its new splendor it housed only fifty students. Over half the one hundred and twenty boys were forced to find board and room with private families. Forewarned of this difficulty, Stephen Longfellow had arranged with a quondam Portland resident, Benjamin Titcomb, to watch over his sons, and their friend Ned Preble, while they lived at his home near Professor Cleaveland's on Federal Street.

Parson Titcomb, an elderly gentleman, formerly coeditor of Portland's first newspaper, had taken upon himself the mantle of Baptist priesthood in later life and supplemented his meagre salary by renting several rooms. The trio from Portland were not overly pleased with what the Parson had to offer. Their plainly furnished quarters, all too well ventilated by loose-fitting windows, depended for heat on one small fireplace. Henry's immediate plea to his sisters that they make him bombazine curtains and some artistic decorations for his blank walls started a flurry of sewing and painting in the Portland home.

The young men quickly fell into the routine of rising in the morning dusk, hustling up the road to the college yard while the chapel bell tolled final summons to the six o'clock prayers, attending their first recitation immediately afterwards, and returning to Parson Titcomb's for breakfast. At eleven they went back to college for midday recitations. If they needed to work in the library they were forced to do so at the risk of losing dinner, for the room over the chapel was open only through the noon hour. John Abbot, the mouselike tutor who served as librarian, was a constant butt for practical jokes, and many were the cruel tricks devised for teasing him. The afternoon schedule began at two, with a second study period in the students' rooms. Later, all gathered at Massachusetts Hall for the second recitation period and closed the day by attending evening prayers in the bleak chapel.

There was a college law requiring all students to remain in their rooms during the evening, but no amount of watching or punishing could enforce it.[2] Groups of less industrious students gathered in local stores or about tavern tables for convivial evenings of card playing and late suppers. A favorite place for carousals was Ward's tavern, conveniently located on the edge of the yard. Especially attractive to the boys was the good-natured and pretty Ward girl who managed the tavern with capable dignity even after the death of her father.[3] Stephen Longfellow was more actively engaged in night prowling than his more studious brother. Yet there was a mutual loyalty which led Henry to avoid any mention of these nocturnal absences in letters. His first was devoted largely to impressions and immediate needs:

"Brunswick September 22nd 1822

"Dear Parents,

"As we have now got comfortably settled, I suppose it is about time to let you know how we go on here. I feel very well contented, and am much pleased with a College Life. Many of the students are very agreeable companions and, thus far, I have passed my time very pleasantly. The students have considerably more leisure than I expected, but as the season advances and the days grow shorter, our leisure moments must necessarily be considerably diminished. I expected, when I got here, that I should have to study very hard to keep a good footing with the rest of the class; but I find I have sufficient time for the preparation of my lessons and for amusement, and that I am not more deficient than some of the rest of the class. I have not been 'screwed' at recitation yet and shall endeavour not to be—So much for egotism!

"I have very little more to write, but I will not forget to mention that by some means or other, I cannot tell what, I have either lost on my passage here, or left at home, all my cotton stockings except the one pair which I wore—And another thing is that I wish some one would get a brass ferrule put on to my cane and send it to me as soon as possible—If you have any good apples or pears I wish you would send me some—and tell the girls to send a whole parcel of Gingerbread with them. My box of tooth-powder may also be put into the bundle—

"Yours affectionately—

"H. W. L.——

"P.S. There is another thing of considerable importance which I had like to have forgotten. You do not know how much we stand in need of a good Watch. When the chapel bell rings for recitation it is only struck a few times and then is done, so that we, living so far from the College Buildings, are liable to be late—however we must do the best we can—Give my love to all and tell the Girls to write soon." [4]

Although the novelty of college life delighted Longfellow, he found his thoughts turning wistfully toward home early in the term, when a few days of mild illness unexpectedly overtook him. He began to realize the contrast between his little room at Parson Titcomb's and the gaiety in the spacious parlor on Congress Street —the hilarious hours his younger sisters and brothers were enjoying with friends who dropped in, after the candles were lit, for evenings of singing and dancing. His faithful sisters, forever writing little notes to him, would not let him forget. Fourteen-year-old Elizabeth, always eager for amusement, wrote: "You cannot think how much we miss you here. The evenings are so dull without your society." [5] But the same sister made fun of him, a few days later, in answer to his confession of homesickness:

"As to being 'melancholy and sad' I should laugh to hear of it. It would be the first time I guess. Nevertheless, I hope you will be homesick enough to come home Thanksgiving Day, for I have set my heart upon seeing you then, and should be *very* sorry to be disappointed. Pa has sent you a chest of apples and nuts supposing you would like to have something to treat your friends with." [6]

Thanksgiving! What an an occasion for celebrating that day

would be! Scheming to surprise their family, the two boys made secret plans for returning to Portland with a flourish: they would hire a horse and carriage, drive posthaste over the thirty miles, and amaze everyone by pulling up before the house in fine style. Nothing was said about the arrangement, even to their mother, who, with Mrs. Preble, surprised them one afternoon by arriving unannounced at Parson Titcomb's during study hour.

Fortunately, they were both at work. The October weather had turned cold, and Zilpah found her two sons sniffling over their books in a chilly room, which caused her some concern. "It seems their time is chiefly taken up with their studies," she wrote proudly to her husband on her return. "I found it so, but would not allow them to omit a lesson on my account. Henry has been unwell, but appeared to be better than Stephen whose cold was just coming on." [7] The Portland ladies spent the night at the home of Professor Cleaveland. Apparently Zilpah had made the visit with the hope of dispelling any protracted gloom of homesickness, for she tried to bolster her son's spirits by writing encouraging letters after her return:

"You find the term very long, it seems. It is rather unlucky your first term should be tedious but you will have more time for improvement and each succeeding term will appear much shorter. You did not say whether you should come home, or not, to give thanks with us next week, but we shall expect you, and be very happy to see you, should not the roads be too bad. In which case we shall certainly have a thanksgiving when you do come.

"I am sorry to find that your room is too cold. You must have some little wedges and make the windows closer. . . . I fear learning will not flourish, or your ideas properly expand, in a frosty atmosphere, and I fear the muses will not visit you, and that I shall have no poetic effusion presented, on the new years day." [8]

Without revealing their secret the boys waited impatiently for Thanksgiving. Unfortunately the idea which they had hit upon seemed to be a Bowdoin favorite, for when the great day came and the brothers hurried to the local livery stable they were told that someone else had accidentally taken the horse and carriage reserved for them—and there was no other conveyance. Heavy-hearted and sick with their disappointment the disconsolate pair

of sophomores sent a message home by Pat Greenleaf, watched
the other students departing, then walked back through the half-
deserted regions of the college to their room to spend the lonely
vacation as best they might. Even the letters from home, intended
for consolation, added to their misery. Their father took time
from his busy practice to commiserate with them on their misfortune. After expressing his own regret he continued:

"On Wednesday the children were all on tiptoe, and the
window seats were filled every time a chaise passed. We waited
dinner some time, & ma kept some tidbits for you by the fire until
night, and our tea was delayed to a late hour. But when P. Greenleaf arrived with the unwelcome tidings that you were not coming, the disappointment was visible in every countenance, & poor
Alexander could not suppress his tears. You see, my dear children, how much we are all interested in every thing that concerns
you, and how tenderly we love you." [9]

Fortunately, the watchful eye of Professor Cleaveland discovered the stranded boys, and with characteristic hospitality he
invited them to spend Thanksgiving Day with his family. Even
the honor of celebrating with such a distinguished host could not
reduce the inner smart caused by "a scurvy trick," as Henry
described it to his mother, "that Fortune (or rather Mis-fortune)
has played." And the original cause of his first homesickness had
not left him, for he wrote in the same letter:

"I have not got well yet & what is more, do not see much prospect of 'a speedy recovery'—However I make two meals on 'pud-
ding & milk,' that is one good thing! We have fixed our fireplace
as you mentioned. I think it may be advantageous as it respects
warming the room, but the chimney is more inclined to smoke &
that, you know, is about as disagreeable as cold is—but to have
both is rather too bad." [10]

His condition remained so unsatisfactory that the winter vacation was spent in recuperation at home. He did feel well enough
to join Ned Preble and his brother in studying a little French at
the home of Charles Nolcini, an Italian who taught music as well
as foreign languages, in Portland.[11] When the winter term opened,
near the middle of February, Longfellow returned to college feeling better but still annoyed by what he described as "a continual

swimming and aching in my head—a fullness & heaviness." [12] To
his mother's suggestion that he take soap and soda pills he replied,
"I would take them if you will send them on to me but I do not
want to taste any more of Brunswick medicine; I have had quite
enough of that already." [13]

As the trouble continued he feared he might be wasting away
under the romantic blight of consumption. Finally, he felt it
advisable to reveal his fears to his father:

"I write to state my situation to you, and to let you know how
affairs stand. I am afraid that my health is declining, and I have
good reasons to think that my suspicions are not without foundation. I am somewhat troubled with an unpleasant feeling in my
head, altho' it is not so bad as it was at the commencement of the
term, and my costiveness continues as usual. My appetite is very
good and I am somewhat inclined to indulge myself, altho' my
food is generally light, especially at morning and evening meals.
I exercise considerably, but my whole frame is so debilitated that
all exercise becomes fatigue, and apparently defeats its own purpose. I know not what this may end in, but unless my health improves I shall be *very averse to continuing here.* I am sensible it
would have been better for me to have gone to West Point, where
they require regular exercise as well as study. Accustomed to so
much relaxation from study as I took before I left Portland, it is
not surprising that I am unable to bear so much confinement as I
here experience. This matter I begin to think deserves some attention and that, too, speedily. I wish you would think upon it and
let me know as soon as possible, what course is best to be pursued.
Why, in the name of Goodness, does not somebody write!" [14]

Answering his son with expressions of sympathy, Stephen
Longfellow recommended the virtues of Congress Water, which,
Henry subsequently confessed, entirely cured his ailments.

Extracurricular diversions at Bowdoin were infrequent except
for the meetings and programs of the two literary societies. But
since the Longfellow brothers had not been residents until the
fall of their sophomore year they had not been sufficiently ap-
praised by their college mates to be elected early in the year. By
February, decisions were reached. Henry was invited to join the
Peucinian Society, which included the best students; Stephen be-

longed with the jolly good fellows of the Athenean Society, which welcomed him into membership with classmates that included Horatio Bridge, Franklin Pierce, and Nathaniel Hawthorne. On March 21, 1823, Henry was initiated with Hawthorne's roommate, Alfred Mason, in the dormitory room of an upper classman. The ceremony was extremely simple. Calvin E. Stowe, the Secretary (and later the husband of Harriet Beecher), greeted the candidate with an extended pine branch, grasped his hand, and said, "This we present you as a symbol of the society and emblematic of our connection. As we now unite our hands in the branches of this bough, may our hearts be united in affections and our endeavors in literary pursuits." [15] Thus ended the ritual.

During the remainder of his first evening, Longfellow listened to a forensic disputation on the question, "Is diversity of opinion beneficial to Society?" As he conversed with his new brothers, who included such scholars as Josiah Little, Gorham Deane, George Cheever, and George Bradbury, he may have sensed that the ideals of the group were to be a stimulus to him; that the encouragement of these friends was to mean far more to him in his discovery of literature than all his classes of English rhetoric under the tutelage of President Allen.

The president, who supervised the sophomores in their writing, reading, declamation, and grammar, was proud of his literary tastes and accomplishments. He boasted that he had been the first to compile a cyclopaedia of American biography and was not averse to being known as a poet and hymn writer. Unfortunately, he was as dogmatic and antagonistic in his teaching of English literature as in his teaching of the Bible and was extremely unpopular. The students called him "Old Gul" behind his back, in derisive ridicule of his pompous Latin given name as it appeared on the broadside commencement programs. Nevertheless, his perfunctory guidance led Longfellow to the discovery of Thomas Gray's odes and to further readings in Doctor Johnson's *Lives of the Poets*. Perhaps these accounts of literary lives may have influenced Longfellow to entertain some thought of his own career. But the only apparent result from his reading was his attempt to analyze in self-conscious and imitative phrases which crowded letters to his mother, his conviction that Gray's seeming obscurity contributed "in the highest degree to sublimity." [16] Zilpah, pleased to find her son interested in his studies, encouraged him to develop his critical powers by continuing to discuss the subjects already mentioned. Displaying a tact and discrimination which surpassed that of the Bowdoin president, she wrote:

"I am not very conversant with the poetry of Gray, dear Henry, therefore cannot tell whether I should be as much pleased with it, in general, as you are. His Elegy I have read frequently, and always with pleasure. I admire it for its truth and simplicity, and think it a charming thing. I presume you will not allow it any sublimity. Obscurity is favorable to the sublime, you think. It may be so, but I am much better pleased with those pieces that touch the feelings and improve the heart than with those that excite the imagination only and raise perhaps an indistinct admiration. That is, an admiration of we know not exactly what." [17]

In a subsequent letter she added:

"To return to our old subject, Gray's Poems, I wish you would bring the book home with you, for I cannot find it in town; I have enquired of several people for it. I have a strong inclination to read the poems, since you commend them so highly. I think I should be pleased with them, though Dr. Johnson was not. I do not think the Dr. possessed much sensibility for the charms of poetry, and he was sometimes most unmerciful in his criticisms." [18]

Probably Longfellow worked into his letters some of the materials he used in his fortnightly essays on literature, which he was obliged to read aloud in class for President Allen to criticize. Nobody seemed to enjoy this requirement. Despite the young man's many literary projects begun with William Browne in Academy days, he showed no delight in this course—probably because of dull teaching.

Certain members of the faculty loyally defended Allen, claiming that his inflexible and impassive exterior concealed a kind and generous nature. But his tactless mannerisms gradually incurred the ill-will of students and trustees alike. The first outburst of public indignation against him came about in the spring of 1823 —and indirectly because of Longfellow's friend Browne. Two years ahead of Henry at Bowdoin, William Browne had earned a reputation for inattention to his studies and occasional intemperance. In April, 1823, this senior made the mistake of attending a Fast Day service in the Brunswick Congregational Church while intoxicated. The preacher, Rev. Asa Mead, who had been ordained only a few weeks earlier as the pastor of this church, was cordially disliked by the students, who were compelled to attend his meetings on such occasions. A general belief prevailed that Reverend Mr. Mead and President Allen were in strong alliance to defend their own narrow sectarianism against the more liberal doctrines which were finding expression among newer members of the Bowdoin faculty. Consequently, when the inebriate senior was suddenly taken ill and led, vomiting, from the chapel service by his friends, Mead quickly altered his sermon to condemn the sin of drunkenness.

Eager to seize any chance for heckling, the students shuffled their feet, made disrespectful noises of protest, and at the close of the service stormed out of the church in wild anger. When they were reprimanded by President Allen, that evening at prayers, the trouble began on a second front. Resentment grew because of the high-handed way in which the President dismissed those who petitioned that they be allowed to attend Parson Titcomb's church instead of Mead's. Apologies and explanations were demanded by the seniors from Mead for some of his Fast Day insinuations. And when the faculty rusticated Browne for his misbehavior and refused him the right to be graduated with his class, a series of violent demonstrations broke out about the campus and in the village. "The whole town is literally 'up in arms,'" Longfellow informed his father, as he wrote his account and asked permission to join those who were petitioning to attend Parson Titcomb's church.[19] Stephen Longfellow curtly refused his son's request and wrote him a brief lecture on the evils of intemperance. Temporary order was restored at Brunswick although the incident had plowed seeds of resentment deep into the minds of the students.[20]

A sudden burst of patriotic fervor distracted the attention of the college during the spring. A group of students began to train as a military corps and named themselves the "Bowdoin Cadets."

Stephen and Henry enlisted with high enthusiasm. They were both with the company on the Saturday afternoon when the astute Professor Cleaveland, perceiving the value of this harmless outlet to animal spirits, sent a "particular request" that the young soldiers parade on review past his house.[21] Within a month, Henry had lost interest in parading and had returned to the society of his less demonstrative friends. Stephen, discovering that the rapidly diminishing band was transforming itself into a convivial club, joyfully retained his membership.

More appealing to Henry than soldiering was the quiet diversion of walking through the shaded forest paths with such congenial companions as Preble, Greenleaf, and his classmate Eugene Weld. Occasionally they walked through the town to the falls of the Androscoggin, where great logs, carried down by the spring freshets, pitched and rolled out over the steep ledges of the falls to the quiet waters beyond. Another favorite walk led them through the pine groves to a little stream that flowed down behind Professor Cleaveland's house and on to the river. Paradise Spring, a favorite rendezvous, poured its cold water into this brook from a hollow in the banking.

Spring and warm weather banished all thoughts of homesickness. Suddenly Longfellow discovered that sunlight, the song of birds returning after the dreary cold, and the appearance of new leaves and grass, transformed the village and yard until he felt a sentimental attachment. He even wrote to his father that his once unpleasant quarters at Parson Titcomb's were very satisfactory: "an excellent room for Summer; cool and comfortable during the heat of the day." [22]

In the pleasant summer atmosphere Longfellow completed his sophomore year. The months had been spent in making adjustments to strange and occasionally irksome routine, in overcoming loneliness, and in making new friends. But he was little changed from the boy who had visited the college with Ned Preble two years earlier. There was no definite cast of his mind toward a career of literature, or any career. He had mastered the peculiarly difficult principles of geometry and had made an excellent showing in Greek and Latin recitations. He had even explored unfamiliar bypaths of English poetry and had made slight attempts to express his critical reactions, with a minimum of originality and insight. It did not matter. He was satisfied to have been one of the Portland boys who had made a good record in his classes; one who had gone through his second year without a single reprimand from an irate professor.

V

NEW HORIZONS

I am reading three or four books at a time—sometimes more! [1]

THE NUMBER of students enrolled at Bowdoin College increased so rapidly after Maine became an independent state that arrangements were made for building a new dormitory. By the fall of 1823 the work was completed and the brick structure stood beside Maine Hall, almost identical in size and general appearance. Longfellow, returning as a junior, was given a corner room with his brother in the third story of "New College," as the authorities agreed to call it until they should select an appropriate name. From one window he could look across the narrow back-campus into the dark grove of whispering pines which were so closely associated by tradition and fact with the history of Bowdoin. Quite naturally the Peucinian Society, eager to emulate the restrained dignity of arboreal conversations, had chosen the motto:

Pinos loquentes semper habemus. [2]

To Longfellow, living almost within reach of the symbolic branches, this view from his window offered a pleasant reminder of the ideals fostered within his literary society. His friends were keenly alive to every new expression of praise or criticism concerning books published in England and America. They subscribed to *Blackwood's,* the *North American Review,* and the *American Monthly,* so that they might decide which books to buy for the society library. Although the fire which had destroyed Maine Hall two years earlier had damaged the Peucinian collection, the misfortune had aroused such generosity that by the fall the library was larger than ever. When plans were made for compiling a printed catalogue, Longfellow was appointed to serve on the committee. [3]

How pleasant it was to handle these books! Here were no battered, dog-eared volumes, but new books, recently printed, sump-

tuously bound in calf or simply bound in boards, with bright
backstrips and neat paper labels. And many of his favorites were
here. Scott's romances and poems belonged on these shelves but
rarely rested long because of the demand for them. An American
Scott had recently published some novels which revealed the rich
and dramatic possibilities in the legends and history of America.
One of his books was *The Spy*, a tale of the Revolution, and another was *The Pioneers*—both of which Longfellow had enjoyed.
Of course Irving had led the way in America with his elegant
sketches and legends. The Peucinian Society had bought *The
Sketch Book* as it appeared serially in parts.

Two other writers were represented in this library because of
their importance in portraying American scenes. One was a
Portland eccentric named John Neal, who had recently published
two novels, *Randolph* and *Seventy-six*. The other, whose works
had recently attracted notice in England, was the late Charles
Brockden Brown, author of *Arthur Mervyn, Edgar Huntly,
Wieland,* and other strange novels. Brown's weird extravagances
had not interested the Peucinians until the English reviewers and
authors began to praise them. In 1819, a reviewer in the *North
American* had complained: "He is very far from being a popular
writer. There is no call, so far as we know, for a second edition of
any of his works." [4] English praise had begun to change all that.
As Longfellow looked over the shelves he decided that he should
know something more about Brown, and put *Arthur Mervyn*
aside for reading before his own fireplace. The Peucinian library
was well buttressed with the classics of literature, from the Latin
and Greek poets to Pope and Johnson. But the young men found
new books and new authors far more exciting than the classics.

Welcomed into this literary atmosphere, Longfellow began to
take a new interest in reading and writing. His first two years of
college work had given him little inclination for continuing the
desultory reading he had done at home. Although he was never a
bookworm he discovered through Irving, Cooper, and Brown
that reading could be a compelling, thrilling experience. What a
contrast between Peucinian books and those on the second floor
of the Bowdoin chapel! Within two weeks after the beginning of
the fall term he wrote to his mother:

"I am reading three or four books at a time—sometimes more! A very foolish way of improving, or rather of wasting time, you will think. I know it—but when a volume grows tedious and uninteresting, I choose rather to lay it aside, than to weary my patience by poring over sleepy pages in such a manner as to derive neither advantage nor amusement. Besides I can never endure that, which is dull, when that, which is entertaining is upon my shelf—and within my reach, and requires but a change of posture to be placed open before me." [5]

Probably the book which began his new discovery of excitement in literature was *The Sketch Book*. "Every reader has his first book; I mean to say, one book among all others which in early youth first fascinates his imagination, and at once excites and satisfies the desires of his mind," he said in later years. "To me, this first book was *The Sketch Book* of Washington Irving." Was he recalling the Peucinian Society library? Or was he thinking of his Academy days? He continued:

"I was a school-boy when it was published, and read each succeeding number with ever increasing wonder and delight, spellbound by its pleasant humor, its melancholy tenderness, its atmosphere of revery,—nay, even by its gray-brown covers, the shaded letters of its titles, and the fair clean type . . . " [6]

Probably he did not see *The Sketch Book* in 1819, when the first numbers appeared. [7] But if he did he returned to it with opened eyes in the fall of 1823, for his letters suddenly took on a self-conscious and Irvingesque flavor. Abruptly he began to make observations on the quaint scenes and situations about him which he had never mentioned before:

"I see by the Portland papers that the Governour and council have appointed the twentieth of November as the day of Thanksgiving! as 'Thanksgiving Day' I suppose I should have said. I think I shall come up to feast with you on the fat of the land and every good thing of Portland. I like to have such days come round. They resemble the 'Merry Christmass of Old England' as the account is given of it in the Sketch Book. Although the 'Christmass Pie' is far surpassed by the 'New England peculiar' baked pumpkin & pan-dowdy! Talking about Thanksgiving Day puts me in mind of the *Pioneers* and ten thousand other things,—

geese, turkies, ducks, chickens, roasted pork, plum puddings, sour
apples and Molasses and pumpkin pies baked in milkpans, &c. &c.
—The Yankee's feast! ! ! . . . .

"The weather has been rainy and very unpleasant to day, with
a high north wind, that whistles well through the key hole and
the cracks around the door. I must have some list and very soon
too, or we shall all blow away up chimney. And now to conclude
my letter, I shall inform you that a few good *sour* apples would
be a most acceptable present from home. I prefer a mild sour to
sweet—or, in fact, any kind of sour, mild or not mild— But the
bell rings." [8]

Here was his response to his discovery of a native literature, and
the beginning of his conscious joy in objects peculiar to the land
of the Yankee. Throughout the fall he continued to reveal a par-
tiality for the writings of American authors, to assume a genuine
pride in his own country, and to take up the already familiar
cudgels of strong language in favor of a native literature. (At this
time and in later years, his literary tastes were in perfect accordance with the current trends.) He explained the situation to his
mother when he wrote a letter which purported to deal with
Charles Brockden Brown:

"You wish to know what I am reading. . . . I have just closed
Arthur Mervyn, a novel—an American novel—from the elegant
pen of C. B. Browne, formerly of N. York, whose writings are
nearly as much read and admired in Old England, as those of
Irving himself. The scene is laid in Philadelphia, at the time, when
that beautiful city was desolated by the wasting breath of pesti-
lence. . . . The author of the book, you will recollect, as an
American has never received from his countrymen that praise and
renown, which was his due,—justly and undeniably his due, and
which the stranger and the foreigner do not hesitate to bestow.
And it is a silent, but eloquent rebuke to the land of his birth and
his childhood, that the country already so great in literary reputation, so jealous of the beautiful wisdom of her rebellious and un-
dutiful child,—so impatient of superiority and so suspicious of
rivalship, should willingly and freely crown the brows of the
offspring of another soil with the laurel, which the unnatural
mother withheld. But the reputation of Brown, as a novelist is

at last breaking forth here also, and dawning upon the grave that holds his ashes. Tired at last of caressing the children of an exotick soil and fostering the offspring of another instead of her own, our country becomes grateful too late to cheer him with hope and smiles upon him when her smiles can no longer gladden the heart that felt her frowns and her rebukes so keenly. Arthur Mervyn is the only one of his novels I have read, though I reccollect I once met with another by the same author some years ago. His writings are numerous and a writer in Blackwood's Magazine speaks highly of them. I have lately understood, that a complete edition of his works will shortly issue from one of the N. York presses. I hope this is true, for I am so much pleased with what I have already seen, that I am impatient for more." [9]

His mother may have smiled as she refolded this letter and put it away. The boy had done his best to grow up by adopting a stilted phraseology which seemed worthy of the thoughts he had found in *Blackwood's* and the *North American*. He had told his mother that he had recently been reading books as diverse as William Wirt's *Letters of a British Spy* and D'Israeli's *Quarrels of Authors*. In answer to Zilpah's references to the writings of their townsman John Neal, Longfellow assured her that his enthusiasm had not run away with him:

"You mention 'Seventy Six' and 'Randolph.' If you call the former of these 'over-*wrought*' I do not know what you will say of the latter. Of Randolph I have heard a good-deal said. I have also seen several long extracts from it. It seems to me, judging from these, to be a compound of reason and nonsense—drollery and absurdity—wit and nastiness. It talks about the ladies of Baltimore—and how they 'eat snuff'! And some other things ten times as bad. And still I believe there are parts of it that go far to prove it the work of Genius." [10]

With unflagging delight he continued to rush through volume after volume. Only one week after he had written his first defense of American writers in general and Brown in particular he began a letter to his favorite sister, Anne: "You must know I have no time to spare—for what little time I can steal from my college exercises, I wish to devote to reading." [11] He explained that the announcement of assignments for the public exhibition of the fall term would give a definite direction to his reading for a time—at least, until he had completed his preparation:

"The part assigned me to perform, is a dialogue with J. W. Bradbury. Or as it was given out by the President, 'English Dialogue between a North American Savage and an English Emigrant.' We have 4 minutes a-piece: and the part is a high one, being the third in this division of the class. I think it will be a very fine subject both to write and speak upon, and although it is not the part I wished for, yet I have this consolation that it is much higher than that, which I expected, so that I have every reason to be satisfied and well pleased with this appointment." [12]

For the purposes of dialogue the two students identified themselves with familiar characters: Bradbury was Miles Standish, and Longfellow was King Philip. Possibly this decision to defend the Indians through the character of King Philip was due to Longfellow's familiarity with Irving's sketch entitled "Philip of Pokanoket." [13] But he needed background reading of a broader nature than *The Sketch Book*. In his search he discovered a big volume recently published by a Moravian missionary who had spent many years among the Delaware Indians: the Rev. John Heckewelder's *Account of the History, Manners, and Customs of the Indian Nations who once inhabited Pennsylvania and the neighbouring States*.[14] Although Heckewelder's prejudiced and romantic stories were not likely to furnish satisfactory information about King Philip, they naturally made a strong appeal to one who read Irving so contentedly.

When the evening of the exhibition came, snow fell hard across the landscape and blew in great gusts along the Brunswick plain. Only a few of the townspeople gathered with the students (who could do nothing else than attend) in the unheated chapel and braved the cold while the exhibition took place. But Longfellow and Bradbury provided them with a lively tilt, in which the savage and the emigrant took turns in hurling recriminations at each other. And yet, in the conclusion, the savage threw a spell and a mood of tragic dignity over the affair by bursting into lyric sentences pitched in a minor key. The last two speeches were these:

"*Emigrant:* Is it thus you should spurn all our offers of kindness, and glut your appetite with the blood of our countrymen, with no excuse but the mere pretence of retaliation? Shall the viper sting us and we not bruise his head? Shall we not only let your robberies and murders pass unpunished, but give you the possession of our very fireside, while the only arguments you offer are insolence and slaughter? Know ye, the land is ours until you will improve it. Go, tell your ungrateful comrades the world declares the spread of the white people at the expense of the red is the triumph of peace over violence. Tell them to cease their outrages upon the civilized world, or but a few days, and they shall be swept from the earth.

"*Savage:* Alas! the sky is overcast with dark and blustering clouds. The rivers run with blood, but never, never will we suffer the grass to grow upon our war-path. And now I do remember that the Initiate prophet, in my earlier years, told from his dreams that all our race should fall like withered leaves when Autumn strips the forest! Lo! I hear sighing and sobbing: 'tis the death-song of a mighty nation, the last requiem over the grave of the fallen." [15]

Having given a creditable performance, Longfellow was relieved. He wrote to his father: "The Exhibition took place last night, and I must confess I feel glad it is past. I feel a great weight is removed from my shoulders, for I could not but feel some solicitude, though I would never confess it. I shall now have a great deal more leisure, which to me is one of the sweetest things in the world." [16]

Returning once more to the quiet of his own room and fireplace, he soon found that he was blessed with an unexpected period of leisure and solitude. The college authorities gave special absence permissions to almost half of the upper classmen so that they might teach school in rural communities from two weeks before the winter vacation to two weeks after. Other students, eager to escape the last classwork in half-empty recitation rooms, managed to find a plausible excuse for absence. Stephen Longfellow departed early on a satisfactory pretext. Henry was happy to stay. Although he had considered teaching school, the idea was not very attractive to him. Earlier in the fall he had discussed the subject quite fully in a letter to his mother:

"I have just awoken from an afternoon's nap, and find all have gone to meeting and left me alone. I dropt to sleep just before the bell rang, as I was sitting with my book by the fire, and as this slip has given me a little leisure I gladly devote it to you. . . .

"I have been thinking about taking a school this Winter Vacation, but have at length concluded, that I had rather not. I have not come to this conclusion without some good reasons for it. One is, that I feel afraid of wasting my time, and wish to have leisure during the vacation for reading. A second is, that the confinement will be injurious to my health. I wish to ride round a little and get over the tediousness that the same things over and over again at College are apt to produce. I know I do not take sufficient exercise at present and I am confident I should not take much more whilst instructing a school." [17]

In spite of such complaints of tediousness associated with his studies he was enjoying most of his courses. Even the annoying difficulties of solid geometry were alleviated by the kindly wisdom of Professor Cleaveland. Under the same teacher's guidance he had progressed in philosophy through Paley's *Evidences* with more patience than pleasure and had found Locke's *Essay on the Human Understanding* "neither remarkably hard nor uninteresting." [18] Occasionally Cleaveland permitted his students to vary the formal recitations in philosophy by introducing informal discussions. He could even muster a benign smile for one student's theory that the soul continued in a state of consciousness at all times because "the souls of the inhabitants of one hemisphere whilst asleep, took up their abodes in the bodies of persons in the other." [19]

Another teacher even more important to Longfellow's development was Samuel P. Newman, Professor of Languages. Through his eyes Longfellow had discovered the personality behind the poetry of Horace. His earlier instructors in Latin and Greek had made language study merely a cold process of analyzing words and sentences; Newman was interested in both language and literature. The son of the headmaster of Phillips Academy, Andover, and a graduate of Harvard, he had come to Bowdoin in 1818 at the age of twenty-one. Immediately he had earned a reputation for the excellence of his teaching. Furthermore he did not present that forbidding and unpleasant severity of classroom manner which was a common characteristic of the older members of the faculty. It was even insinuated that Professor Newman was not a Congregationalist at all, but a Unitarian. At once his popularity increased anew among certain students.

Although there was no chair of rhetoric and oratory established at Bowdoin until 1824, Newman had already assumed the duties of such an office in the fall of 1823. To no other man on the Bowdoin faculty did Longfellow owe a greater debt of gratitude at the end of his course than to this professor who revived his earlier interest in writing verses, prose essays, and translations. Shortly before Christmas of 1823 Longfellow told his father in a letter why he preferred to remain at Bowdoin until the beginning of vacation:

"The Term is about closing, and many of the students, at least half, have gone. I should know it was the close of the term, even from the almost universal silence that prevails, though I had no further evidence. Now and then there is a solitary footstep heard in the entry, a solitary rap at the distant door, the noise of the falling latch, and then all still again. I dare say you can imagine it much better than I can write it, especially if you were ever among the few that linger to the end of the fall-term. . . . I may well say alone, for I am the only person in the third story of this end of college. It seems pretty solitary to be sure, but I had about as lief be alone, and rather on some accounts, than have another with me. For my part, I feel no great desire to return yet. Our lessons are generally far from being difficult, the recitations short, and the evenings long. About three fourths of our class are absent, so that the time taken up in reciting is not half what it used to be. The Term closes on Friday the 9th. I do not think of leaving until very near the end. Wednesday is the day I have pitched upon as my νόστιμον ημαρ, or day of returning. We read themes this forenoon—or more properly we did not read them, for the plan pursued by our professor is this. The themes are given to him for criticism, once a-fortnight. He returns them to us marked for correction, or not, as it may happen. We hand them to him again, and on a fixed day he reads extracts from the best written before the whole class, not mentioning the name of the writer. This course has apparently done much good, for it makes us all

ambitious to excell, and the Themes are evidently written with
much greater care than they were before, when we all read our
own to the President. And he (Professor Newman) has also made
another new regulation with regard to our writing, which I
should think equally beneficial with the former. This is having a
strict rule of punctuality. Unless the Themes are given to him
upon the day appointed, the student is fined for omission of writing, except he give a satisfactory excuse. This has had the desired
effect, and where before everything seemed to lag as it were, we
now go on in great order and regularity." [20]

He did not tell his father that he had been writing poetry. His
mother would listen with greater sympathy. Also, the poem on
which he had been working in the silence of his dormitory room
was a matter for secrecy. Announcements had been made in
various newspapers that the Boston Shakespeare Jubilee was spon-
soring a prize competition for an ode to be read at the opening
of the Jubilee in February, 1824. And long before the beginning
of vacation Longfellow had submitted an ode. Possibly he might
get to Boston for the event. Eugene Weld, his classmate, was
driving from Brunswick to Boston on business during the vacation and had invited Longfellow to accompany him. First, there
was the need for permission from his father, then in Washington.
With characteristic foresight Stephen Longfellow had written to
his sons just before he left Portland in the fall of 1823: "From this
time till thirty days after Congress rises you can write to me by
mail free of postage, if your letters do not weigh more than two
ounces. You will therefore direct your letters to the family, to
me." [21] Here was a thrifty, practical man, who would be influenced only by the strongest arguments his son could devise. Conscious of this difficulty, Henry did his best to compose a convincing letter:

"PORTLAND Jan. 11 1824

"My Dear Father,

"I write to you at this time to inform you of a plan I have
formed for passing a part of the present College vacation. 'Amusement reigns man's great demand' as Dr. Young says, and my plan
is this. To go to Boston, and spend a week there. My classmate

Weld is going on in the course of a week or two, and offers me a seat in his sleigh, which invitation I feel much inclination to accept. I have written to you for your approbation of this plan, which I think is a very good one. That you may the more readily think as I do, I would inform you that I was never fifty miles from Portland, in all my life, which I think is rather a sorrowful circumstance in the annals of my history. When I hear others talking, as travellers are very apt to do, about what they have seen and heard abroad, I always regret my having never been from home more than I have hitherto. So that I often wish I had not been so fond of a sedentary life. I am of an opinion, that it is better to know the world partly from observation than wholly from books. You, who have seen so much of it, at least of one division of it, will know how this is, and I dare say, will think so too, since most others do. This visit then may on this account be advantageous as well as agreeable. Besides I do not think it will be very expensive, since if I go in the manner before-mentioned the cost of travelling will be greatly reduced. My companion that is to be, should this plan go into operation, has numerous relatives in Boston, and as he will take the horse to his own account, that expense will also be removed. He is going on for his sister, who is visiting there, in consequence of which, if he has my company, I shall be under the necessity of returning in the stage. I do not know as there is any kind of utility to arise from thus being minute in the statement of particulars, but I wish you to know everything 'pro and con.' I think you will be inclined to express your approbation of this measure. I wish you would write me as soon as convenient upon this subject, that I may know what answer to give Mr. Weld in regard to this." [22]

In answer to this carefully worded petition, Mr. Longfellow wrote an enlightening polemic on the subject of travel. His letter expressed the prudent moral dignity and stiff righteousness which contrasted so strongly with the pliant loveliness of Zilpah's character. This distant seriousness, an unintentional barrier between himself and his son, strengthened respect but hindered intimacy:

"Nothing affords me more pleasure than to gratify the reasonable desires of my children, especially when they evince a disposition to promote the happiness of their parents, by diligent improvement of their time & talents, & uniform attention to those rules of morality, which adorn the human character. . . .

"It is certainly desirable to know the world from observation, as well as from books. A careful & accurate observation of men & manners is necessary to correct many erroneous opinions, which we find in books & to guard us against false impressions, and impositions, to which the young & inexperienced are exposed in their first intercourse with the world. But there is danger on the other hand, that youth & inexperience by launching into the world too early, may imbibe many false & extravagant notions, that may prove injurious to them through life. To travel with advantage requires a maturity of understanding & an extensive knowledge of books. Youth is therefore the proper period for study, manhood for traveling, & intercourse with mankind. The ardor of youth is apt to place a false estimate on the novelties of the world, & is easily led astray by the allurements of pleasure, & enchanted by the visions of fancy, or the splendor of a deceitful world.

"These are general observations, & not intended to have a particular bearing on your proposed visit to Boston, but designed to guard you against too ardent a desire to become a traveler early in life, which frequently injures rather than improves very young persons.

"As the opportunity you mention will be a good one, if you are very desirous of availing yourself of it, I shall not object, if your mother thinks it best." [23]

Significant warnings these, and many of them worth Longfellow's renewed consideration two years later. For the present, a compromise was arranged: Henry took the stage for Boston, but with his Aunt Lucia on the morning of February 11. Apparently Zilpah, at least, had been allowed to share the secret of why it was so important that her son be in Boston. In Salem, Aunt Lucia left the stage. She had no fears about her nephew, for she knew that he was to visit the Doanes and the Wellses on Beacon Hill. But to Henry, the adventure of entering the "Literary Emporium" was exciting beyond words. Night had come, and the windows in the city were yellow with candlelight as the coach rattled down cobblestone streets and stopped before the Exchange Coffee House on Congress Square. Alone, and happy in his freedom, Long-fellow decided that the hour was too late for arousing his host, and took a room for the night high under the eaves in the Exchange House.

After he had found his friends the next morning, he began crowding days with activity—visits to the State House, the Boston Athenaeum, Stewart's painting room, Dagget's Repository, Charlestown, the Navy Yard, Breed's Hill, Cambridge, and the Harvard College Yard. There were social events, also. The private ball given by Miss Emily Marshall, the most celebrated of the city belles, afforded an evening of what Longfellow described as "indeed a most *splendid* entertainment, more so by far than any I had ever beheld before." [24]

Even feminine loveliness, to which Longfellow was always susceptible, could not make him forget his prize poem and the Shakespeare Jubilee. He attended, but to his disappointment learned that the honors had been awarded to Charles Sprague, already a professional master in the art of manufacturing poetry to order.[25] Since Longfellow had kept the entire matter pretty much a secret, he felt no disgrace attached to his failure. But one evening at dinner, he sat next to Judge Minot, who had helped award the prize to Sprague. And he felt his face grow red, suddenly, as the Judge turned to ask if he were by any chance the Longfellow who had written a poem for the festival and sent it from Portland. The boy pretended not to hear, and the subject was not discussed. "It is fortunate I think that H. did not receive the prize," Zilpah wrote, confidentially, to her husband after the details of this incident had been shared with her. "That would have turned his head. It shews a good share of confidence in his own powers to make the attempt to win the prize. It has never been mentioned to him at home." [26]

There were consolations in Boston. In the home of Dr. John Doane Wells,[27] where Longfellow was visiting, was an attractive young cousin of the doctor, named Caroline Doane. Her genuine interest and wide reading in modern poetry led the guest to talk quite freely with her and finally to confess the beginning of his own literary endeavors. Her response was flattering. Before he went back to Portland the Bowdoin junior had become quite a literary lion within the narrow circle of the Wells household. Zilpah described the arrival of the travelers in one of her faithful letters to Stephen in Washington:

"Friday evening we had the pleasure of seeing Lucia and Henry return. Dr. Wells was with them. They arrived about 7 in the mail stage. As we had a little party of half a dozen *young* ladies and as many gentlemen, their arrival was very opportune. Henry came home quite in spirits; he danced in the evening, and walked home with Miss E. Scott, after being awake all the night before, and riding a hundred miles in a day. But he complained of fatigue at last. . . . Stephen went back to college on Saturday morning, Henry concluded to stop till Monday. He wished Dr. Wells to pass a day or two with us but could not prevail on him to stay, though we said every thing we could. Mr. Cleaveland had written to him to be on a week beforehand, and he must go, as the lectures were to commence on Monday. Henry staid at Mr. Wells, and was most kindly entertained. He will tell you himself about his delightful visit." [28]

VI

SELF-DISCOVERY

The fact is,—and I will not disguise it in the least, for I think I ought not,—the fact is, I most eagerly aspire after future eminence in literature, my whole soul burns most ardently after it, and every earthly thought centers in it.[1]

SHORTLY after his return to Bowdoin from Boston, Longfellow wrote to his father that he had come back with some reluctance— and added significantly, "Yet here I am again, and well contented to be here, since I am to stay but a little more than a year longer." [2] His visit had revealed even wider horizons, and had set loose in his head grand ideas which hindered him from regaining his earlier interest in classes.

Gradually, he had been developing a strong desire to direct his life toward a literary career. In spite of his failure to compete successfully with Charles Sprague, he had reasons for optimism, for he had found editors who were willing to publish his writings. Before his departure for Boston he had sent to the editor of the *Portland Advertiser* four ten-line stanzas welcoming the New Year. Modelled after his favorite "Ode on a Distant Prospect of Eton College," the verses were flavored with the same eighteenth century conceits and tricks which he had worked into his Shakespeare ode. This was the final stanza:

And thou art fair, thou New-born Year,
  Though, heralding thy birth,
The night-wind moan'd through woodlands sere,
  And wav'd their branches forth,—
Though the night-dirge, above the grave,
Was the sole musick Winter gave,
  To bid thine advent speed!
For his rude hand had broken in pride
The lute of Nature's Summer tide,
  And Autumn's mellow reed.[3]

His good fortune in securing the publication of these verses and his eager hope of success in the Shakespeare ode competition had whetted his desire for literary eminence and had increased his impatience with the confining requirements of college. But what would his father say to such chimerical plans? Not long after his return to Brunswick from Boston he determined to sound his father out on the subject. After writing an account of lectures on chemistry by Professor Cleaveland, he granted that they were of importance to medical students but of little interest to him. Then he cautiously approached the more important matter:

"I feel very glad that I am not to be a physician,—that there are quite enough in the world without me. And now, as somehow or other this subject has been introduced, I am curious to know what you do intend to make of me!—Whether I am to study a profession or not! and if so, what profession? I hope your ideas upon this subject will agree with mine, for I have a particular and strong prejudice for one course of life, to which you I fear will not agree. It will not be worth while for me to mention what this is, until I become more acquainted with your own wishes." [4]

Although he watched the mails for a possible answer to this pertinent question, he received none. Apparently his father, busy with congressional duties, did not believe that there was any need for an immediate decision.

As Longfellow's junior year drew to an end he became more thoroughly absorbed in the relationship between what he read and what he wrote. The translating of Horace was a delight which caused him to assert, "I have not met with so pleasant a study since the commencement of my college life." [5] Probably Professor Newman encouraged his talented student to combine his assignments in Latin with those in Rhetoric, and to make metrical translations. The Honorable Benjamin Orr, a trustee of Bowdoin, serving on the committee of examination at the close of the year, was so impressed with the grace and smoothness of Longfellow's translation of an ode from Horace that he made particular enquiries concerning the student. Mr. Orr knew the young man's father and had occasionally dined with the lawyer in his Portland home. His friend's son would bear watching, Orr decided. One year later he recalled this incident when the trustees began to search for a professor of modern languages. [6]

The unanswered question was still troubling Longfellow when he returned to Bowdoin as a senior in the fall of 1824. He must convince his father that there was only one path for him, and that he should not be happy if circumstances denied him access to this path. Stephen Longfellow did not need to say, "*You shall study the law*," for Longfellow had been made to understand this unspoken decree. Nevertheless, his father could not ignore an argument fired with ardent conviction. Having pondered many weeks over the conflict between his hopes and his father's plans, the Bowdoin senior mapped out a definite course of action. Recognizing the inadequacy of his education, and convinced that a man of letters needed a firmer grasp of languages than that afforded at Bowdoin, Longfellow wrote a pointed exposition to his father early in December:

"I take this early opportunity to write to you, because I wish to know fully your inclination with regard to the profession I am to pursue when I leave college. For my part, I have already hinted to you what would best please me. I want to spend one year at Cambridge for the purpose of reading History, and of becoming familiar with the best authors in polite literature; whilst at the same time I can be acquiring a knowledge of the Italian language, without an acquaintance with which I shall be shut out from one of the most beautiful departments of letters. The French I mean to understand pretty thoroughly before I leave College. After leaving Cambridge I would attach myself to some literary periodical publication, by which I could maintain myself and still enjoy the advantage of reading. Now I do not think that there is anything visionary and chimerical in my plan thus far. The fact is,— and I will not disguise it in the least, for I think I ought not,—the fact is, I most eagerly aspire after future eminence in literature, my whole soul burns most ardently after it, and every earthly thought centers in it. There may be something visionary in *this*, but I flatter myself, that I have prudence enough to keep my enthusiasm from defeating its own object by too great haste.

"Surely there never was a better opportunity offered for the exertion of literary talent in our own country than is now offered. To be sure, most of our literary men, thus far, have not been professedly so, until they have studied and entered the practice of Theology, Law, or Medicine. But this is evidently lost time.

"I do believe that we ought to pay more attention to the opinion of Philosophers, that 'nothing but Nature can qualify a man for knowledge.'—Whether Nature has given me any capacity for knowledge or not, she has at any rate given me a very strong predilection for literary pursuits, and I am almost confident in believing, that if I can ever rise in the world it must be by the exercise of my talents in the wide field of literature. With such a belief I must say, that I am unwilling to engage in the study of the Law. Had I an inclination to become an orator, not this inclination, nor any application to the study of oratory, could constitute me one, unless Nature had given me a genius for that pursuit. This I think will hold good in its application to all the professions of life, and of course to literary pursuits. Here, then, seems to be the starting point; and I think it best for me to float out into the world upon that tide, and in that channel, which will the soonest bring me to my destined port;—and not struggle against both wind and tide, and by attempting what is impossible, lose everything.

"I have sent three pieces of Poetry to Mr. Parsons for the U. S. Literary Gazette, and he has thought so well of them as to invite me to become a regular correspondent. I intended to have shown you his letters at Thanksgiving, but forgot to take them with me when I left Brunswick. I am very much pleased with the kindness he has already shown me, and am willing to leave to his own judgement the amount of compensation, which I am justly entitled to by my contributions, and which he promises shall be satisfactory. Mr. Parsons says,—I speak it without vanity because I speak it to *you*—that he is 'well satisfied that my literary talents are of no ordinary character,' and he judges from the three short pieces I have already sent him, and speaks with so much apparent sincerity, that I should be unwilling on that account, had I no other, to think that he spoke otherwise, than as he thought." [7]

Again his father made no immediate reply, and the silence seemed to confirm Longfellow's belief that he was being forced, without words, to an acceptance of the law as a profession. So great was the boy's sense of filial respect and obedience that he did not dare to rebel further against even this unspoken command. His next letter showed a gradual yielding to the pregnant silence, although it contained a determined plea for the one year of respite at Cambridge:

"I am very desirous to hear your opinion of my project of residing a year at Cambridge. Even should it be found necessary for me to study a profession, I should think a twelve-months residence at Harvard before commencing the study of that profession would be exceedingly useful. Of Divinity, Medicine, & Law, I should choose the last. And whatever I do study ought to be engaged in with all my soul—for I *will* be eminent in something. The question then is, whether or not I could engage in the Law with all that eagerness which in these times is necessary to success?—I fear that I could not!—Ought I not then to choose another path in which I can go on with better hopes of success?—Let me reside one year at Cambridge,—let me study Belles Lettres;—and after that time has elapsed it will not require a spirit of prophecy to predict with some degree of certainty what kind of a figure I could make in the literary world." [8]

When his father's answer came, it was exactly what was expected. Stephen Longfellow did not insist that his son devote himself to the study of law immediately—he did not need to insist. He even admitted that a year of graduate work at Harvard "might be beneficial." But he expressed severe doubts as to the advisability of supposing a man might earn a living with his pen—in America:

"The subject of your first letter is one of deep interest, and demands great consideration. A literary life, to one who has the means of support, must be very pleasant. But there is not wealth & munificence enough in this country to afford sufficient encouragement & patronage to merely literary men. And as you have not had the fortune (I will not say good or ill) to be born rich, you must adopt a profession which will afford you a subsistence as well as reputation. I am happy to observe that you are ambitious of literary distinction, and I have no doubt but you possess genius & taste which, if properly cultivated will secure you high respectability in the literary world or in a profession if you should devote your attention to one. You have every inducement to cultivate with care & diligence the faculties which you possess, and with the blessing of a kind Providence, & a careful attention to your health & morals, I feel a comforting assurance that you will succeed.

"My ambition has never been to accumulate wealth for my children, but to cultivate their minds in the best possible manner, & to imbue them with correct moral, political, & religious principles, believing that a person thus educated with proper diligence & attention, will be certain of attaining all the wealth which is necessary to his happiness. . . ." [9]

The obedient son accepted this rejoinder as a command from which there could be no immediate appeal. But he found great consolation in his father's tentative promise that he should be given a year of study at Harvard. Such a year would give a temporary escape from reading law—and what might not happen in a year? Outwardly resigned, but inwardly planning and dreaming methods of escape, he wrote his capitulation:

"From the general tenor of your last letter, it seems to be your fixed desire, that I should choose the profession of the Law for the business of my life. I believe that I have already mentioned to you that I did not wish to enter immediately upon any profession. I am very much rejoiced to hear that you accede so readily to my proposition of studying general literature for one year at Cambridge. My grand object in doing this will be to gain as perfect a knowledge of the French and Italian languages as can be gained by study without travelling in France and Italy, though to tell the truth I intend to visit both before I die. The advantages of this step are obvious,—the means of accomplishing an end so desirable exertion must supply. I am afraid that you begin to think me rather chimerical in many of my ideas, and that I am ambitious of becoming a 'rara avis in terris.'—But you must acknowledge the propriety and usefulness of aiming high—at something which it is impossible to overshoot—perhaps to reach. The fact is,—what I have previously said to you upon the subject leads me to exhibit myself without disguise,—I have a most voracious appetite for knowledge. To its acquisition I will sacrifice anything; and I now lament most bitterly the defects of my early education that are attributable in part to myself and in part to my instructers. My advantages have been from infancy almost boundless—and by reflecting but one moment I see how awfully I have neglected them.

STEPHEN LONGFLLOW, 1825

I knew neither the value of time nor of these advantages. I now refer to the years which I passed at the Academy. Of having misspent the portion of my College life already passed I cannot reproach myself so severely, although I have left undone a multitude of things that ought to have been done. But fortunately for me, as I grow older I grow more studious. Nothing delights me more than reading and writing—and although this assertion, unqualified as I have made it, may savour of vanity, yet I feel the truth of it: and nothing could induce me to relinquish the pleasures of literature—little as I have as yet tasted them.

"—But this is a wide digression. And in returning to our former subject I can only say that of all professions—I would say of the three professions which are sometimes called the learned professions—I should prefer the Law. I am far from being a fluent speaker:—but practice must serve as a talisman, when talent is wanting. I can be a lawyer, for some lawyers are mere simpletons. This will support my *real* existence, literature an *ideal* one.

"I purchased last evening a beautiful pocket edition of Sir Wm Jones's letters and have just finished reading them. Eight languages he was critically versed in—eight more he read with a dictionary, and there were still twelve more which he had studied less perfectly, but which were not wholly unknown to him; making in all twenty eight languages to which he had given his attention. I have somewhere seen or heard the observation, that as many languages as a person acquired, so many times was he a man. Mr. Jones was equal to about sixteen men, according to that observation." [10]

Having thus qualified his surrender to his father's wishes, Longfellow still hoped he might prove that writing could furnish a real means of earning one's daily bread. Since the visit to Boston he had been writing, writing, writing, and his first letter to his mother thereafter had contained a significant postscript: "Please to send me a quire of letter-paper!" [11] Furthermore, he had been selling his literary productions to editors in Boston and Philadelphia. During the month before he had returned to Bowdoin as a senior, he had published over one hundred and fifty lines of poetry in the *Portland Advertiser*.[12] More satisfying still was the flattering praise of James McHenry, editor of the *American Monthly Maga-*

zine, who had accepted one dramatic sketch, one poem, and one essay, with words of high commendation and promises of liberal payment.[13] He had told his father about Theophilus Parsons, and the *United States Literary Gazette*. The first letter from Parsons was very satisfying, and had contained a few lines so genuinely cordial as to turn the head of any seventeen-year-old boy:

". . . almost all the poetry we print is sent to us gratis, & we have no general rule or measure of repayment. But the beauty of your poetry makes me wish to obtain your regular aid. Will you be good enough to let me know how large & how frequent contributions it will be agreeable to you to furnish us, & what mode or amount of compensation you would desire." [14]

Spurred to greater energy by this praise, Longfellow sent to the *Gazette* editor one manuscript after another in rapid succession during the fall and winter of his senior year.[15] Occasionally, Parsons was forced to refuse certain offerings. The young author was gratified when the kindly editor, unable to use his review essay on Grattan's *Highways and Byways*, wrote that he would send it on to his friend Jared Sparks, editor of the *North American*, because that periodical did not "seek for novelty so much as a Gazette must." [16] Sparks, in returning the article to Parsons, commented, "Many of the thoughts and reflections are good, but they want maturity, and betray a young writer. The style too is a little ambitious although not without occasional elegance. With more practice the author cannot fail to become a good writer." [17] Sparks's advice was taken to heart, for the Bowdoin senior practiced so diligently during his senior year that his contributions to the *Gazette* alone included sixteen separate poems, five prose essays, and two book reviews—an amazing output, for a college student.

Longfellow also found time for participation in various college activities. His first letter home in the fall had made this introductory apology for failure to write sooner: "The fact is, I have been much engaged of late in writing my Latin Oration, which is to be delivered at the Exhibition on Friday next." Professor Newman seems to have been an early exponent of correlating various subjects, for he approved Longfellow's selection of *Angli Poetae* as the subject of his oration, delivered October 29, 1824. Shortly after this occasion came the annual anniversary celebration of the Peucinian Society.

To the Bowdoin students, nothing except commencement was as important an event during the college year as the public celebrations of the two literary societies. Rivalry for honors was keen. Graduates returned for the occasions, townspeople assembled to fill the chapel, and each participating member did his best to make an oral offering worthy of the society tradition. To Longfellow was assigned the significant honor of delivering a poem of some four hundred lines. Having saturated his mind, since Academy days, with Scott's tales of knights and fair ladies, novices in convents, joustings on fields of honor, and ancient chivalry, he chose as his subject "The Poetry of the Dark Ages." So well received was his reading that favorable reports reached the ears of Theophilus Parsons, who wrote asking if he might use it in the *Gazette*. But Longfellow protested that it was too long and declined to send it.[19]

Poetry did not interest Henry's brother Stephen. The two boys offered revealing contrasts. Although Stephen held the advantage in age, Henry was obliged to urge him on in his studies. There was no need for tutoring assistance from Henry, for Stephen was the more brilliant of the two when he wished to be. Yet, while the younger brother sat late over his classroom preparations, Stephen preferred to prowl about the dormitory or to enjoy the forbidden pleasures of visiting Ward's tavern. When his fines began to mount his parents reprimanded him—without changing his ways. Discussing these matters, while her sons were juniors, Zilpah had written to her husband:

"Your plan for the education of your sons was liberal and judicious, and as it respected one of them perfectly right. Henry I believe will fully answer your expectations, his bill was perfectly free from fines, and his brother says that his part at the exhibition was very handsomely performed, he thinks I should have been much pleased to have witnessed it. But our sons are different, very different. I think they are so naturally, and it cannot, I think, be imputed as a fault to one that he is not like the other, that he does not delight in the same employments." [20]

The danger of violating college rules was a very practical

weapon of caution which Henry Longfellow used on his older brother. The conflict between the government and the students had increased at Bowdoin until one scrape followed another in quick succession and the action of the faculty became so severe that suspensions were given out almost as freely as fines. These facts could be pointed out to Stephen without having any apparent effect. Finally, under the direct questioning of his mother, Henry was forced to give accounts of his brother's behavior. But his letter left unsaid far more than it told:

"Stephen did not show his letter to me, nor mention that he had received one. I have said nothing about it to him, and do not know whether he has yet received the one you refer to. If you desire the whole truth I must not conceal it. His conduct seems to be pretty much as it was last term. He is absent from his room most of the time, and I do not know how much he studies, although he does not appear very well at recitation. I am now almost sorry I have told you, what I have told. It is too near the beginning of the term to judge of what he will do. Excepting this apparent negligence, his conduct is perfectly regular. You see in what a very unpleasant situation you have placed me, by setting me as a spy upon him. If I do not tell you the truth of the matter, I shall not be doing my duty, and yet when I tell you the truth, I am afraid you will interpret things worse than they really are. Don't write to papa about it for I am certain he will be more apt to do so than you are. I cannot say any more." [21]

President Allen had been trying to discover who was responsible for the continual outbreaks of disorder in the yard and dormitories. He seemed powerless to stop the hoodlum noises and mysterious bonfires which disturbed the intended quiet of evening study hours. He also seemed to have little success in curtailing the drinking of certain students. All the inns sold liquor freely, and the more daring members of the college boldly smuggled strong spirits across the yard and into their dormitory rooms in new kerosene cans which looked innocent enough. Stephen Longfellow joyfully participated in much of the mischief until late December of his senior year, when he was caught in an evening rumpus. Convicted of having violated three major interdictions he was promptly rusticated to the home of a Congregational minister in Kennebunkport for a period of four months.[22]

Doubtless Stephen was not concerned when he found that his absence deprived him of the first lecture delivered by a new "Professor of Mental and Moral Philosophy" at Bowdoin. The name of Thomas Cogswell Upham and the appearance of this young Dartmouth graduate at Bowdoin were certain to mean more to Stephen's brother, who knew him as the author of a poem on the battle of Lovewell's Pond. Ironic, indeed, that this flesh-and-blood reminder of original literary sin should walk before the guilty one; that he should come to lead the culprit out of the darkness of plagiaristic iniquity into the light of goodness, beauty, and truth. An added touch of distaste was given by the accepted rumor that young Professor Upham had been called from his Congregational ministry to defend the losing cause of orthodoxy at Bowdoin, against the infidel ideas and insinuations of Kant and Cousin. Fortunately the students soon found that Upham did not fit well into the hated group represented to them by myopic Parson Mead and officious President Allen. Longfellow was pleased to find, through classroom relations, that his new teacher was not only agreeable but also eager to establish intimate friendship with his students. This was an amazing precedent. When the occasion permitted, Longfellow arranged for his new friend to call at the Congress Street home during one of his frequent visits to Portland. Mrs. Longfellow was well pleased with what she heard of the gentleman, although she did not see him when he delivered the following note at her front door:

"My dear Mother,

"I take this opportunity to write you a line, in order to introduce to you our new Professor, Mr. Upham, with whom you will doubtless be much pleased. No one of our government,—no—not even a student is so universally admired in college, as he is. His 'sayings & doings' are altogether different from anything we have hitherto met with from our instructers & officers of college. He associates with us as if he were one of us—he visits us at our rooms & we visit him at his:—so that the formality, which has heretofore existed between the officers & students of college is fast wearing out of use, and giving place to a more agreeable, & doubtless a profitable,—familiarity. He has politely offered to be the bearer of any letters, & I have given him this, that you may see him:—of course inviting him to call." [23]

As young poets, both Upham and Longfellow reflected the spirit of the day in their desire to help America bring forth an indigenous literature. In his preface to *American Sketches,* Upham had pointed out that stories about the first settlers, the missionaries, the explorers, the frontier villages, and especially the Indian savages, offered "enchanting topicks as well for the pencil of the limner as the lyre of the bard." In another part of that preface he had written:

"Every rood of Scotland, her hills and moated castles, her bleak mountains and threatening precipices are as dear to the memory and as classical, as the isles of Greece and the plains of Italy. . . . If then other countries almost universally cultivate in a greater or less degree the arts of song, and contrive to encircle with a sort of local enchantment their mountains, waters, and windshaken woods, . . . shall not our native country listen to a single 'witch-note' in the commemoration of its glories?" [24]

Longfellow had followed Upham's exhortations—and possibly his acquaintance and conversation with Upham at Bowdoin during his senior year was responsible for a renewed interest in Indian subjects. Four of his poems, written in the spring of 1825, were entitled, "The Indian Hunter," "Lover's Rock," "Jeckoyva" (Chocorua), and "Burial of the Minnisink." [25]

Another poem, written at this time, was still more closely associated with Upham. When the centennial day of Captain Lovewell's historic battle approached, the town of Fryeburg decided to commemorate the heroic tragedy. An elaborate local holiday was planned, with ceremonies including speeches, a social levee, and a ball in the evening. Eager to participate, Longfellow wrote appropriate verses which he offered to be sung during the occasion. On May 19, he drove up through the woods to Fryeburg with his friend Ned Preble, attended the celebration, participated in the singing of his own "Ode Written for the Commemoration of Lovewell's Fight," mingled with the guests of honor at Judge Dana's mansion where the levee was held, and danced at the ball in the local tavern that evening. The following day they stopped at Hiram, on their way home, to visit with Peleg Wadsworth and his family.[26] The entire affair was a gay outing for the Bowdoin seniors, and perhaps Longfellow, reading his second poem on Captain Lovewell, as it was printed in a Portland newspaper a few days later, was satisfied that he had thereby redeemed himself.

The last term at Bowdoin was extremely pleasant. The summer days and the realization of imminent partings colored the appearance of familiar scenes and endowed them with richer significance. And when the commencement day parts were announced shortly after the beginning of the term, Longfellow wrote to his sister Anne, who would be eager to share his happiness:

"The appointments for commencement were given out this afternoon. Little has the first Oration in English—Bradbury the second—your brother Henry the third. You must not think from this that I am the third schollar in the class, for that would be a sad mistake. Weld has a disquisition—Mellen a poem—and so forth & so on.

"The moon is just rising over our beautiful pines, and the twilight grows too dark for me to write without a lamp—Good night —I shall have a word or two more for you in the morning.

"Thursday Morning, June 30.
"My appointment, they tell me, is considered the fourth in the class, having only Little, Deane & Bradbury above me—How I came to get so high, is rather a mistery to me, in as much as I have never been a remarkably hard student, touching College studies,— except during my Sophomore year, when I used to think that I was studying pretty hard—though I might possibly have been mistaken.—In five weeks we shall be set free from College—for one month—Then comes Commencement—and then—and then—I cannot say what *will be*, after that." [27]

The subject which had been assigned to Longfellow, and which had been duly recorded with the other subjects in the faculty minutes under date of June 28, 1825, was "Native Writers." Another subject had made such a strong appeal to him, however, that he asked for permission to make a change. In April he had purchased from a dealer in Boston a three-volume edition of Chatterton's poems, and had paid for the set from honorariums owed him by the *Gazette*. Having grown particularly fond of melancholy tales, and graveyard poets, Longfellow very naturally found a strong appeal in Chatterton's pathetic story. He had written to his mother about it:

"Your frequent rebukes in reference to my negligence in writing have not been to me vain chidings:—I have felt them all, though you may have had reason to think otherwise. With all my usual delinquency, however, I should have answered your letter of the 13th before this, had I not received, on Monday, 'Chatterton's Works,' for which I had some time since sent to Boston. It is an elegant work in three large Octavo volumes, of 536 pages each, and since Monday noon I have read the greater part of two of them—besides attending two Lectures a day of an hour each and three recitations of the same length together with my study-hours for preparation. Of course I have no time for writing letters. . . ." [28]

The immediate outcome of his reading Chatterton was an essay, in his newly acquired literary style of elegance tinged with melancholy. His former collaborator, William Browne, who had been given his degree from Bowdoin *in absentia*, was studying law in Portland, and conducting a column in the *Portland Advertiser*, under the title, "Pedestrian." To this column Longfellow sent his essay, "Reminiscence of Genius." [29] Later, he had asked that he be allowed to choose for his commencement oration "The Life and Writings of Chatterton." In July he wrote to his father concerning the approved change, confessed that he had written his essay, but expressed some hesitancy as to whether he had done well to choose the subject of Chatterton's brief career. "I hardly know how this will answer," he wrote, "but am rather of the opinion that it must do." [30] His father expressed doubts as to whether the subject would interest practical and matter-of-fact people:

"To the man of genius, the poet & the scholar, the life & writings of Chatterton will be an interesting subject; but so few of your audience ever heard of his name or know anything of the untimely fate of that uncommon youth, that I fear you will not be able to make the subject interesting to them. . . . If you doubt on this subject it is not too late to make another choice." [31]

Although Longfellow had been requested by his classmates to prepare a farewell poem which was to be read at a final private meeting of the class on the day following graduation, he decided to abandon his essay on Chatterton and to return to the original subject assigned. Again he obtained permission to change, although Professor Cleaveland was not a little disturbed. The programs had already been printed, and there was nothing for the busy professor to do but take his pen and correct the title of Longfellow's oration on every sheet.[32]

Because the class of 1825 was the largest which had ever been graduated from Bowdoin the occasion brought a great assemblage of people. Commencement was the most important day of the year not only for the faculty and students but also for the merchants and townspeople, who prepared for the large crowds by building booths along the fences of the yard and decorating them colorfully to attract customers to partake of pies, gingerbread, root beer, and stronger drinks. The relatives and friends arrived in stagecoaches, chaises, phaëtons, and outlandish rigs. Conveyances lined Maine Street so thickly that the row of fly-troubled horses pounded their hooves in the dirt along the yard fence from Ward's tavern to the end of College Street. The college authorities, experienced in their tasks, always estimated the number of people who would attend the exercises by studying the row of horses and wagons along that fence. And since no building could house the throng, the custom was to erect a platform in the open region near the pine grove. Here assembled the trustees, the overseers, the clergymen, and the notables of Maine to witness the graduation of the class of 1825.

The crowd, the excitement, and the importance of the moment must have brought strange thoughts into Longfellow's mind as he sat on the platform, in his black robe, under the shadow of the whispering pines. Gone were the unpleasant memories: the early discouragement, the disappointment of the first Thanksgiving, the illness and homesickness of his sophomore year, the drab room at

Parson Titcomb's, so bleak through the long winter. Gone were the recollections of dull classes in mathematics, the incessant Sunday drone of Rev. Asa Mead, the plodding stagecoach rides in the rain after vacations, the loneliness of half-deserted dormitories, and the bitter clashes between the students and the President. Friendships suddenly became strong and imperishable. Equally strong were the bonds of intimacy which had been fashioned in long conversations outside the classroom with such teachers as Parker Cleaveland, Samuel Phillips Newman, and Thomas Cogswell Upham. But his most important memory was the joy of self-discovery; the excitement of working secretly, late in the night, to fetter newly caught ideas with written words; the inner glow that came with reading letters of praise from appreciative editors in the enchanting city of Boston and the unknown city of Philadelphia. What would this new discovery mean to him? At last he was free. Commencement—and then?

He already knew the answer. Against his wish, he would become a lawyer, for there was no alternative. This thorn in his side had bothered ever since his father had decided for him so firmly and quietly. The hurt was aggravated, however, by the young man's certainty that his father was wrong: that a national literature could be created if only enough American authors worked devotedly and with a singleness of purpose; if only the readers wanted a native literature enough to support it. Out of these very thoughts he had written the commencement oration which he was about to deliver. And when his turn came, he spoke no mere words of conventional graduation day discourse but words which reflected his own cherished aspirations. It is not difficult to imagine him standing erect on the wooden platform, his well formed head up as his sensitive blue eyes looked out over the upturned faces that stretched from the platform edge to the very shadow of the dark pines in the background. The light must have brought out the heightened color in his cheeks and glinted through his profuse brown hair as he launched vigorously into his subject:

"To an American there is something endearing in the very sounds,—Our Native Writers. Like the music of our native tongue, when heard in a foreign land, they have power to kindle up within him the tender memory of his home and fireside;—and more than this, they foretell, that whatever is noble and attractive in our national character will one day be associated with the sweet magic of Poetry. Is then our land to be indeed the land of song? Will it one day be rich in romantic associations? Will poetry, that hallows every scene,—that renders every spot classical,—and pours out on all things the soul of its enthusiasm, breathe over it that enchantment, which lives in the isles of Greece, and is more than life amid the 'woods, that wave o'er Delphi's steep'? Yes!—and palms are to be won by our native writers!—by those, that have been nursed and brought up with us in the civil and religious freedom of our country. Already has a voice been lifted up in this land,—already a spirit and a love of literature are springing up in the shadow of our free political institutions. . . .

"Of the many causes which have hitherto retarded the growth of polite literature in our country, I have not time to say much. The greatest, which now exists, is doubtless the want of that exclusive attention, which eminence in any profession so imperiously demands. Ours is an age and a country of great minds, though perhaps not of great endeavors. Poetry with us has never yet been anything but a pastime. The fault however is not so much that of our writers, as of the prevalent modes of thinking which characterize our country and our times. We are a plain people, that have had nothing to do with the mere pleasures and luxuries of life: and hence there has sprung up within us a quick-sightedness to the failings of literary men, and an aversion to everything that is not practical, operative, and thorough-going. But if we would ever have a national literature, our native writers must be patronized. Whatever there may be in letters, over which time shall have no power, must be 'born of great endeavors,' and those endeavors are the offspring of liberal patronage. Putting off, then, what Shakespeare calls 'the visage of the times,'—we must become hearty well-wishers to our native authors:—and with them there must be a deep and thorough conviction of the glory of their calling,—an utter abandonment of everything else,—and a noble self-devotion to the cause of literature. We have indeed much to hope from these things:—for our hearts are already growing warm towards literary adventurers, and a generous spirit has gone abroad in our land, which shall liberalize and enlighten. . . .

"Our poetry is not in books alone. It is in the hearts of those men, whose love for the world's gain,—for its business and its holiday, has grown cold within them, and who have gone into the retirements of nature, and have found there that sweet sentiment, and pure devotion of feeling can spring up and live in the shadow of a low and quiet life, and amid those, that have no splendor in their joys, and no parade in their griefs.

"There shall the mind take color from things around us:—from them shall there be a genuine birth of enthusiasm,—a rich development of poetic feeling, that shall break forth in song. Though the works of art must grow old and perish away from earth, the forms of nature shall keep forever their power over the human mind, and have their influence upon the literature of a people.

"We may rejoice, then, in the hope of beauty and sublimity in our national literature, for no people are richer than we are in the treasures of nature. And well may each of us feel a glorious and high-minded pride in saying, as he looks on the hills and vales,—on the woods and waters of New England,—'This is my own, my native land.' " [33]

As he finished and returned to his place among his classmates, Longfellow must have been watched by a few who felt the sincerity of his words. Professor Newman had every reason to be particularly proud of this student whom he had encouraged so successfully in his composition, and surely he felt the underlying implications of this oration. Perhaps the Honorable Benjamin Orr repeated to himself the conviction that this scholar who had shone in the classics would stand even further watching in whatever endeavor he pursued. And what of Longfellow's father, listening and watching intently? Had he and Orr already talked with members of the faculty about a possible position for the boy on the Bowdoin faculty? Did these ringing sentences soften Stephen Longfellow's stiff prejudice in favor of the law? We wish we could know.

On the following day, the class of 1825 met for the last time in the room of Cullen Sawtelle to hear Longfellow read his farewell poem.[34] There were only a few of them left, for some had already gone home. But one who had stayed—a quiet, dark-eyed lad with a shock of black hair—planned to carry out Longfellow's call to "a noble self-devotion to the cause of literature." He would return to his Salem home, seclude himself hermit-fashion in his little room with its flag-bottomed chair and its pine table—and give himself over to writing, writing, writing. How strangely different these two classmates who were not to meet again for twelve years! From Bowdoin they set out on different paths for the same goal of literary success—and each was to know the same anguish of heart and loss of faith, when the way grew dim. Yet who could say which path would be the better?

VII

ESCAPE FROM THE LAW

. . . it seems to be your fixed desire, that I should choose the pro-
fession of the Law for the business of my life. . . . I can be a lawyer,
for some lawyers are mere simpletons. This will support my real
existence, literature an ideal one.[1]

BEFORE commencement, Stephen Longfellow had agreed that his
son should devote one year to graduate study at Harvard College
before beginning to read law at Portland. Although such an outlook was pleasant it was not entirely acceptable to Longfellow.
Intolerable to him was the prospect of isolating himself in a Portland law office after enjoying a rich year of literary activity at
Cambridge. During the vacation preceding commencement he
had puzzled over this apparently inevitable trap and had looked
about secretly for some definite proof with which to contradict
his father's almost scornful conclusion that there was not enough
wealth in America to support merely literary men. That the father
had condemned his proposal to secure an editorial position with
some periodical, had not destroyed the son's plan. Several months
after his apparent surrender to his father's wishes, Longfellow
had written to Theophilus Parsons:

"PORTLAND, August 13, 1825

"Dear Sir,
    "Being apprehensive that you did not receive a letter, which I
wrote you from Brunswick, a few weeks since, I take the liberty
to write again. I shall trouble you with but few words, at this
time; in as much as I have but little leisure, and you will have but
little patience with me in warm weather. The letter to which I
refered above contained some suggestions upon the plausibility—
or rather the possibility of my becoming connected—for one year
—with the Editorial department of the Literary Gazette:—whether
Mr. Carter would like an assistant Editor—etc. etc.
    "I did not write directly to Mr. Carter upon the subject for I

74

might have been intrusive: but thinking that you could easily learn of Mr. C. his inclination upon the subject, I thought it would be best to write to you touching this matter, as an affair, for the present, 'inter nos.'

"I wish to breathe a little while a literary atmosphere, and as I shall not probably enter upon the study of my profession for a year, I wish to be connected in some way with a literary periodical. Of course, the Literary Gazette is first in my thoughts, and I wish that it might be my lot to be associated with Mr. Carter in a capacity different from that of an occasional writer for the paper.

"If you will be kind enough to discover his sentiments upon the subject without mentioning my name, unless he should approve of the scheme, you will confer a great obligation upon me. It strikes me that a single Editor must be very much confined with such a work as the Lit. Gaz. and that he would be willing for the sake of more liberty and less solicitude to have a partner in the business. Pray write me as soon as possible, as it is of some importance for me to be acquainted with my prospects in this way before commencement. . . .

"By the way—I hope to see you at Bowdoin this fall; that you may be present when a parcel of us poor fellows receive the parting benediction of our young Alma Mater. We are, to be sure, too poor in gifts to offer you any great inducements—but one I will offer you—and that is a hearty welcome.

"Yours affectionately
"HENRY W. LONGFELLOW." [2]

Parsons was qualified to understand the aspirations of Longfellow, for he had also been tempted from the law to try his hand at earning a living through literary endeavors. But after editorial experience had convinced him that no writer in America could support himself well with his pen he had returned to the law. Longfellow's letter forced Parsons to disillusion a young man whose dreams were similar to his own. Yet, he had convincing truths with which to dissuade the boy. If Stephen Longfellow had sat down with Parsons the two of them could not have contrived a more effective document opposing any attempt to establish *writing* as a profession in America. Parsons began his letter mildly. He pointed out that, in all probability, Carter would not be able to share his meagre profits with an assistant. Then he turned to far more discouraging observations:

"I should think it would be exceedingly difficult for any one to earn a living by literature, just now. There are very few in our country who actually provide for themselves in this way except newspaper editors. No one of them would pay you enough to live on, because an unsuccessful editor could not, and as a successful editor must have succeeded by being able to take care of his own paper he need not & so would not pay another. You can easily earn a little anywhere, but I think you will find it difficult to earn much as a mere scholar.

"You may rely upon it, my dear Sir, that the kind of love of letters which you & all men of taste & talent have at a certain age, is proper to an unripened intellect. It is grounded partly on vanity; as it seems to be, & often times truly, an indication of superior powers; but there is a more general reason for it. There is a stage in the progress of a bright mind, when the boy has thrown away his toys and marbles, but the young man is still so far a child as to value things more by their elegance and power of amusing, than by their usefulness. He plays with his books, and thinks he is working when he is only playing hard. At this stage he thinks it more worthy and becoming him who has gifts while his neighbors have not, to bury himself with his books, live like a 'Lay Monk,' and be refined, delicate, and unconnected with passing events, than to plunge at once into the business of life & help it along vigorously, & fix upon ourselves its yoke. Now all this is a folly, which sooner or later you will surely discover; and for your sake I wish it may be *sooner*.

"The yoke of society is heavy—but he who will not bear it, had better not live; for however much the amount of eloquent nonsense which may be uttered about the happiness and dignity of solitude, nothing is more true, than that our best means of improvement and of happiness are offered and must be availed of in society. Get through your present delusion as soon as you can, & then you will see how wise it will be for you to devote yourself to the law. In one year you can by obstinate perseverance, create a love of labour and a relish for legal pursuits, which will not only secure success, but, allowing for poor human nature, win it with little pain or sacrifice. There is no fear of your losing your hold upon letters; at least, the danger of any young man's neglecting literature too much if he really loves it, is so remote, it hardly needs to be guarded against." [3]

If Longfellow grasped the entire meaning of Parsons' hard words, he must have felt the lustre fade from his dreams. And quite naturally he began to write with less frequency thereafter. [4] He had not lost faith in his ability, [5] but such words of discouragement, deliberately aimed, could not fail to take effect on a nature so easily dissuaded. But Parsons had taken a dig at the "Lay Monk" without having noticed the well aimed plea for American poets and poetry which Longfellow had sent to the *Gazette* just when Carter took over the reins. Perhaps, if the retiring editor had read that plea, he might not have written quite so harsh a letter to the boy. At the time when Longfellow had been pestering his father with long letters urging that he be permitted to begin his literary career immediately after graduation, he had written a "Lay Monastery" essay which got at the very roots of the trouble: indifference to literature as a "calling" in America.

The title of the essay had been "The Literary Spirit of Our Country." The central idea, so close in design to Longfellow's secret aspirations, was very plainly a piece of the same cloth from which the senior had cut his "Oration." After preliminary remarks on the bright prospect for rapid strides in the advance of literary talent in the United States, he held a light behind the very stumbling-block which his father had pointed at, and which Parsons had referred to, indirectly: no literary spirit could blossom in a country where it was not cultivated seriously. Readers of the *Gazette*, thumbing through the crisp pages of the issue for April 1, 1825, while they were still fresh with the smell of undried printer's ink, may have found only familiar ideas when they came to Longfellow's essay. William Cullen Bryant, disillusioned by his own experience during this same period, later summed the matter up thus, in a letter to Richard Henry Dana:

"After all, poetic wares are not for the market of the present day. Poetry may get printed in the newspapers, but no man makes money by it, for the simple reason that nobody cares a fig for it. The taste for it is something old fashioned, the march of the age is in another direction; mankind are occupied with politics, railroads and steamboats." [6]

But what was already an old story to Bryant was new and still unbearable to the ambitious young poet who had written his essay from the fulness of his heart by the light of his kerosene lamp in a Bowdoin dormitory:

"Perhaps the chief cause which has retarded the progress of poetry in America, is the want of that exclusive cultivation, which so noble a branch of literature would seem to require. Few here think of relying upon the exertion of poetic talent for a livelihood, and of making literature the profession of life. The bar or the pulpit claims the greater part of the scholar's existence, and poetry is made its pastime. This is a defect, which the hand of honourable patronage alone can remedy. . . . It is the fear of poverty that deters many gifted and poetic minds from coming forward into the arena, and wiping away all reproach from our literature." [7]

How well he knew what he wrote! Longfellow himself could not break down his dependence on his father's wishes and decisions. (He never did break it down completely.) And in this most important moment he was faced with the necessity for making up his own mind while his youth and his filial loyalty made any independent decision impossible. Then too, his avowed passion for writing was circumscribed by an inner Yankee prejudice which led him, personally, to place respectability and material comforts above the satisfaction in self-expression. Partly, therefore, because of his own need for living comfortably and partly because of his father's insistence, Longfellow was obliged to accept compromise—a course always easier for him than any struggle which was liable to become grim. After all, he would not lose his love of writing; it would still remain the pleasant avocation of his leisure hours. The law, then, must be accepted as the profession to support his real existence, much as he hated the thought of it.

Apparently without warning there came an attractive means of escape from the law. At commencement the governing body of Bowdoin College voted to establish a chair of modern languages,

and the trustees recommended that Henry W. Longfellow, then
eighteen years old, be offered, informally, the newly created professorship. Undoubtedly many of the trustees besides the Hon.
Benjamin Orr knew, at least by hearsay, of Longfellow's ability.
Of particular influence with the trustees in securing this tentative
appointment was a member of the faculty, Professor Parker
Cleaveland. But Longfellow was poorly qualified, since he had
studied only French—and little of that. The trustees suggested
that he might prepare for the position by studying in Europe, at
his own expense, for two years. Stephen Longfellow, himself a
trustee, returned to his home in Portland with the momentous
announcement.[8]

Europe! The land of his dreams! Since boyhood Longfellow
had revelled in thoughts of mouldering castles, the ruins of ancient temples, the snow-capped wonders of Alpine peaks, the soft
breathing of musical night-winds over moonlit waters in Italy.
Europe and poetry were one to him—all the mystery of antique
tradition and legend was wrapped up in the very sound of the
name. At Portland Academy one of the poems he had copied into
his commonplace book had been Samuel Rogers's "Venice, an
Italian Song." His discovery of Scott had rapidly developed his
fondness for tales of chivalry and legends of medieval times. Just
what Europe was like, he had no definite idea, because his visions
were blurred by mists of romance. But *The Sketch Book* had
transformed his vague imaginings into a persistent longing to
travel in those regions of quaint peculiarities. How perfectly Irving's "Account of Himself" had summed up Longfellow's unexpressed thoughts:

"Europe was rich in the accumulated treasures of age. Her
very ruins told the history of times gone by, and every mouldering stone was a chronicle. I longed to wander over the scenes of
renowned achievement—to tread, as it were, in the footsteps of
antiquity—to loiter about the ruined castle—to meditate on the
falling tower—to escape, in short, from the commonplace realities
of the present, and lose myself among the shadowy grandeurs of
the past." [9]

What solution could be more propitious than to avoid the law
by embarking for Europe? Blinded by this immediate fulfil-

ment of long cherished hopes, Longfellow did not think beyond the projected visit—he did not need to. Europe had been a mine of literary gold to Irving. To Longfellow, walking in paths similar to those Irving had chosen, Europe would also lead him surely to a successful career as a man of letters. He was ready to start at once. But there were preparations to be made, and the dangers of ocean passage in the late fall. He was advised to wait until spring.

In the meantime, Stephen Longfellow insisted that a good taste of law would be wholesome nourishment for his son. Early in the fall, Henry settled down to read Blackstone with some of his classmates in the front-room office of his Congress Street home.

The law office was a hilariously noisy place whenever Mr. Longfellow was absent during the next few months, for the five young men studying there were not too seriously inclined. They were all college friends. With the two Longfellow brothers were Frederic Mellen, the class poet, Patrick Greenleaf, intimate with Henry since Academy days, and George Pierce, a particularly close friend of the Longfellow boys and a devoted suitor of their sister Anne. Each day these five cronies managed to find diversions which alleviated the dulness of law books. Before they had been together one month they had organized themselves into a secret brotherhood, "Knights of the Temple Bar," designed primarily for the advancement of nonsense. The vehicle chosen for public expression of the society was a column in the *Portland Advertiser*, where the knights published a series of essays intended to pique the curiosity of the good citizens. In the early numbers the reader's attention was attracted by a crude woodcut silhouette of a head with an enormous nose. Beneath the cut, the curious might learn that the article was written at the Temple Bar by a member of an ancient social club known as "Brazen Nose College." Undoubtedly Longfellow was the instigator of this literary hoax, directly descended from the *Salmagundi* essays of another society. Writing the first number, Longfellow described himself as one of Portland's oldest inhabitants, Nathan Bonithan by name, who clearly remembered the beginnings of "Brazen Nose College" and even the first mysterious appearance of its founder, Benedict de Nez. The satirical purpose of the series degenerated very soon until there was no unification or merit which justified continuance. The second, and last, essay which Longfellow wrote, entitled, "My School Boy Days," gave a complete account of the circumstances under which he had written and published his first poem. After fourteen appearances of the essays had completely failed to arouse any criticism or protest, the gentlemen of the Temple Bar abandoned their efforts, and the snorings of the Brazen Nose ceased.[10]

William Browne, who was still conducting the "Pedestrian" column in the *Advertiser*, included occasional veiled jests at the expense of his friends at Temple Bar and played one practical joke at this time by publishing one of Longfellow's poems beneath these words of explanation:

"The following lines were written by a young man who died last summer of the dysentery. . . . Next week I will send another performance from the same pen." [11]

The poem, entitled "Youthful Years," had been sent to Browne by Longfellow early in the fall of 1824, but had never been published by the author. Apparently the victim of dysentery arose from his grave with such violent protests that the self-appointed editor was forced to reconsider his promise, for no further lines of poetry appeared in his column.

The failure of the "Brazen Nose" enterprise did not quite end Longfellow's writing during the winter. A little room no bigger than a cupboard opened from the law office and permitted one or two serious students to escape from the noise of the main office. Here Longfellow hid occasionally to fashion new verses or to revise the old. "With regard to Poetry," he wrote at this time to Caroline Doane in Boston, "I have not stopped writing, tho' I have stopped publishing for certain reasons which I cannot go into at length in a letter." [12] To let her sample a few lines, he copied into his letter a "Song" of four quatrains which he sent to the *Gazette* soon after. It was his last contribution to that magazine.[13]

As spring approached, Longfellow made last preparations for departure by calling on certain people who might give him letters of introduction. One Portland friend was Hon. Charles S. Daveis, already recognized as an authority on maritime law. With him Longfellow had shared the honors at the Fryeburg celebration of Lovewell's fight less than a year earlier, where Daveis had delivered the oration. Having studied law in Boston, Daveis was able to direct Longfellow to influential friends there. Particularly valuable to anyone going abroad to study languages was the advice of Professor George Ticknor at Harvard. Daveis had studied law with him in Boston, until fondness for literature had tempted Ticknor to abandon his newly established practice. Daveis could remember what difficulty his friend had encountered in finding any German grammar or dictionary in New England in 1814. At that time no college in New England offered regular courses in the modern European languages. At Harvard, if French were desired, arrangements could be made with a private tutor. Daveis could also show Longfellow some of the letters Ticknor had written him from Göttingen, filled with strange and entirely new information about the German language and literature. But while Ticknor was still in Europe a Boston merchant had bequeathed to Harvard a sum of money for the maintenance of a teacher of French and Spanish. Professor Kirkland had written to Ticknor, then twenty-five years old, asking him to accept an appointment as Smith Professor of Modern Languages and Literatures. In the fall of 1819, Ticknor opened the second department of modern languages in any American college. The first had been established at William and Mary College, through the influence of Thomas Jefferson, in 1779–80. Jefferson, who had been completing his plans for an ideal university in Virginia, succeeded in establishing the third department of that nature and scope at Virginia one year before he died.[14] Obviously, Bowdoin was continuing to copy the pattern of Harvard, and Longfellow was preparing to open a fourth department of modern languages. When he was ready to leave Portland, Mr. Daveis gave Longfellow letters to Mr. Ticknor and to other friends in Boston.

"I dined to-day with Mr. Ticknor," the traveler wrote to his mother after having spent a few days in Boston. "He is a little, Spanish-looking man, but exceedingly kind & affable."[15] It seemed strange to find a Harvard professor living in a fine house commanding a view of the Common from the head of Beacon Street and not in Professors' Row at Cambridge. After his experiences in Brunswick, Longfellow must have been delighted to be entertained in Ticknor's splendid and impressive library. Here were many of the books which the learned scholar had brought home with him from Europe. Here also was Leslie's painting of Sir Walter Scott, done expressly for Scott's Yankee friend. Although Ticknor had been gracious in his greeting to Longfellow, he was a bit surprised to discover that the young man intended to study in France and Spain. Who had ever heard of such a plan? These countries were important to the traveler but not to one who wished to learn the new, scientific approach to scholarship. "He strongly recommends a year's residence in Germany," Longfellow continued in his note to his mother, "and is very decidedly and strongly in favor of commencing literary studies there." [16] Precedent enough for such a plan. Five American students had gone abroad during the last eleven years to complete their education, and each had gone first to Germany—to the University of Göttingen. No matter what one wished to study, one could study it best in Germany. Edward Everett had gone there with Ticknor to concentrate on the classics, George Bancroft had been sent there on a Harvard fellowship to study theology, and Joseph Green Cogswell, who had but recently resigned his position as Librarian and Professor of Mineralogy at Harvard to establish a school on the Fellenberg model at Northampton, had taken courses in a variety of subjects in Germany. Ticknor believed that the educational advantages in Paris were extremely poor in comparison with those in Göttingen or Berlin. Possibly Longfellow listened with the unexpressed belief that, regardless of library advantages, there was little sense in going to Germany when one wished to learn to speak French and Spanish. Furthermore, his plans were already made. He would not trouble himself over Professor Ticknor's strong feeling until he discovered what his father wished to do.

He also visited Harvard and there met President Kirkland, probably through the courtesy of Professor Ticknor. To the visitor, this round-faced gentleman seemed "a jolly little man," [17] but to Ticknor he personified the essential conservatism and backwardness which kept Harvard, to his way of thinking, the provincial college it was. Longfellow could not have guessed the inner disappointment caused Ticknor by this man. Returning from Germany with enthusiastic plans for improving the educational facilities of his country and particularly of Harvard, Ticknor had met bitter opposition. President Kirkland disliked change, and so did most of his faculty. Such German ideas would never be forced upon the college while Kirkland was able to prevent them. Cogswell and Bancroft, meeting the same opposition, had given up and had left to found a school of their own. Ticknor urged Longfellow to call on these two scholars, as he passed through Northampton.

The Round Hill School, happily situated, surveyed from its eminence the quiet village below and, not far beyond it, the lazy undulations of the Connecticut River. Longfellow was delighted with the school and with the friendly reception given him by Professor Ticknor's friends. They corroborated all that Ticknor had said about Germany although they did not recommend that the student spend all his time in Göttingen. They had both begun their studies there, but had not returned to America until they had traveled throughout Europe.

Cogswell had gone on foot farther than most American travelers had gone in carriages. On his seventeen-hundred-mile walking trip he had visited the famous schools of Fellenberg and Pestalozzi. In fact, he had been entertained with great cordiality from Marseilles to Edinburgh. But most memorable of all was his friendship with Goethe, whom he had visited several times. "Keep me, I beg you, in friendly remembrance," the old German had said, his eyes filling with tears, as he kissed Cogswell on both cheeks at parting.[18]

Bancroft in his turn could tell Longfellow much about the pitfalls and difficulties of going abroad for study while still young. He had been only eighteen when he embarked for Germany with young Frederic Henry Hedge in his charge. Professor Andrews Norton had worried lest his favorite student be engulfed in the popular fallacies of German teaching; but Bancroft had survived all temptations to evil, except that he had learned to waltz on Sunday and had brought home a few barbarous mannerisms. The two resounding kisses he had planted on Professor Norton's cheeks, at their first meeting, offended the sedate gentleman so greatly that Bancroft had difficulty in mending the breach between them. As Emerson said, he came back needing "a great deal of cutting and pruning." [19]

But Bancroft could give Longfellow the secret formula for turning his absence to good account: unceasing study, from half past five in the morning to very late at night. Cogswell agreed that no other course would enable an American to acquire a scholarly training. He had devised a schedule at Göttingen which allowed for eight hours in the lecture room and eight hours of study each day. Such a program could be carried out only in Germany, they repeated to their young guest, as they wished him a pleasant voyage and watched him making his departure. Two days later Longfellow wrote an account of this visit, to his father:

"With the village of Northampton I was highly delighted. The mountain and river scenery near it are certainly very beautiful, and from Round hill—the seat of Messrs. Coggswell & Bancroft's school—you have an extended view of the village and its environs. These gentlemen received me with the greatest kindness—and have furnished me with a number of excellent letters. They coincide with Prof. Ticknor of Cambridge in recommending a year's residence at Göttingen. Mr. Ticknor says that the expenses there will not be so great as at Paris, & that it is all-important to have a knowledge of the German language. The Lectures on literary history, which he wishes me to attend there, commence in October, and he says I could before that time become sufficiently advanced in the languages to understand them. I should take rooms there as at Paris, and should pay about one guinea for a course of Lectures. It will, he thinks, be removing me from a great deal of temptation, and moreover be laying a solid foundation for future literary acquirements.

"For my own part—I must confess that this change in my original plan did not strike me very favorably at first—but the more I reflect upon it the better I like it.—I wish you to write me, at New York, as soon as you receive this—and tell me what you think of the change in my plans. Mr. Ticknor and Mr. Bancroft have both studied at Göttingen, and of course their opinion on the subject is of much weight." [20]

He was relieved to shift the responsibility for such a decision to his father. All this advice about German universities, and lectures given in languages which he could not yet understand, did not fit exactly with what he had imagined lay ahead of him. But he need not worry about the choice between Paris and Göttingen for several weeks, and that was comforting. Was he to spend all his time in dreary study? His longing for Europe had been fostered by Washington Irving and not by George Ticknor. He would go abroad, and he would acquire such knowledge of the languages as would lead him into nooks, corners, and by-places of literature. But above this expectation was his desire to view the lands which, through Irving's eyes, had fascinated him.

Traveling down the valley of the Hudson, he recalled the sketches which had made Dutch names familiar. In a letter to his sister Elizabeth he confessed that his scheme for seeing the region had not been entirely fulfilled:

"I was very desirous on leaving Albany to pass the highlands of the Hudson, and the hills of Wehawken by daylight, and consequently made arrangements to stop at Caatskill, and to ascend the mountains, my head being full of Hendrick Hudson and his crew at nine-pins—the Doolittle Inn—and Rip Van Winkle.—I found it however too early in the season to put my plans into execution, in as much as travellers have not yet begun to ascend the hills and of course the means of conveyance were not at hand. I therefore stopped at Hudson, and went down by land to Red Hook, where I passed Sunday afternoon. The scenery on the North River between Albany and Hudson is very beautiful, especially where the river makes a gradual sweep round a low point of land, and you catch the last view of Albany." [21]

Once in New York, Longfellow began making final visits to friends and relatives in the vicinity. A hasty trip to Philadelphia was prompted in part by a letter received a few weeks earlier from Carey & Lea, publishers of *The Atlantic Souvenir*, America's first gift-book annual. The letter read:

"It is our intention to publish during the next summer another volume of '*The Atlantic Souvenir*' a work which has lately been brought out by us & which you have probably seen.

"We take the liberty of requesting your aid in furnishing a few poetical articles of a suitable character, & not long. We shall feel flattered by being enabled to add your name to our list of contributors & will cheerfully pay such sum as you may consider a reasonable compensation for your time & labour." [22]

Undoubtedly the editors were somewhat surprised to find that the author to whom they had written, and who appeared at their office with three poetical articles [23] for them, was a very young man. Their welcome was so hearty, however, and their appreciation so genuine that Longfellow remembered it three years later and offered them the honor of publishing his first book. Aside from his pleasure at having met Messrs. Carey and Lea, he was not particularly pleased with Philadelphia and returned to pass the few remaining days in New York. His first letter, sent from Boston, had reached his family, for he found an answer from his mother:

"It was very fortunate for me that your Boston stage was late, as it gave me the pleasure of receiving a letter from you, which is no small consolation in your absence. I will not say how much we miss your elastic step, your cheerful voice, your melodious flute; but will say farewell, my dear son, may God be with and prosper you. May you be successful in your pursuit of knowledge; may you hold fast your integrity, and retain that purity of heart which is so interesting and endearing to friends. I feel as if you were going into a thousand perils. You must be very watchful & guard against every temptation.

"Your affectionate mother,

"ZWL." [24]

His letter from Albany, concerning the advice of Cogswell and Bancroft, had not reached his father, for Stephen Longfellow filled his last letter with many specific instructions as to conduct, but made no mention of a possible change in plans:

"It is impossible, with all my solicitude, to give you all the instructions which your youth and inexperience require, but permit me to conjure you to remember the great objects of your pursuit. Keep them constantly in view, and let not the solicitations of pleasure, nor the allurements of vice lead you from the path of virtue. Your tour is one for improvement rather than pleasure, and you must make every exertion to cultivate and improve your mind. . . . Be careful not to take any part in opposition to the religion or politics of the countries through which you pass, or in which you reside. They are local concerns, in which a stranger has no right to interfere. I want to say a thousand things, but the time for the mail to close has arrived, and praying God to protect and preserve you, I must bid you an affectionate adieu." [25]

The packet ship *Cadmus*, Captain Allen, was waiting down the bay. On Monday morning May 15, Longfellow was escorted to the pier by Eugene Weld and Patrick Greenleaf, two of his classmates who had come to celebrate the event. The three sailed down the bay in the *Nautilus*, enjoyed a merry luncheon of ham and porter aboard the *Cadmus*, and finally parted with many promises and rejoinders as the packet ship weighed anchor in the early afternoon.[26]

Ahead of him lay Europe, and the thirty long days of the voyage were made doubly tedious and dreary by his impatience. "I had little else to do than to busy myself with my own thoughts and meditations," he later confessed to his mother, "so few circumstances were there at sea to call me away from them." [27] At last the day came when he was startled out of his reverie by the excited cries of "Land!" The thin gray line on the horizon was enough to thrill him. The land beyond the sea! The land he had dreamed about since boyhood. To be sure, he had embarked with serious intentions and was prepared for the necessary hours of study. But this first glimpse was entirely shrouded in a romantic haze of adventure. His own words described the moment perfectly:

"For to my youthful imagination the Old World was a kind of Holy Land, lying afar off beyond the blue horizon of the ocean; and when its shores first rose upon my sight, looming through the hazy atmosphere of the sea, my heart swelled with the deep emotion of the pilgrim, when he sees afar the spire which rises above the shrine of his devotion." [28]

The dream had at last come true!

VIII

THE PILGRIM DISAPPOINTED

If I had known before leaving home how hard a task I was under-
taking, I should have shrunk. . . . I never imagined the business I
have taken in hand a very light affair, but I thought there would be
fewer perplexities attending it.[1]

THE WATER FRONT of Havre de Grâce was no shrine for adoration. Even before the pilgrim had disembarked, he was staring in
surprise at the peculiar and shabby sailing-vessels in the harbor,
the dilapidated houses that lined the quay, the narrow and dirty
streets. His eyes, ready to worship, began to twinkle with mirth
as he caught sight of "a grand display from every upper window,
of blankets and bed-clothes, old shirts and old sheets—flapping in
the wind." [2] As he walked along the streets, more humorous
scenes caught his attention. The fierce whiskers of the *gendarmes*,
the wooden shoes, tight pantaloons, and paper hats of the women,
were all funny. He was particularly amused by the "dames of
Normandy, with tall pyramidal caps of muslin—reaching at least
two feet above their heads, and adorned with long ear-lappets." [3]
Everything struck him as such a good joke that he wished Ned
Preble were there to enjoy the circus with him.

The overland trip to Paris which began on the following day
afforded a continuation of amusing novelties which Longfellow
glimpsed from atop a strange vehicle which he soon learned to
call a "diligence." His companions on his lofty perch, "a subaltern
with fierce mustache, and a nut-brown village beauty of sweet sixteen," [4] were pleasant enough, but not nearly so amusing as the
postilion, short of stature, and garbed in a purple velvet jacket
with a red collar, and with "tight breeches of bright yellow" covering his "pipestem legs." [5]

Rouen and the Golden Lion Inn were new sources of diversion.
He continued to laugh even when assigned to a room seven flights
above the ground floor and derived compensation from his excel-

lent view of the market place. Later, he wandered about the town
until he came unexpectedly into the very shadow of the cathedral.
Thrilled by the massive towers on either side and by the graceful
upward sweep of the spire, the pilgrim stood and lifted his eyes in
romantic adoration. This was a part of his dreams. Such a moment he had often imagined after reading stories of medieval
times. Now, coming upon the reality without warning, as he
walked out of a narrow alley in the town where Joan of Arc was
burned to death, he felt an overpowering sense of awe. If the
strong walls with their delicate ornaments had risen out of the
earth as he watched, the effect could not have been more powerful:

"It completely overwhelmed my imagination, and I stood for a
long time motionless, gazing entranced upon the stupendous edi-
fice. I had before seen no specimen of Gothic architecture; and
the massive towers before me, the lofty windows of stained glass,
the low portal, with its receding arches and rude statues, all produced upon my untravelled mind an impression of awful sublimity. When I entered the church, the impression was still more
deep and solemn. It was the hour of vespers. The religious twilight of the place, the lamps that burned on the distant altar, the
kneeling crowd, the tinkling bell, and the chant of the evening
service that rolled along the vaulted roof in broken and repeated
echoes, filled me with new and intense emotions." [6]

No moment of ecstasy which he would experience during his
entire stay in Europe could equal the thrilling discovery of this
cathedral at Rouen. Disillusion, with its attendant moods of homesickness and discouragement, would come soon enough. He had
set out with dreamy optimism, confident that he could master two
or three languages and at the same time give himself over to the
worship of quaint beauty and antiquity so perfectly blended in
the architecture of this church, but he was to learn how false his
hope had been. Yet, even if the remainder of his travel and residence abroad should be marred by perplexities, his expectation
had found this early fulfilment. Buoyed by his eagerness for other
new sensations, he continued to Paris, arriving at dusk on the 18th
of June.

Somewhere across the Seine, in the Faubourg Saint-Germain,

Longfellow knew that he should find his cousin, Eben Storer, who had come to Paris several months earlier to study medicine. He had written that he was living in the home of a Madame Potet, 49 Rue Monsieur-le-Prince, and that his Portland cousin would find cordial welcome there.[7] As soon as his bags were unloaded from the diligence, he found transportation in a cabriolet, gave the strange address, and before long was knocking at the door of Madame Potet.

His reception was so friendly that he felt almost as though he were returning home. Madame Potet received him with great kindness and quickly adopted him as her "son"—the seventh recent adoption, as is proved, since there were already six other American students over whom the good lady had spread maternal wings. She took an immediate interest in his desire to speak French. Longfellow had been advised to put himself under the guidance of a tutor in Paris, but there seemed to him to be no need for this when his hostess was so eager to help him. She had encouraged all her American boys to speak only French during meals and had cordially approved their agreement to fine each person a sou for violation. Naturally this cramped conversation so seriously that all spoke English as soon as chairs were pushed back from the table.

At first Longfellow felt impatient with such hindrances to mastering the language. But there were compensations. The two daughters of Madame Potet added an atmosphere of home to the boarding house and delighted him with their accomplished playing of the piano. Certainly he could find no better lodgings in all Paris, he finally concluded, although there was some need for reassuring his father and for making perfectly obvious the wisdom of this first decision. After describing his situation, he explained:

"If I had my chambers at a Hotel I should have a thousand solitary hours, because I cannot speak French well enough to go into French society—but now if I wish to be alone I can shut myself up in my chambers—if I wish for society I can go at any hour into Madam's parlour—and talk my kind of French with her and her daughters—besides the pleasure of hearing most delicious music." [8]

In subsequent letters, he was obliged to confess that other disappointing aspects of his position had developed. Although he had hoped to understand the French lectures at the University of Paris, near by, two or three attempts proved that he merely sat through the period, catching an occasional isolated sentence which was of no importance. And within five weeks of his arrival the lectures were interrupted for at least two months by the summer vacation. A further misfortune, Madame Potet was obliged to point out, resulted from Longfellow's poor accent. In one letter he complained of his French instruction in Maine:

"D'Eon was a very poor instructor—his pronunciation very bad. It is impossible that he should have been a Parisien—He was a German. . . . And this has been not only unfortunate but absolutely discouraging:—to find myself so far speaking French with a German as well as an English accent." [9]

Even the city of Paris proved disappointing. It appeared at first a gloomy city of yellow-stone houses, with dirty streets full of "noise and stench enough to drive a man mad." [10] The treasures of the Louvre pleased him little until he found a painting of Venus which caught his eye because it seemed to be "an exact portrait of Miss Knight," [11] a lady in Portland whose friendship he treasured. The New Englander accepted the memory of favorite scenes and people in the state of Maine as a touchstone for appreciation. But frequent strolls in the Luxembourg Gardens, walks to the Pantheon, and a few evenings at the theatre wore away the first strangeness.

Soon he was even pretending that he had become completely Parisian. To his brother he confided, perhaps in jest, that he had entered into the spirit of the Luxembourg promenades:

"After five weeks' residence in Paris I have settled down in something half-way between a Frenchman and a New Englander: —within, all Jonathan—but outwardly a little of the Parlez-vous. That is to say, I have good home-feelings at heart—but have decorated my outward man, with a long-waisted thin coat—claret-coloured—and a pair of linen pantaloons:—and then on Sundays and other fête days—I appear in all the glory of a little hard French hat—glossy—and bushed—and rolled up at the sides:—it makes my head ache to think of it.—In this garb I jostle along among the crowds of the Luxembourg, which is the favorite promenade in St. Germain." [12]

In spite of such sartorial diversions, he remembered his original purpose. Seemingly Paris in summer was no place to study. Perhaps he might escape to some rural spot, safely removed from the temptation to speak his own tongue with American friends. With this worthy notion in mind, he visited Montmorency and was tempted to make a short retreat there from the heat of Paris. By no process of divination could he know the effect his decisions might have upon his parents in far-away Portland. But it behooved him to support his choice with arguments. He wrote that Montmorency would offer distinct advantages over Paris: "In the first place, I hope to live cheaper there—in the second place, I shall be more studious there, and consequently become more proficient in the French language, and consequently better able to attend the public lectures in the city during the winter . . ." [13] When his parents received and read this volley of arguments, they could not guess that the boy had meanwhile changed his mind. But the next letter, which informed them, reversed the financial reason. "Besides," Longfellow added, "I am unwilling to leave Madame Potet —it is such an excellent situation for one to learn the language— and Madame takes such unwearied pains to instruct me—I am coming on famously, I assure you." [14]

Stephen Longfellow and his wife were destined to receive many more of these contradictory letters, each well larded with supposedly convincing ideas. For the first time in his life, the boy was thrown utterly on his own resources. Thus the account of his stay in France and of his travel in Europe becomes particularly valuable in revealing his immaturity. The pilgrim never seemed quite certain where to seek his shrine. And, as we shall see, the vacillation and confusion of his first trip explain clearly why Longfellow did not succeed in carrying back to America the scholarly training which Ticknor, Cogswell, and Bancroft had brought with them. Again and again, the boy's inexperience and romantic wanderings from the strait path of duty innocently vitiated the original purpose of his travels, until his father was forced to write stern and only partially effectual letters of warning. Moreover, we can easily read between the lines of the son's defensive answers. Impelled to build up arguments in support of his aberrations from study, he met his father's criticism (and the prick of his own conscience) by boasting, in later months, that he could write and speak the languages he was learning, just as well as he could write and speak English. But, like Stephen Longfellow, we are aware of the defensive feeling and make allowances. We cannot, as many commentators have done, take the young man's rationalization at its face value and claim that the pilgrim made superlative scholarly progress on this first excursion to Europe. With each change of his purpose, he marshalled arguments calculated to assuage his father's doubts. To report linguistic advance was a sure defense for a sudden shift in plan.

At the beginning of his stay in Paris, when Longfellow did not feel that he need waste money in hiring daily instruction, because he was making such good progress with Madame Potet, he was certain that his father would approve of his saving money. But he continued to think of escaping from the heat of Paris. Not long after the Montmorency episode, he was led to make new plans when a young Frenchman told him of a pleasant boarding house in the village of Auteuil. Together, Longfellow and his new friend visited the place, walked through the grounds, enjoyed the beautiful gardens, and talked with the landlord. The situation appealed so strongly that the Yankee completed the bargain then and there —and secured a fine room by paying a month's rent in advance. As he left he was a bit troubled by the faces of the people staying there; they seemed so pale and sickly. His friend explained that there was a good reason, since all were invalids who had sought the bracing tonic of country air. A *maison de santé!* He had made the discovery too late. His money was paid, and he had no choice but to become a patient with the others.

The month spent at Auteuil seemed pleasant enough when he described it later in *Outre-Mer*,[15] although he suffered moments of deep depression and loneliness there. During his first week he took much pleasure in walking and talking with his companions. ("I can at any time hear French conversation," he wrote, "for the French are always talking." [16]) He was delighted to meet people who seemed like celebrities to him: an old gentleman who had known Louis XVI; Madame de Sailly, whose father was a famous French advocate; and a young law student who became a faithful substitute for Madame Potet, correcting Longfellow's mistakes in pronunciation. But when the novelty wore off, after two weeks, feelings of homesickness led to discontent. To his mother he revealed his longings in a letter which began bravely concerning "this pleasant village of Auteuil." Yet, this nineteen-year-old son of Maine had found the country of France unsatisfactory because it lacked the picturesque details of home:

"There is so little about it—except, indeed, its quiet and tranquility,—to remind one that he is out of town—no corn-fields garnished with yellow pumpkins—no green trees, and orchards by the road side—no slab-fences—no well-poles—no painted cottages, with huge barns and outhouses,—ornamented in front with monstrous piles of wood for winter-firing; nothing in fine to bring to the mind of an American a remembrance of the beautiful villages of his native land." [17]

He continued in uncomplimentary fashion by describing the houses of French towns, possibly elegant within, surely "always much more so than the dirty entrance would lead one to anticipate:—for there is generally a pile of filth & decaying vegetables garnishing the outer-door, and an odour of anything but sanctity upon the stair-case." [18] The final betrayal of his homesickness came in the last paragraph, where he confessed how frequently he returned, in his thoughts, to his family in Portland. He concluded: "This is almost the only consolation which I have in my absence from you,—and this at best is a very melancholy one." [19]

IX

PATERNAL GUIDANCE

The truth is, that the heavy responsibility which I have taken upon myself . . . together with the continual solicitude about the final result of my studies, and the fear that you will be displeased with my expenses—are hanging with a terrible weight upon me.[1]

EARLY in September, Longfellow turned his back on the cool garden plots, the shaded hedgerows of Auteuil, and set his face resolutely toward a winter of serious study in the ugliness of Paris. First of all, he decided that his progress in learning to speak French had not been satisfactory at Madame Potet's, and that some change was imperative. With reluctance he left the attractive home, took rooms with a family which spoke no English, and discovered almost immediately that he had exchanged one set of evils for another. The grasping and deceptive attitude of his landlord, purely mercenary in his interest, and the dinginess of the small room made him dislike the change.

His mood was not relieved by the discovery that the lectures which he had expected to attend immediately did not begin until November. Thwarted and discouraged in all his groping endeavors to solve problems made doubly difficult by youth and inexperience, he considered making a new start in some other city such as Tours. He might even be permitted to follow Professor Ticknor's advice and go to Göttingen. But he did not care to alter his father's decisions on this point without permission.

In early October, nearly four months after his arrival in France, he received his first letter from home. Stephen Longfellow had been considering the advice of Ticknor, Bancroft, and Cogswell, but this matter was not the parent's most serious concern. He had read the first few letters written by his son from Paris, and had been forced to suspect that the student had not begun his study properly. The father may have felt that although many young men were prepared to meet the exigencies of travel while still in their teens, Henry had been too well protected. Consequently he had originally made out for his son a simple itinerary and plan of study to be followed during the sojourn in Europe. The boy would spend two years abroad, learning at least the French and the Spanish, and would pursue these studies in France and Spain. If there were time for further travel and study, Henry might continue to Italy and Germany.

But Stephen feared that his son had not been making proper use of his time. "I had supposed," he wrote, "that by diligence & close application to your studies you would be able to acquire competent knowledge of the French so as to visit Spain early this winter or this autumn . . ."[2] Other details warranted specific paternal counsel. After dealing with the projected itinerary from France to Spain, then possibly to Italy and Germany, Stephen concluded his letter:

"Your expenses are much more than I had been led to expect, and though I wish you to appear respectably you will recollect the necessity of observing as much economy as you can with propriety. And as your great object is to acquire a knowledge of the modern languages, the importance of great diligence will strongly impress your mind and influence your conduct. You are surrounded with temptations and allurements and it will be necessary for you to set a double guard upon yourself, and a close attention to your studies will be one of the most effectual securities against dissipation—Go but little into company, & be careful to associate with none but the virtuous. Such is your youth, & inexperience that I feel great solicitude for your safety, and therefore give you line upon line & precept upon precept, knowing that you will duly appreciate my motives, and be disposed to relieve my anxiety."[3]

As Longfellow studied his father's letter in the solitude of his dingy little French room, he realized that his early letters had given an unfortunate impression. Certainly his father misunderstood, if he thought it necessary to urge diligence and close attention to studies—if he thought that even the closest application could result in mastery of the French by fall. October had already begun and the student had not yet been able to start his classes at the University of Paris. But how could his father blame him for these circumstances? The lectures had been meaningless when he had arrived and had ended before Madame Potet had proceeded far with her coaching. He had tried to improve the vacation time by making a sojourn into the countryside. Surely, his father should understand. Defensively, Longfellow answered:

"I am convinced that what you say of Spain, will be impossible. You either over-rate my abilities and my advantages, if you think that I am already master of the French: or I have sadly misimproved them both, which I do not wish to allow. But I will confess that I had no idea of the difficulties attending my situation—no idea, that it was indeed so difficult to learn a language. If I had known before leaving home how hard a task I was undertaking, I should have shrunk. My friends at home, and especially my young friends, imagine that I am enjoying a most delightful existence, without care and without labor, surrounded by all the allurements of a splendid metropolis, and living in continual delight. But nothing can be further from the truth. There are allurements enough around me, it is true, but I do not feel myself at liberty to indulge in them:—and there is splendor enough, but it is a splendor in which I have no share. No! The truth is, that the heavy responsibility which I have taken upon myself—the disappointments I have met with,—in not finding my advantages so great as I had fancied them—and in finding my progress comparatively slow:—together with the continual solicitude about the final result of my studies, and the fear that you will be displeased with my expenses—are hanging with a terrible weight upon me. I never imagined the business I have taken in hand a very light affair, but I thought there would be fewer perplexities attending it." [4]

Having spoken bluntly on this score, he also made direct answer to his father's implication that he might be able to learn Italian and German after he had completed learning the French and Spanish:

"I am convinced that if I remain here but two years I had better relinquish the Spanish language for the German—since I cannot acquire a thorough knowledge of four languages in so short a time. This was the advice, which Mr. Bancroft & Mr. Cogswell gave me, who of course are well qualified to judge upon the subject. If you are of the same opinion,—the plan which strikes me as being most plausable is to pursue the French most vigorously for a few months—then commence Italian—learn its principles thoroughly—spend the spring in Italy to speak the language, and then spend the summer and succeeding winter in Germany. This to be sure is changing our plans, from the very foundation, since the year which I intended to pass in Paris will be essentially shortened.—I think, however, that this change will be a good one, in as much as the German language is infinitely more important than the Spanish, being infinitely more rich in literary resources." [5]

Another change of plan which he suggested in this letter was his removal to Tours during the fall months. In support of the idea he called attention to heavy expenses already incurred in Paris, his disappointment in being forced to wait until November for the University lectures, and the need for escaping from his American friends in Paris. He would, of course, return during the winter, to deliver certain letters he still had and to attend the lectures. After having devoted nearly two pages of explanation to the projected stay in Tours, he added a postscript on the margin of the letter: "Upon more mature reflexion I have renounced the idea of residing at Tours. I fear that too many changes in my situation will not be advantageous." [6]

In the light of this sage conclusion, Stephen Longfellow might have been somewhat surprised if he had seen his son starting out on a ten-day walking trip through the Loire valley on the day after he had written this letter of confused hopes and protests. But he would have been convinced that Henry had decided rather impulsively upon this venture, had he seen the unfortunate picture the boy made upon his arrival in Orléans that evening. His knapsack, containing his clothing for the journey, had not been placed in the diligence as he had supposed, and his entire costume gave a forlorn impression:

". . . when I reached Orleans I found myself wandering about in a dirty shirt—with my travelling cap on my head—two pair of dirty socks—with holes in the toes—together with a cake of Windsor soap stowed away in my pockets—having put them there in the hurry of moving the evening before.

" 'A proud man in a dirty shirt, is an imposing character in the literary world.' Washington Irving." [7]

The hasty decision to run away from the unpleasantness of Paris was a surrender to his longing to saunter through Europe in emulation of his countryman Irving, or after the fashion of Oliver Goldsmith, who had actually described the Loire valley. Here was no language student like Ticknor, with an insatiable hunger for the advanced methods of German universities; here was no Cogswell, pressing on over mile after mile of country, absorbing all sorts of valuable knowledge. Here was the pilgrim who had come to the Old World eager to worship in sequestered regions that might charm him with quaint scenes and pensive moments.

Having recovered his knapsack, he set out along the Loire the following morning and wandered through the vineyards then filled with harvesters. At evening he joined a group of workers returning to their village. Hoping to win the confidence of a pretty companion he asked one of the girls if she liked to dance and added that he had a flute in his knapsack. "I thought it would be very pretty to touch up at a cottage-door, Goldsmith-like," he later wrote, "though I would not have done it for the world without an invitation." [8] Disconcerting indeed was the maid's reply that she liked to dance, but that she had no idea what a flute was. Thereafter the instrument, never mentioned, remained in the knapsack through the trip.

Day after day he continued his rambles through the towns of Tivher, Blois, and Amboise, often turning aside from roads and paths to examine the ruins of old châteaux. Once he sat down with an Englishman for dinner at an inn where he was spending the night, and struggled to carry on a conversation in French with him. That night, recording the incident in his journal, he commented: "—knew that he must be English by his accent—how ridiculous for us to have talked bad french together when we might have conversed in our natural tongue." From Tours he returned to Paris by way of Vendôme, arriving October 12.

Undoubtedly Longfellow spent many moments, during his walking excursion, wondering how best to explain this deliberate violation of parental counsel. He had already learned that it was advisable to save for letters to his father those details of practical accomplishment or financial astringency which would please him. When confessions of romantic digressions were to be made, he always wrote to his mother. Choosing her as the one more easily persuaded of his wisdom in the present instance, he began his apology: "I was melancholy—downhearted, dispirited—almost disconsolate—and I therefore resolved to take a short vacation, and leave my cares behind me." After describing the pleasures of the trip he returned to a stronger defense:

"I was induced thus to run away from my studies—perhaps from my duties—by the consideration that perhaps I should never have an opportunity of seeing that part of France—certainly never in the season of the vintage. At the same time I found the excursion of the greatest advantage to me every way—It nursed my funds a little—for I travelled very cheaply—being most of the way on foot —and moreover exercised me in speaking the language and gave me confidence in my own powers, which a man who is learning to speak a language can never have too much of. . . . I wished first of all to make my apology for taking such a journey without leave —though I have no reason to think that you will call the step an unwise one—when I enumerate its advantages and tell you that I spoke not an English word the whole route—and that it is impossible to pass ten days in Paris without conversing as many times in one's native tongue:—So that in fact I was a gainer rather than a loser:—and I assure you that I shall remember that foot excursion with delight to the latest day of my life—even were I to live a century." [9]

On his return to Paris, Longfellow had once again changed his lodgings. This time he took a single room in a *pension* in Rue Racine, Faubourg Saint-Germain, not far from the home of Madame Potet. His new quarters pleased him, since the privacy afforded a better chance to escape from friends.

Less than a week after he had taken his new room he received a letter from Ned Preble, who secretly announced that he was planning to visit Europe in the spring and was eager to study with Longfellow at Göttingen. The prospect was too strong an inducement to be resisted. To his father Longfellow had already suggested that the original schedule be modified by omitting the study of Spanish and substituting Italian and German. Preble's letter led to a new scheme: going direct from France to Germany. He marshalled various reasons in favor of such an arrangement, although it would mean abandoning any thought of going to Spain or Italy. "Yes—I had rather give up the Spanish and the Italian for the present," he wrote to his father, "than leave the French half-acquired and miss a glorious opportunity of acquiring it." [10] He had become quite a genius at marshalling reasons. Spain, he added, was badly torn by civil wars which made all travel there extremely dangerous. "We get most terrible accounts from every quarter—and as I never desired to come to my end by the dagger of an assassin or the pistol of a robber, I think it at least prudent to leave Spain like the 'man who fell among thieves'. . ." [11]

Having weighed the arguments very carefully, he summarized his position. "Hence," he wrote, "I am for remaining here in my comfortable winter quarters until March or April and then for passing into Germany to remain a year." [12] Up to this point in his letter, Longfellow had not mentioned any new influence which tempted him to sacrifice even his early and romantic longing to see Italy. But since his father had already refused to approve the idea of going to Germany before going to Spain, Longfellow confessed the pull of friendship:

"And now I will tell you a secret which every one who reads this letter must keep as a profound secret, since it was imparted to me in confidence. Edward Preble writes me that he will come out in the Spring and attend lectures with me at Göttingen . . . Please to talk to him upon the subject and advise him to the step, if you conclude to let me go." [13]

In reply, Stephen Longfellow wrote sharply. He expressed himself no longer with the indulgent patience of his first letter. Bluntly he stated that he was not pleased with so much tinkering and so little accomplishment. The new arrangement was impossible because it would deliberately violate the entire purpose of this visit to Europe. His sentences, no longer suggestions, were commands heavily underscored to give added significance:

". . . Your ulterior objects cannot be accomplished unless you obtain an *accurate* knowledge of the *French & Spanish* languages. The *situation you have in view cannot be obtained unless you qualify yourself to teach both these languages correctly.*" [14]

With continually growing trade relations between the United States and South America, the father pointed out, the acquisition of a firm grounding in Spanish was particularly valuable, even if it were to be secured by studying in France. He added:

"Permit me however to say that I consider the knowledge of the *Spanish* of more importance to you than *German & Italian both*. These latter languages are very desirable but are by no means so important to *you* as the *French & Spanish*. Indeed if you neglect *either of them* your whole object will be defeated and *you may be sure of not obtaining the station which you have in view*. And I should never have consented to your visiting Europe, had it not been to secure that station. You must recollect, my dear son, that your great object is to obtain an accurate knowledge of Modern languages & particularly of the *French & Spanish*, and during your absence it will be necessary that your constant & particular attention should be exerted to that object. . . . I did suppose you would have placed yourself under the care of some able instructor, and think your labours would have been greatly facilitated and your progress accelerated by that course but as you say nothing about it I presume it is not the case. What reason have you for not doing it?" [15]

While this letter was still traveling across the ocean, Longfellow had again changed his mind and modified his plans. The impulsive desire to meet Preble in Göttingen in the spring, and the words of Professor Ticknor, had eclipsed, for a time, his longing to see Italy—the country which had fascinated him in literature and in imagination since Portland Academy days. Knowing that his father had already expressed his disapproval of the initial proposal to go immediately to Germany, but not yet aware of parental pressure which would force him to study Spanish immediately after completing his work in French, Longfellow reconsidered. His new proposal, written to his mother, was plainly stimulated by a reversion to his vision of Italy as a land of poetry and romance. But he offered as his immediate excuses, his mother's reluctance to have him visit Germany, and his recently acquired understanding that the German language was not easily mastered. He wrote:

"You seem no way pleased with my idea of visiting Germany, and your first reason is my own personal safety, which you think would be in danger. Now for my own part, I have not the least

apprehension on this score for I never had any particular fondness for a duel.–Your second reason for my not visiting the country is much more plausable–its lengthening my stay in Europe. It
would be useless to go into Germany unless I could remain at least
a year–and I suppose you would object to this on more than one
account. When I wrote my last letter upon the subject, speaking
of my going to Göttingen as a matter almost certain, I thought I
could learn the language and get some insight into the literature
in a shorter time than a twelve month, but those who are best acquainted with the subject tell me no–The language is so exceedingly difficult that it will not be worth while to attempt to speak
it unless I have much time to devote to it. I must come back again
to my original destination–France–Spain and Italy. But Italy
before Spain on many accounts–The dangerous state of the country–the suspicion naturally attached to an Englishman if the War
continue long–would not detain me though I once thought they
would. But then I should wish to make sure of Italy and its language first–for fear that if I went first into Spain I should lose
Italy by some untoward circumstances–such as being under the
necessity of returning before the time anticipated &c.

"Thus we see how much the events of life depend upon momen-
tery circumstances–and how much the apprehension of some
mischance will change one's plans and resolutions. I have been
talking considerably with Mr. Carter [16] upon the subject, who
advises me most decidedly to go to Italy in the first instance–and
then to Spain. You will hear from me soon, then, in Italy–What
a delightful prospect for me! With how much delight I shall leave
the populous and noisy streets of Paris for the sunny regions of
the south, and the eternal summer of the Italian valleys! Then
indeed the distance between us will become more perceptible,
because our intercourse by letters will be more interrupted and
more uncertain. I shall instead of regular letters keep a journal for
you–a thing that I have not done in France on many accounts and
chiefly on account of the little interest attached to anything in
Paris, and a thorough disgust for French manners and customs." [17]

So definitely settled was this new plan that Longfellow began
studying Italian in Paris, with an instructor named Ferranti, as a
preliminary gesture. But his father's heavily underscored sen-

tences arrived in time to haul him back on the path of duty. Happily, Longfellow's weathervane impulses veered suddenly toward Spain at almost the very time when his father's letter reached him. Through his cousin, Eben Storer, he met two young men from New York who had come but recently to Paris from Spain. One of them, Pierre Irving, was a nephew of Washington Irving. Undoubtedly the prospect of meeting the author of *The Sketch Book* was strong enough to blow away all clouds of fear aroused by talk of bloodshed and danger. Pierre Irving and his companion, David Berdan, assured him that there was no serious reason for alarm, and that he should not fail to go to Madrid, where Washington Irving was working on his study of Columbus.

At last, his own wishes coincided with those of his father, and he made preparations to leave Paris on February 21, 1827. He was fairly well contented with his accomplishment, in retrospect, and wrote his father a defensive summary of his success:

"It is now exactly eight months since my arrival in Paris—and setting all boasting aside—I must say that I am well satisfied with the knowledge I have acquired of the french language. My friends all tell me that I have a good pronunciation—and although I do not pretend to anything like perfection—yet in comparison with what others have done—I am confident that I have done well. I cannot imagine who told you that six months was enough for the French. He would have been more correct if he had said six years—that is— speaking of perfection in the language.

"I shall leave Paris for Spain on Wednesday—day after to-morrow." [18]

The journey across southern France by coach was a slow one, requiring five days and four nights of travel by way of Orléans, Limoges, and Périgueux to Bordeaux, which he reached on the eve of his twentieth birthday. He found little to make him sorry that his sojourn in France was so nearly over, for his disappointments had been far greater than his joys. There was the vivid memory of the cathedral at Rouen and there was the charming idyll of the Loire valley excursion. But he had shown no pleasure in studying the French language and listening to lectures on French literature. Annoyed by the sights and smells of Paris, the gloomy days of winter, and the loneliness of his solitary room in

the Rue Racine, he felt no regret in turning his back on them.
His pensive hours of sentiment and adoration had been purchased
at a cost far higher than he had anticipated when he embarked
for Europe. Paris in winter had not been conducive to the pleasant
melancholy of dreams. Bordeaux was different; a sunny city
breathing spring warmth even in February. Within two days he
would leave France for an even warmer land—and he was glad.

X

SPAIN AND A NEW BEGINNING

*Thus you see me on my way to Spain: and I cannot say that I
leave France with much regret:— It may be, that my curiosity leaves
no room for feelings of this kind, by painting the land to which I
am going as fairer than that I am leaving—or it may be a secret
disappointment lurking in my heart,—at having found more perplexities to escape—and more difficulties to encounter than I had anticipated;—but true it is that I look forward to a happier life in Spain,
than I have led in France.*[1]

THE JOURNEY into Spain was a pleasant interlude. As Longfellow
watched the countryside through the windows of his clumsy
diligence his spirits revived. Even the rumors of highwaymen
attacking travelers and tales of banditti in the hills ahead increased his enjoyment. The Basque girls along the road were
beautiful, with their tanned faces, flashing teeth, dark eyes, and
black, glossy hair. He watched some of them on horseback outside the city of Bayonne. Attached to the saddle was a double
seat which seemed to balance across the horse's back in such a way
that girl and passenger rode, one on each side, with feet dangling
in the air beneath them. How charming! One girl, with a large
straw hat tied by a bright ribbon and pushed back on her shoulders, smiled in at him as she passed, and he could not forget her
face. Stupid to be boxed in a diligence when he might be journey-
ing in company with a pretty nut-brown maid and talking French
with her.

South of Bayonne, the blue waters of the Bay of Biscay came
into view for the first time, unexpectedly. He had not looked out
over such an expanse since Havre de Grâce, where he had landed
nearly a year ago. Had he been away from home a year? Memories of Casco Bay brought new longings. "It seemed but a step—
a little step—from one shore to the other; and with my mind's eye
I saw White Head, looming thro' the mists, that gathered on the
horizon." [2] Like the blending mists, his homesickness and his

romanticism ascended from a common source. And the vapors of
sentiment which welled up continuously from the young man's
heart were frequently conducive to mirage.

The leisurely progress toward Madrid across northern Spain
carried him through Burgos, the capital of Old Castile, where the
glorious Cid Campeador was entombed. Rich, indeed, was Spain
with legend and tradition recorded long since in song and narrative. Greedily his memory absorbed scenes and incidents which
would furnish literary provender. In France there had been little
to record. But his wanderings on foot through the Loire valley
had turned his mind toward literary channels; had led him to compare himself with Scott's young Quentin Durward, with Goldsmith and Irving. These authors had turned their travels to good
account: why shouldn't he? The country, even in its sombre aspects, was picturesque. "You will remember," his father had
advised, "that a description of the wonders of the old world will
always be interesting to us, who are so far removed from you and
them." [3] Here was an abundance of material for letters—strange
pictures, stirring the imagination. The gloomy, barren regions of
the mountains created in his mind a grim melancholy that he
enjoyed:

"In broad daylight, too, one who travels in this country has
always something to remind him of the perilous ways he is treading in. The cold, inhospitable, uncultivated look of the country
itself—the dark, fiendish countenances which peep at him from
the folds of the Spanish cloak in every town and village, but more
than all, the little black crosses which one comes upon at almost
every step—standing by the roadside in commemoration of a mur-
der or other violent death which has taken place upon the spot—
these keep his fancy busy." [4]

Lost in this pleasantly creepy reverie, Longfellow cared not a
fig for looking beyond the picturesque; for concerning himself
with those social and historic causes which had made Spain a prey
for lawbreakers and bandits. When this American traveler had
been only a year old, Napoleon Bonaparte had invaded Spain—
and ever since that time, the country had known no protracted
years of peace. The return of Ferdinand VII to the throne, after
Napoleon had been driven out by the concerted effort of the

Spanish, had led to a long series of uprisings and clashes between the Liberals, demanding the reëstablishment of the Cortes, and the reactionary Absolutists. By the time Longfellow reached Spain, the land was exhausted after intermittent periods of rebellion, terrorism, and coercion. But the young romantic, whose vision was blurred by his love of the bizarre, could not work up any interest in the age-old struggle between the oppressed and the powerful. Enough for him to enjoy an added sense of possible danger, as he rode slowly through the desolate countryside.

Madrid was different. Arriving there on the 6th of March, Longfellow found Lieutenant Alexander Slidell, of the United States Navy, in his quarters at the foot of Calle de la Montera near a public square called Puerta del Sol.[5] Pierre Irving, who had urged Longfellow to go to Madrid, had told him of Slidell, then helping Washington Irving on historical research concerning the life of Columbus. Probably at Slidell's suggestion, Longfellow engaged rooms in the home of Valentín González. Finding that he must wait a few days for lodgings there, Longfellow accepted Slidell's invitation to make a ten-day jaunt to the ancient city of Segovia and into the Guadarrama Mountains.

Conveniently, he had forgotten his father's warning that his object could be obtained only through diligent application to his books, for this venture was far more appealing than Spanish grammar. The two young men traveled on foot, by mule, and even in covered wagons, through the mountainous country—over snow-filled passes and into desolate wilderness.

Slidell was merry company. And the trip would have been worth while if only for the visit to the magnificent Escorial. Again the pilgrim found himself worshipping within the mysterious twilight of a holy place. It was far more than a church, he discovered, for Philip II had intended it for both palace and sepulchre. But history was not so important to him as the emotions he felt as he moved through the church aisles:

"I could not help lingering among its gloomy arches, and indulging in that pleasant kind of melancholy which such scenes are apt to inspire. I heard mass said in the twilight of its aisles—and as the chant of the priests reached my ear at intervals, with the peal of the organ echoing amid the arches and dying away in indistinct murmurs along the roof and vaults—the effect was most powerful." [6]

Again in Madrid, he felt obliged to make another explanation to his parents for this latest departure from duty. Perhaps it would be enough to mention his difficulty in finding immediate lodgings. Obediently, he began an account of his travels, however, according to the wishes of his father. "As it will be impossible to write very fully and frequently from such a distance—I shall endeavour to supply the deficiencies of my correspondence by a kind of journal." [7] The fulfilment of this plan required hours of labor, and page after page of narration, broken occasionally by a brief salutation of a new section to some particular member of his family. Not until nearly two months after the end of his trip with Slidell did he complete the final written account of the return to Madrid from the Escorial.

The lodgings for which he had waited proved more delightful than he had imagined. "The whole house is goodness—from the mistress down to the domestic," he wrote, "and the daughter, a young lady of 'sweet sixteen' with the romantic name of Florence, supplies the place of a sister much better than I had anticipated could be possible." [8] In another letter he wrote concerning his newly adopted sister, "Under her attentions I hope to find the acquisition of the Spanish a delightful task." [9] But, lest his critical father misinterpret the sincerity of his intention, he made a pointed statement that he had arranged for professional tutoring. Long before Longfellow had left France, his father had mistakenly advised him that Barcelona was reputed to be a better place for learning the language than Madrid; that the pronunciation was purer there.[10] To be sure, Pierre Irving had corrected this erroneous notion and had added other arguments strong enough to eclipse those of Stephen Longfellow. But they might not sound so convincing when relayed to Portland as they had sounded in Paris. Longfellow's only defense was a casual one:

"It will not of course be necessary to explain very fully my motives in coming to Madrid in preference to any other city in Spain—with a view of making the language my study:—because I know that the same reasons which actuated me will suggest themselves forcibly to your own mind. The metropolis of a country is always the great literary mart:—then—literary advantages are always greater—books always more numerous and more accessible . . . I dare say that I shall not regret my coming." [11]

His friendly association with the author of *The Sketch Book* was unquestionably the most important literary event he had ever known. The genial author revealed in his personality the same qualities of humor, sentiment, and poetic charm which had drawn his admirer so strongly to him many years earlier. "He has a most beautiful countenance—and at the same time a very intellectual one—but he has some halting and hesitating in his conversation," Longfellow wrote, "and says very pleasant, agreeable things, in a husky—weak—peculiar voice. He has a dark complexion—dark hair:—whiskers already a little grey. This is a very off-hand portrait of so illustrious a man." [12]

Day after day Longfellow grew better acquainted with his famous countryman. He learned that Irving had been in Madrid over a year, and that he had been invited by the United States Ambassador Alexander H. Everett to translate Navarette's recently published book on the voyages of Columbus. To facilitate his travels in Spain, the American minister had made Irving an attaché of the Legation. He had taken rooms under the roof of Obadiah Rich, a native of Cape Cod and a zealous book collector then serving his second year as American consul in Madrid. Although Longfellow called on Irving occasionally, he always found him busy. "Sit down," he invariably said, "I will talk with you in a moment, but I must first finish this sentence." [13] His constant industry was due in large part to his ill-timed promise to Murray, his English publisher, that he should have the manuscript of the *Life of Columbus* (he had abandoned the idea of translation) soon after Christmas of 1826. But the discovery of new and conflicting material led him to make deliberate and careful revision. Spring moved on into summer, and still the manuscript remained unfinished. One summer morning Longfellow noticed, as he walked by the house, that Irving's study window was already wide open. "Yes," Irving later explained, "I am always at work as early as six." [14]

Although Longfellow's knowledge of Spanish was too slight to allow full appreciation, he developed a friendly respect for

Obadiah Rich, who was collecting Spanish books and manuscripts relating to the discovery and settlement of America. A simple, kindly, hospitable gentleman, he eagerly opened the doors of his library to any who wished to work there. "His house at Madrid was a literary wilderness," Irving later wrote, "abounding with curious works and rare editions, in the midst of which he lived and moved and had his being." [15]

From Hon. C. S. Daveis of Portland, Longfellow had brought letters of introduction to Mr. and Mrs. Alexander Everett, who were as charmed with their young countryman as he was with them. "His countenance is itself a letter of recommendation," wrote Mrs. Everett to Mrs. Daveis.[16] To his father, Longfellow described Mrs. Everett as "a very pleasant lady," and added, "She has not all the 'pomp and circumstance' which Ambassadors' wives sometimes put on—and receives one in a friendly—not an official way." [17] What opportunity for such enlightening comparison Longfellow had, he did not divulge. Nevertheless, he was happy to take part in the informal social life of these Americans in Madrid. In the evenings he never hesitated to call on them, for he was assured of a cordial welcome. Particularly pleasant were his evenings spent with Rich, for he could be fairly certain that Irving would join the circle. It amused him greatly to hear this man, who seemed to him such a learned historian, hesitate when someone asked him the exact year of a famous Spanish event. "When was that, Peter?" he used to question in a troubled voice. And the invariable answer from his helper was, "Well, Washington, I don't exactly recollect." [18]

Even attendance at the opera with the ambassador or conversation with Irving could not eclipse the pleasure which Longfellow derived from daily association with the members of the González family—and particularly with the sixteen-year-old Florencia. To his mother he wrote:

"The daughter of the old lady with whom I am residing is one of the sweetest-tempered little girls that I ever met with:—and added to this, the grace of the Spanish women and the beauty of their language makes her conversation quite fascinating. I could not receive greater kindness than I receive at the hands of this good family, who on all occasions exhibit the greatest, and most disinterested affection for me. I shall feel the most sincere regret in bidding them farewell for ever. There is also another family in the house, with which I am acquainted. It is a Malaga lady with her daughter—a very handsome young lady of about seventeen— a very white skin—light blue eyes—and fine auburn hair. She frequently reminds me of sister Anne, and by the way, has the same name. As the two young ladies are very intimate together, I have a great deal of good society. Whilst I write, I see them in the balcony below me, busy with their needles and their tongues—little dreaming that I am sending tidings of them across the sea. I confess that I feel very little desire to leave Madrid, as you may imagine." [19]

His letters from Madrid made almost no mention of his progress in learning Spanish. There were so many more pleasant occupations. With his Spanish sisters, Florencia and Anita, he walked about the Prado or the Puerto del Sol in the cool of the day. He liked listening to their pretty stories of tradition, legend, or gossip. Several times during his stay in Madrid he attended the bull fights with them and seemed to share the lusty spirit of the crowd with unfeeling sensibilities which were surprising for a sensitive novice. One brief journal entry described his favorite: "May 21. The Bull-fight. The best of the season. A great number of horses killed. A great many hair-breadth escapes of Picadores:—a banderillero tossed in the air.—one of the afficionados:—a good lesson for him." [20]

Late in May he made an excursion into the country with the González family to the village of El Pardillo, four leagues from Madrid, to "see if the shepherds, which inhabit the green valleys of Castile are the same with those that sigh through whole pages of pastoral romance." [21] He found a satisfactory answer: "One almost thinks he has got back into old pastoral times; and the peculiar dress of the Spanish peasantry adds much to this romantic self-deception." [22] Participating in the village festival, he engaged in the celebration, and even experimented with the gestures and gyrations of the dancers. In one moment of abandon he sent the manager's hat flying off his head with an outflung arm and immediately afterwards, "the first swing of my leg brought my dirty boots into collision with a pair of nice white Sunday stock-

ings—manoeuvres which excited universal approbation and unbounded applause." [23]

The language student found such rural pleasures far more
diverting than the rare volumes in the library of Obadiah Rich.
After two weeks of absence from Madrid, he wrote in his journal:

"June 6th, This will probably be my last day at Pardillo—making preparations to return to Madrid tomorrow—Thus I have
seen a little of Spanish rural life & am much delighted with it. I
like to see things in reality—not in painting—to study men—not
books.—

> "Jucundum est, rerum radices scrutare, nam,
> 'Dulcius ex ipse fonte bibuntur aquae'!—" [24]

As Longfellow sent letter after letter across the Atlantic filled
with descriptions of his travels and accounts of his pleasant social
activities, yet with very few references to his supposedly primary
purpose, he may have wondered what effect his past course of
action was having on his father. But answers were slow in coming,
and over two months elapsed before he could expect a reply.
Shortly after he had reached Madrid, he had received letters calculated to find him in Italy. True enough, he had written that he
would go there before going to Spain. In referring to this misunderstanding he explained:

"To be sure, it was my own fault: as I wrote you from Paris,
that I should go there first. But after forming twenty different
plans—comparing them together as many different times—considering and reconsidering—reading old letters from home, and consulting your wishes—and the best method of attaining the end for
which I crossed the sea—I concluded that it would be more advantageous to visit Spain first, and trust to future circumstances
for a poetic pilgrimage through Italy." [25]

Spain had afforded him several poetic pilgrimages and he was
not impatient to leave. His father, trusting that Henry was preparing himself satisfactorily for teaching French and Spanish, was
under the impression that the enterprise would be completed by
the summer of 1828. Having accepted the student's explanation
that Spain, not Italy, had been the second objective, he wrote:

"Will it be necessary for you to stop a short time in France as you return for the purpose of refreshing or perfecting your knowledge of the French language? Or would it do to pass from Italy, through Germany to England, or shall you prefer coming directly home from Italy without visiting those countries?" [26]

The answer to this questioning was that Longfellow had not abandoned his intention of meeting Preble in Germany as soon as he had finished his studies in Spain. He was even willing to sacrifice his long anticipated visit to Italy, but he was not willing to return without going to Germany. From Madrid, on July 16 (a full month before he had received these questions) he wrote to his father:

"I am still in my former intention of going to Germany by way of Marseilles, unless some objection should offer itself previous to my departure from the South of Europe. Pray do not think me too changeble in my designs—many of them are rather suggestions than mature plans—but rest assured that I shall do what will result most to my advantage, so far as I am capable of judging. Do not believe too much of what people tell you of learning the French language in six months and the Spanish in three. Were I guided by such counsellors I should return a sheer charletan: and though I might deceive others as to the amount of my knowledge, I cannot deceive myself so easily: for whatever vanity I may possess with regard to my natural abilities, I have very little with regard to my acquisitions." [27]

With no illusions concerning the extent of knowledge he had acquired in Spain, Longfellow determined to push on toward Germany early in the fall of 1827. At the end of six months, he ended his studies in Madrid and departed for the south of Spain on September 2, intending to sail from Gibraltar to Marseilles. Traveling slowly overland in one sort of conveyance after another, he reached the barren and desolate regions of La Mancha, recently plundered by the Peninsular Wars. Again, the young traveler was more concerned with the picturesque than with war history. The very name La Mancha stirred within his mind visions of romantic ghosts wandering about the countryside:

"No one can enter the province of La Mancha, without a reverie of faithfulness in love and chivalry in arms. The memory of Don Quixote has made it classic ground. The history of his achievements is written in everything that meets the eye: and one cannot get a view of a windmill perched on an eminence by the roadside, without fancying that he sees the figure of the wandering knight tilting valiantly against the imaginary giant!" [28]

Approaching Cordova, he felt the wild landscape of Andalusia strike reminiscent chords. "The scenery resembles that of the White Mountains," he wrote in his diary, "but it is not so fine. Indeed—I have seen nothing in Europe to compare with the White Hills." [29] At Gibraltar a serious disappointment awaited him, for he was unable to find immediate passage by boat for Marseilles and was forced to remain there a full month. Having met in Cadiz a Mr. Maynard who had relatives in Portland and who was then living in Gibraltar, Longfellow had traveled with him to the British stronghold and had visited pleasantly for some time before becoming impatient. Finally he determined to wait no longer and set sail from Gibraltar to Málaga.

He had not intended visiting Granada and the Alhambra when he made his itinerary, but after spending a week in Málaga, he found an American companion who was eager to go there with him. Quite unexpectedly Longfellow was lifted to a new height of romantic adoration, for his entrance to Granada was the beginning of a rich emotional experience. In his journal he described his arrival:

"We reached the city after nightfall. As we crossed the beautiful Vega—those delicious and luxuriant meadows which stretch away to the south and west of Granada—I felt as if I were indeed treading in fairy lands. The thousand lights of the city glimmering in the distance—and the sound of the evening bells . . . called my thoughts away from the realities of life to the musings of romance. The gradual closing of twilight added enchantment to the scene: and as my companions crossed some eminence in the road, and wrapt in their Spanish cloaks became relieved against the dusky sky—I could not help fancying them a silent band of Christian knights of olden time—bound on some chivalrous adventure by the walls of the besieged city." [30]

Having found a room almost under the shadow of the towering Alhambra, Longfellow could not wait until morning to begin

MALAGA TO GRANADA, NOVEMBER 1827

From a pen and pencil sketch which Longfellow made in his journal while in Spain. Beneath it he wrote:

"*To horse—to horse—he quits, forever quits*
A scene of peace, though soothing to his soul."
—BYRON

his pilgrimage. The mood of reverence came over him as he looked out into the dimly lit city from his window:

"It seems a dream to me—I am within the walls of this ancient city of the Moorish kings. From my window I see the ruined towers of their palace overlooking the city—and at midnight I hear the solemn bell calling the silent watches from its mouldering turret! How my spirit is stirred within me!—how my heart is lifted up!—how my thoughts are rapt away in visions of other times!—Is it not a dream?

". . . It is now past midnight. The bell has tolled the hour. The crowded street has become lonely and deserted, and echoes only to the song of the watchman on his nightly round—'Ave María puríssima!—las doce y serena!' At my window the faint glimmer of a light from the ruined towers of the Alhambra falls upon my eye, and I faintly discern the dusky and indistinct outline of its mouldering turrets rising amid the uncertain twilight of the hour, like a shadow of departed years and departed glory." [31]

For five days he continued his sentimental wanderings about the Alhambra. As he concluded his stay and prepared to make his departure he looked back over those days as endless hours of enjoyment. "No portion of my life has been so much like a dream," he wrote in his journal. "It was a season of most singular excitement to me. How much I wanted in those happy moments some early bosom friend to share those feelings with me! . . . How many solitary moments a traveller has! There is some truth in Madame de Staël's remark that 'of all the *pleasures* of life, travelling is the *saddest*!'" [32] But he could not turn away. Again he returned to the walls of the Alhambra, and came back to write, "Visited for the last time the Alhambra and the valley of the Darro and took a last lingering look of those scenes of romance, which I thought I could gaze on forever." [33]

His joyous pilgrimage through Spain had found its perfect ending. Never again was he to know greater heights of romantic fervor. And never in years that lay before him would he spoil the rapture of his memory by revisiting Spain.

XI

ROMANCE IN ITALY

I suppose the very names of Florence—the Arno—and Vallombrosa are full of romance and poetry for you who have not seen them:—and that you imagine me sitting at night in the shadow of some olive grove—watching the rising moon—and listening to the song of the Italian boatman, or the chime of a convent bell! Alas! distance and poetry have so much magic about them! Can you believe that the Arno—"that glassy river"—"rolling his crystal tide through classic vales"—is a stream of yellow, muddy water almost entirely dry in summer!—and that Italian gondoliers—and convent bells—and white-robed nuns—and all the rigmarole of midnight song and soft serenade, are not altogether so delightful in reality as we sometimes fancy them to be? But I must not tell tales! I may spoil the market for some beautiful effusion . . .[1]

AFTER SPAIN, he was ready to go home. There he had climbed higher into the clouds than he had ever soared even in dreams, and he was content to ask nothing more. What was there left to expect? Against his early prejudices, he had been persuaded to visit the bandit-infested country without any thought of finding a land of sunshine, delicious fruits and flowers, orange blossoms, and romance. But the surprise had enriched the pleasure. All that he had thought to find in a poetic pilgrimage through Italy, he had found in Spain, and he had no sooner left than he longed to return.

But he must be practical. According to those constantly shifting plans which he had made and broken by letters to his father, across the Atlantic, the departure from Spain marked the end of necessary study and left the approaching winter for less diligent application and travel. He would go to Germany overland from Marseilles, without bothering, now, to enter Italy. Surely, Preble would join him as he had promised. If inclination led Longfellow to study at Dresden (as Washington Irving had suggested) or at Göttingen, there would be time for that as well as travel, during the winter. But he had heard that the German language was very difficult. Of course he could not be expected to master the language in a few months. The very thought of it discouraged him.

Unexpectedly, his plans were modified sharply by two letters from his father which were waiting at Marseilles. Stephen Longfellow had suddenly been persuaded by Professor Ticknor that his son should not return without studying German at Göttingen. Consequently he wrote to say that Henry should remain abroad another year:

"I have recently seen Mr. Ticknor who appears very anxious that you should go to Germany. He says the acquisition of the German language will be of more importance to you as a literary man than any two other languages within his knowledge, as it unlocks a vast store of learning and you find in that language the best treatises on French, Spanish & even English literature there are to be found in any language. Although you may be correct in your supposition that generally speaking a situation in a private family in a retired town would be better than a University, I should doubt whether a situation of that kind in Germany would be so advantageous to you as a residence at the University at Göttingen. Mr. Ticknor says the advantages there for perfecting your knowledge of all the languages are very great, and the expenses are much less than at any other place in Europe—The Lectures also are of very great advantage to a literary man—

"I am disposed to do all in my power to make your education as perfect as possible, and as you are now abroad, should be sorry for you to omit any thing which would occasion regret hereafter. The only objection is the procrastination of your return & the increase of your expenses, and these are serious objections. But if on the whole you think it best to go to Germany and find the expenses will not be too great I will endeavor to meet them reminding you at the same time that you must make them as light as you can with propriety, as they will come out of your patrimony, and will I fear entirely consume it.

"I have understood that the lectures at Göttingen commence in the fall. In that case you would not reach there in a favorable time if you go directly there, for you would be entirely ignorant of the language & not able to draw any advantage from them. By spending the winter in the mild climate of Italy you would avoid the cold winter of the north and might make your journey as early in the spring as you could cross the Alps." [2]

In the second letter waiting at Marseilles, Stephen Longfellow wrote at more length concerning the advisability of going first to Italy, but left to his son the decision as to whether it would be expedient to study the language there, "or only view the country & its curiosities." [3] Somewhat weary of travel, Longfellow expressed neither gratitude nor enthusiasm for the new arrangement. "What a pity that those letters did not reach me before I left Spain!" he wrote in answer. "If they had, I could have arranged a journey of a much finer route, by embarking for Naples instead of Marseilles. But at present I must do the best in my power, which is to go to Florence, where I hope to master the Italian in a very short time." [4]

He was hiding his longing for home, and continued successfully until the last sentence of the letter: "Tell mama and all the family, not forgetting my good Aunt Lucia—that before I left them I did not know how much I loved them."

The overland journey to Genoa was relieved from tediousness by Longfellow's good fortune in meeting and traveling with several officers from the American schooner *Porpoise*. One of his companions on the trip was George Washington Greene of Newport, Rhode Island—a grandson of General Nathanael Greene—who was not a naval officer but, like Longfellow, a student intending to spend a few weeks in Italy. Attracted by similarity of purpose and temperament, the two struck up an acquaintance which quickly grew into close friendship. Together they continued from Genoa to Leghorn where they parted with promises to meet a few weeks later in Rome.

In Florence, Longfellow took rooms with an Italian family on the Piazza Santa Maria Novella and immediately began his study of Italian. He was eager to be on his way again. At first, he believed that he should make short work, for his knowledge of Spanish enabled him to read Italian. But he was constantly annoyed by the confusion of the two languages when he tried to speak them. After all, since there was no necessity for mastering Italian, the problem need not trouble him seriously. However, he was aware of a greater disappointment than confusion of words and the harshness of the Tuscan pronunciation: Italy was not the romantic country he had imagined it to be. Since boyhood he had dreamed of this magic land of song, with soft moonlight drenching the grandeur of old ruins and slow rivers bearing graceful black gondolas. From his reading he had pictured it all so clearly that he had written lines, during his junior year at Bowdoin, which were entitled "Italian Scenery":

> Night rests in beauty on Mont Alto.
> Beneath its shade the beauteous Arno sleeps
> In Vallombrosa's bosom, and dark trees
> Bend with a calm and quiet shadow down
> Upon the beauty of that silent river.
> Still in the west a melancholy smile
> Mantles the lips of day, and twilight pale
> Moves like a spectre in the dusky sky;
> While eve's sweet star on the fast fading year
> Smiles calmly:—Music steals at intervals
> Across the water, with a tremulous swell,
> From out the upland dingle of tall firs,
> And a faint footfall sounds where dim and dark
> Hangs the gray willow from the river's brink,
> O'er-shadowing its current. Slowly there
> The lover's gondola drops down the stream,
> Silent, save when its dipping oar is heard,
> Or in its eddy sighs the rippling wave. . . .[5]

But the pilgrim had come once again to be deluded. Nothing was as he had expected. In Spain he had enjoyed reading "Childe Harold's Pilgrimage" and the first canto of "Don Juan" as guidebooks.[6] Once in Italy, however, he felt that such poetic guides as Byron and Samuel Rogers had deceived him. Florence, where he had hoped to dwell pleasurably for a short time, had none of the charms associated in his mind with the mouldering walls of the Alhambra or with the mysterious gloom of the cathedral at Rouen. With sardonic bitterness, he wrote to his mother that he had been cheated.

Despite many delightful evenings at the theatre and hours spent in the distinguished company of the daughter of Joseph Bonaparte

or with the Countess de Survilliers, Longfellow was impatient
with Florence. He was anxious to leave Italy behind him. Why
should he tarry in such an unpleasant land? After only three
weeks there he wrote:

"I shall stay but a few days longer in Florence—I feel anxious to
get into Germany—at least as much so as I do to see Rome and
Naples. I must confess it!—It is rather singular—but I must confess it—I am travelling through Italy without any enthusiasm—
and just curiosity enough to keep me awake!—I feel no excitement—no—nothing of that romantic feeling which every body
else has—or pretends to have. The fact is I am homesick for
Spain—I want to go back there again—The recollection of it
completely ruins Italy for me: and next to going home—let me
go to Spain." [7]

In this listless state of mind he lost interest in his study of the
Italian. "I got quite out of humor with the language," he wrote to
his mother, "and concluded that I would not give further attention to speaking—but would make my way through Italy with the
little I had acquired—and be contented with reading:—without
making much pretension to speaking it." [8] In Rome he found
solace in the company of his friend Greene and took rooms in the
same home with him. Rome would not detain him long, he was
convinced, for Venice and Milan were also to be visited in his
rapid itinerary toward Germany. Spring had already come, and
he wished to reach Göttingen by early summer.

But he found in Rome a romantic fascination to which he had
shown himself susceptible in both France and Spain: the daughters
of his hostess. The Persiani family, living on the Piazza Navona
("the very heart of the city, and one of the largest and most
magnificent squares of modern Rome" [9]), had lost great wealth
because of political changes, but had retained a high social standing. The three attractive sisters in the family were well educated
and able to converse with Longfellow not only in their own language—which, in their mouths, became suddenly beautiful to him
—but also in French and English. Furthermore, here were musi-
cians far more skillful and talented than either Florencia González
or the daughters of Madame Potet. One played the harp, another

played the piano and sang beautifully. "The youngest of the three —is not so highly gifted," he confessed, "in these particulars."

As Longfellow lingered in this delicious atmosphere he forgot about hurrying on to Germany—and the knowledge of the Italian language, which had seemed so unimportant in Florence, became imperative. Describing his good fortune to his mother, he continued:

"But the family is so very kind—so very genteel—we see so much good society in the evening—and I have so good an opportunity for practicing French, Spanish, & Italian, that I shall make my residence in Italy something longer than I had intended on leaving Florence." [10]

How easily the impulsive student could be swayed from despondency to bliss! Two months earlier he had expressed a complete boredom toward any travel except that which would carry him home—or to Spain. But even in Spain he had written no letters filled with his joy in studying the language or in reading Spanish authors. Neither had he made any mention of his enthusiasm for French literature. His few defensive comments on satisfactory progress had always been elicited by his father's questions and criticisms.[11] Yet from Rome he expressed his first joy in the study of language. He even wished that his brothers and sisters in Portland might be given immediate instruction so that they should continue to pursue their learning with him when he returned. With lyric rapture he added: "Let the youngest learn it also—it is never too young—and the more I study myself the more I am interested. The fact is, I am completely engrossed with the subject—With this study of the languages I am completely enchanted —Indeed I am very passionately fond of it." [12]

After such an outburst of reiteration, who could doubt? Obviously, the charming influence of the Persiani sisters was not entirely responsible for his new interest. But his stay in Rome (which was protracted for various reasons until he had been in Italy twelve months) was devoted more to pilgrimages among ancient ruins and to hours of diversion in company with his new friends than to poring over volumes in the public libraries. Into his notebook he tucked occasional descriptions of such festive events as the Summer Carnival in Rome and his visit to the suburbs —and once even attempted to write a poem on the "Eternal City." [13] But almost no passage made mention of his reading.

More characteristic of Longfellow's stay in Italy was the three-week visit to Naples he made with George Greene in the month of April. His disillusionment in Florence was entirely forgotten as he looked from a window of their rooms, out across the Bay to the broken cone of Vesuvius, to the slow curving shore and the white houses. At the end of the shore line rose the blue promontory of Sorrento, and beyond, in the blue-green waters of the ocean, he could discern the celebrated island of Capri.

Greene shared his fondness for romantic dreamery. Years later, recalling this scene, he caught in his description the very atmosphere which had charmed them both: "And over all, with a thrill like that of solemn music, fell the splendor of the Italian sunset. We talked and mused by turns, till the twilight deepened and the stars came forth to mingle their mysterious influences with the overmastering magic of the scene." [14] How easily, how naturally, the two young men talked to each other of intimate longings. Greene, impressed by the deep seriousness of their conversation, later wrote: "It was then that you unfolded to me your plans of life, and showed me from what 'deep cisterns' you had already learned to draw. From that day the office of literature took a new place in my thoughts." [15]

When the two friends took leave of each other late in April, Greene continued his travels across southern France to Spain and Longfellow returned to Rome. Knowing that his father had urged him to reach Göttingen before the heat of the summer, he later made excuses that he was obliged to wait for letters of credit from his banker in Paris. Apparently the delay did not trouble him, for he hinted to his brother that there were other inducements: "I have been so much delighted with Rome, that I have extended my residence much beyond my original intention." [16] Then, lest his father become suspicious, he hastened to describe the fascination of "the ruined temples—the mausoleums—and the old mouldering acqueducts." [17] Two weeks later, he made another self-conscious explanation to his mother: "You can judge from my long residence in Italy, that I am much pleased with it.

Its language is very beautiful; but more difficult than the Spanish." [18] He added that he had dipped into the German but that he had learned little except that it was also difficult.

Why had he lost all interest in moving on to Göttingen? Even the news that Ned Preble had left home in April failed to arouse the earlier impatience to join him. His parents began to wonder and ask questions. The truth, which he very carefully concealed from them, was that he had lost his heart to Julia,[19] the eldest of the Persiani sisters, and was willing to make any number of excuses if only he might continue to live on the Piazza Navona. Fortunately he was given an incontrovertible excuse. In the middle of July he was taken ill with a serious fever and was confined to his bed for a week or ten days. As soon as he was able to write a letter, he described his misfortunes at great length, and was careful to make his account a plausible explanation of protracted dalliance:

"L'Ariccia, August 4, 1828

"My dear Father,

"You will doubtless be not a little surprised to find by the date of my letter that I am still in the environs of Rome; it being probably your intention as well as my own, that long ere this I should have been established and pursuing my studies at the University of Goetingen. But circumstances out of my power either to foresee or to prevent have broken in upon these plans. Since the first week in January, I have not received any letters from America, nor any from Mr. Welles in Paris. To Mr. Welles I have written repeatedly—and one of my letters at least must have reached him . . . however I do not get a word in reply. . . .

"As I have no letters of credit for Germany, and of course look to Mr. Welles for them, this long and unaccountable silence had been very unpleasant to me. Consequently when I was ready to leave Rome, and felt myself well enough advanced in the Italian Language to set out for another foreign country, I was greatly incommoded by this want of letters:—from you, to know your decisions upon the course I was to take, after knowing my expenses thus far . . . and also from Mr. Welles forwarding me letters of credit for Germany. I was thus delayed by 'hope de-

ferred, that maketh the heart sick.' Thus week after week slipped
away—whilst I waited patiently in daily expectation of the arrival
of letters. The season advanced, and warm weather came on.
The summer, you know, in Rome is very unhealthy for foreigners:
and so it proved to me:—and I who have hardly known until this
what sickness is—am now an invalid seeking my health in a little
village among the hills in the vicinity of Rome. I am however
happy to tell you that I am no longer in danger: and find myself
gradually gaining strength and activity.

"In the beginning of July I took a violent cold, which of course
gave me no alarm, as I am seldom free from some affection of the
kind. Feeling, however, a little feverish at night, on going to bed
I took the usual remedy of something to throw open the pores,
and in a day or two felt well enough to venture out. But I had
anticipated my time. For a few days afterwards I felt poorly—and
took the advice of a physician. . . . For my own part I grew
worse, and was at length obliged to take to my bed with a raging
fever. Of course another physician was instantly called—but there
was no checking the fever—we were obliged to let it have its
course—and come to a crisis. It proved to be an inflamatory rheu-
matic fever—and grew very high and dangerous. It was one of
those fevers, however, which are violent and rapid in their course,
and throw the die of life and death in a very short space of time.
My medical aid was of the highest order—and the crisis passed
favorably for me. Medical aid might however have been of no
avail had I not very fortunately been situated in a very kind family,
whose attentions were most zealous and unremitting. Indeed, next
to the hand of Providence, it is to the care of this most excellent
and kind hearted family, that I owe my life. I have been in the
house ever since my arrival in Rome, and have always experienced
from them the greatest kindness. Had I been a son of the family
nothing more could have been done for me, during my sickness,
than what has been done. The extent of my gratitude, it would
be difficult to concieve: and more so perhaps, when I mention as
an instance of the attention I received, that during the seven days
I was languishing upon a sick-bed, every moment some one of the
family was by me, both day and night. I am, however, most indebted to the ever-watchful care of Mrs. Julia, the oldest daugh-

ter, who having the freedom of a married woman,[20] which the other daughters had not, was of course my nurse:—and a better one I think could not be found. It is to her, I may say, I owe my life, for having administered to me a gentle dose of medicine, as I lay almost gasping for breath, from violent oppression of the chest, and having prevented the surgeon from bleeding me a fourth time;—and this too without orders from the doctor, who on coming in and finding me so much better and the dangerous crisis thus past—was loud in his praises.

"It is now four days since I left Rome, and am residing at this village where the air is pure and delightfully cool—even in the heat of August. My strength is slowly returning: but I shall not take a step upon my travels northward, until I find myself entirely restored. This is quite a new sphere of existence to me, who have never before been a valetudinarian." [21]

After spending less than a month at Ariccia, Longfellow felt strong enough to return to Rome. Instead of bidding farewell, he settled down again in the Piazza Navona and remained there through September, October, November, and on into the middle of December. Even a letter from Preble, already established at Göttingen, and eagerly awaiting Longfellow, failed to move him. Although the gossip of his love affair with Julia resulted in some mild banter from his friends in Rome,[22] Longfellow was blissfully unmindful.

Disturbed by well-grounded fears that some peculiar temptation had deflected his son from his intended course, Stephen Longfellow wrote a sharp letter of warning which drew forth a hasty protestation: "I have only to assure you that whatever suspicions my long stay in Italy may have occasioned you, they are wholly without foundation, as you will be satisfied of, in reading my last letters." [23]

Suddenly, out of this blue summer-sky of romance, a thunderbolt fell, shattering the idyll. Stephen Longfellow wrote that Bowdoin had voted to offer Longfellow, not the expected professorship but a mere instructorship, at a greatly reduced salary. Blasted out of his complacency by this announcement, the boy packed his bags and fled northward from Rome in consternation. In Venice

his feeling of guilt was smothered under a resentment which over-
flowed in an angry letter:

"Venice, December 19, 1828

"My dear father,

"On receiving yours of the 15th Septemb. I left Rome immediately. I unsealed your letter with the usual delightful feelings of
hearing from home: but I assure you the perusal of it caused me
great pain. The tidings that the anticipated appointment at Bowdoin had been refused me, were very unexpected and very jarring
to my feelings. And more so, because it was a situation, which
neither yourself, nor I, had solicited, but which had been gratu-
itously offered me upon certain conditions—the which I have
scrupulously fulfilled.

"I assure you—my dear father—I am very indignant at this.
They say I am too young! Were they not aware of this three years
ago? If I am not capable of performing the duties of the office,
they may be very sure of my not accepting it. I know not in what
light they may look upon it, but for my own part I do not in the
least regard it as a favor conferred upon me. It is no sinecure: and
if my services are an equivalent to my salary, there is no favor
done me: if they be not, I do not desire the situation.

"If they think I would accept the place which they offer me,
they are much mistaken in my character. No Sir—I am not yet reduced to this. I am not a dog to eat the crumbs, that fall from
such a table. Excuse my warmth, but I feel rather hurt and indignant. It is a pitiful policy,—that, whilst other institutions send
abroad their professors to qualify themselves for their stations and
pay their expenses—they should offer me an uncertain and precarious office—for it is a probationary one, if I understand them,—
in which the labours of six years would hardly reimburse the sum
I have expended in three. I do not think so meanly of myself as to
accept such an appointment. It was not necessary to come to
Europe for such an office as they offer me: it could have been had
at a much cheaper rate—and at an earlier hour.

"I am led to employ such language as this, because I feel no great
anxiety for my future prospects. Thanks to your goodness, I
have received a good education. I am ashamed to touch upon this

point again: I thought that what I said in my last letter would be the last I should ever have occasion to say in my own justification. But now I feel it a duty I owe to myself to speak even more fully. I know you cannot be dissatisfied with the progress I have made in my studies. I do not speak this from any feeling of self-complacency, nor do I wish that parental partialities should bias your judgment. I speak honestly—not boastingly. With the French and Spanish Languages I am familiarly conversant—so as to speak them correctly—and write them with as much ease and fluency as I do the English. The Portuguese I read without difficulty:—and with regard to my proficiency in the Italian, I have only to say, that when I came to this city, all at the Hotel where I lodge took me for an Italian, until I gave them my passport, and told them I was an American. Do you, then, advise to accept of such a situation as is proffered me. No, I think you cannot. For myself, I have the greatest abhorrence to such a step. I beg of you not to think that this springs from any undue degree of arrogance. I arrogate nothing: but I must assert a freedom of thought and of speech.

"I intend leaving Venice in a few days for Dresden, where I think of remaining until the opening of spring. I do not wish to return without a competent knowledge of German—and all that I can do to acquire it shall be done. The time is short—but I hope to turn it to good advantage.

"In the meantime please to give my kindest remembrances and most cordial thanks to those friends who have taken so much interest in my behalf; particularly to Judge Preble and Prof. Cleaveland. I should be sorry that my refusal of what had been so kindly solicited by them should cause them any pain: but more so should it cause you any." [24]

For several days, Longfellow kept this letter, undecided as to the advisability of speaking his mind so bluntly. Finally he concluded to send it, and added an apologetic, subservient note: "If my language is too violent, excuse me:—it was not written in passion—but I feel too sensitive upon the subject. Such were and still are my sentiments: but they are always subject to your own wishes. I will do as you desire." [25]

In answer the father admitted that he could forgive his son's indignation, but that, after having talked with Dr. Ichabod Nichols and others who had used their influence to secure the position for Longfellow, he had decided that there would be no wisdom in refusing the offered instructorship since the move was obviously a temporary postponement of the appointment to the professorship. With new conviction he emphasized his belief that Longfellow should remain until he had learned the German language—"whether you accept your appointment or not, for it will be of great importance to you as a literary man." [26] He was not willing, however, to extend his son's stay in Europe, and wished him to return before commencement of 1829.

XII

WITH PREBLE IN GERMANY

Finding Göttingen everything I had imagined it, my desire to pass a year here springs up anew. Allow me at least, then, to pass the Summer here; and in the meantime my friends can probably think of some other situation equally good for me as a professorship at Brunswick.[1]

THOROUGHLY confused by the sudden collapse of his expectations, Longfellow could not decide whether to go to Dresden or to Göttingen, for his study of German. From Trieste he wrote to his father that he had been urged by Washington Irving to study in Dresden, that the author of *The Sketch Book* had given him several letters of introduction, and that these letters would be of great value. "This makes me desirous of remaining there in preference to any other place," he wrote. But his indecision expressed itself in postscript:

"I feel so very melancholy and downhearted—that I am more disposed to go as soon as possible to find Mr. Preble at Göttingen —and seek the consolation of friendship in his society. This step would doubtless be the best, on some accounts, that I could take: but it would impede my progress in German." [2]

The idea was a tempting one; so tempting that he found room for an additional postscript before he sealed the letter:

"I can hardly reconcile myself to the idea of relinquishing my studies at a German University. I become daily more and more impressed with the importance of it. My familiarity with the modern languages will unlock to me all those springs of literature, which formerly would have been as sealed books to me. I have often had to lament, that I was obliged to leave the different countries I have visited, at the critical moment when the knowledge I had attained of these several languages rendered a longer residence peculiarly desirable. You see how it was with Washington Irving. He had remained in Spain upwards of three years—and you see what profit he reaps from it. Whoever first makes a

Sketch Book of Spain will necessarily make a very interesting book. I see by the papers that Mr. Irving has collected from old Mss. in the archives of the Libraries of Arch Bishop of Seville a series of Moorish Tales. I have no doubt they will be delightfully interesting. He is a fortunate man: and deserves to be so, for he is a good man." [3]

Continuing with himself this train of thought Longfellow fixed his attention more steadily on the prospect of converting his own European experiences into the popular literary form of "sketches." The refusal of the Bowdoin Professorship spurred him toward some literary enterprise which might enable him to put the College to shame for such a bungling mistake. From the time he had reached Madrid he had been keeping improvised notebooks recording experiences, incidents, and descriptions which might serve as material for sketches. Mrs. Alexander Everett had urged that he write some account of his visit to Spain, and thereafter his letters bore traces of a self-conscious elegance which had not been apparent before. The idea of a European sketch book had been a nebulous possibility which now seemed more substantial.

A curious twist was given to this literary dream by the dismal pains of homesickness which overcame him when he arrived in Dresden on the 13th of January. The accumulated despair and bitterness in his heart enervated all ambition for further study. If he could have had one wish fulfilled he would have chosen to be transported instantaneously from the loneliness and discouragement of his Dresden room to the comforting arms of his family in far-away Portland. Over and over again he had compared the wonders of the Old World with the beauties of America, and invariably had decided that his native land excelled in every way. The scenes which he remembered, and which he now longed to see, were far more quaint and fascinating than European scenes. As he recalled the Down East which he knew so well, his longing touched each remembrance with golden outlines until he wondered that he had been tempted to write sketches of less charming people and places.

A sketch book of New England was exactly the sort of work he could undertake with pleasure. In the mood of those first few

days in Dresden he continued to recall and jot down a series of
subjects for sketches about his homeland.[4] On the second day
after he reached Dresden he was so far advanced with his plans
that he was ready to offer his prospective volume to a publisher.
Carey & Lea of Philadelphia had solicited poems from him for
The Atlantic Souvenir, and had been so hospitable to him that
he felt they should have his first book. He wrote:

"DRESDEN 15 Jany 1829

"Messrs. Carey & Lea:
   "Dear Sirs,

     "Permit me to renew an acquaintance, which has been
long interrupted by time and absence, with the usual congratulations of the season, and the friendly good wishes, that always sig-
nalise the advent of a New Year. I recur with pleasure to the circumstances of my first acquaintance with you, and often recall
the kindnesses I received at your hands, during the few days I
passed in Philadelphia.

     "My object in visiting Europe has been a literary one. Since
my residence on the continent the difference between the Old
World and the New has struck me very forcibly; and I have
thought that a series of papers upon the scenes and customs of my
Native Land might not be an unacceptable offering to the literary
world. Accordingly I have commenced a Sketch Book of New
England, in the stile of Irving's Sketch Book of Old England and
from the variety of topics which naturally present themselves to
the mind of an American, when in a foreign land, he recalls the
blessings and endearments of home. I hope to give sufficient interest to the work to secure its success. Of course every thing will
depend upon the stile of the work, and the manner in which its
subjects are treated. Upon my own stile it does not become me
to speak, and with regard to the subjects of my papers, they are
such as recollection furnishes me with. Thus far, I have written
but two Nos.—the contents I here subjoin. Each no. I suppose if
printed in a fair type, and an ornamental manner, will make, with
the usual 'remplissage' of index—title pages &c. about a hundred
pages 8°. Perhaps I over-rate: you can judge when you see the
manuscript.

"No. 1

" 'The Author'—his account of himself.—
" 'Home Feelings'—recollections of my Native Land.
" 'Rural Scenery.'—peculiarities of New England.
" 'The Bald Eagle Tavern'—humorous description of the preparations made by the inhabitants of an inland New England village for the reception of General Lafayette, when on his tour in America.
" 'The Indian Summer' a Tale.

———

"No. 2

" 'Scenes of Childhood.'—return to them after long absence.
" 'The Village Graveyard'—
" 'Blind Tom'—a Tale
" 'Harvest Home in New England.'
" 'Dixy Bull, the Pirate'—a Tale.

"Thus you have an inventory of my literary wares: a kind of 'Programme du Spectacle.'—Instead thereof I would send you the Ms. did I know of any mode of conveyance. You shall have it as soon as possible: with the title, mottos, &c &c all in order.

"With regard to the terms of publication, I leave that to you: only I should wish to retain the copyright in my own hands—as the publication is an experiment. With regard to the rest, I will enter into what arrangements you may propose: Allowing you whatever share of the profits you may deem just, on condition that you share with me the risk of failure:—

"The Nos. are not to appear at any fixed periods—but as the work may accumulate on my hands. Be kind enough to write me upon the subject, directing to the care of Messrs. Welles & Co. 24 Rue Taitbout, à Paris:—

"With sentiments of esteem & respect, I am
"Your Obt Servt—
"HENRY W. LONGFELLOW"

"P.S. In thus making known to you my secret, Gentlemen, I have confidence in you, that you will not betray me: for in case of failure, it might injure my after-prospects as a literary man, were my name known. For the same reason I publish in nos. since in putting out a pamphlet, one has not much at stake—and at all events the loss cannot be great in any point of view—. Further— the two nos. I have written, I have written with the utmost care, and attention to the stile. I intend to do the same with the others; and, in so doing, I assure you I do not anticipate a failure. Only let me again pray you not to let my name be known. I have a good many materials on hand and in part worked up for future nos. I wish always to keep one no. in advance." [5]

Having relieved himself of such a weighty secret, Longfellow was able to turn with a modicum of interest to the business of learning German grammar. His occasional peeks into German books while in Italy had been of no value to him, and therefore it seemed sensible to facilitate progress by studying with a tutor. Even this arrangement proved unsatisfactory because of an un- happy choice. There were still the letters from Washington Irving, which opened many doors and provided evenings of diversion and entertainment. Unfortunately the dinners, con- certs, operas, tableaux somehow added to the stranger's loneliness, for he felt constantly that he was an outsider courteously per- mitted to stand at the edge of the circle and look on. Although other letters offered him the use of excellent libraries, he could derive no meaning from German texts. Fortunately he found several ancient volumes concerning Spanish and French litera- ture, one of which contained a good account of the troubadours and their poetry. Discovering his interest in Spanish literature, Irving's friend Karl August Böttiger lent him several books from which the student made so many copious extracts in his journals that he was able to lay the foundation for a study of the history of the languages of southern Europe. [6]

After nearly a month of residence in Dresden, Longfellow had built himself a heavy burden of unhappiness. In his journal he wrote: "Feel decidedly *blue*—blue—deep blue—as blue as Mr. Warren's map of Jerusalem." And his entry for the following day: "The counterpart of yesterday in weather and feeling." [7] The tutor was partly to blame for this melancholy, for he was too queer a creature to be tolerated as a daily companion. [8]

At the end of one month, Longfellow had convinced himself that Dresden was a very unsatisfactory place to study the German language. He had been mistaken—in fact he had been mildly mistaken in his vague belief that he *wanted* to study the German language; but it would be fun to surprise his old friend Preble in Göttingen. Near the middle of February he paid his last calls to those who had been politely hospitable to him, and set out for the university town of Göttingen.

The morning after his arrival he wandered through the streets enquiring for "Jew Alley," where Preble had taken rooms. This was to be a great surprise. Even the discovery that Herr Preble was not at home did not discourage Longfellow; he would step in and wait. And such rooms! There was a college atmosphere about the wall decorations which delighted him in every detail—from the two crossed broadswords and the four-stringed guitar to the long-stemmed porcelain pipe and accompanying tobacco pouch.[9] This promised infinitely more pleasure than he had known in Dresden. When the unsuspecting Ned finally sauntered into the room, Longfellow knew how wise he had been to leave Dresden. Two Portland boys, far from all their other friends, had suddenly found each other in the university town of Göttingen, and their delight was unbounded.

There were subjects of conversation that would last them indefinitely: news from home, doings in Portland, the activities of friends and former classmates at Bowdoin. Alfred Mason, the fellow-Peucinian whom Longfellow had once visited in Portsmouth, had recently died while studying law in New York. Pitt Fessenden had at last culminated his courtship of Elizabeth Longfellow with proposals of marriage, and almost everyone was pleased with the match. John Neal, who boasted that he had stimulated considerable intellectual progress in his home state by his preface to *Niagara*, had opened a law office in Portland and was publishing a literary magazine called the *Yankee*. Ned had brought three copies with him—and two precious Portland newspapers!

The entire membership of Temple Bar had sent greetings from Congress Street. They were all as indignant over the ruling of Bowdoin College as Longfellow could possibly wish them to be.

Ned and Henry had letters from them to be read aloud. One in particular, from the clever pen of young Stephen, had a story connected with it. From Rome, Longfellow had written to his brother:

"You at home must not keep me long in want of letters from you. Every little circumstance which takes place in Portland is interesting to me: from the Brazen Nose of Temple Bar (which I understand has been again snoring its inspiration among the Boeotians of Fish Street) down to David Ross going round Trull's corner on a windy day. By the way, I wish you of Temple Bar would keep me a kind of journal or day-book recording interesting facts, and send it to me once a month. Amongst so many of you it would cost you nothing to make a few loose notes and illustrations . . .

"I most heartily wish that one of you Templars would come out and spend with me the rest of my sojourn in Europe. You must make Ned Preble—'Chargé d'affaires et Envoyé Extraordinaire' to my Court at Göttingen." [10]

In reply Stephen had written an elaborate letter of gossip, illustrated with an amusing sketch of the law office, and its several young students busy in curious ways. This creation of news and nonsense was a challenge which Ned, with his fondness for drawing, and Henry, with his love of writing, eagerly accepted. On their first Saturday night together—which happened to fall on Longfellow's twenty-second birthday—they concocted a manuscript news-sheet for their friends of Temple Bar, and entitled it the *Old Dominion Zeitung,* to be issued, according to the masthead, "every Saturday evening at Göttingen—Jew Alley—462."

The first number was devoted very largely to expressions of disgust concerning the disturbing news from Bowdoin. Although President Allen was not directly implicated, he made a very satisfactory target for ridicule. As a background for the title of the paper one of the editors drew a sketch of the College with a great pot of jam standing out in the middle of the campus, protected from the dissolving rains by a battered umbrella. Lest any Portland reader fail to recognize this idealized portrait of the offensive "Gul," the sketch was supported with a quotation from Thomson: "a little, round, fat, oily man of God." [11] Six numbers were issued. In the fourth number was a news item:

"We have been creditably informed, that a professorship being offered to a young man by the government of Bow. Coll. on condition of his passing two years in Europe *at his own* expense—at the expiration of that time the situation of *Tutor* was offered him, with little more than half a professor's salary! *We are happy to add*—that such a proposition has been treated with all the contempt it deserved."

The poet's corner of this issue carried further correlated scorn:

> Said the Old Professor to the young professor
> Thou shalt be Tutor now!
> Said the young professor to the old professor—
> I can teach as well as thou!
>
> Said the old Trustee to the young professor
> We'll make a cheap bargain with *you.*
> Said the young professor to the Old Trustee
> No—I'll be —— if you do. [12]

Having discussed the entire subject of the appointment at great length with Preble, Longfellow grew stronger in his determination to refuse any kind of position offered by Bowdoin. Undoubtedly, each boy reminded the other of many unpleasant incidents which had antagonized them as undergraduates. On the very day when the first number of the *Old Dominion Zeitung* was made, Longfellow wrote to his father:

"For my own part, I shall remain here this vacation: and should like to, the next term, unless circumstances should render my return this summer absolutely necessary. With regard to Bowdoin College, the more I think of it, the more I am dissatisfied. So much so, indeed, that I am averse to going there at all, if any other situation can be procured me. I dislike the manner in which things are conducted there. Their illiberality in point of religion—and their narrow-minded views upon many other points, need no comment. Had I the means of a bare subsistence, I would *now* refuse a Professorship there. I say *now:* I mean since they have offered me a lower office. I am inclined to think that the opposition came

PAGE OF THE *Old Dominion Zeitung*
From the original manuscript in the Craigie House.

from the younger professors. I suppose they did not like the idea of seeing so young a man step at once into the chair of prof. without serving the usual apprenticeship. I have but one question to ask—Do the Professors of Bowdoin College speak the language they teach? No—not one of them. I have another plan to suggest to your consideration which to me holds out better inducement than the first.

"Finding Göttingen everything I had imagined it, my desire to pass a year here springs up anew. Allow me at least, then, to pass the Summer here; and in the meantime my friends can probably think of some other situation equally good for me as a professorship at Brunswick. If they cannot, upon my return I might be permitted to deliver a course of lectures on modern literature at the Portland Atheneum, and in the mean time, I could look out for myself. As I have already told you, upon this point I feel not the slightest anxiety or mistrust. But I will not anticipate—at present let us speak of the present. I find living at Göttingen very cheap. As I have just arrived I cannot give you any just idea of what my expenses will be monthly: but as soon as I have been here a little longer I will send you a continuation of what my last letter contained. The Library here is the largest in Germany and is full of choise rare works and the advantages for a student of my particular pursuits are certainly not overrated in the universal fame of the University of Göttingen.

"Whilst at Dresden I felt no other desire than that of returning home once more to the bosom of the family. I had got discouraged and a little downhearted. But meeting with an old and good friend, has given new elasticity to my spirits:—they have again taken their wonted tone, and I am contented and happy. In this disposition, I am a little unwilling to give up what is now in my reach: and as I shall never again be in Europe, I should think it were better to lengthen a little my absence from home at present, than by not so doing to have subject for future regret. I brought letters to several of the Professors here from Bancroft and Ticknor: and have been well received. Göttingen is a small city—and there are no amusements here whatever: so there is no alternative but study. With regard to duelling, for which all the German Universities are more or less notorious, you will find a description of them in the North American for July 1828—page 87. They are considered by the students as sport: and it is not uncommon to hear of six being fought in one afternoon and on the same spot. There is however no possibility either of Preble or myself being engaged in these affairs, as we do not know the broad-sword exercise, and are of course *hors de combat*. There are about 14 or 15 hundred students here: as in all Universities some *scholars*—and others high wild fellows. He who wishes to be distinguished among the latter, must fight his way into distinction: but he who wishes to pursue his studies quietly, is no more molested here than at one of our colleges.

"I find Preble improved every way. He is everything I could wish a friend to be. His associates are entirely from the studious class:—and if his mother could see every action of his during the twenty four hours of the day, she could not wish one of them changed. This is saying a great deal, but it is so.

"Please write me immediately upon the subject of this, and tell me if you think my suggestions practicable. In the mean time, I have other literary projects in view, which shall be duly set in order and made known to you, when the time arrives in which I can put them into execution. Pray set your mind perfectly at rest upon all points, that may have occasioned you any uneasiness . . .

"What Preble tells me of the improvements going on in Portland delights me. It might be made one of the most beautiful cities in the world. I have never seen a finer situation in all the countries I have visited. Besides, he tells me the 'march and mind' goes forward with great strides. I see Mr. Neal attributes it to his 'preface to Niagara.' Mr. de Beaufort—who by the way refused the situation of Instructor at Bow: Coll:—has probably done something in this way.

                              "Most Affectionately your son" [13]

The request for a fourth year of study in Europe was prompted probably by a sudden fear that he had misused too much of his time there. Had he acquired such a knowledge of the languages that he was prepared to teach courses as Professor Ticknor was teaching them at Harvard? Or had he merely gathered nosegays from European literature which could be pinned into sketches of his travels? A quick glance at his three years of residence in the Old World showed him how much he had fed romantic long-ings at the expense of scholarly duties. When he had arrived in Europe, ignorant of even the fundamentals of modern languages, he had fumbled his way to a superficial understanding of French and had prided himself that all requirements were satisfied when he had learned to speak and write that language. He had repeated the process in Spain. But he had not explored the treasures of literature which these keys were intended to unlock for him. If he had returned according to the original plan, at the end of two years, his training would have been pathetically incomplete.[14] And only his father's decision concerning a year of extra study in Germany had avoided this awkward revelation. He had even squandered the extra year in romantic Italy. In Göttingen at last, and jolted to his senses by news from home, he feared to assume responsibility for teaching in three or four months. Further-more, he was not at all sure that he wanted to teach at Bowdoin.

Longfellow did not clearly perceive the alternatives. Vaguely he looked down two paths which stretched into his future: he could reject the Bowdoin offer and hope to return to the literary career he had first sought, or he could yield to the practical de-cision of his father that he subdue his pride and accept whatever Bowdoin offered. There were arguments in his own mind for each path of action. The tempting solution of treading Europe as a road to literary pursuit rather than to linguistic knowledge had been in his mind, certainly, since his stay in Spain, and possibly since the day he had escaped the law by the teaching compromise. The same thought had been partially responsible for the mention to his father of "other literary projects in view" when he asked for a fourth year of study. He was quite sure that he could make such a desirable plan work.

But if he should take the other course, if he should play safe and accept the Bowdoin offer (as he feared his father would expect him to do) he must be ready for teaching. To begin at Bowdoin after the next commencement meant intensive study in more than speaking and writing French and Spanish; it meant the need for erecting some superstructure of literary knowledge on his slight language foundation. Bluntly, he must get to work; he must make up for lost time.

He would have preferred the first alternative, but he was not in a position to take any action. His friends in Brunswick and Portland had secured the Bowdoin offer for him, and he could not break away from obligations already accepted. Writing to his mother from Göttingen, he expressed a petulant impatience with the trap which he had set for himself and into which he had so blithely wandered:

"It is today three years since I left America. In running my eye over this lapse of time, it seems to me more like an interlude in the drama of life, than a part of the play. My own part of this world's comedy is so connected with the parts my friends at home have to act on the same stage, that without their presence I am not sure of my own identity:—and hence I look upon this visit to Europe as a song sung between the acts: and I am sorry that some of the variations lately introduced have not gained me much applause." [15]

In this half-concealed fashion, Longfellow permitted himself to admit a trace of guilty conscience for some of the decisions which he had made, contrary to the suggestions and commands of his parents. Finally, he had reached a point where choice was no longer his. If his father should fail to grant him a further extension of time and money, he must go home. And if he were given the position he had expected, he must devote himself largely to the languages he would teach (French and Spanish), even though his father had sent him to Germany for the express purpose of learning German.

Impelled by this conclusion, Longfellow settled down to an intensive schedule of studies. For a short time he did not concern himself with walking trips about the picturesque and ancient town of Göttingen or with visits to German villages in the environs. During the spring vacation, which began not long after his arrival there, his friend Preble set out on a journey of several days. Longfellow remained. "I am the only American here," he wrote to his ailing sister Elizabeth. "It is now vacation—and every body but myself is travelling. For my own part I remain—entrenched behind a rampart of books—and with intellectual provisions enough to hold out a siege quite through Vacation." [16]   He carefully avoided any mention of his spending so little time on German, although he did write to his father that he was studying it "under the guidance of an able professor." He added:

"For the rest—my fervent wish is—and long has been, to return home. I would not remain a moment, were it not for the persuation of its necessity:—but the German language is beyond measure difficult—not to read—no—that is not so hard:—but to write it— and one must write, and write correctly too, in order to teach. I can only promise you to do my best—I can most assuredly lay a good foundation, and much more I cannot expect to do." [17]

Unfortunately, no lectures were offered, during the spring term, on subjects of immediate value to Longfellow. Occasionally he and Preble attended the courses of Professor Wendt on Natural Law and Professor Heeren on Ancient and Modern History. It little mattered what the learned men chose to discuss, for the newly arrived American could not understand much German.

While he continued in perfunctory fashion his study of German grammar he spent most of his time, as he had done in Dresden, on Spanish language and literature. Into his notebooks he copied liberal passages from works on the Spanish literary history under such diverse headings as, "La Lengua Castellana," "Obras periódicas Españolas," and "Poetas Españoles del siglo xvi," and continued his work so assiduously that he assembled over one hundred pages of notes for later use. [18]

His interests in Göttingen were divided between imperative study and dilettante rummaging for pretty verses, quaint passages, or entertaining narratives which might be salvaged from some forgotten volume for use in sketches of the lands and literatures of Europe. A special notebook was reserved for gathering such material. Like Irving, Longfellow lacked the inner resource for purely imaginative writing, but was learning to adorn old stories with an elegant embroidery of words. His plan took shape so rapidly in Göttingen that he included an account of it in the letter intended to prove that he was studying assiduously:

"I am also writing a book—a kind of Sketch Book of scenes in France, Spain, and Italy—one volume of which I hope to get finished this summer. This is what I spoke of [in my] last letter; I

hope by it to prove that I *have not* wasted my time: though I have
no longer a very high opinion of my prudence or my own talents.
—The farther I advance, the more I see to be done—and the less
time to do it in. The more, too, am I persuaded of the charlatanism
of literary men." [19]

Loneliness was again the cause of dejection. While Preble had
been away during vacation, Longfellow had stayed at his books
as long as he could. Then, impatient for more excitement than
he found in study, he had broken his resolves and had made a
hasty trip across Germany and Holland to England. The journey was very unsatisfactory to one who preferred to loiter. "If I
hurry you along with too much speed," he wrote to his mother in
describing his stay in London, "bear in mind that I was also hurried along through scenes in which I fain would have lingered." [20]
Furthermore, this respite from study did not shake off loneliness.
On his way back to Göttingen he was overwhelmed with what he
described as a "violent attack of the Blue Devils," and tried to
ward them off with poetry. Sensations of melancholy and of
poetry were so closely associated in his mind that he hoped his
unpleasant feelings might fashion themselves into felicitous
verses. The results were not much:

> I am not sick—nor sad! but there are times
> When thoughts of other days, and distant friends
> Pass o'er me like a funeral knell.

———

> Spring to her youthful bosom presses
> The icy temples of the imprisoned year,
> And cheers his wintry dungeon with her voice,
> Like the fair Roman girl—that History boasts of—
> Who on her fruitful bosom warmed and suckled
> The second childhood of her poor old father. [21]

Obviously, such meagre success in literary endeavor was
enough to dim aspiration. He had tried to write poetry only once
before, during his stay in Europe, and had met with no better
satisfaction. Spanish ballads and lyrics were pleasant exercises
for translation and versification, but even these caused him much

effort. Not long after his arrival in Göttingen, he had written to his sister on this subject:

"After spending an idle hour in a vain attempt to put into English verse a lovely little Portuguese song, which I got from the library today, I have thrown the book aside for some other and perhaps more fortunate moment, and will devote the remnant of daylight which remains, to kindly recollections of an absent sister. My failure in the translation, I attribute solely to a cold in the head, which does not allow the requisite circulation in the *bump:* —and to show you how very badly I have succeeded, I will here transcribe you one verse of the song just as it lies before me on my paper . . . premising that the subject is the Poet's farewell to his Lyre:

> "How oft—alas! when lonely,
>   Awakening from my slumbers,
>   Thou lyre of gentle numbers,
> My hand hath tun'd thy strings!
> Thou, said I, and thou only,
>   Canst soothe my soul!—I borrow
> From thee my joy in sorrow,
> From thee — — — ings!!!

You must get Sammy to fill up the hiatus. Now, after reading this, I think you can easily imagine me sitting alone in my chamber, at the close of a chill melancholy day in March—with a leaden sky over-head, and twilight stealing in at the window. It is a disheartening, gloomy day—'and then its hue, Who ever saw so fine a *blue?*'—One of those days, which makes us just sad enough to translate a sad ballad—and just poor enough in spirit to make a poor translation. . . .

"My poetic career is finished—Since I left America, I have hardly put two lines together. I may indeed say, that my muse has been sent to the House of Correction—and her last offspring were laid at the door of one of those Foundling Hospitals for poor poetry—a New Year's 'Souvenir.' So you see the Dark Ages have come upon me;—and no soft poetic ray has irradiated my heart— since the Goths and Vandals swept over the Rubicon of the 'front entry' and turned the Sanctum Sanctorum of the 'Little Room' into a China Closet." [22]

The loneliness disappeared as soon as Preble returned. The two good friends were constantly together, struggling to make some sense out of the lectures, sharing the pleasant comfort of the same room, and studying beneath the brow of one lampshade. Yet Longfellow had lost the zest of his earlier desire to stay much longer in Europe. As June came he watched for letters from home which would answer his now regretted request for permission to remain abroad during a fourth year. His longing to see those he loved was increased by the disturbing news that his sister Elizabeth was afflicted with serious illness. And then, if he decided to accept the Bowdoin offer, he must make some answer to them soon. Cautiously he had softened his previous outbursts on that score, and had written to his father, "If I can have the Professorship at Bow. Coll.—I should like it—but I must have it on fair grounds:—with the same privileges as the other professors. No state of probation—and no calling me a boy—and retrenching my salary. That was a very unlucky attempt at Economy." [23]

Before the middle of June a letter from Stephen Longfellow settled the question of longer absence. The student's father was willing to let the boy stay through the summer, but a heavy heart urged him home. His sister Elizabeth had not improved, and there was no expectation that she would ever get better. With some haste and with few regrets he made arrangements for departure. After leaving Göttingen he spent a few days in Paris, crossed to England and sailed from Liverpool on the ship *Manchester*. In Paris he had received from his father a long and pitiful account of Elizabeth's death which added a heavy burden of sorrow to his returning. His years of absence had been curiously patched with joys, trials, and disappointments. So buoyantly enthusiastic had been his setting out; so bitterly sad was his return. On the 11th of August, 1829, he reached New York.

XIII

PROFESSOR AT BOWDOIN

*For my own part, buried in the dust and cobwebs of this country
college, moth and rust begin to consume me. I am with them, but
not of them, may I truly say of those around me.*[1]

"I AM now in Boston," Longfellow wrote, six days after he had
landed. "All friends here are well:—They insist upon it that I am
Professor at Bowdoin."[2] But the question was by no means
settled in his own mind, and he was anxious to consult with his
father and friends as soon as he reached Portland. Although Dr.
Nichols and Judge Preble considered it advisable to accept the
offer of the reduced salary and the instructorship, Longfellow
would not submit to such humiliation. There was no need for
histrionics, his father felt certain. The Bowdoin authorities
would undoubtedly make the necessary concessions if the boy
stood firm in his refusal. Stephen Longfellow understood the
ways of the Bowdoin trustees and overseers. With parental consent Longfellow wrote President Allen a dignified statement
which managed to veil without complete concealment the fierce
indignation which had rankled in the young candidate ever since
that unpleasant announcement had reached Rome:

"PORTLAND August 27, 1829.
"Dear Sir,
"Your letter to my father dated Sept. 26, 1828, and enclosing a
copy of the vote of the Trustees and Overseers of Bowdoin College, by which they have elected me Instructer of the Modern
Languages in that institution, has been duly handed me.
"I am sorry, that under existing circumstances, I cannot accept
the appointment. The Professorship of Modern Languages, with
a salary equal to that of the other Professors, would certainly not
have been refused. But having at great expense, devoted four
years to the acquisition of the French, Spanish, Italian, and Ger-

147

man languages, I cannot accept a subordinate station with a salary
so disproportionate to the duties required.

"I have the honor to be, Sir,

"Very respectfully
"Your Ob^t Ser^t
"HENRY W. LONGFELLOW." [3]

Guided by ingrained Yankee wisdom, the board of trustees
adopted a compromise calculated to satisfy the overseers as well
as Henry Longfellow. They voted to offer the candidate the title
of Professor, although they requested, tactfully, that he serve an
apprenticeship before formal induction into office. Furthermore,
they agreed upon a compromise salary of $800, which was neither
that of a professor nor that of an instructor. But by appointing
him to serve as college librarian at an additional salary of $100, the
trustees were able to approximate the regular full professor's
salary of $1,000. In weighing this neatly balanced agreement, the
board casually rested a hand on the scales in order to give the
College a bargain: a harmless clause was added, providing that
the President might, if he wished, ask the new teacher of modern
languages to give instruction to the lower classmen as well as to
the upper classmen.

Details were unimportant to Longfellow. He had won the
desired victory, for he received an announcement that he had
been appointed "Professor of Modern Languages" at Bowdoin.[4]

These teaching years at Bowdoin were to prove heavy traveling—and the coveted professorship a Pyrrhic victory. During this
important period of his development, Longfellow revealed a
primary and very natural objective: eminence—an insistent desire
to get ahead. This prodding ambition showed in all he undertook.
At first he plunged bravely into his teaching, determined to make
a success of it. Soon he saw the chance to make a name for himself by editing much-needed textbooks. Conscious of the growing
market for any kind of information on foreign subjects, he
quickly took advantage of invitations to write prose essays for
magazines.

Before long, as we shall see, he grew impatient with all these
tedious stepping-stones to fame. He began to dream of ways to

escape from the backwoods of Maine—and his dreams took fantastic, futile shapes. We expect to find him filling these years of his life, from the age of twenty-two to twenty-eight, with a spontaneous flood of original writing. But he could find little impulse for original work while classroom hours exhausted his energy. His greatest satisfaction came from finishing and publishing his sketches of travel—and even these failed to keep his interest to the end of the story. His impetuous efforts to get away from Brunswick subsequently increased until he seemed at times almost frantic. Yet he was jubilant at the beginning, when first he returned to Brunswick as a fledgling professor.

The town had changed little since he and his classmates had left it, four years earlier. The elms along Maine and Federal streets reached a little farther out above the thoroughfares; the mall which had been fashioned with great diligence, by students and townspeople, from the swampy region in the middle of Twelve Rod Road, had lost its bare appearance so thoroughly that it added a new touch of green refinement to the square-sided mansions which faced it. Although a few more houses had been built nearer the college, the yard within the white rail fence bore few marks of change. One new brick building, Commons Hall, afforded much-needed advantages by giving all the students a convenient dining room—even though many of them were still obliged to find rooms outside the dormitories.

Several private families kept their spare rooms to rent to the unmarried instructors and professors. But Longfellow found that he was not to be a professor, in this respect. He was assigned to a dormitory room in the south end of Maine Hall, for his first year, and was required to accept the unpleasant duties of a proctor. Thus he was harnessed into the position of an instructor without any ado. His window, facing on the main yard, did not afford him the familiar view of dark pines. Instead, he looked out through the scrawny branches of a balm of Gilead tree toward the unpainted wooden chapel, beyond which was the President's barn and the dusty highroad to Portland—not an inspiring vista. But he was resolved to prove himself capable, no matter how arduous his duties might be.

At first he taught only junior and senior classes in elementary

French and Spanish. Beginning his day at six, he attended morning prayers in the conveniently located chapel, conducted his morning recitations, climbed the chapel stairs to the second floor to open the library for an hour, conducted afternoon recitations, walked with his friends before supper, and struggled through great piles of classroom papers each evening.[5]

In less than a month he began to find fault with this once coveted position. To Alexander Slidell, with whom he had shared so many sparkling hours in Spain, he revealed his first delusion in a letter written not long after the beginning of the fall term:

"BOWDOIN COLLEGE, Oct. 15, 1829

"Dear Slidell,

"I trust to your friendship to pardon my long silence, after having promised you, as I held your hand at parting, to write you immediately. You will find my apology in what I am now about to say of myself. Having concluded to accept my appointment as Prof. at this college, I was some time busy in making the necessary arrangements for taking up my abode here: which arrangements, together with visiting of friends in town and country—completely consumed the vacation: and since the commencement of the term I have been very much occupied—as the business of instruction is new to me, and I have also the charge of the Library, which occupies one hour every day. You know very well how the little everyday occurrances of life are linked into each other, so as to form one long continued chain; and though each one of them separately is insignificant, yet all together make up no small portion of our existence. Besides after having corrected upwards of forty exercises from Levisac's grammar—which I have to do daily—I hate the sight of pen, ink and paper.

"I am also very busy in translating an elementary grammar from the French—intended for my own use as instructer here—and for the use of Schools. It is already in a state of forwardness—and I shall put it to press without delay. I will send you a copy as soon as it is out.

"Your book on Spain is very much admired here. It makes me, however, very melancholy when I read it, for open where I will, I find something unknown to me before. I was as long in Spain as

you were—enjoyed the same advantages whilst there—and now
having before my eye a record of what you did, and the information you collected there, I feel rather sad, that I should have
effected so little, where you have effected so much: for instead of
a treasure of useful and valuable information, such as you have
brought away from Spain, I have only dreamy sensations, and
vague recollections of a sunny land. I quarrel with myself every
day for not having seen more Bull fights—and sometimes fret
myself into a fever for not having been hard hearted enough to
see the tragedies of the Plaza de Cehada. Nothing, which I
omitted seeing, but now rises up in judgment against me: and I
shall ere long be driven back to Spain in despair.

"How unstable and precarious an acquisition is that of the languages! I refer to the facility of speaking them. My foothold is
sliping from under me daily: and it is a subject on which I feel
pretty sensitive *now:* having placed myself in a situation peculiarly liable to animadversion. The only consolation I have is
that at some future day I shall be forced to go back to Europe
again for nobody in this part of the world pretends to speak anything but English—and some might dispute them even that prerogative.

"I am little in the 'penseroso' tonight, so farewel. I must turn
from the indulgence of friendly recollections to wallowing in the
mire of Levisac—or rather I should say to the contemplation of
such sublime truths as 'L'âme de l'homme, sans culture, est comme
un diamant brut!'—and so on to the end of the chapter.

"Write soon—and let me know what you are doing and what
you mean to do this winter—and whether I may indulge the hope
of seeing you at the North.
                    "Very affectionately your friend
                              "HENRY W. LONGFELLOW." [6]

In spite of these brief periods of restlessness, he dug deep into
the labors of school work. The French grammar which he had
chosen to adapt to his classroom needs was that of C. F. Lhomond,
formerly a professor in the University of Paris. In editing
suitable translations of grammars, Longfellow was by no means
a pioneer in America, nor was he the first to discover the merits

of Lhomond's grammar for use in American schools, since reprints of the *Eléments de la grammaire française* had been published in New York in 1814 and in Boston in 1826. Professor Ticknor's language instructors at Harvard had also published their own textbooks in French, Spanish, and German before Longfellow began to teach.[7] Even his colleagues in Brunswick had already supplied the local printer with considerable work of a similar nature.[8]

But Longfellow found difficulty in convincing his father that the enterprise warranted an investment of over one hundred dollars to cover the cost of publication. The young professor argued that there were excellent reasons for bringing out such a text; that the study of French was spreading rapidly through the secondary schools of the country; that, although there were several French grammars in print, they were so large that they needed the abridgment which Monsieur Lhomond had so carefully made. Furthermore, he was able to buttress his remarks by pointing out that Hon. Albert Gallatin, former minister to both France and England, and a noted linguist, had recently recommended Lhomond's grammar as the best in use.[9]

After winning his father's reluctant financial support, Longfellow took his neatly stitched copy to the small two-story printing establishment and bookstore of Joseph Griffin to the north of the mall on Maine Street.[10] Samuel Colman, a Portland bookseller, agreed to publish the work. But Longfellow preferred to have the book bound by a small firm in Brunswick. He enjoyed keeping an eye on the progress of this his first book. Griffin's typesetters seemed inexcusably careless and were forever ignoring his proof-sheet corrections or making new errors in place of the old. In his eagerness to share every detail of the exciting work, he consulted with Griffin about a suitable quality and weight of paper. To his sister Mary he wrote letters about the cotton cloth to be used for the binding. Having decided that purple would give a dignified touch, he arranged for her to buy the cloth for him in a Portland dry-goods store.

Everyone moved so slowly! "I am waiting for the purple cloth to bind the Grammars in," he wrote to his sister. "Pray get it for me soon. It must be two thirds of a yard wide—otherwise it will cut very much to waste." [11] The many details of printing and correction delayed the completion of the work beyond his expectation. Also, college duties interfered in an unexpected manner, for the President exercised his prerogative by adding to Longfellow's schedule several new classes. When the winter vacation began, conflicting duties led him to write a long letter to his father to explain his absence from Portland:

"Our examinations are at length over, and the college closed. I now occupy Dr. Welles's room at Mrs. Barnes' near Prof. Cleaveland's—where I intend to pass a greater part of the vacation. The reasons which induce me to do this, instead of passing the winter with you, as my intention was when I last saw you, are very simple ones, but such as I did not anticipate three weeks since.

"The Executive government have thought it advisable to introduce some considerable changes into the proposed plans of studies for the year, upon which plan we have acted thus far. The new arrangement puts a hard-laboring oar into my hands, and will give me four recitations per day, besides the hour occupied in the Library.

"The Junior Class will as usual recite French every afternoon. The Seniors will have three recitations a week in French—and three in Spanish—at noon. The Sophomore class will recite French every morning. This you perceive, gives me three recitations per diem through the week, Saturday afternoons excepted. Besides this, I am to have a private lesson in German: and the prospect before me seems thick-sown with occupations, promising me little leisure for my private studies, which on account of my busy life the last term, already begin to assume a retrograde march. Before closing this catalogue, I must add, that I have also an Inaugural Address to write for next term, and a Poem before the Phi Beta at Commencement.

"What detains me in Brunswick at the present moment is my Grammar, which is not yet from under the press. The notes and additions have rendered it larger than I anticipated, and the trouble of correcting Griffin's proofs, is not to be expressed in words. This, however, does not discourage me from engaging farther in the same occupation. Among the French books in the

Library, I have just found a few volumes, which have pleased me
so much and are so much what is wanted for a text-book, that I
have concluded to make a selection from them, for the use of my
pupils, and such other scholars as may want. The Book is intended for those who are already a little advanced in the language,
and who wish for a manual of polite conversation on familiar
topics. The work from which I make the selection is a collection
of Dramatic Proverbs, or small plays, such as are performed in
Paris by ladies and gentlemen in private society. The book is so
exactly what we stand in need of, that I am only surprised that
something of the kind has not appeared before. I need not tell
you, how delighted I am with the idea of having found the
treasure. The more I see of the life of an instructer the more I
wonder at the course generally pursued by teachers. They seem
to forget, that the youthful mind is to be *interested* in order to be
instructed: or at least they overlook the means, by which they
may best lead on the mental faculties, at an age when amusement
is a more powerful incitement than improvement. In proof of
this, look at the text-books generally in use. What are they?
Extracts from the best and most polished writers of the nation;
food for maturer minds: but a fruit that hangs without the reach
of children, and those that ignorance of a foreign language puts
on the same footing with children. But the little collection of
dramas which I now propose to publish, unites all the simplicity
and ease of conversation, with the interest of a short comedy,
whose point turns upon some humorous situation in common life,
and whose plot illustrates some familiar proverb, which stands at
its head by way of motto.

"I think you cannot but approve my plan, which can better be
discussed face to face than in a letter. For my own part, I am so
much engrossed with the idea, that for the present I should be ill
at ease anywhere but just where I am. I shall, however, pay you
a visit as soon as I get my grammar finished, if the roads should
then be in a good state for travelling.

"I wrote Dr. Nichols a few days since, and sent him the outline of a Prospectus for the new Female High School, which I
drew up at his request. I hope they do not mean to let the subject

die. If you should see Mr. Furbish, pray assure him from me, that I have the matter as much at heart as ever." [12]

Before the *Proverbes dramatiques* (containing seven sketches) and the *Elements of French Grammar* had passed through the press, Longfellow was at work on an intermediate text of *French Exercises*, for his beginners. For his Spanish students he undertook to edit a reader which proved to be a curious literary boomerang. The two Spanish stories selected were "El Serrano de las Alpujarras" and "El Cuadro Misterioso," written by George Washington Montgomery, an American in Spain, in close imitation of Washington Irving's "Rip Van Winkle" and "The Young Italian." This text was printed by Griffin and published by Colman with the other three, late in the spring of 1830.[13]

Absorbed by the task of editing, proof reading, and teaching, Longfellow thought of gaining a reputation as a scholar as soon as his textbooks should be introduced to American schools and colleges. Having found this apparently easy road to eminence, he was misled into exclaiming to his friend Greene, "I am delighted more and more with the profession I have embraced." [14] Nevertheless, a few tedious days in the classroom clouded his optimism and made him fret against the provincial isolation of Bowdoin. The infinite advantages and experiences of travel beckoned to him so often in memory that his longing for escape made the chains of routine grow tight.

In his leisure there was so little to do. He could not be forever calling on such friends as Dr. Welles, Professor Upham, and other favorite members of the faculty. At meal times, he walked from his room in Maine Hall, across the northwest corner of the yard to Mrs. Fales's boarding house on Main Street; but he took little pleasure in conversing with his associates at table there. Gradually he fell into the habit of taking solitary walks along familiar paths through the pine groves, down to Paradise Spring or out across the plain to Maquoit Bay. Another diversion, he told James Berdan, was gained from "capering about on a white horse with one eye." He added: "The exercise I take all alone, for I lead the life of an anchorite; to be sure I have many *acquaintances*,—mais elles ne sont pas du bois dont on fait les amis." [15]

Happily, Professor Cleaveland's home was a certain refuge from loneliness, for the Cleaveland family welcomed Longfellow cordially. Evening after evening, he walked down Federal Street to enjoy a pipe with the genial professor before his fireplace and to indulge in pleasant gossip about college affairs. Occasionally Cleaveland's three daughters, reticent and timid, added musical diversion by gathering about the piano with Longfellow to sing favorite songs of Moore and Burns.[16]

This home breathed a cultural atmosphere akin to that in which Longfellow had been raised. Like Stephen Longfellow, Professor Cleaveland still preserved the social refinement of that liberal tradition which he had absorbed at Harvard in the days when Joseph Story and William Ellery Channing were young men. Despite his self-effacing humility and modesty, Cleaveland revealed in his conversation wide horizons of interest and knowledge. His friends in Cambridge had never ceased to nurse a jealous grief at having lost such a man to Bowdoin after he had once been an instructor at Harvard. But no kind of tempting offer could induce him to leave Brunswick. He was happy to live out his days humbly, always serving his townsmen in any practical capacity, and even acting as Chief of the Volunteer Fire Department. Longfellow loved his quiet friend and drew closer to him as the years passed.

He grew conscious of a keener loneliness when Pierre Irving wrote a letter describing his joy in settling a home with his new bride. George Greene, recently returned to Rhode Island from Italy, was also married. "My wife is a Roman girl not yet sixteen," Greene had written. "I met her at Florence—she was my fellow traveller to Paris and there our acquaintance concluded in marriage."[17] Simple, apparently, for the dashing grandson of General Greene. But Longfellow considered the art of love to be a more deliberate and courtly affair, with the lady dwelling so far beyond the reach of the worshipping knight that adoration could be expressed only after the legendary fashion of the troubadours. During his college days he had often paid homage to some excellent piece of divinity, but each new subject of devotion had eventually become, not a sweetheart, but a "sister."

In the loneliness of his dormitory room, however, the young

professor's thoughts turned persistently toward one to whom he intended to pay court most seriously—Mary Storer Potter, one of three attractive sisters over whom a suspicious father, Judge Barrett Potter, watched with scowling eyes. Mary Potter had been a younger schoolmate with Longfellow at the Portland Academy several years earlier. She had continued her education at Miss Cushing's fashionable female school in Hingham. During Longfellow's absence in Europe she had changed from the child he had known to a young woman of fragile and appealing beauty. Her delicate, pale face, blue eyes, and dark hair had held Longfellow's gaze as he was leaving the Meetinghouse with his sisters on the first Sunday after his return from Europe. Who was she? Would his sister Anne call with him at the Potter home on Free Street that afternoon? [18] Since that day, Longfellow had made only occasional visits to Portland and to Free Street, but his mind was fixed in its purpose, as he revealed to Berdan, early in the spring:

"How very singular, that I should not have heard a word about Pierre's marriage! . . . I hope you will never place me in a similar dilemma: at all events I will not place you in one. I say this because you manifest some anxiety upon the subject of my matrimonial speculations. Upon that subject you may set your heart at rest: for I am not a whit nearer 'that bourne etc.' than when I last saw you. I must confess however, that the lively colours in which Pierre describes his happy lot—make me very discontented with my present inglorious estate, and I take this occasion to publish my manifesto, declaring my intention to enter into the holy alliance, as soon as circumstances shall permit me to commence negociations with the other party concerned. But I promise you at the same time, that this shall not interfere in the least with your visit in the summer, upon which I count with certainty. As I am not yet engaged, there is no danger of my being married then." [19]

To woo a daughter of Judge Potter was an undertaking fraught with difficulty, Longfellow learned. Secretly he enclosed most of his letters to Mary within his notes to his faithful sister Anne with instructions that they were to be smuggled into a certain house on Free Street. In sending one important billet containing an invitation to a Portland ball, Longfellow cautioned his sister to take special care: "For I fancy that if the Judge finds out that I have written a letter to his daughter, he will stand on the defensive. So please hand it to her ladyship when no one is nigh." [20]

During the summer vacation he was far too attentive in his courtship to remember his assurances given to Berdan. Shortly before the beginning of the fall term in 1830, he came to Portland from Brunswick for a short vacation, confident that he had won the hand of his lady but fearful lest he should fail to gain the sanction and blessing of her father. Some people said that Judge Potter had sown his portion of wild oats in his youth and consequently hesitated to place any trust in the young men who called on his daughters. But Longfellow found comfort in his knowledge that the Judge and his father were intimate friends. When the ordeal was concluded and the austere gentleman had given his approval, the suitor felt obliged to contrive a formal letter of thanks. In stilted phrases which suggested an uncomfortable respect he wrote:

"Dear Sir,

"I regretted that I had not the opportunity of conversing with you before leaving town on Wednesday morning, but the hurry of departure rendered it impossible. I wished to express the grateful acknowledgment I owe you, for the confidence you have reposed in me in placing in my hands the happiness of a daughter, and in part your own. I most ardently hope, my dear sir, that you may never have the slightest occasion to think that your confidence has been misplaced. I certainly believe you never will have: and this belief is founded upon the attachment I feel for Mary, in whom I find the inestimable virtues of a pure heart and a guileless disposition—qualities which not only excite an ardent affection, but which tend to make it as durable as it is ardent.

"I think I have formed a just estimate of the excellence of Mary's character. I can say to your ear, what I would not often say to hers—that I have never seen a woman in whom every look and word, and action seemed to proceed from so gentle and innocent a spirit. Indeed how much she possesses of all we most admire in the female character!

"On this account I esteem myself highly privileged beyond the common lot in having engaged her affection and secured your approval. I hope to merit both by attention and tenderness to her, and promise myself a life of happiness in the social intercourse of your fireside and the domestic quiet of my own.

"I am, dear sir, most respectfully and affectionately yours,

"HENRY W. LONGFELLOW" [21]

XIV

POET TURNS SCHOLAR

I am proud to have your favorable opinion of those little poetic attempts, which date so many years back. I had long ceased to attach any kind of value to them, and indeed to think of them—and I concluded it was so with others. . . . Indeed I find such an engrossing interest in the studies of my profession, that I write very seldom, except in connection with those studies.[1]

AT THE commencement exercises of his second year of teaching, Longfellow was given formal induction as Professor of Modern Languages at Bowdoin. The probationary period had been satisfactorily completed and the "instructer" was invited to make an inaugural address. Climbing to the platform of the Congregational church, before the eyes of the President, faculty, trustees, students, and guests of Bowdoin College, the young man delivered a long lecture on "The Origin and Growth of the Languages of Southern Europe and of Their Literature." With sentences calculated to make the dignitaries nod their heads in approval, Longfellow launched into a prefatory salutation:

"Mr. President and Gentlemen,—

"I have looked forward to this day with feelings of pleasure and solicitude. Having been engaged already one year in the duties of my profession, it is natural for me to have desired an occasion on which I might express to you how grateful to my feelings has been the confidence you have reposed in me in conferring on me the Professorship of the Modern Languages in this institution. When a man's duty and his inclination go hand in hand, surely he has no small reason to rejoice, no feeble stimulus to act. The truth of this I feel. I regard the profession of teacher in a far more noble and elevated point of view than many do. I cannot help believing that he who bends in a right direction the pliant disposition of the young, and trains up the ductile mind to a vigorous and healthy growth, does something for the welfare of his country and something for the great interests of humanity." [2]

Impressive words! Whenever Longfellow confined his discussion of education to theory, he spoke with enthusiasm and sincerity. His background of genuine interest had accumulated, since his residence in Dresden and Göttingen, where he had read a number of treatises on education which ranged in variety from Roger Ascham's *Schoolmaster* to current articles in the *North American Review*. Like Ticknor and other American predecessors in Göttingen, he had found the German methods of instruction far superior to the secondary-school methods of study and recitation still in use at Harvard and Bowdoin.

The immediate outcome of his European reading and thinking had been a very long letter to his father, outlining the need for reform in American colleges and proposing specific action. After advocating the need for copying the methods of the University of Göttingen, he had applied his suggestions by pointing out that Portland, Maine, was ideally located for a model university; that he and his father should begin it modestly by giving lectures on literature and law. The essential part of his plan was contained in two paragraphs of the letter:

"Take this [the Sorbonne] and the German universities for models. Let two or three Professors—begin the work—let them deliver lectures in some *town* (Portland seems to me better adapted for it than any other place in our part of the country) —not in a village—not in the woods if their lectures be worth any-thing—they will have hearers and disciples enough—and a *nucleus* will thus be formed around which is to grow an University. In the outset, lectures could not be *gratis*—no, the profits arising therefrom should be the Professor's support. Every one should rely upon his own talents for support—and his pay would in consequence be in proportion to his ability.

"I am now coming to the application of my remarks told you in my last, that I wished to have nothing to do with Bowdoin. The system is too limited and superficial. Instead of going there I wish if possible to sow the seeds of an University after the models of those quoted above, in our own state and our own town. Portland is just the spot for an *University*—(not a college)—it is neither too large nor too small. Yes, let Portland set an example to the whole U. States. Let us begin forthwith: As soon as I return—if the matter seems at all plausible—I mean to proffer my humble endeavours to the execution of such a plan—and put my shoulder to the wheel. The present is just the moment: we must now take the tide there is in the affairs of men. Even before I left home, you had seriously thought of reading Law Lectures—and of gradually giving up the practice of law. This is just what is wanted: and should it meet with good success, as it doubtless would, you would benefit your health thereby—and remove a weight of care and anxiety from your mind. When I return I will also read those lectures I had proposed reading elsewhere. Let not a word be said about an University but let lectures upon different subjects be read—and students will collect. Thus we may steal silently upon the world with these innovations—and without Legislative grants, or College buildings, our State will see an University springing into existence in its very bosom—without its having even an intuition of its origin." [3]

This plan, basically identical with the lyceum programs which had begun in America nearly three years before Longfellow's letter was written, did not receive the approval of his father. "It contains much good sense," Stephen had written, "but is perhaps rather sanguine in its anticipation of our cold climate. I should prefer the Professorship at Bowdoin as it would be more certain and permanent." [4] And Longfellow, combining filial obedience with the practical sense of accepting the easiest course, had abandoned his dream of creating a university in Portland.

But he had not entirely relinquished his hope of bringing educational reforms to his home town. In discussing with Dr. Nichols proposals for a new female high school,[5] Longfellow had stressed the importance of instruction in modern languages. Furthermore, during his first year at Bowdoin he prepared voluminous notes on French, Spanish, and Italian literature which he hoped to use in a series of lectures to be delivered in Portland during the winter of 1830.[6] But his courtship of Mary Potter had left little time for planning a lyceum course in modern literatures and languages, and the lectures were revised to serve as the basis for the inaugural address.

After the beginning of his second year of teaching, Longfellow was requested to deliver two lectures on education: one before the Benevolent Society of Portland and another before a convention of teachers at Augusta.[7] Educational reforms were being discussed by many leaders, and Longfellow's remarks in his inaugural address brought him into prominence as one whose recent study in Europe had made him something of an authority. To him, however, lecturing in public was most exciting, not when he was talking to societies about education but when he was describing the quaint and picturesque features of a foreign language and its literature. Appreciating the growing interest in the lyceum movement, he was eager to take advantage of it. He advised his friend Greene to consider delivering lectures in Providence, Rhode Island, on the Italian language and literature rather than to waste time preparing an Italian grammar. "You will find most delightful occupation in it," he wrote, "—and you will have an opportunity to distinguish yourself, and I can assure you it will be more profitable than the grammar." He added: "If I were you I would not trouble myself about Greek for the present: believe me, my dear fellow, the mod. lang. are more in demand." [8]

Longfellow brought to his literary profession a shrewd opportunism. Here, at last, was a method of capitalizing on his knowledge of French, Italian, and Spanish. He had already taken advantage of a growing demand for simple, elementary textbooks, and had explained frankly to his practical father that the publication of the French grammar was a sound financial investment. His remarks to Greene were equally bald: modern literature was a commodity in demand, and those who could offer it for sale were in a position to command profit and prestige. Longfellow would be eminent in something, he had insisted, earlier. Here was an obvious road.

If he happened to be a purveyor of Old World culture, and a missionary of linguistic enlightenment, at this time, such happy coincidences were fortuitous, but only indirectly associated with his intention. His primary interest was self-advancement as a scholar and as a literary man. Irving had made successful use of his knowledge acquired in Europe; Longfellow would also make use of his knowledge—in a different fashion. But he was bluntly outspoken to Greene. He urged Greene to concentrate on modern languages, instead of Greek, not because the literature of modern Europe was richer than the literature of ancient Greece, but because such a course of action was more profitable.

He discovered other possibilities for converting his knowledge into remunerative expression. Finding that Alexander H. Everett had recently returned from Spain to become editor of the *North American Review*, he sent him copies of his grammars and received a letter of appreciation which concluded:

"I avail myself of this occasion to express the hope that you will employ a part of your leisure from other more important occupations in furnishing me from time to time with an article for the Review. I should consider your aid & cooperation as highly valuable. The compensation which has been allowed hitherto to the contributors is a dollar a page and this will be continued for the present but may perhaps be raised hereafter." [9]

Having compiled his long inaugural address on the growth of the languages of southern Europe, he could divide it into a number of sizable studies which would lend themselves to easy elaboration for magazine articles. He proposed to send a paper on the origin and progress of the French language, and Everett was delighted. "The subject is very interesting," the editor wrote, "and belongs to a department of literature in which we find it less easy to obtain assistance than in most others." [10] Everett may have regretted his rather apologetic remarks about the size of the honorarium when he received the article, which took forty pages of the *Review* for January, 1831. As the cornucopian inaugural address continued to furnish article after article, Everett was finally obliged to ask his exuberant contributor to limit himself. [11]

One factor which added considerable length to Longfellow's *North American* papers was his frequent use of translations to illustrate his remarks. His first article included six generous English versions of French poetry. Although apparently devoid of inner thoughts which sought expression in original poetry at this time, Longfellow brought to the work of translation a facility and grace which increased rapidly with practice. He was not troubled at all by his loss of interest in writing original poetry, as he revealed to Greene at this time, in mentioning his writing:

"I am proud to have your favorable opinion of those little poetic attempts, which date so many years back. I had long ceased to attach any kind of value to them, and indeed to think of them—and I concluded it was so with others. Since my return I have written a piece and a half but have not published a line. You need not be alarmed on that score—I am all prudence, now, since I can form a more accurate judgment of the merit of poetry. If I ever publish a volume it will be many years first. Indeed I find such an engrossing interest in the studies of my profession, that I write very seldom, except in connection with those studies." [12]

Was this partly rationalization, to conceal the unpleasant feeling that he had nothing to say? For ten years, from 1826 to 1836, when one might expect him to be most prolific, as other poets have been in their twenties, Longfellow wrote only a half-dozen pieces of original verse. Here and throughout his life his chronic need was, as in the case of Washington Irving, literary subject-matter. Experience rarely moved him to an expression of his own emotions or thoughts. To his sister he had defended his failure to burst into rapturous praise over the glories of ancient Rome by protesting, "But with me, all deep impressions are silent ones." [13] He could not follow Wordsworth on this score. With Longfellow, impressions were too rapidly volatilized into sentiment, preserved not as emotional remembrances but as vague, dreamy recollections. Such memories were suitable for romantic and elegant trimming about the edges of prose descriptions but were not strong enough to demand expression in poetry. And so, impelled by literary ambition, he had no course at this time but to be an opportunist in his writing.

So much delving into European literature for the *North American Review* and for his classes, prompted him to consider the advantages of combining the descriptive travel sketches which he had begun in Europe with analytical commentaries on, and translations from, foreign literature. Here again Irving served as a model, in such a sketch as "A Royal Poet." Longfellow would guide his reader from the picturesque thoroughfares of French and Spanish towns into the quaint byways of French and Spanish literature. Furthermore, this type of writing seemed to be in more demand than the material which he had intended to use for the "Sketch Book of New England" refused by Carey & Lea. In

returning that manuscript, the Philadelphia publishers had concluded their apologetic remarks with these discouraging observations:

"You ask our opinion of the sale of such a work to which we
reply that it is not probable that it would afford very much for the
author. Books are generally sold here at prices that will only pay
the publisher, as most books pay no copyright, & the affect upon
original books is very bad—so much so, that it appears to us there
is less inducement for writing now than 10 years since." [14]

Perhaps his father had been right—there was not enough wealth
or interest to afford encouragement to *merely* literary men. Perhaps a professorship held decided advantages over the precarious
life of a free-lance writer. But Alexander Everett spurred him
toward further effort on his plan for a European Sketch Book by
soliciting contributions for a new literary periodical to be edited
by James T. Buckingham as the *New-England Magazine*.[15] For
the first number Longfellow sent an introductory essay entitled,
"The Schoolmaster." Faithfully copying Irving, he began by
giving an account of the author:

"I am a Schoolmaster in the little village of Sharon. A son of
New-England, I have been educated in all her feelings and prejudices. To her maternal care I owe the little that is good within
me; and upon her bosom I hope to repose hereafter, when my
worldly task is done, and my soul, like a rejoicing schoolboy, shall
close its weary book, and burst forth from this earthly schoolhouse. My childhood was passed at my native village, in the
usual amusements and occupations of that age; but, as I grew up, I
became satiated with the monotony of my life. A restless spirit
prompted me to visit foreign countries. I said with the Cos-
mopolite, 'The world is a kind of book, in which he, who has seen
his own country only, has read but one page.' Guided by this
feeling I became a traveler. I have traversed France on foot;
smoked my pipe in a Flemish inn; floated through Holland in a
Trekschuit; trimmed the midnight lamp in a German University;
wandered and mused amid the classic scenes of Italy; and danced
to the gay guitar and merry castanet on the borders of the blue
Guadalquiver. When I had read thus far the volume of the world,
I closed it with a sigh, and turned back to that long neglected

page, in which are recorded the name and history of New-England." [16]

Like Irving, Longfellow might have recounted, after such a beginning, legends of his native land as well as memories of his travels. But true to his romantic sentimentalism and his ingrained feeling for what was wanted, he turned to scenes and lands far away. If he had written these sketches for the *New-England Magazine* while still in Dresden, he might have continued to incorporate the New England material which he had outlined at that time. Because he wrote them while a discontented young professor in a country college, he naturally turned his eyes with yearning toward the countries beyond the sea. The second paper was entitled "The Norman Diligence" and recounted his first day of travel in France after landing at Havre. And through four subsequent sketches he fished up other literary matter from the pool of his French pilgrimage.

The pleasure of writing for the *New-England Magazine* increased Longfellow's impatience with the hindering drudgery of classroom drill in French and Spanish grammar. His recollection of distinguished friends in Paris, Marseilles, Madrid, and Rome accentuated his distaste for uncouth students and the provincial, narrow-minded members on the Bowdoin faculty. Escape he must. As the year closed, his bitterness increased. It had already found expression in letters to James Berdan in New York. Writing about a friend who intended to visit Manhattan soon, he had concluded impatiently: "To him I refer you for all that can possibly interest you in this land of Barbarians—this miserable Down East. I feel as if I were living in exile here." [17]

XV

SCHOLAR ATTACKS AMERICA

*With us, the spirit of the age is clamorous for utility, for visible,
tangible utility,—for bare, brawny, muscular utility. We would be
roused to action by the voice of the populace, and the sounds of the
crowded mart, and not "lulled asleep in shady idleness with poet's
pastimes." We are swallowed up in schemes for gain, and engrossed
with contrivances for bodily enjoyments, as if this particle of dust
were immortal. . . . But the truth is, the word utility has a wider
signification than this.*[1]

Mary Potter and Henry Longfellow had chosen September 14,
1831, as their wedding day; and during the weeks immediately
preceding, the young professor was frequently absent from
Brunswick. But even the happy prospect did not decrease his annoyance with the irksome duties of the classroom. His resentment burst forth unexpectedly in a letter to his sister Anne concerning the approaching wedding:

"We *would* postpone our wedding, dear Anne, on your account, if circumstances would permit; but the vacation is but 3
weeks—and we have now fixed the wedding-day in the second:—
so that we shall have barely time to get comfortably settled in
Brunswick, before I shall be forced to commence grinding in the
knowledge mill again. You call it a dog's life: it is indeed—my
dear Anne: I do not believe that I was born for such a lot. . . ."[2]

Within two weeks after the wedding, which took place at the
Potter home in Portland, Longfellow brought his bride to Brunswick. A slight girl of but nineteen years, she won an immediate
place in the hearts of Longfellow's friends, because of her delicate
beauty and charm. Stimulated by the advantages of her education, she had developed an exceptional fondness for mathematics
and literature. She took delight in reading the poetry of Campbell, Moore, Burns, Gray, and Goldsmith; enjoyed criticizing the
writings of contemporary authors; and showed a lively interest in
her husband's work as a teacher, scholar, and author.[3]

To Longfellow's chagrin, he had not been able to find a suitable house for his bride. He was obliged to ask that she be content to live for a time in his rooms at Mrs. Fales's boarding house and accept such cooking as their landlady supplied to her boarders.[4] With characteristic forbearance Mary Potter Longfellow accepted the necessary arrangements, although a hint of disappointment crept into her first letter to her sisters from Brunswick: "I like it as well as I can upon so short a residence here. The ladies have been very kind and polite to me, and it would be very wrong for me not to be contented and happy with such a husband and so pleasant a home." [5]

The first term of the new college year followed the customary routine. When classroom preparations permitted, Longfellow worked at his "European Sketch Book" and made translations of Spanish poetry for future numbers of the *New-England Magazine*.[6] Other literary doors opened for him. Gray & Bowen, the Boston publishers, who were preparing the second edition of his grammars, wrote asking him to contribute to their gift-book annual, *The Token*, edited by S. G. Goodrich. In reply he sent one prose sketch, taken from the rejected manuscript "Sketch Book of New England" and one short poem translated from the Spanish.[7] A more scholarly undertaking during the fall was the careful elaboration of another part of his inaugural address into a forty-page article entitled "Spanish Devotional and Moral Poetry."

During his first three years of teaching at Bowdoin, he built a remarkably large superstructure of literary and linguistic study on the somewhat meagre foundations laid down in France, Spain, Italy, and Germany. The change of heart in Göttingen and the brief but faithful application to his books there had prepared the way for an intensive period of scholarly devotion. Perhaps he remembered Irving's example in Madrid, for he developed the habit of rising each morning at five in order to have hours of quiet study before the routine work began. The quantity and range of his reading in European literature was phenomenal. In his researches for the series of *North American Review* articles, he exhausted the slight offerings of the Bowdoin Library, then began borrowing books by mail from friends and from the Harvard

Library. At the same time he prepared his classroom lectures with utmost faithfulness until the students who heard him were fired with rare inspiration.

Although Longfellow was being diverted from his ultimate goal as a poet, he put heart and soul into his language study. The European experience flowered into an idealistic concept of the wide opportunity to be found in teaching and learning modern languages. In his "Inaugural Address" he had talked enthusiastically about his ideal:

"I cannot regard the study of a language as the pastime of a listless hour. To trace the progress of the human mind through the progressive development of language; to learn how other nations thought and felt, and spake; to enrich the understanding by opening upon it new sources of knowledge; and by speaking many tongues to become a citizen of the world; these are objects worthy the exertion their attainment demands at our hands.

"The mere acquisition of a language then is not the ultimate object; it is a means to be employed in the acquisition of something which lies beyond. I should therefore deem my duty but half performed were I to limit my exertions to the narrow bounds of grammatical rules: nay that I had done little for the intellectual culture of a pupil, when I had merely put an instrument into his hands without explaining to him its most important uses. . . . And it will be my aim, not only to teach the turns and idioms of a language, but, according to my ability and as soon as time and circumstances shall permit, to direct the student in his researches into the literature of those nations whose language he is studying." [8]

Although Professor Ticknor at Harvard taught with similar objectives in view, such exceptions were peaks in the flat landscape of dull, unimaginative linguistic drill which characterized most of the teaching of foreign languages in America at that time. No better illustration of this may be found than by looking sixteen years beyond this "Inaugural Address" to an altercation which arose at Harvard when Longfellow, as Ticknor's successor, tried to impress on the executives that his ideal demanded an extension of a shrinking program; that modern languages should be taught not only during the last two years but also in the sophomore year, to permit students time for exploring the literatures of new-learned languages. The committee appointed to consider possible revision, showed how reluctantly the old order gave way: how entirely unsympathetic it was toward Longfellow's suggestions. Here is the report:

"With regard to the Modern Languages, the majority of the committee are of opinion, that the perfect acquisition of any modern language, meaning thereby the ability of reading and speaking it correctly and fluently, does not form a part of the scheme of the College; these languages are looked upon as literary auxiliaries, and the College does not extend its instruction in this department any further than is necessary to enable the student to read the language taught, without the aid of an instructor." [9]

This was the very attitude which Ticknor had fought so hopelessly. Longfellow was to have better success. It was encouraging to Ticknor to watch him grow at Bowdoin. In working toward his ideal there, Longfellow rapidly became proficient as an American authority on European languages. The boyhood pleasure in wandering as a pilgrim through Europe was translated into a more mature delight in a vicarious sort of foreign travel in the realm of books. Even in the study of German, which had been slighted at Göttingen, he made some progress. As a result of his growing interest, he added many volumes by German authors to the inadequate Bowdoin Library—the works of Klopstock, Gellert, Goethe, Herder, and Körner, good editions of the *Nibelungenlied* and *Heldenbuch*, together with several collections in the fields of literature, history, and language. But his early love of the Spanish remained so strong that Ticknor, writing a letter of recommendation for him later, when he was ready to leave Bowdoin, spoke high praise:

"Soon after he was graduated from Brunswick, he became known to me by an interest quite remarkable at his age, and still more so, perhaps, from the circumstances in which he was placed, —an interest, I mean, in the early Provençal literature, and in the literatures of Spain and Italy. He passed some time in France and still more in Italy and in Spain; and his knowledge of the language and literature of each of these countries, has, for several years past, seemed to me extraordinary. He writes and speaks Spanish with a degree of fluency and exactness which I have known in no American born of parents speaking English as their vernacular. His knowledge of Spanish literature is extensive and is to be relied upon; and several publications he has made on the subject have been accompanied with poetical translations of much spirit and fidelity." [10]

With all the study necessary for such advance, Longfellow also wrote occasional book reviews—one of the best being inspired by the publication of an American edition of Sidney's *Defence of Poesie*. This review-essay is too important for us to hurry past. It deserves careful scrutiny, for it contains some of Longfellow's most vigorous prose, directed against those irritating shackles which cramped the growth of a truly American literature. As an undergraduate he had attacked the same matter twice—in his *Gazette* article on "The Literary Spirit of Our Country" and in his "Commencement Oration." But he had matured since then. And in this essay, inspired by Sidney, he spoke out more vehemently and more specifically against the current indifference to the function and place of the poet. Here was his own declaration of the independence which he desired and dared not take by force. Many of the same ideas found more penetrating and significant expression in Emerson's "American Scholar," five years later.

But where were the authors who should fulfill Longfellow's dream of men bold enough to make a profession of writing? Emerson, who had as yet published not even a pamphlet, was still serving the Second Church of Boston as its pastor and had not yet objected to the administration of the Lord's Supper. Hawthorne, who now occasionally ventured out of his Salem world, and into the White Hills for inspiration, had published one novel of Bowdoin origin, *Fanshawe*—and had immediately regretted it. Most of the New England authors who would become famous in the next quarter-century were still schoolboys. Lowell was in grammar school; Thoreau was getting ready for Harvard, at the Concord Academy; Melville was a favorite pupil at the Albany Academy. And which of the poets had already begun? Holmes had acquired some fame for a single poem, "Old Ironsides," published at a particularly happy moment, in a Boston newspaper.

Poe had published three precious volumes (the first "By a Bostonian") without arousing anyone except John Neal to great enthusiasm. Whittier, living in Hartford, Connecticut, and editing a magazine there, had published a volume of prose and verse entitled *Legends of New England*—also without success. And Walter Whitman was a mere boy beginning to learn the duties of a printer's devil in a Long Island newspaper office. But to such as these, who showed an interest in a native literature—and to those like Halleck, Bryant, Sprague, and Dana, who had grown discouraged—Longfellow held out cheer by championing the coming of a better day. I must quote his "Defence of Poetry" at some length here, because it has never been given its proper due as a summary of the time and as an autobiographical document:

". . . As no 'Apologie for Poetrie' has appeared among us, we hope that Sir Philip Sidney's Defence will be widely read and long remembered. O that in our country, it might be the harbinger of as bright an intellectual day as it was in his own!—With us, the spirit of the age is clamorous for utility, for visible, tangible utility, —for bare, brawny, muscular utility. We would be roused to action by the voice of the populace, and the sounds of the crowded mart, and not 'lulled asleep in shady idleness with poet's pastimes.' We are swallowed up in schemes for gain, and engrossed with contrivances for bodily enjoyments, as if this particle of dust were immortal,—as if the soul needed no aliment, and the mind no raiment. We glory in the extent of our territory, in our rapidly increasing population, in our agricultural privileges, and our commercial advantages. . . . We boast of the increase and extent of our physical strength, the sound of populous cities, breaking the silence and solitude of our Western territories,—plantations conquered from the forest, and gardens springing up in the wilderness. Yet the true glory of a nation consists not in the extent of its territory, the pomp of its forests, the majesty of its rivers, the height of its mountains, and the beauty of its sky; but in the extent of its mental power,—the majesty of its intellect,—the height and depth and purity of its moral nature. It consists not in what nature has given to the body, but in what nature and education have given to the mind. . . .

"But still the main current of education runs in the wide and not well defined channel of immediate and practical utility. The main point is, how to make the greatest progress in worldly prosperity,—how to advance most rapidly in the career of gain. This, perhaps, is necessarily the case to a certain extent in a country where every man is taught to rely upon his own exertions for a livelihood, and is the artificer of his own fortune and estate. But it ought not to be exclusively so. . . .

"Now, under correction be it said, we are much led astray by this word utility. There is hardly a word in our language whose meaning is so vague, and so often misunderstood and misapplied. . . . We are too apt to think that nothing can be useful, but what is done with a noise, at noonday, and at the corners of the streets; as if action and utility were synonymous, and it were not as useless to act without thinking, as it is to think without acting. But the truth is, the word utility has a wider signification than this. It embraces in its proper definition whatever contributes to our happiness; and thus includes many of those arts and sciences, many of those secret studies and solitary avocations, which are generally regarded either as useless, or as absolutely injurious to society. Not he alone does service to the State, whose wisdom guides her councils at home, nor he whose voice asserts her dignity abroad. A thousand little rills, springing up in the retired walks of life, go to swell the rushing tide of national glory and prosperity; and whoever in the solitude of his chamber, and by even a single effort of his mind, has added to the intellectual pre-eminence of his country, has not lived in vain, nor to himself alone. . . .

"If this be true, then are the ornamental arts of life not merely ornamental, but at the same time highly useful; and Poetry and the Fine Arts become the instruction, as well as the amusement of mankind. They will not till our lands, nor freight our ships, nor fill our granaries and our coffers; but they will enrich the heart, freight the understanding, and make up the garnered fulness of the mind. And this we hold to be the true use of the subject. . . .

"We apprehend that there are some, and indeed not a few in our active community, who hold the appellation of scholar and man of letters in as little repute, as did our Gothic ancestors that of Roman; associating with it about the same ideas of effeminacy and inefficiency. They think, that the learning of books is not wisdom; that study unfits a man for action; that poetry and non-sense are convertible terms; that literature begets an effeminate and craven spirit; in a word, that the dust and cobwebs of a library are a kind of armor, which will not stand long against the hard knocks of 'the bone and muscle of the State,' and the 'huge two-fisted sway' of the stump orator. . . .

"And yet such men have lived, as Homer, and Dante, and Mil-ton;—poets and scholars, whose minds were bathed in song, and yet not weakened; men who severally carried forward the spirit of their age, who soared upward on the wings of poetry, and yet were not unfitted to penetrate the deepest recesses of the human soul, and search out the hidden treasures of wisdom, and the secret springs of thought, feeling, and action. . . . It does not, then, appear to be the necessary nor the natural tendency of poetry to enervate the mind, corrupt the heart, or incapacitate us for performing the private and public duties of life. On the contrary, it may be made, and should be made, an instrument for improving the condition of society, and advancing the great pur-pose of human happiness. . . .

"From all these considerations, we are forced to the conclusion, that poetry is a subject of far greater importance in itself, and in its bearing upon the condition of society, than the majority of mankind would be willing to allow. We heartily regret, that this opinion is not a more prevailing one in our land. We give too little encouragement to works of imagination and taste. The vocation of the poet does not stand high enough in our esteem; we are too cold in admiration, too timid in praise. . . . The prospect, how-ever, brightens. But a short time ago, not a poet 'moved the wing, or opened the mouth, or peeped;' and now we have a host of them,—three or four good ones, and three or four hundred poor ones. This, however, we will not stop to cavil about at present. To those of them, who may honor us by reading our article, we would whisper this request,—that they should be more original, and withal more national. It seems every way important, that now, whilst we are forming our literature, we should make it as original, characteristic, and national as possible. To effect this, it is not necessary that the war-whoop should ring in every line, and every page be rife with scalps, tomahawks and wampum. Shades of Tecumseh forbid!—The whole secret lies in Sidney's maxim,—'Look in thy heart and write.' . . .

"A national literature, then, in the widest signification of the words, embraces every mental effort made by the inhabitants of a country, through the medium of the press. Every book written by a citizen of a country belongs to its national literature. But the term has also a more peculiar and appropriate definition; for when we say that the literature of a country is *national*, we mean that it bears upon it the stamp of national character. . . .

"We repeat, then, that we wish our native poets would give a more national character to their writings. In order to effect this, they have only to write more naturally, to write from their own feelings and impressions, from the influence of what they see around them, and not from any preconceived notions of what poetry ought to be, caught by reading many books, and imitating many models. This is peculiarly true in descriptions of natural scenery. In these, let us have no more sky-larks and nightingales. For us they only warble in books. A painter might as well introduce an elephant or a rhinoceros into a New England landscape. We would not restrict our poets in the choice of their subjects, or the scenes of their story; but when they sing under an American sky, and describe a native landscape, let the description be graphic . . . the figures and imagery of poetry a little more characteristic, as if drawn from nature and not from books. . . .

"We have set forth the portrait of modern poetry in rather gloomy colors; for we really think, that the greater part of what is published in this book-writing age, ought in justice to suffer the fate of the children of Thetis, whose immortality was tried by fire. We hope, however, that ere long, some one of our most gifted bards will throw his fetters off, and relying on himself alone, fathom the recesses of his own mind, and bring up rich pearls from the secret depths of thought." [11]

If only he could have taken his own advice a bit more closely to heart! Truly, the very faults of his time were all wrapped up in this Bowdoin Professor who spoke through the mouthpiece of the *North American Review*. He bitterly resented being told by his father and by Theophilus Parsons that writing must always take second place, and he sincerely disliked the American emphasis on the primary value of money and material prestige. Yet he could not hurdle these very prejudices, because they were too thoroughly a part of his own Yankee heritage. Attack them, yes. Escape them, never. As for his criticism of that kind of second-hand poetry which grew out of books, there again he was powerless to carry out his own advice. Throughout his life, Longfellow drew far more material from books than he ever drew from his head or heart.

But there were duties other than defending American poetry, to occupy the scholar. From Boston the proof sheets of his various textbooks came constantly to his desk at Bowdoin. Intending to publish a series of four books to form a "Cours de Langue Française," he made a trip to Boston with his wife during the winter vacation, to consult with his publishers and to visit friends. Charles Folsom, a scholar of the classics who had resigned a position as tutor and librarian at Harvard College to become a valuable editor for Colonel Metcalf's University Press, where Longfellow's textbooks were being printed, entertained the Longfellows at his home.[12] Folsom took a keen interest in his new acquaintance because of his surprising knowledge of foreign languages and proudly introduced him to those at Harvard who would appreciate him. In this way Longfellow met Cornelius Conway Felton, a stout, jocular young man who had recently become a tutor in the classics at Harvard.

During the visit, he also renewed acquaintance with other members of the Harvard faculty—Professors Willard, Ware, and Ticknor. If he were to devote his life to teaching (a prospect which he did not particularly relish), the more cultured and literary atmosphere of Cambridge seemed far more attractive than the rural simplicity of Brunswick. Since his first visit with Professor Ticknor in 1826, Longfellow had been considering the possibility of securing a position at Harvard. Rev. Ichabod Nichols had put the thought into his head shortly before he had sailed for Europe. Failing to understand what Nichols had meant, Longfellow had asked his father about it:

"I recollect that when I last saw Doct. Nichols, he said something about '*my friends at Cambridge*' taking an interest in my situation abroad.—Not understanding what he could mean by this I said that he meant my friends at *Brunswick*. 'No'—he said—'my friends at *Cambridge*'—and from other casual expressions which he dropped in the course of conversation, I thought he intended to hint, that he had a plan for obtaining a situation for me at Harvard—as being more to my taste than Brunswick . . . If there is a plan formed in his mind, with regard to situation at Harvard, what situation can it be?—Pray satisfy my curiosity as soon as possible." [13]

Apparently Longfellow remembered Dr. Nichols's earlier remarks, and his frequent visits to Cambridge from Brunswick were intended to advance such designs.

Shortly after his return to Brunswick for the beginning of the winter term, he prepared the third paper of his series for the *North American*—a study of the Italian language and dialects. But more ambitious plans were beginning to conflict with scholarship. He had been dreaming of giving up teaching in order to secure a position as an undersecretary of the Spanish legation in Madrid. Knowing that Alexander Everett was not only friendly but also in a position to advise, he asked his assistance. In answer, Everett discouraged any further thought concerning such a scheme and concluded: "I am not sure that the place—if you obtained it—would realize your anticipation. It is not a very agreeable one especially for a married man without fortune. I have tried it, married and single, and can speak from experience." [14]

Not to be put off with general remarks, Longfellow wrote again, expressing in more definite terms his desire to find some change in occupation and pointing out specific reasons for his dissatisfaction with affairs at Bowdoin. Everett agreed that a position as secretary of a legation "—although not on all accounts a very eligible one especially for a married man—is better than the one you hold." He added, "Not that the office of a Professor is in itself objectionable but that the college is in a tottering—uncertain state." [15]

Everett was right. The policy of the government at Bowdoin was so muddled at this time that none could be sure the institution would continue under the same organization for another year. The trouble was fundamentally caused by a chronic conflict between the dominant Congregational orthodoxy of the Bowdoin authorities and the hostile liberalism of the state legislature. Since the day when the petition for a Maine college had been drawn up by a group of Congregational ministers, the control of the college had remained in clerical hands. Incorporated as an institution free of state control, Bowdoin had been surrendered to the whim of politicians by President Allen, who had permitted such interference for the sake of much-needed appropriations.

During Longfellow's undergraduate years there had been many moves to strengthen the college as a bulwark of orthodoxy against the insurgent liberalism of the times, until the state legislature, disgusted by such bitter sectarianism, refused to make any appropriation in 1825. President Allen's pompous manners had continued to annoy the legislature so greatly that a bill was introduced in March, 1831, to oust him. The bill, which was passed, required that the president should hold office only by a two-thirds vote of the college trustees and overseers. Aimed deliberately at Allen, the law proved two-edged, for when the governing bodies voted at commencement of 1831, Allen did not gain a two-thirds vote—nor did any of the other candidates nominated to take his place.

Thus the college year of 1831–32 began with no president in office at Bowdoin. Acting by vote of the faculty, Professors Cleaveland and Newman served in executive capacities, and the year continued with a minimum of internal friction.[16]

But a battle of words was waged in the Maine newspapers. Criticism and ridicule were levelled at both college and legislature by leading voices throughout New England. To Longfellow, the entire quarrel seemed a natural outcome of President Allen's unwise policies, which he had detested ever since the famous "scrape" between the students and Rev. Asa Mead. These circumstances prompted him to appeal to Everett and to express his desire to sever relations with an institution which had come so precariously near to dissolution.

Furthermore, his own Unitarian beliefs had not made him popular among the orthodox members of the faculty. Since his return to Brunswick he had affiliated himself with the small Unitarian group which met regularly, and had assisted by singing in the choir and conducting a Bible class. Such deliberate and flagrant disagreement with the conventional religious belief at Bowdoin did not strengthen his position. Viewing the affair from the outside, Everett expressed his attitude to Longfellow:

"The ingratitude which appears to be shown by your Legislature to gentlemen who are rendering them such important services as are now performed by the Professors at Bowdoin College is truly revolting. For the sake of the institution and the interests connected with it I should regret your departure from it, as it is certain that the loss could not at present be supplied. To you it would be comparatively a matter of indifference. Your talents and industry would secure you an honourable and advantageous position wherever you may choose to place yourself."

And again he wrote on the same subject:

"I am sorry to learn that you are likely to be molested by the State authorities, but derive consolation from the expectation that all your troubles of this kind have a certain indirect tendency to bring you into this quarter." [17]

Such genuine interest was encouraging to Longfellow. From various sources he learned that he had other friends in Boston and Cambridge who were working for his interests. Their good intentions were of no immediate avail, however, and he could only settle down and wait a little longer.

During the winter term of 1832 he experimented with an uncommon method of teaching Italian. The Bowdoin curriculum of modern languages had been steadily enlarged during his first two years by the introduction of German and Italian as elective courses. Since no student was eligible to study Italian until he had completed the required course in French, Longfellow ventured to combine the teaching of French and Italian by compiling a simple Italian grammar in French and publishing it as a *Syllabus de la grammaire italienne*. To supplement this text he also edited an Italian reader entitled *Saggi de' novellieri italiani*.

Unfortunately, Colonel Metcalf at the University Press in Cambridge was not able to print these texts fast enough to have them ready for the winter term of 1832, and Longfellow was obliged to ask the printer to send him sets of unbound sheets as the book progressed. These he distributed to his students. As he neared the completion of one set, he urged the printer to greater haste. Unavoidable delays of stagecoaches and the accidents of printing resulted in some confusion. One letter from the printer, demanding more copy, brought a distracted reply from the teacher:

"Yours of the 26th inst. has just reached me. You can hardly imagine the *consternation* it caused me. Why—a fortnight ago I sent Mr. Folsom additional matter to continue the Italian Reading-book with—and have been waiting to hear from him again—in order to supply more which I have prepared. My letter must have been lost. I regret this more than you can—because I hoped that in the course of a week or ten days I should have the books to go on with my classes—I have now a class of 8 or 10 who have finished what was sent in sheets—and in about ten days shall commence with another class of about 30! What is to be done? Would it not be well to do up 40 or 50 copies in paper—and then when the remainder is finished all can be bound up together." [18]

Apparently the scheme was carried out, for before the spring term had started Longfellow recorded in his carefully kept student-account book, "Rec^d of Gray & Bowen . . . 40 Novellieri (Imperfect)." [19]

Such an informal method of study added a pleasant element of friendliness between the students and the instructor. Longfellow made a constant effort to win the good will and friendship of his students by making his classes interesting. His youthful appearance and his lack of that uncomfortable severity which made older members of the faculty detested was instrumental in adding to his popularity. "We were fond of him from the start," one of his students recalled later; "his earnest and dignified demeanor inspired us. A better teacher, a more sympathetic friend, never addressed a class of young men." [20] Occasionally Longfellow entertained some of his students in his home. One such gathering was recorded by a boy thus favored:

"Wednesday evening, I had an invitation to Prof. Longfellow's and found there quite a select coterie of gentlemen. Dr. Sweetster and two or three medical students. The object for which we were called together, was to partake of a delicious wild goose, and some other good things, and a bountiful table was spread before

us, as I can assure you. The evening passed off very pleasantly
with conversation, and though it was twelve o'clock when I returned to my own room I consoled myself that my dissipation had
been in the company of learned Professors . . . Mrs. Longfellow is to appearance an interesting, amiable woman, though not
of much energy. Prof. Longfellow is a very interesting man, has
travelled much and is well versed in the literature of modern
Europe." [21]

Even such friendly evenings with his associates in his new home
could not exclude from Longfellow's mind a persistent and increasing desire to escape from the backwoods of Maine. In the
spring of 1832 George Greene gave him some information concerning a possible opportunity of obtaining a position as professor of modern languages at New York University. With impulsive eagerness he responded:

"Your suggestions concerning the chair of Mod. Lang. in the
University of New York please me very much. I would gladly
make the exchange; and yet I know not why I say so, for I know
nothing of the proposed endowments in the N. York University,
nor of the salary, or tuition, or perquisites of the Professors. Will
you be good enough to write me upon this point; and tell me
what will probably be the duties, and what the income of the Prof.
of Modern languages? It would be wrong, you know, to solicit
a situation of this kind, without having first resolved to accept the
appointment, in case I should prove successful in my application: . . .

"On first commencing my Professorial duties, I was actuated
by the same feelings which seem now to influence you. I sought
retirement; and I am confident I did wisely. Next September
completes 3 years, that I have been laboring on in this little solitude; and I now feel a strong desire to tread a stage on which I can
take longer strides and spout to a larger audience." [22]

For three years after the writing of this letter, Longfellow was
obliged to remain at Bowdoin, but continued to hope that the
situation at New York University might develop to his advantage. Here again, as in so many of his other expectations, he was
disappointed.

XVI

RESTLESSNESS

I do not believe that I was born for such a lot. I have aimed higher than this: and I cannot believe that all my aspirations are to terminate in the drudgery of a situation, which gives me no opportunity to distinguish myself, and in point of worldly gain, does not even pay me for my labor. Besides, one loses ground so fast in these out of the way places: the mind has no stimulus to exertion—grows sluggish in its movements and narrow in its sphere—and there's the end of a man. We will see.[1]

THE PHI BETA KAPPA SOCIETY of Bowdoin College invited Longfellow to deliver a poem at the annual fall meeting in 1832. Averse to the unpleasant process of grinding out poetry to order, he nevertheless contrived a lengthy dissertation of over four hundred lines, in which he traced the progress of education by contrasting the intellectual servility of medieval times against the freedom of thought stimulated by modern teaching. Possibly he drew freely from his equally long poem entitled "The Dark Ages," which he had delivered before the Peucinian Society during his senior year at Bowdoin. But even if the new production was merely an expanded revision, it met with so much praise that Charles Folsom heard of it in Cambridge. "I congratulate you on the success of your Phi Beta Kappa poem," he wrote, "and charge you to keep the same lyre ready strung." [2] Five weeks later, Folsom explained himself by writing as secretary of the Harvard Phi Beta Kappa Society to invite Longfellow to appear in Cambridge as poet for their next anniversary. He added:

"This appointment I would privately as a friend urge on you to accept, unless there be insuperable objections. Hereafter the reasons of my urgency for your accepting the appointment for the *next* anniversary will be apparent. I go on the supposition that you are, at *some* time, to be our Poet. Now is the *best* time, from various circumstances, which you will hereafter know. Nor let the fact of your having been the Poet at Brunswick this year have any weight with you to make you decline. The audience you will address, *not one* of them, probably, was at Brunswick. Nor let the time of our celebration (the day after Commencement) have more weight with you. You are called abroad to illustrate your Alma Mater, while she sits with proud complacency at home. She will dismiss you on such an errand with a special benediction, & be content to be less well served by another, or even go unserved in your absence.

"You have a year for preparation. If your song lasts *twenty minutes or half an hour*, the measure of delight will be as great as a Poet *is bound* to give at once, though you may be bountiful as you please beyond that measure.

"Again I repeat it, as a friend, I think you ought to accept *this present* appointment, for reasons, which you will hereafter pronounce good, and weightier than any reason for deferring which I am acquainted with." [3]

Obviously, Longfellow's friends at Cambridge were watching out for him with the same interest which Dr. Nichols had shown several years earlier. After Longfellow had accepted, Folsom explained that his urgent words had been prompted by the wish that his friend might share honors with the distinguished former United States President John Quincy Adams, who had been invited to deliver the prose discourse. "Was I not right," he asked, "to wish to bring a minstrel from Maine, if the best was to be had there; and if I had a regard for that minstrel, ought I not to wish to find him 'fit audience *and many*'?" [4]

Meanwhile, there were prosaic affairs demanding attention at Brunswick. In October, 1832, the Longfellows moved their household goods from the cramped quarters of Mrs. Fales's boarding house to a pleasant home under the elms of Federal Street, not far from Professor Cleaveland's. Here the spacious rooms afforded more seclusion for the scholar-poet and more freedom for entertaining friends from Portland, Boston, and Rhode Island. Unfortunately the task of moving proved too strenuous for the delicate state of Mrs. Longfellow's health. Referring to the confusion of this untimely illness, her husband wrote, "I have been quite indisposed—my wife is still confined to her chamber—we are just half-moved—so that I stand Colossus-like astride—one foot in my own

house and one in a boarding-house." [5] Impatient to be done with
the semipublic unpleasantness of his old quarters, he was happy to
tell Folsom, a little later:

"I have at length got seated in my new house. It is one of the
pleasantest in town, and one of the most convenient. It suits me
exactly. The only thing that annoys me is the style of the paper-
hangings, which cry aloud against the taste of my landlord and
predecessor. *Stripes* of the most odious colors in all the parlors
and chambers—and in the front entry *green parrots dancing on
the slack wire*." [6]

As soon as peace settled over the house Longfellow gave much
of his time to literary opportunities. When the editor of the
annual *Token* had solicited further contributions for the 1833
edition, the author drew from his portfolio a prose sketch originally intended for the abandoned "Sketch Book of New England"
and one original poem, conveniently snipped from his long "Phi
Beta Kappa poem." [7]

Charles Folsom wrote to tell of his projected quarterly, a *Select
Journal of Foreign Periodicals* which he had agreed to edit with
Professor Andrews Norton in Cambridge. For the first issue the
editors wished Longfellow to make a translation of a long and
scholarly article on Medieval French Romances which had recently appeared in the Paris *Bulletin Universal*. "The price of the
labor in our journal is hardly yet settled," wrote Folsom, "but in
this case it will be to your satisfaction." [8] In spite of these demands Longfellow also began a fourth study of modern languages for some future number of the *North American*.[9]

When scholarly labors and classroom duties permitted, he wrote
and revised sketches of his wanderings about France and Spain
for Buckingham's *New-England Magazine*. After relating his
pleasantest experiences and impressions in France he suddenly
abandoned the scheme of scattering his essays through the pages
of a periodical. For some time he had been reconsidering his
original plan of publishing the work in parts, as Irving had published *The Sketch Book*. How much more exciting such an enterprise would be than the laborious copying of excerpts for French
readers and Spanish texts. "This teaching boys their a, b, c, is
growing somewhat irksome," he confided to Folsom. "Morning,

noon, night—*toujours perdrix!* I mean to turn author and write
a book—not a *grammar*." [10] Carrying on his scheme for feeding
the current curiosity about foreign literature, he tucked many
scattered translations of poems into appropriate places—and even
managed to incorporate his long translation of Manrique's "Coplas." [11] Such work delighted him more than anything he had done
since he had begun teaching. To Greene he wrote:

"And shall I tell you what I am engaged in now? Well I am
writing a book—a kind of Sketch-Book of France, Spain, Germany, and Italy;—composed of descriptions—sketches of character—tales illustrating manners and customs, and tales illustrating
nothing in particular. Whether the book will ever see the light is
yet uncertain. If I finally conclude to publish it I think I shall put
it out in Nos. or parts:—and shall of course, send you a copy as
soon as it *peeps.* However it is very possible that the book will
remain for aye in manuscript. I find that it requires little courage
to publish grammars and school-books—but in the department of
fine writing, or attempts at fine writing—it requires vastly more
courage." [12]

Relying on the practical judgment of his father, he sent a section of his manuscript to him for criticism. "If your papers had
been written in a legible manner," Mr. Longfellow answered, in a
bearish mood, "I should have read them with more pleasure. With
great difficulty I spelt them out, and derived much pleasure from
the perusal, even under these unfavorable circumstances." [13] He
confessed, however, that he was troubled by the probable cost of
publishing such a book; furthermore, what sense would any
reader make of such a meaningless title as "Outre-Mer"? Undismayed, Longfellow refused to change it. "Outre-Mer: A Pilgrimage Beyond the Sea." Such a quaint phrase not only gave
the exact connotation desired but also prepared the reader for the
vein in which the book was written. And there was the explana-
tory introduction for those who were too stupid: "The Pays
d'Outre-Mer, or the Land beyond the Sea, is a name by which the
pilgrims and crusaders of old usually designated the Holy Land.
I, too, in a certain sense, have been a pilgrim of Outre-Mer." [14]

His father's cautionary remarks about the difficulty of finding
a publisher were not so easily brushed aside. At length he secured

the advice of Frederick T. Gray, a member of the firm which had published his textbooks in their second edition, and through him began negotiations in April with Lilly, Wait, and Company in Boston. When this firm finally decided against printing the first number, Longfellow impetuously forced the issue. He would go ahead with the printing—and find a publisher afterwards. Again he carried his manuscript to the reliable Griffin in Brunswick. In May the compositors began their work. Thus the author's original wish was realized, for he was able to supervise the layout and design. With flattering emulation he copied all the important details of Irving's *Sketch Book*, even to the large type, the tall pages, wide margins, and mottoes.

While this first part of *Outre-Mer* was being printed, Longfellow tried a new tack. Would any publishers like to bring out his volume of translations from Spanish poetry? After various houses had refused, Messrs. Allen and Ticknor wrote a half-hearted acceptance, but were so unkind as to remark, "We presume it [the book] would find a slow and perhaps limited sale; yet as it is not large the expense cannot be great. We therefore believe it will pay for itself at least." [15] It never did.

In the meantime, *Outre-Mer* had been completed at Griffin's press, except for the printing of the title page. But no publisher had been found. Experienced in such trade details, Joseph Griffin departed for Boston late in June to use his influence. He returned with the gratifying news that Hilliard, Gray & Company were willing to buy the book at very good terms. Immediately Longfellow wrote to his new publishers:

"BRUNSWICK June 30, 1833

"MM. Hilliard, Gray & co
    "Gentlemen,
        "Mr. Griffin reached town to-day, and has just handed me your proposition in regard to the purchase and publication of my little book of sketches. The offer you make me is better than I expected; and all that prevents me from accepting it at once is the obligation in respect to any future Nos. of the work.

    "Whether any future Nos. are to see the light must depend upon circumstances beyond my control;—after September next, the place of my residence is uncertain; I may be so far from this part of the country, that even if the work should be completed it would be impossible or inconvenient to comply with that part of the contract which relates to the printing. These circumstances lead me to refuse an offer, which under other circumstances, I should be glad to accept.

"I wish, however, that you would have the goodness to act as Agent for the work. I put the *nominal retail* price at .62½ per No. upon which I make you a discount of 35 per cent.

"500 copies have been printed. 425 I shall send you; 25 of which are for gratuitous distribution; 25 more, I shall myself distribute; and 50 copies will remain in Mr. Griffin's hands for the market here and in Portland.

"The books shall be sent as soon as they can be done up.

"I wish you to take out a copy-right in your name, for I do not wish to appear as the author of the work. I am well aware, that this would be no *remedy* against any one who should choose to pilfer, but it would be a strong *preventative*.

"Allen & Ticknor, who are now publishing for me a work of a different kind, have offered to act as agents in this. For certain reasons, however, which it would be unnecessary to mention, I have given you the preference. As this might create hard feelings on their part, were it known, I wish that the arrangement between us may be kept secret.

"Thanking you for your generous offer, and for any interest you may take in the success of my little work, I am

"very respectfully yours
"Henry W. Longfellow."

"P.S. In regard to time of pay^t, I shall be satisfied with whatever is customary. Upon this point and others, which may arise, I will converse with you in August next, when I shall have the pleasure of seeing you in Boston." [16]

His comment concerning the uncertainty of his remaining at Bowdoin another year was an indication of his persistent hope of finding a more congenial occupation. In May he had sought the aid of Dr. Nichols concerning the possibility of going to Harvard —possibly as a lecturing assistant to Professor Ticknor. Dr.

Nichols enlisted the support of Stephen Longfellow's college friend, Judge Joseph Story, a Harvard overseer, formerly acting chief justice of the United States after Marshall's death, and now the head of the Harvard school of law. In reply to Longfellow, Dr. Nichols referred specifically to the young man's eager confession that he would be glad to spend some additional time abroad in preparation for such a position:

"I have been waiting with impatience for a letter from Judge Story which I have this moment received. He informs me that he has been interesting himself in the object—and conferring with the gentlemen proper to be consulted—but the result, he is sorry to discover, is, and I can appreciate the sincerity of his regret from the strong feeling of regard he manifested for yourself—that 'we would gladly avail ourselves of Mr. L's talents & known devotion to this valuable department, if we could, but unless some gentleman of fortune would give the College a suitable foundation (and unfortunately there seems to be no such person) the project seems to our friends impracticable. All our means are now absorbed in the existing arrangements.' The Judge in several conversations with me upon the subject, spoke of yourself and of his wishes as to your connexion with Cambridge in such terms as left me convinced that nothing would be wanting on his part, to secure your services there. The extent of your proposed plan as to Europe, is not within any particular means of judging which I possess. I am aware of certain disadvantages at Brunswick. But I think I can clearly see that your reputation—ever advancing as it is by your literary exertions, and productions, will sooner or later give you a choice of situation such as would be every way convenient to your pursuits. I should not deem it at all requisite for this purpose that you should exile yourself again from your native land.

"With the sincerest affection and regard, yours,

"I. Nichols." [17]

Clearly, Longfellow had set his heart on making another protracted visit to the countries of Europe. He continued to believe that, if only he could live there indefinitely as Washington Irving had done, he might find infinite literary mines from which to dig ore for his refining. In July, only a month after he had heard from

Dr. Nichols, an obituary notice in a Boston paper excited him with the belief that his dream might come true. The secretary of legation in Madrid had recently died, and Longfellow saw no reason why he should not secure the appointment through the aid of friends. With trembling haste he wrote a postscript in a letter to Alexander H. Everett:

"I have taken my letter from the office to say that I have seen by this morning's papers the death of Mr. Walsh, Secretary of Legation at Madrid. I am very desirous of making application for the place, thus left vacant; and as you have much experience in such matters I wish you to advise me how I am to proceed. I hope you will not refuse me your influence in this thing. I wish you would be kind enough to write immediately to the Secretary of State at Washington, or to him who has the disposal of such places. You being a leading man in the Opposition, will not I think diminish your influence at the present time. It is a kind of era of good feelings now; and doubtless the President entertains very friendly feelings towards you all in Boston, after the splendid reception you gave him. I shall certainly be under very great obligations to you if you will write to Washington upon this subject without delay. Will it be necessary for me to make a personal application? If so to whom?—and how?

"You will excuse me for importuning you so much, but here I am in a corner, beyond the reach of almost every body, and with only one or two friends, to whom I must apply in every emergency. The present seems to be an opportunity of realizing some of my fondest wishes, which I ought not to let slip without an effort." [18]

Everett crushed this hope by answering that the place had already been filled; that Mr. Walsh was superseded several months before his death. He also dissuaded Longfellow from expecting to secure any such appointment during the administration of President Andrew Jackson, because, he added, "appointments under the present administration are so entirely and exclusively a business of political jobbing—and especially where New England is concerned." [19]

Deeply disappointed by this intelligence, Longfellow considered an even stranger prospect of escape. Since his return from

Europe, he had taken an interest in the movement for offering greater educational advantages to young women. His lectures, in Portland and Augusta, upon that subject, had stressed European methods, already popular in America. And so he might turn his growing reputation to account by opening a girls' school. To Charles Folsom he wrote:

"You must know, that my prolific brain has conceived the mad project of leaving this College, and establishing a Female School in the city of New York, where I understand great things may be done in that way. I am anxious, however, to have more definite information upon the point; and as I understand that your friend W. C. Bryant takes a good deal of interest in the subject of female education, you would do me a great favor if you would write him two or three lines requesting information in the matter." [20]

With loyal devotion, Folsom constructed a thoughtful letter to Bryant, already a proprietor and editor of the *New York Evening Post:*

"Dear Sir,

"I am happy to bring myself to your recollection by addressing you in behalf of an esteemed friend, whose merit is not wholly unknown to you.

"Mr. Longfellow (whose early promise is likely to be verified, if his lot should be well cast) after spending some years in Europe, has been professor of modern literature at Bowdoin College, in Maine. He is dissatisfied with his situation, and sighs for a more public scene. He has conceived the plan of establishing a female school of higher class in the city of New York, where, he has been told, great things may be done in that way. In the cultivated languages of Modern Europe, and in elegant literature generally, he is accomplished to a degree rare among his countrymen. His amiable temper, and the simplicity & frankness of his manners, must make him an engaging teacher. Mrs. Longfellow (who I suppose is to come in for a share, but of this I am not certain) partakes of her husband's tastes, and is commended for her proficiency in all that is good.

"Now Mr. Longfellow has understood that you, Sir, take a

strong interest in female education, which you have, he says, manifested in various ways. On the strength of this he has requested you to pass judgment on his plan. Would such a school as he would be likely to set up, in your opinion, have a good chance for success in New York? The modern languages & polite literature would of course be his forte, but I suppose his plan to embrace all things beautiful & true which young ladies ought to learn.

"I wish we could have him in this neighborhood, for I think he would be an ornament to any community. If he should succeed in establishing himself in New York, I should think him happy. He needs only the influence which he would receive from a few minds, such as he would find there, to become an efficient litterateur, a real promoter of the good learning in the country." [21]

Again Longfellow was disappointed, for Bryant gave him no encouragement. The school year dragged on, leaving the Bowdoin professor stranded in the backwaters where he had been carried by his reckless eagerness for Europe in 1826. True, he had escaped the law. But at what cost? The colorful visions concerning the noble calling of the teacher were rapidly vanishing. Impatiently he continued to watch for some high tide of opportunity which might float him out to freedom. His romantic longings fashioned strange dreams, but the moon and stars were not propitious. And the fourth year of drudgery in a Down East village ended, leaving him still a prisoner.

XVII

VAIN PROJECTS

*I heard that Mr. Cogswell of Northampton was about to re-
linquish the Round Hill school . . . It seemed to me a glorious
opening. . . .*

*My ardent desire is, to obtain an appointment as Secretary of
Legation in some foreign Embassy. . . .*

*I mentioned to you casually that I contemplated removing to
your city. . . . It is proposed to me to take a situation in the New
York University. . . . could I assist you in the discharge of your
duties connected with the Mirror.*[1]

In the fall of 1833, Longfellow traveled overland by stage to
Cambridge to deliver his revised Phi Beta Kappa poem, "The Past
and the Present." On the platform with him was the renowned
orator Edward Everett, in place of the previously invited John
Quincy Adams. Like Longfellow, Everett had returned from his
years of study in foreign universities with a desire to reform the
educational practices of his country, but had soon chafed under
failure in the narrow restrictions of Harvard. Popular, successful,
brilliant, he too had longed for the glamor of a larger stage and
had gladly escaped from teaching through his election to Congress in 1824. In deference to such a noted superior, Longfellow
asked that he be allowed to deliver his poem as a preliminary to
Everett's oration, lest his lines seem colorless in contrast to the
elegant phrases of his colleague. The audience was enthusiastic
beyond the poet's expectation. As Mr. Everett rose to follow him
he prefaced his oration with the gracious remark that his subject
was also "Education," but that he found himself "but a follower
in a field where the flashing sickle had already passed." [2] Plainly,
Longfellow had made a favorable impression. His friends were
delighted, and urged him to publish the entire poem. Wisely, he
refused.

Returning to Bowdoin to begin his fifth year of instruction, he
fell into the accustomed round of classes in French, Spanish,

Italian, and German, using his own textbooks in all classes except the German. Because there was nothing new in the routine to inspire fresh interest, he gave much of his spare time to writing. The second number of *Outre-Mer*, which had been prepared for the printer during the preceding summer, was to have appeared in the fall, but was delayed by Longfellow's indecision as to whether he should be long enough in Brunswick to see it through the press. To the editors of various periodicals he sent occasional contributions: translations of Spanish poetry for Buckingham's magazine, a long article on "Old English Romances" to Alexander Everett, and a review of R. H. Dana's volume of collected *Poems and Prose Writings*. For *The Token* he found little remaining from his "New England Sketches," and was obliged to offer something else—a Spanish tale entitled "The Convent of the Paular." [3]

At the beginning of the winter vacation, a letter from Joseph Green Cogswell at Round Hill electrified him with an immediate prospect of escape. Cogswell wrote that for various reasons he had decided to sell his school:

"I should be truly pleased to have you for my successor at Round Hill; I mean no flattery, but I cannot help saying that a place so beautiful ought to be in the hand of a gentleman of a mind and character like yours. I have made no disposal of the buildings as yet, and as there is no great probability that I shall be able to sell them at once, I would transfer the remainder of my lease, which runs until Jan. 1, 1836, to you on favourable terms: the property belongs to a corporation, a certain number of the shares being mine. The buildings are in fine order and as convenient for the purpose, as any could be, even if they have not originally been built for the present appropriation." [4]

Even the discomfort of cold winter traveling in a stagecoach on runners could not restrain Longfellow from departing, a few days later, to discuss the plan with Cogswell and to consult with Boston friends. On his return he gave a complete account of the journey to Greene:

"I suppose you think I am dead. But it is not so; I am only *buried*—in Brunswick, again, after a most fatiguing and almost useless journey *west*ward ho! which I am about to lay before you in detail.

"About the time I received your first letter, and the books—whose arrival I should have made known to you at the time, had not my brain been too full of thick-coming fancies, to allow me to write even a letter—I heard that Mr. Cogswell of Northampton was about to relinquish the Round Hill School at that place—a school, whose renown must have reached your ears. It seemed to me a glorious opening; and I determined *instanter* to go and see for myself, what were the situation, capabilities, and prospects of this school. So off I started on the coldest day, this *mild* winter has vouchsafed to the children of the North. I stopped a day or two in Boston, to attend to some business of a friend and to get disappointed in a way, which you shall hear of anon. I reached Northampton safe and sound—and remained there two days, devoted to the business of investigating the school. The spot is lovely indeed—lovely even beneath its mantle of snow. I have seen it in summer—and I believe it one of the most beautiful places in New England. But I will not pause to describe it now.

"Mr. Cogswell's propositions were these: Rent of the buildings from next June to January *1836*, including taxes, etc. $1,400. For use of furniture during same time $350; in addition to which he required an advance of $1600—These terms—though they seem high—are not unreasonable when everything is taken into consideration.—The school however is *run down*; and as nothing could warrant such an outlay, but certainty of success—I found it would be necessary to pause and consider. On my return to Boston I consulted with those whose opinions I most valued—and they said the scheme was a bad one—that the school was out of favor with the public—and that it would be very difficult to get it upon its feet again—in short, that I ought not to think of such an undertaking. My friends in Portland are of the same opinion—so that I consider the whole business as blown into thin air—and I awake as from a dream—vanished the pleasant visions of our wandering together through those romantic groves—and of the *golden age* we were to lead in that still retirement.

"And now for my disappointment in Boston—and the reason I had for not paying you a flying visit in Prov'. which, by the way, you must have thought deuced strange. When I left Portland I took only money enough to pay my way to Boston, expecting there to receive money from my books etc. Silly swain that I was! One of my publishers said up and down, that he could not pay me a farthing—and what was most mortifying of all—Allen & Ticknor—to whom I repaired in full-blown confidence—told me with the greatest sang-froid, that not enough copies of the Coplas de Manrique had been sold to defray the expenses of publication! So, not a farthing from them. In fine I was obliged to borrow money to defray my expenses to Northampton. . . .

"I reached Brunswick last night—My wife comes tomorrow; I precede her to get the house in readiness, and the rooms warm, like a dutiful and affectionate husband, as I am.

"Addio. I shall write you again soon, for I have not had room to say half what I wished to." [5]

Mrs. Longfellow was disappointed for her husband, but was relieved to feel that he was not to undertake such a financial burden. "I hope Henry has given up all hope of going to Northampton," she wrote soon after his return to Brunswick. "In doing so he sacrifices very much to the wishes of his friends. The poor fellow has set his heart upon it & I believe he detests Brunswick most cordially." [6] Even an attempt to conceal his critical attitude toward the inhabitants of Brunswick did not deceive certain of the townspeople, who resented his aloofness and superior manners. His failure to conform to the Congregational orthodoxy of Bowdoin accentuated his outspoken disgust for the hysteria of fanatical revivalism which strangled the Bowdoin campus in the spring of 1834. His wife told of the growing tension in a gossipy letter to one of his sisters:

"The 'town is in a great toss' indeed. There is nothing going on or thought of now but these revivals. . . . There has been much excitement. . . . The students are so much excited that they cannot attend to their studies, and Pres't and most of the Professors are in the same state. One of the students had a fit the other day, and Dr. Mussey told them (the revivalists) if they did not let him alone they would kill him. . . . There is not a single house in town that has not been visited by some of them, excepting this. I believe they think we are among the doomed. . . . The other evening at the meeting of the Fire Company Dr. L[incoln] motioned that if Prof. Longfellow's house should burn down no one should move to put it out. Peter O'Slender said it was a very unchristian motion. The Dr. got very much excited, and made the motion again; no one would second it. It was reported that it was because Henry is a Unitarian. . . . The true reason was that Henry has not been to any of their meetings. . . . It ended by turning Henry out of the society. . . . In these exciting times you must not be surprised to hear that our house is set on fire. . . . Henry cares nothing about it, of course, but it is making quite a talk. . . . I suppose if Henry saw this he would not let me send it." [7]

The gradual accumulation of unpleasantness, real and imaginary, tempted Longfellow to force the issue by handing in his resignation at Bowdoin during the spring of 1834. Instead of making any categorical statement to the authorities he said that he intended to resign as soon as he could secure one of the many positions for which he was angling, and received permission from the government of the college to leave his position in the fall of 1834, if he wished. He even went so far as to suggest his friend Greene as a candidate for the vacancy which he was so eager to make.[8]

News of a change in the language department of the University of Virginia set him to writing more letters, one of which asked for the personal influence of a Maine Senator, Hon. Peleg Sprague, in Washington:

"For reasons, which I need not here mention, I have become desirous of leaving Brunswick. My ardent desire is, to obtain an appointment as Secretary of Legation in some foreign Embassy; but this I suppose is impossible at the present moment. I have no friends in power under the present Administration; though I hope hereafter to procure such a situation. *En attendant* a gentleman from Virginia—a friend who is much interested in my success in life—informs me that in all probability I should be able to procure the professorship Mod. Lang. in the University of Va. . . ." [9]

Such enquiries demanded tedious days of waiting before any answer could be expected. Even the appearance of the second part of *Outre-Mer* failed to divert his attention from his prospects. The thin book appeared in May, under the imprint of a new publisher, Lilly, Wait, & Company. Two months later he made a passing mention of the publication in a letter to Greene: "Outre Mer No. 2 seems to succeed admirably. The critics say 'he is a fine boy, and looks like his pa.' " [10] But his main object in writing to Greene was to discuss the situation at New York University:

"Well, the upshot of the whole matter is, that at so great a distance it is impossible to obtain *satisfactory* information. Therefore, on the 31st day of this month I shall leave Brunswick, and on the third of August I shall be in New York. Having started in this matter, I shall not abandon it without having seen with my own eyes.

"The postponement of the election at N. Y. is a *contre-temps* for our arrangements here. All that I can do shall be done—n'en doutez pas. Your name is already before the Executive government of the College backed by my recommendation. I have also spoken with my father upon the subject; and shall converse with other members of the Boards, as soon as I have an opportunity; but all this is of course conditional. I cannot do anything decisive until I have been in N. York. But more of this when we meet. All I can feel sure of is, that if any one takes my place here next autumn you will be the man." [11]

To his hopeful and blindly optimistic eyes the visit to New York University seemed quite promising. Longfellow was admittedly one of the candidates being considered, although there could be no definite answer for anyone until after the University commencement. While in the city, he met a few of the literati—including the Clark brothers, who had recently taken over the editorship of the *Knickerbocker*, George Pope Morris, an editor of the *New York Mirror*, with Nathaniel Willis, a native of Portland. He also paid a visit to the Harpers to ask if their publishing house would bring out the third number of *Outre-Mer*. Unfortunately, Lilly, Wait, & Company had become entangled in financial difficulties and their bad credit had seriously impeded the distribution of the second part. The Harpers were willing to publish the entire series in a single book, but found that Lilly, Wait, & Company wished to use the surrender of their copyright as a means of relieving themselves of the remaining stock. Finally the arrangement was made, and the New York firm promised to publish *Outre-Mer* complete in two volumes as soon as Long-fellow could finish the manuscript.[12]

Shop talk of this sort was wine to Longfellow. He returned to Brunswick filled with new ambitions for participating in the literary activities of the New York circle. He had promised to write for the *Knickerbocker,* the *New Yorker,* and the *Mirror,* and his head was full of a variety of plans for tales, translations, and sketches. But the hope of becoming an editor, not a mere contributor, led him to write to George Pope Morris:

"I mentioned to you casually that I contemplated removing to your city. . . . It is proposed to me to take a situation in the New York University—a professorship of modern languages. This professorship, if created, will be without a salary. I shall be obliged to look for my support, in part at least, to sources disconnected with the university, and I wished to inquire of you whether it would be possible and desirable for me to make some arrangements by which I could assist you in the discharge of your duties connected with the Mirror." [13]

Morris had nothing to offer. The University of Virginia had reached no decision before the Bowdoin commencement took place. And a few days before commencement, a letter from New York University caused Longfellow to relinquish any anticipation of a satisfactory arrangement there. Thus, to his mortification, he was obliged to inform President Allen that he would like to remain at Bowdoin for another year. He reserved permission, however, to resign at short notice.

XVIII

GOOD–BYE TO BRUNSWICK

Everything is in utter confusion in our poor deserted home. All day long rap! rap! ting-a-ling-ling! at the door. Hurry-skurry up-stairs and down! Both tables—the chairs and the carpet are already gone from my study.[1]

BRUNSWICK inspired Longfellow to write one prose tale which won him a prize of fifty dollars in Horace Greeley's *New Yorker*. Giving vent to his long accumulated impatience with back-country manners, he satirized the town and its inhabitants with Irvingesque drollery. Nobody familiar with the appearance of Brunswick could have failed to recognize the picture at the beginning of the story:

"Upon the margin of one of the blue rivers that pour their tributary waters into the broad lap of Merry-meeting Bay, stands the village of Bungonuck,—a drowsy land, where the rush of a waterfall lulls the inhabitants into a dreamy state of existence, leaving them neither quite asleep, nor quite awake. The village is intersected by a wide street, which yawns to receive the weary traveller; while around it are pleasant woodland walks, and groves of pine, that perfume the air, and are cheerful with the bark of the squirrel and the twitter of birds. On an eminence at one extremity of the village stands a meeting-house, all windows. . . . A dial without hands ornaments the front of the tower, and the steeple is surmounted by a weathercock in the shape of a boot-jack; so that instead of asking which way the wind blows, it is customary to say, 'Which way is the boot-jack?' "[2]

The name of Bungonuck was familiar to every inhabitant of Brunswick. The hero of the tale, a gentleman who wore gosling-green clothes, and whom Longfellow called John Schwartkins, was indeed an actual character of that name—an eccentric foreigner who had come to Brunswick from Holland many years earlier. Although the narrator garnished his mystifying tale of the Dutchman's quiet life with a generous sprinkling of satire, the thrusts at his neighbors were characteristically gentle. Longfellow never tore a passion to tatters. Yet he found relief in describing his townsmen with winking malice:

"The choice of town clerk and select-men, or some occurrence of equal importance, occasionally arouses the drowsy villagers from their wonted repose, and rakes open anew the ashes of some half-extinguished family feud. . . . Having very little business of their own, they have ample leisure to devote to the affairs of their neighbors; and it is said, that even to this day, if a Bungonucker wishes to find out what is going on in his own family, the surest and most expeditious way is to ask the person who lives next door." [3]

The story, entitled "The Wondrous Tale of a Little Man in Gosling Green," was submitted to the *New Yorker* contest under the assumed name of Charles F. Brown, through the harmless collusion of Lewis Gaylord Clark. "Well, the Man in Green succeeded in part," wrote Clark as soon as the awards were made, "and should in whole, but for the overpowering solicitude of that venerable spinster Miss Leslie, who inflicted two *pretty* good tales upon the committee, and 'hoped that one would be found worthy the prize.' In consideration, therefore, of her manifold labors, we did award to her one half of the $100 and to Mr. Brown the other." [4]

As a gesture of appreciation for Clark's assistance, Longfellow began to make frequent contributions to the *Knickerbocker*, little dreaming that he should never be paid for any of them. Clark was well-meaning, and if he was not able to pay his writers immediately, he was always prompt with promises. Longfellow sent him two sets of random sketches and observations which were ostensibly pages from the "Blank-Book of a Country Schoolmaster" [5]—seemingly an indolent cousin of the "Schoolmaster" that had appeared in the *New-England Magazine*. This new series enabled him to publish assorted fragments which were not directly related to his travels in Europe or to each other. But he thought that he might eventually use the title to hold together in book form much of the magazine material he had published. In his journal for October 24, 1834, he elaborated the idea:

"Fate seems to decree that my next book after Outre-Mer shall be The Schoolmaster of Bungonuck. Among other matters it will contain:

"1. The Table Book—being sundry sentences and sketches, and scraps of erudition, such as creep into my mind unawares, or are noted down from my reading. Critical remarks on Modern Literature, &c.

"2. Down East—a history of that land of shadows—more pleasant than authentic.

"3. The Wondrous Tale of the Little Man in Gosling Green.

"4. Essays on various topics:

"The Defence of Poetry." [6]

None of his plans at this time included ideas for original poems. Although he had written a dozen translations from the poetry of French, Spanish, and German authors, during the previous years, he had published only one. Yet he liked to think of himself as a poet. "I am flattered that the committee of the Society should have thought of me as a poet," [7] he had written, after receiving the invitation from the Harvard Phi Beta Kappa Society. Perhaps his longing to preserve this thin reputation led him to clip out several lyrics from his Phi Beta Kappa poem in the fall of 1834. Two, entitled "The Dead" and "The Soul," were sent to the *Knickerbocker*. Another, entitled "Truth," was sent to the *Boston Notion*. One good poem, subsequently taken from the same source, was not published until 1842. [8]

Delighted with these various literary enterprises, Longfellow continued to believe that he could become a successful magazine editor. He hated to surrender that dream which had been associated with his earliest ambition. Theophilus Parsons had discouraged him at that time; Morris had offered him no place on the *Mirror*; the Clark brothers were self-sufficient. Yet many men were supporting themselves in such positions. Why should he not start his own magazine? Boston or Cambridge would be a splendid location. In Boston he had met George Hillard, a friend of Cornelius Felton, who was about his age and apparently a brilliant young man. If Hillard would leave the law for a literary career as his partner, Longfellow believed the two of them could make a success of a new and original periodical. In response to such a proposal, Hillard wrote:

"I am sorry that the course of events has not opened some loophole through which you might escape and wend your way to 'fresh fields and pastures new.' With regard to the plan of the literary paper which you propose—you need not be told how much pleasure it would give me to be associated with you or how much confidence I have in your ability to conduct a journal—but the proposal does not at all meet my views, which are altogether professional and not literary. . . . I am afraid, too, that your scheme is hardly desirable or at least advisable, since the ground is very much occupied with every sort of weekly monthly and quarterly periodical and though there is no such one as you propose to support, many take the N. Y. Mirror and many are contented with the wishy-washy stuff they get from the Evening Gazette and such like trumpery. . . .

"I want very much to have you here and I cannot help feeling a conviction that there is a place for you." [9]

Was it possible that Hillard knew something that he could not tell; that a secret plan was under way? Or was this the same answer that he had heard so often before? Everyone assured him that he could expect something soon. But so much unwarranted optimism was depressing. He had filled his mind with so many futile visions of eminent positions for himself—secretary of legation at Madrid, at Paris, at Rome; head master of a school for girls; an editor of the *Mirror;* an editor of his own magazine; owner of the Round Hill School; professor of modern languages at Virginia or at New York University. Such diverse prospects were unified by the common motive of escape. And each seemed to be ending in failure.

Whether Hillard knew or not, Ichabod Nichols and Judge Story were very actively making plans in Cambridge for Longfellow. They knew that the chair of the Smith Professor at Harvard might soon be vacated. In such an event, letters of recommendation would enable them to be forearmed. Simon Greenleaf, a Portland lawyer who had been a trustee at Bowdoin, in 1825, and who had but recently accepted a position at Harvard as Royall Professor of Law, joined the forces of Nichols and Story by writing a letter of enquiry concerning Longfellow's ability as a teacher. He sent it to his friend Ebenezer Everett, a Brunswick resident, and the secretary of the Bowdoin board of trustees. With sly humor, Everett answered:

"BRUNSWICK, October 21, 1834.

"Dear Sir,

"I took up my pen with the intention of giving you a good honest recommendation of my friend, Prof. Longfellow, in reply to your letter of the 17th inst. But recollecting that in case of his removal from this place, I shall lose a valuable neighbor and that the College Corporation of which I am a member, would feel themselves much disconcerted by his resignation, and perplexed to find a suitable successor, I have altered my intention, and must give you a character of him corresponding to the circumstances in which I am placed.

"You can judge what a poor disciplinarian he must be when you find that he keeps himself on such easy friendly terms with the students that discipline has nothing to do in the connection. A scholar, ever so turbulent, would be a singular fellow not to be willing to study French and Spanish from a set of entertaining class books; and if his instructor acts like a gentleman, what has he to quarrel with? Besides this, Mr. Longfellow resides in the village at a considerable distance from the College and has not had so good opportunities practically to perfect himself in governmental tactics, as those have, who are near the scenes of real action and are obliged to leave their warm beds five or six times a term to quench a bonfire, or to close a *vocem et praeterea nihil*. He is young too and it takes many winters to wrinkle up a forehead into real stern majesty, without which no discipline can be efficient.

"Moreover he is not a Clergyman, and how can a man not wearing black, as all but one other of the College Faculty do, and all of every College Faculty ought to do (yourself excepted) carry sufficient gravity *in fronte* to inspire respect, much less awe? I think any serious difficulty with the students would make him feel quite uneasy. If he were a good disciplinarian, he would be more complained of, and I scarcely ever heard anything said against him.

"Bowdoin College has recently had some pretty strict rules from yourself and your respected Colleagues in the Law School on the subject of *vested rights*. The Trustees have lately been taught, that if they or their predecessors have chosen an officer, it is ten to one, but they must choose to keep him so long as he chooses to stay. At our last meeting the subject of Prof. Longfellow's willingness to leave was incidentally brought before them, and a few words were dropped among them about *mutuality*, tho the term of his office seems not to have been expressly defined. In this case the Trustees will be as slow to unlearn your doctrine of vested rights, as they were slow to learn it before; and I suppose in your present situation you would not like to abandon it yourself. Even equitable obligations ought to be reciprocal.

"I believe his attempt to change his situation has not been encouraged by his father nor by his best friends. How far an offer from Harvard might alter their views, I do not know. I should be very sorry to have the experience tried.

"Excuse my evading your plain questions and believe me however very sincerely your friend,

"EBENE^R EVERETT" [10]

This letter was added to others that began to accumulate in President Quincy's office concerning Longfellow. Professor Ticknor, who had retained the Smith Professorship only until he should be satisfied with the department which he had worked so hard to create, was glad to support the candidacy of Longfellow as his successor. He would remain, however, until Longfellow was able to assume the duties at Harvard. Early in December, a letter from President Quincy informed Longfellow that Professor Ticknor was to resign and that he was invited to take his place, with a salary of fifteen hundred dollars. "So here it comes at last," Longfellow wrote almost wearily in his journal,"—the offer of the Professorial chair of Mod^n Lang^e at Harv^d University. Before accepting, let me learn more in detail the duties of the office." [11]

The truly tempting part of the offer was contained in President Quincy's final sentence: "Should it be your wish previously to your entering upon the duties of the office, to reside in Europe, at your own expense, a year or 18 months for the purpose of a more perfect attainment of the German, Mr. Ticknor will retain his office till your return." [12] In his correspondence with Dr. Nichols, Longfellow had asserted that he wished to spend some time in Europe. Apparently his friends had not failed to inform the President. In sending the letter to his father, Longfellow wrote: "Good fortune comes at last, and I shall not reject it. The last paragraph of the letter though put in the form of a permission seems to imply a request. I think I shall accept that also." [13] With the memory of moral and financial worries over the first voyage still fresh in his mind, Stephen Longfellow was not eager to have his son increase his heavy debts or absent himself from home so long a time. He answered:

"It is what I had anticipated, although it has arrived sooner than I expected. . . . With respect to the idea of going again to Europe we all think you must not indulge it or give any reason to expect it. . . . Your compensation at Cambridge will not be better, considering the expenses there, than it now is at Brunswick. It will not more than support you, & you will have nothing to pay debts with. . . .

"Mary was here day before yesterday. She seems delighted with the prospect of change, but not with the idea of going to Europe." [14]

Not even the reluctance of Mary Potter Longfellow could dissuade her husband from his insistence on going abroad. Some unexpressed and secret plan caused him to write to President Quincy that he could give no definite answer, however, until he had made an important visit farther south during the approaching winter vacation. Possibly he still cherished the belief that he might obtain some appointment in a foreign legation, or related capacity, for he went to Washington in the early part of January. Whatever he sought he did not divulge even to such friends as George Greene and Professor Cleaveland. Returning to Portland early in February, he wrote an account of the trip to Professor Cleaveland, mentioning only such incidents as would be of immediate interest to the professor of chemistry and geology. At the close of the letter, Longfellow resumed a subject already thoroughly discussed, no doubt, in front of Cleaveland's fireplace before his departure from Brunswick:

"Well—I have concluded to accept the offer at Cambridge, and shall go to Europe in the Spring. I want to sail, if possible on the first of April; and in order to do this must dissolve my connection with Bowdoin as early as the first of March. Or would the Gov^t prefer that I should not enter on the duties of the next term? I will do as they think best. Mr. Greene says he is willing to supply for me till the close of the College year; so that on that point there will be no embarrassment, if the Gov^t wish the course of instruction to go on unchanged. Please communicate this to the other gentlemen.

"I intend to be in Brunswick about week before the beginning of the term—probably on Monday next. I am not perfectly satisfied with all the manœuvres of the Cambridge corporation; but have concluded after much debate to accede to their terms. This is *sub-rosa*. I will tell you more when we meet; and if you do not exclaim '*That is just like them*'—I am mistaken." [15]

The decision of the Bowdoin government was that the college would use only tutors to complete the year of teaching modern languages and that Greene's services would not be needed, even though they permitted Longfellow to complete his duties early in March. To increase his slender funds for travel, Longfellow sold some of his books to Greene and privately disposed of his furniture. Describing the domestic chaos precipitated by his impatience to be off for Europe, Longfellow wrote, late in February:

"Everything is in utter confusion in our poor deserted home. All day long rap! rap! ting-a-ling-ling! at the door. Hurry-skurry upstairs and down! Both tables—the chairs and the carpet are already gone from my study; the bookcases stand ajar, and beneath yawn sundry boxes, ready to receive their precious freight of books." [16]

Leaving Brunswick on March 11, the Longfellows completed their packing at Portland and stored the books which were not to be sold. To Greene, Longfellow outlined his plans:

"I have concluded you see to go first to London. I shall remain there two or three weeks, and then make the best of my way to Stockholm, where I shall remain until October. The winter will be passed in Berlin—and the succeeding summer in Copenhagen. This is in brief the plan of my journey.

"We go in a company of *four;* two Boston ladies Miss Goddard and Miss Crowninshield having joined our party. This will be very pleasant—and leave me more leisure than if Mary went alone, for being in such a goodly number the ladies will amuse each other, without too much of my assistance. This is a very uncivil speech for me to make; but as I go for the purpose of studying, I shall want as much of the time to myself as possible. I hardly need say that we are all on tip-toe to be gone." [17]

On a bright morning in early April, the party sailed out of New York harbor aboard the ship *Philadelphia*. Behind him, Longfellow left all the gloom of ambitious restlessness which had clouded the past six years. Once again he was running away, much as he had run away from his father's law office nine years earlier. He had not known, then, that he would dislike what he was to find at the end of his running; that he would describe the teaching of foreign languages as *"toujours perdrix."* Setting sail on his second trip he knew all that; he even knew that he would be dissatisfied with teaching at Harvard almost as much as at Bowdoin. That did not matter now, for he was on his way to Europe.

He had grown wiser than the dreamy pilgrim he had been on his first voyage. Gondolas floating lazily on moonlit canals were no longer a part of his vision. And yet he was not going to Europe primarily to prepare himself for his position at Harvard. Vaguely hungry for something the Old World could give him, he was returning to find it. Was his hunger a part of his spiritual and mental dearth? Did he hope to find in his travels and studies a replenishment? He planned to go, not to Germany immediately, but first to England, then to Holland, Denmark, Norway, and Sweden, although his courses would not require a knowledge of Scandinavian literature. But his curiosity needed to be satisfied. He had skimmed the cream from what interested him most in French and Spanish literature and had not yet developed any particular enthusiasm for German and Italian. Because Scandinavian countries were unknown to him, they attracted him with that romantic appeal associated with everything strange.

Thus, in a new sense, he was setting out for Europe once again as a pilgrim, eager to store his mind with recollections and knowledge on which he might feed long after his return to a barren routine.

XIX

EUROPE AND TRAGEDY

Far back stands the peaceful home I have left—and the friends I love are there—and there is a painful parting, and leave taking of those that are never to meet again on earth—and from that far distance my father's face still looks towards me sorrowfully and beseechingly. Thus the year began in sadness. It has closed in utter sorrow. Through the darkness in which it ended, moves a grim and spectral form, armed as with a flail; and the flower my heart cherished—the blessed one—is dead;—and the young tree is smitten down at a blow ere its fruit was ripe.

And now it is, that for the first time in my life,—a life of nearly thirty years—I feel that I am indeed a Pilgrim to the Holy sepulchre. Henceforth let me bear on my shield the holy cross.[1]

ALTHOUGH Longfellow reached England with his heart set on meeting the literary celebrities immediately, he failed to count on the delaying influence of the three attractive ladies who accompanied him. They easily persuaded him to forget, for a few days at least, the precious letters of introduction which would open many doors for him in London. Landing at Portsmouth on the evening of May 8, 1835, the party arranged an intensive itinerary of sight-seeing in the south of England. They began by visiting the Portsmouth Navy Yard and chuckling over the strange cockney pronunciation of their boatman, then took a steamboat ride to the Isle of Wight, went to Newport, and saw Appuldurcombe, the estate of Lord Yarborough. When finally they reached London, the ladies expected their guide to know the name of every park, street, and square, because he had been there in 1829. But he recalled little. Everything about the great city seemed new to him. For a week he played escort to his companions, discovering for them objects of interest that ranged from the Coliseum in Regent's Park to the graves in St. Paul's cathedral. Sir Philip Sidney was buried there, he found, and John Donne, as well as Christopher Wren, who had designed the cathedral after the great fire. How moving were the thoughts inspired by these associations! The Sunday service in St. Paul's was a strange experience for Longfellow. "A thousand echoes mock the hymn," he wrote, "and the peal of the organ; and the continuous rattling of coaches on the pavements without seems like the unbroken roar of the sea." [2] He had come for new sensations and had already begun to find them.

After two weeks of riding and wandering about the city, Longfellow felt free to deliver some of his most important letters. One of these, thanks to his young Boston friend, R. C. Waterston, who had secured it for him, was from Mr. Ralph W. Emerson to Mr. Carlyle. What their connection was, Longfellow scarcely knew, except that Emerson had traveled in Europe a few years earlier and had been greatly impressed with Carlyle. This Englishman had published "Sartor Resartus" in *Fraser's Magazine* and a *Life of Schiller*—neither of which Longfellow had read. Although he found only Mrs. Carlyle at home when he called with Emerson's letter at Number 5, Great Cheyne Row, Chelsea, he was cordially received. As soon as the name of Emerson was mentioned, she began asking questions about America. She wanted so much to go there, she told her caller, and especially wished she might see Emerson again. Longfellow was given a full account of that memorable visit his countryman had made to the Carlyles on their lonely farm in Scotland, and of how the quiet young American had won their hearts. His stay had left an indelible impression. "It was like the visit of an angel," she said, "and though he stayed with us hardly twenty-four hours, yet when he left us I cried —I could not help it." [3]

The loveliness of this alert woman, with her black hair and spirited glances, made Longfellow glad to have her continue talking. The Carlyles, having lived in London less than a year, were acquainted with only a few people. Occasionally their neighbor Leigh Hunt would come in, of an evening, for a bowl of porridge with Carlyle while Mrs. Carlyle played on the pianoforte and sang Scottish ballads. John Stuart Mill, the son of a Scotchman, and like his father a servant of the East India Company, was a younger friend. Mrs. Carlyle could not help repeating the story of the dreadful day when young Mill, wretched with remorse, had stood in this room trying to tell her husband how the manuscript of his work on the French Revolution, which Mill had borrowed, had been destroyed accidentally, by a stupid housemaid. The work was to have been Carlyle's first serious bid for literary fortune after his arrival in London. Its loss was an ill omen. They had begun life so hopefully in the city after selling the farm at Craigenputtock. Chico, their canary, had burst into song, on the morning they had driven with their belongings in a hackney coach to Chelsea—and that had seemed a happy portent. But now— Longfellow nearly wept with her, as she finished.

A few days later, Carlyle appeared at Longfellow's lodgings and carried the American back to Chelsea for the evening. Such a strange man, this Scotchman! Tall, with coal-black hair and a wind-burned complexion. There was nothing prepossessing about his clothes: an old blue coat, brown trousers, and carpet slippers. His actions and gestures were at times almost clownish, Longfellow thought. But when he began to talk, his listener was spellbound. He was not accustomed to such a vehemence of sincerity and such a glorious explosion of words. In speaking of Napoleon, Carlyle said that the General would have made a successful author, as anyone knew who had read his precise and forceful written commands. "He spoke pistol bullets." His guest felt that such a characterization was not unbecoming to Carlyle himself. When he turned to talk of Germany and particularly of the writings of Goethe, Longfellow felt his own contrasting ignorance. He had once looked into *Wilhelm Meister* (which he was surprised to find that Carlyle had translated), but had not liked it. The *Life of Schiller*, he intended to read immediately, although Carlyle spoke slightingly of it and wondered "how anyone can read so tame and colorless a production." [4]

Sitting over his coal fire in his hotel room the following morning, Longfellow began the *Life of Schiller*. Here was the same blunt power of expression which he had liked in yesterday's conversation. But as he read further, he felt the force of new ideas. He had not gone into German literature beyond the occasional lyrics and prose excerpts which he had translated with his small classes at Bowdoin. When he had studied in Göttingen he had spent most of the time on Spanish literature and had found enough trouble mastering even the rudiments of German grammar before returning. Now, under the persuasive enthusiasm of Carlyle he discovered Schiller and was ready to discover Goethe. Late that night he closed the volume with strange emotion. He had been nurtured in a different school—had learned to feel rather than to think. But this book made him sense new and deeper meaning and purpose, suffusing all action. Opening his journal he fumbled vaguely for phrases which might express the new yearning within him: "It is nearly two o'clock in the morning, and I have just finished The Life of Schiller; a truly noble delineation of the life, character and writings of that great and good man. I shall lie down to sleep with my soul quickened and my good resolutions and aspirations strengthened. God grant that the light of morning may not dissipate them all." [5]

At breakfast with the Carlyles a few mornings later, Longfellow was glad to have the discussion return to German literature. Goethe, his host assured him, was the most powerful and important of all German writers. His excitement increased as he discussed the noble character of his hero. As her husband left the room for a moment at the end of the meal, Mrs. Carlyle, answering questions concerning his love for Goethe, said quite simply, "He thinks him the greatest man that ever lived, excepting only Jesus Christ." [6]

Later that morning, Carlyle walked down the street with his guest, to call on Leigh Hunt. Several years older than Carlyle, this early friend of Byron, Keats, and Shelley was no longer the reckless liberal. To Longfellow he appeared as "a thin man of medium stature, with a mop-head of iron gray hair, parted carelessly over his forehead like a girl's and a lively intelligent countenance furrowed deeply with the marks of thought or sorrow." [7] The observer, ignorant of the months Hunt had spent in prison, of the constant hounding of creditors, or of his unhappy life in Italy, concluded from his glance about the room, uncarpeted and very plainly furnished, that Hunt must be an author whom the booksellers had used ill.

At Hunt's door, Carlyle took leave with German warmth of feeling. "God bless you!" he said. "A pleasant journey to you; and when you return to London do not forget to inquire us out!" [8]

Not all of Longfellow's experiences with literary people in

London were so pleasant or fruitful as these visits with Carlyle.
Truly, nothing else compared with them. He had been eager
to meet the author of *Pelham*, but his one encounter with the
gentleman was unpleasant. As he called one morning with a letter
from Lewis G. Clark, Bulwer and his brother were just walking
down the steps. They were handsome men, but dandies, dressed
according to the most fashionable taste of the day.

"Is this Mr. Bulwer?" Longfellow ventured.

"I am Mr. Bulwer, and this is Mr. Bulwer," said the author, with
a silly, lisping accent.

Longfellow, delivering the letter without answer, waited while
Bulwer broke the seal and played with the letter. He made no
pretense to read it. When told that it was from Mr. Clark in
America he asked,

"A letter of introduction?"

"Yes, sir."

"Oh—I am very glad to see you." He extended his hand. "At
this moment I am engaged, but shall be happy to have you call any
morning."

Longfellow felt that some further word of explanation or
apology was due and spoke of his hesitancy in delivering a letter
from Clark without having ascertained the relation of the two
authors. Bulwer confessed that Clark was a "correspondent,"
added that he hoped Longfellow would call again, then walked
off, leaving young Brother Jonathan at the foot of the steps, hurt
and angry. From that day, Longfellow lost some of his taste for
the novels of Sir Edward Lytton Bulwer.[9]

Another distressing occasion arose when he was invited to
breakfast with Sir John Bowring, the poet, translator, and reviewer, to whom he had brought a letter from Jared Sparks.
Describing the visit in his journal, he wrote,

"Breakfasted with Bowring, hoping to have a pleasant tête-à-
tête with him—and an opportunity of correcting my former impression of his talents—if incorrect they were. In this I was disappointed. Another gentleman was with him when I arrived—
and soon after his wife came in, and we sat down to tea and toast.
There was a large package of letters by the morning post upon
the table, which the Dr. & his lady proceded to open and read,

while the other gentleman who seemed to be one of the family pored over the columns of a newspaper. This is a novel fashion, thought I, of receiving a guest. But as the Germans say, 'Ländlich, sittlich'—every country has its customs; and calling to mind the old proverb of Rome and the Romans, I reached back to a side table, and seized upon a book, in which I forthwith began to read, thereby conveying a gentle hint unto mine hosts, though they heeded it not.

"There was very little conversation at breakfast, and I felt some relief when it was over; though before we left the table an artist was introduced, who is now occupied in taking a bust of Bowring—and not long afterwards, a French gentleman . . .

"But after all, I heard nothing worth recording or remembering; and came away more than ever impressed with the idea, that Dr. Bowring is not a profound man—and very much overrated." [10]

Perhaps the greatest causes for concern and mystification on Longfellow's part were the manners and habits of his fellow-townsman Nathaniel Parker Willis, who, in spite of some antagonism in London, resulting from his recent and indecorous remarks concerning English society, still claimed a degree of popularity extraordinary for an American author. Mrs. Longfellow thought Willis had improved in appearance since last she had seen him in Portland. She agreed with her husband that he had become quite as much a dandy as Bulwer, dressed in his carefully fitted snuff-colored coat, with a rose in his buttonhole, and always bustling from one social engagement to another: breakfast with Lady Blessington, an afternoon with the Duchess of St. Albans, or a week-end at Mrs. Skinner's in Shirley Park. The Longfellows, attending some of the social functions with Willis, were amused to see how the ladies fawned about their countryman. Mrs. Skinner ("a lion-feeder," according to Willis) confided to Mrs. Longfellow that she thought Willis's writings far superior to those of Irving. She was so charmed with his graces that she felt certain "the Americans had sent him out as a *specimen* of their elegant and polished manners, in order to contradict Mrs. Trollope's remarks!" [11] Writing to Greene a few days later, Longfellow confided his own reaction:

"I saw Willis in London. His orbit is *high* among the stars and *garters* of the fashionable Zodiac. He was very polite;—but there was no very hearty fellowship between us. It was evident that I hung heavy upon his skirts, like a country cousin. He is too artificial. And his poetry has now lost one of its greatest charms for me—its sincerity. This is strictly *sub rosa*. I do not wish to join the hue and cry against him." [12]

Another friend of former days whom Longfellow found in London was Obadiah Rich, the Madrid consul, now a bookseller. His collection of books and manuscripts relating to America, enhanced by his knowledge of this specialized field, had enabled him to establish a flourishing business with little trouble. To him Longfellow carried questions concerning the purchase of books for Harvard. Commissioned to buy whatever he thought valuable to his department at Harvard, he was glad to share such a problem with this learned bibliographer. But no book could be purchased until Longfellow had made sure that the title was not in the clumsy five-volume Harvard Library Catalogue which he was obliged to cart about with him.[13]

Rich also helped him to secure an English publisher for *Outre-Mer*. There was a certain Thomas Tegg, he said, the successful editor and proprietor of a "Family Library," who had expressed his interest in *Outre-Mer*. Longfellow called, and found a shrewd fellow who had learned to make easy money by pirating editions from British and American publishers. Would Mr. Tegg like to have the rights to *Outre-Mer* for one hundred pounds sterling, the Yankee asked. The pirate's great eyes bulged with incredulity.

"Oh no! Impossible!" he exclaimed. "Why, in three weeks I can get it for nothing!" [14]

Obviously, the British publishers were not averse to retribution for American thefts whenever they could find anything worth stealing. Cooper and Irving had already perfected systems whereby they avoided such losses. Obadiah Rich suggested that Bentley might bring out Longfellow's book, but would not pay much. "They tell me he is a good publisher," Longfellow wrote, "for those who are willing to give their books away." [15] An arrangement was made with this man whose white hair and courteous ways softened the blunt practicality of his red face. "I am

to have half the profits," Longfellow told Greene, "which I suppose means, what he chooses to give me—that is, nothing. I have
no golden dreams." [16]

After spending a month in London, Longfellow and his party
embarked for Hamburg aboard the packet *William Joliffe*. As
the boat swung away from the dock and headed down the Thames
in the dusk of an early June evening, he looked back at the slightly
blurred outlines of the city and was immediately caught in the
dreamy atmosphere of the picture. Here was the literary sustenance which he had learned to seek. Here was material from
which he could fashion Irvingesque broideries. The seeds of
maturer thought, which Carlyle with his impassioned monologues
on German literature had imbedded firmly in Longfellow's mind,
would need the quickening stimulus of grief before they would
germinate. Although the time was near, Goethe and Schiller
were not yet able to compete with Irving's influence. The sketch
of this evening scene was recorded in his journal with all the soft
pastel shades of a Claude Lorrain:

"Went on board the steamer at sun-set. Sat on deck, and
watched the gradual fall of evening on the river. Lamps gleaming
along shore—and on the bridges—a full moon rising over the borough of Southwark, and silvering the scene with a ghostly light.
The moonbeam crinkles on the ripling water—wherein also flares
the reflection of the shore-lamps with a lambent, flickering gleam.
Barges & wherries move to and fro; and heavy-laden luggers are
sweeping up stream with the rising tide, swinging sideways, with
loose-flapping sails. Either side of the river is crowded with various sea-craft, whose black hulls lie in shadow, and whose tapering
and mingling spars rise up into the moon-light like the leafless
branches of a grove in winter. The distant sound of music floats
on the air—a harp and a flute and a horn—It has an unearthly
sound; and lo! like a shooting star a light comes gliding on. It is
the signal-lamp at the mast-head of a steam-vessel, that flits by
like a spectre; unseen, save as a cloud, above which glides a silver
star;—unheard, save by the beating paddles and the fairy music
on its deck. And from all this scene goes up a sound of human
voices, curses, laughter and singing—mingling with the monoto-

nous roar of the city—as its living tides ebb at evening through their paved channels—slowly settling like the ocean-currents to their bed.

"Gradually all sound and motion cease; the river tide is silent at its flood; and from the slumbering city comes only now and then a voice—a feeble murmur.

———

"Midnight is passed. Hark! the clock strikes. One—two. Far distant from some church-tower in the suburbs comes the first sound, so indistinct as hardly to be distinguished from the crowing of a cock. Then nearer—close at hand, with a heavy, solemn sound the great bell of Saint Pauls—with a long interval between the strokes—one!—two!—It is answered from the borough of Southwark; then another bell at a distance like an echo—one, two —and then all around you with various and intermingling clang, like a chime of bells—the clocks from thirty towers strike the hour —One—two! One—two!

———

"The moon is already sinking,—large and fiery—through the vapors of the morning. It is just in the range of the chimneys and house-tops, and seems to follow us with great speed, as we float down the river. Day is dawning in the east—not with a pale streak in the horizon—but with a faint silver light spread through the eastern sky almost to the zenith. It is the mingling of moonlight and daylight. The water is tinged with a green hue melting into purple and gold, like the brilliant scales of a fish. The air grows cool. It comes fresh from the eastern sea, towards which we are swiftly gliding." [17]

Such an experience spelled peace, and a return to the moments of hushed reverence which he had known at midnight in the shadow of the Alhambra many years earlier. Far behind him was the drudgery and isolation from which he had so joyously escaped—far, far away, in both distance and time. To float dreamily on the current of life after such industrious years was a pleasant recompense for unhappiness.

The remainder of the voyage to Hamburg was uneventful except for diverting conversations with the Scotch captain—"a rough old fellow, with a carrotty wig, and a face like a rotten apple." [18] From Hamburg the party continued through Lübeck and Copenhagen to Gothenburg, where they intended taking ship passage to Stockholm. But the fortnightly boat had left shortly before their arrival and this misfortune led the party to choose overland travel to Stockholm rather than to wait. The carriage journey of five days was made without incident, but also without particular pleasure, for the heat of the sun and the tedious miles grew irksome.

Misfortune began to press hard after Longfellow. When he tried to make arrangements for studying the language in Stockholm he found that many of the notables to whom he had brought letters were absent from the city for the summer. Nicander, the Swedish poet whom he had met in Italy eight years earlier, was spending some time in a distant part of the country. Berzelius, the professor under whom he had wished to study, left Stockholm for Paris two days after Longfellow's arrival. To add to these unpleasant conditions, the summer rains began at the end of June and continued, with raw and dreary days, for two weeks. After some searching, Longfellow discovered that Professor Lignel of the University of Upsala was in the city and would help him with his studies. Within a fortnight he had made a little progress. "I am slowly picking up crumbs in the Swedish language," he wrote, "while old Lignel *scratches* for me. Slow work —slow work. It comes word by word, and phrase by phrase." [19] Not satisfied, however, with this single study, he began to explore the Finnish language.

The summer passed uneventfully. Mary Longfellow, who had not been well since the party left England, began to need close attention. Troubled by the delicacy of her condition, Longfellow was willing to cut short his unsatisfactory stay in Sweden. He spoke candidly of his disappointment in a letter to Greene:

"We have now been about two months in Sweden; and shall leave it without regret in about a fortnight, to return no more for-ever—I trust. From which pious ejaculation you will infer, that I have not been much pleased with my 'Summer in the North.' It is indeed so. Stockholm is a very pretty city;—'et quand on a dit cela, on a tout dit.' There is no spirit—no life—no enterprise—in a word—'*no nothing*.' Literature is in an abject condition; and notwithstanding the many great names, that adorn the armorial bearings of Sweden, you cannot help seeing all around you that 'la stupidité est d'uniforme.' And then it is so cold here! It is August —but it is not Summer. The rain it raineth every day; and the air is like November. I was simple enough to go out yesterday without a greatcoat and umbrella; for which scandalous conduct I was drenched through by a tremendous rain; and pelted for fifteen minutes with hail-stones as large as peas. I was on the water, in an open boat. 'O for a beaker full of the warm south!' I shall seek one soon. I wish it were to-day." [20]

Leaving Stockholm, the party went by water to Gothenburg, but was delayed there once again. "Here is 'the devil to pay and no pitch hot!' " Longfellow wrote in exasperation. "The steamer has arrived from Christiania, with so many passengers, that we can have no place except on deck, which will not do for a night-passage. So here we must stay for a week!" [21] His anxiety was increased by Mary's illness, which made him eager to be done with traveling. If only he could bring her safe to Heidelberg, where he intended to spend the winter, he would be free from worry. After five days of impatient waiting at Gothenburg, he turned to his journal: "Monday 7. Heigho! the time drags lazily on. . . . If I were not in such a hurry to get to the Rhine, I should not care a fig. But as it is, every hour is precious." [22]

Yet he did not go there directly. He had arranged to stay two weeks in Copenhagen, that he might have at least a nodding acquaintance with the Danish language, under the tutelage of professors at the University there. To increase his cares, Miss Goddard received a letter from Boston bringing the sad intelligence that her father had died. Arrangements were made for her immediate departure, which reduced the party to three.

From London, Longfellow learned that the English edition of *Outre-Mer* was being given favorable reviews; and from George Pierce in Portland he received clippings from American papers. In acknowledgment he wrote:

"The puffs you sent were quite luxuriant; yet not to be compared with the *palmy exuberance* of the London press. Take the following 'beautiful morceau' as a sample.

" '—The scenes among which our traveller loves to linger are the gothic temple, the neglected, the deserted or the ruined castle, and the softer kind of landscape. His favorite stories are the humorous, with a touch of the satirical, or *the elegantly pensive —melancholy, yet not despairing!* (O, Cockney!) Either the author of the Sketch Book has received a warning, or there are two Richmonds in the field.'

"If you do not laugh heartily at this, I shall feel hurt. Notwithstanding all this, I believe the book is doing well in London; but having received no exact intelligence from the publisher, I cannot speak with certainty. I have not even seen a London copy." [23]

The circumstances under which he first examined a copy of the English edition were amusing even to him. The day after he wrote to Pierce he called upon a Mr. Woodside, recently come to Copenhagen from England as minister in the English legation. The episode was recorded by Longfellow in detail:

"As I was looking over his small library, I discovered on the lower shelf a copy of Outre Mer; and exclaimed;

" 'Ah! you have a copy of that book, I see.'

" 'Yes. I brought it from London. It is very highly spoken of there, but for my part I do not discover so much merit in it.'

" 'Hem!'

" 'By the way; have you a copy of *your* book?'

" 'This is my book'—uttered solemnly; at the same time holding up the volume of Outre Mer, which I had in my hand.

"The minister looked blank; and the author continued;

" 'I am glad to hear your opinion of the book before you knew me to be the author of it.'

"This was said with one of those desperate smiles which conventional politeness obliges us to put on, when we swallow a bitter pill and are ready to swallow the doctor after it. He replied;

" 'I have spoken more candidly in my ignorance than I might otherwise have done; but had I known you to have been the author I should not have given my opinion quite so abruptly. And now I must give you my reasons for the opinion I have expressed. There are many pretty things in the book; but I had heard it so highly spoken of, that I was disappointed. I will tell you what I do not like.'

"Here he turned to the chapter on the 'Old English Prose Romances.'

" 'This paper I think is too trivial. A man of your talents'— (sweetly put in, that)—'might employ his time to more advantage than writing about such foolish stories as Robert the Devil.'

" 'That objection would apply to the whole book. True—in a certain sense you are right. But let me set the matter before you in another point of view. These old stories—though trivial in themselves, are not so as scraps of literary history. I put the paper into my book as you put a Chinese ornament on your mantlepiece, not for its intrinsic value, but because it illustrates manners, customs and feelings of another age or country.'

" 'Yes; you explain this in the paper itself.'

" 'Have you read both volumes of the work?'

" 'No; I have read only the first.'

" 'I think you will like the second better!' " [24]

The question which Mr. Woodside was asking was related closely to those which John Neal and others had already asked. In Copenhagen, as in America, he dismissed the subject casually with rationalizations about quaint ornaments for literary mantelpieces. Most of his readers, happily, were not so critical, for they liked having two Richmonds in the field. Fortuitously, the cultural tastes of the period helped to conceal the true answer.

Occasionally there is a perversity about chance which seems to endow it with malicious power over all human precautions. For Mary's sake, Longfellow arranged to travel from Copenhagen to Hamburg by boat rather than by carriage, and by boat from Hamburg to Amsterdam, where he wished to study Dutch briefly before going to Heidelberg. But the passage to Amsterdam was so rough that medical care was needed for Mary Longfellow immediately after her arrival there. That night she was brought to the verge of death by the premature birth of her child. For several days she remained dangerously ill. Three weeks later, after slow recovery, she felt well enough to travel, and was eager to continue to Rotterdam. Although the overland journey was made slowly in three days, the effort proved so exhausting that she suffered a relapse.

Pleasant and quiet rooms were found for the unhappy party

at the Hotel des Pays Bas. Longfellow believed that the worst of the illness was over; that nothing was needed but patience and a long rest. Even during days of hopeful improvement, however, Mary was not able to leave her bed. While waiting for her expected recovery, Longfellow continued the study of Dutch which he had begun at Amsterdam. Occasionally he varied his research by delving into books of Danish and Scandinavian literature at a near-by library. There he found a newly published English translation of Tegnér's *Frithiofs Saga* which seemed so poor that he was tempted to undertake a translation of his own.

Such thoughts recalled the long interval which had elapsed since he had found time or inclination for making verses. Here was leisure for trying. "Sat up late at night writing poetry," he wrote in his journal, "—the first I have written for many a long, long day. Pleasant feelings of the olden time came over me; of those years when as yet a boy, I gave so many hours to rhymery! I wonder whether I am destined to write anything in verse, that will live?" [25]

One of Longfellow's acquaintances in Rotterdam was Dr. Samuel Bosworth, a scholarly Episcopal clergyman who had been working for the past fifteen years on the compilation of an Anglo-Saxon dictionary. Learning that Bosworth was in Rotterdam, Longfellow remembered how he had once imported from England an Anglo-Saxon grammar which Bosworth had edited, and decided to call on the gentleman. The friendship thus established was to continue for many years. Occasionally the clergyman called on Mary Longfellow, to offer his sympathetic ministrations.

As day followed day she grew so much weaker that Longfellow gradually lost his optimism. On November 24 he wrote: "My poor Mary is worse to-day. Sinking—sinking. My heart is heavy; yet still I hope—perhaps too fondly." In the early morning of November 29, 1835, she died. "This morning between one and two o'clock, my Mary—my beloved Mary—ceased to breathe. She is now, I trust, a Saint in Heaven. Would that I were with her. This morning I have knelt beside her, and kissed her cold lips, and prayed to God, that hereafter in moments of temptation, I might recall that solemn hour, and be delivered from evil." [26]

Overwhelmed with this unexpected tragedy, he wrote to Judge Potter in Portland:

"ROTTERDAM, Dec. 1, 1835

"My dear Sir,

"I trust that my last letter to my father has in some measure prepared your mind for the melancholy intelligence which this will bring to you. Our beloved Mary is no more. She expired on Sunday morning, Nov. 29, without pain or suffering, either of body or mind, and with entire resignation to the will of her heavenly father. Though her sickness was long, yet I could not bring myself to think it dangerous until near its close. Indeed, I did not abandon all hope of her recovery till within a very few hours of her dissolution, and to me the blow was so sudden, that I have hardly yet recovered energy enough to write you the particulars of this solemn and mournful event. When I think, however, upon the goodness and purity of her life, and the holy and peaceful death she died, I feel great consolation in my bereavement, and can say, 'Father, thy will be done.'

"Knowing the delicate state of Mary's health, I came all the way from Stockholm with fear and trembling, and with the exception of one day's ride from Kiel to Hamburg we came the whole distance by water. Unfortunately our passage from Hamburg to Amsterdam in the Steamboat was rather rough, and Mary was quite unwell. On the night of our arrival the circumstance occurred to which I alluded in my last, and which has had this fatal termination. . . . In Amsterdam we remained three weeks; and Mary seemed to be quite restored and was anxious to be gone. To avoid a possibility of fatigue we took three days to come to this place—a distance of only forty miles; and on our arrival here Mary was in excellent spirits and to all appearances very well. But alas! the same night she had a relapse which caused extreme debility, with a low fever, and nervous headache. This was on the 23rd October. In a day or two she was better, and on the 27th worse again. After this she seemed to recover slowly, and sat up for the first time on the 11th, though only for a short while. This continued for a day or two longer, till she felt well enough to sit up for nearly an hour. And then she was seized with a violent rheumatism, and again took to her bed from which she never more arose.

"During all this she was very patient, and generally cheerful, tho' at times her courage fainted and she thought that she should not recover,—wishing only that she could see her friends at home once more before she died. At such moments she loved to repeat these lines, which seemed to soothe her feelings:—

> "Father! I thank thee! may no thought
> E'er deem thy chastisements severe.
> But may this heart, by sorrow taught
> Calm each wild wish, each idle fear.

"On Sunday, the 22nd, all her pain had left her, and she said she had not felt so well during her sickness. On this day, too, we received a letter from Margaret [her sister], which gave her great pleasure, and renovated her spirits very much. But still from day to day she gained no strength. In this situation she continued during the whole week—perfectly calm, cheerful and without any pain. On Friday another letter came from Margaret, and she listened to it with greatest delight. A few minutes afterwards a letter from you and Eliza was brought in, which I reserved for the next day. When I went to her on Saturday morning I found her countenance much changed, and my heart sank within me. Till this moment I had indulged the most sanguine hopes;—but now my fears overmastered them. She was evidently worse, though she felt as well as usual. The day passed without change; and towards evening, as she seemed a little restless and could not sleep, I sat down by her bedside, and read your letter and Eliza's to her. O, I shall never forget how her eyes and her whole countenance brightened, and with what a heavenly smile she looked up into my face as I read. My own hopes revived again to see that look; but alas! this was the last gleam of the dying lamp. Towards ten o'clock she felt a slight oppression in the chest, with a difficulty of breathing. I sat down by her side and tried to cheer her; and as her respiration became more difficult, she said to me, 'Why should I be troubled; If I die God will take me to himself.' And, from this moment she was perfectly calm, excepting for a single instant, when she exclaimed, 'O, my dear Father; how he will mourn for me.' A short time afterwards she thanked Clara for her kindness, and clasping her arms affectionately round my neck, kissed me, and said, 'Dear Henry, do not forget me!' and after this, 'Tell my dear friends at home that I thought of them at the last hour.' I then read to her from the Church Litany the prayers for the sick and dying; and as the nurse spoke of sending for Dr. Bosworth, the Episcopal clergyman, Mary said she should like to see him, and I accordingly sent. He came about one o'clock, but at this time Mary became apparently insensible to what was around her; and at half-past one she ceased to breathe.

"Thus all the hopes I had so fondly cherished of returning home with my dear Mary in happiness and renovated health have in the providence of God ended in disappointment and sorrow unspeakable. All that I have left to me in my affliction is the memory of her goodness, her gentleness, her affection for me—unchangeable in life and in death—and the hope of meeting her again hereafter, where there shall be no more sickness, nor sorrow, nor suffering, nor death. I feel, too, that she must be infinitely, oh, infinitely happier now than when with us on earth, and I say to myself,—

"Peace! peace! she is not dead, she does not sleep!
She has awakened from the dream of life.

"With my most affectionate remembrance to Eliza and Margaret, and my warmest sympathies with you all, very truly yours,
"HENRY W. LONGFELLOW." [27]

What should he do now? Arrangements had been made for sending his wife's body to America. But to what purpose should he accompany it? He might try to carry out his original plan for study in Germany during the winter, although he had little courage for beginning against the knife-edge of grief. At least, there was no longer anything for him in Rotterdam except bitter remorse. His father's words of persistent dissuasion returned to torture him—together with the memory of Mary's reluctance. Sick at heart, he set out for Heidelberg.[28]

XX

WINTER IN HEIDELBERG

I cannot recover my energies, either mental or bodily. I take no interest in anything—or at most only a momentary interest. All my favorite and cherished literary plans are either abandoned, or looked upon as a task which duty requires me work out, as a day-laborer. Other tastes and projects have begun to spring up in my mind; though as yet all is in confusion. In a word, sometimes I think I am crazed—and then I rally—and think it is only nervous debility:— sometimes I sit at home and read diligently—and then for days together I hardly open a book.[1]

MARY's death had thrown Longfellow's world into such confusion that he wondered how he could ever study in Heidelberg. Although the ancient and picturesque town was pleasant, and the sisterly thoughtfulness of Clara Crowninshield (who had taken rooms near by) was comforting, there was no heart in him for work. The heaviness that restrained him from almost any exertion was compounded with remorse stronger, at times, than grief itself. Now that the reproachful faces of his friends and relatives kept crowding his imagination, he remembered how stubbornly and blindly he had refused advice; how he had insisted on going to Europe. And such thoughts tended to place on his shoulders more of the blame than he could stand.

After taking rooms in the home of Frau Himmelhahn, only two doors west of the Karlstor, he spent many hours walking about the ruins of the old castle on the hill that towered above his lodgings, or along the banks of the river Neckar, below. But there was no escape from his thoughts. As best he could, Longfellow tried to rearrange values in accordance with new perceptions.

In the shadow of death, all desire for eminence seemed pitiably absurd. Was it possible that such an empty prize as fame had been his objective from the day when his success in publishing his college verses had led him to dream of a literary career? Even his years of teaching at Bowdoin had been filled with industry deliberately aimed to increase his reputation as a man of letters and a scholar. Those long articles for the *North American,* so conveniently fashioned from histories of literature; the many translations of poems which he had sent to the *New-England Magazine;* the extracts from his Phi Beta Kappa poem which had helped preserve his reputation as a poet—all these had been prompted more by a passion for eminence than by a genuine desire to express himself or to contribute to the cultural growth of his culture-hungry land.

Suddenly this kind of literary aspiration appeared shameful. George Greene, again in Italy because of failing health, wrote complaining of his own unfulfilled desires. From Heidelberg, Longfellow answered him:

"Above all put your heart at ease, and banish that '*corroding ambition*' which you speak of. O I wish I could be with you, speak with you for one half-hour. I think I could set the matter in such a point of view, that you would feel the tooth of the destroyer no more. You have a higher and nobler motive of action within you, believe me. . . .

"Look into your own heart, and you will find the motive there. It is the love of what is intellectual and beautiful—the love of literature—the love of holy converse with the minds of the great and good—and then speaking the truth in what you write, and thereby exercising a good influence on those around you, bringing them so far as you may, to feel a sympathy with 'all that is lovely and of good report.' Think of this, my dear George, and your heart will be lighter.

"For my own part, I feel at this moment more than ever, that fame must be looked upon only as an accessory. If it ever has been a principal object with me—which I doubt—it is now no more so." [2]

That same night, after completing the letter to Greene, he elaborated the same ideas in his journal. Here for the first time occurred some of the basic thoughts which found sincere expression in "A Psalm of Life" less than three years later:

"Answered Greene's letter. He complains of 'corroding ambition.' Thank heaven, I feel it not. If I know my own heart, I labor from a higher motive than this; and so does my friend Greene, tho' he knows it not.

"Literary ambition! away with this destroyer of peace and quietude and the soul's self-possession! The scholar should have a higher and holier aim than this. He should struggle after truth; he should forget himself in communion with the great minds of all ages; and when he writes it should be not to immortalize himself, but to make a salutary and lasting impression on the minds of others. A speaker, whose thoughts are occupied solely or mainly with himself, generally speaks badly; but when he feels the truth and importance of what he is saying, and forgetful of himself strives only to fix this truth in the hearts of his hearers, he generally speaks well. Is it not likewise so to a certain extent with writers?

"Let our object, then, be, not to build ourselves up, but to build up others, and leave our mark upon the age we live in, each according to the measure of his talent. To oppose error and vice, and make mankind more in love with truth and virtue—this is a far higher motive of action than mere literary ambition." [3]

Here were new ideas springing directly from experience. Underlying them was the ingrained utilitarian New England principle of service which Longfellow had kept so well in mind when, in his *Defence of Poetry* essay, he had justified poetry by concluding that it should aim "to give us correct moral impressions, and thereby advance the cause of truth and the improvement of society." [4] At present, these ideas were being given corroboration by the writings of the German authors whom Longfellow was reading.

Although Carlyle's worshipful enthusiasm for German writers had been the strongest influence in guiding the young American's interest, his sudden bereavement had enabled him to understand how completely appropriate to his own heartache was the sentiment of German romantic literature. The verses of Uhland, Salis, and Matthisson, which he had begun to read in Rotterdam, quickened the poet in Longfellow. But the lines of Novalis found largest response. This young German, who had wept alone over a grave in the twilight and had fashioned "Hymns to the Night" in his grief, spoke an emotional language which Longfellow, schooled in New England reticence, had never learned. And yet he could now understand and accept the mystical communion such as Novalis held with the spirit of his beloved in the holy solitude of night. Like Novalis, he also brooded over his loneliness and at times lost the bitterness of his sorrow, in remembrance. For she returned to Longfellow in the hours of darkness. "I will be with you," she had promised, as she lay dying.[5] In Heidelberg, this strange old medieval town on the Rhine, he found solace in that assurance:

"The clock is even now striking ten. I am sitting alone in my new home; and yet not all alone—for the spirit of her, who loved me, and who I trust still loves me—is with me. Not many days before her death she said to me: 'We shall be so happy in Heidelberg!' I feel assured of her presence—and am happy in knowing that she is so. O my beloved Mary—teach me to be good, and kind, and gentle as thou wert when here on earth . . ." [6]

Always, he returned to his reading—page after page, book after book—and into each he read the story of his own life, his own sorrow. The strange weird sentiment of *Sturm und Drang* literature was palatable food for his hunger. Without coherent direction he devoured Goethe's *Sorrows of Werther, Faust,* and *Wilhelm Meister,* Jean Paul's *Titan* and his fantastic sketch entitled "The Death of an Angel," Schiller's *Don Carlos* and Novalis's *Heinrich von Ofterdingen.*

George Ticknor, who had been crushed one year earlier by the loss of his only son, wrote Longfellow that salvation lay in "constant and interesting intellectual labor." [7] He would try that; he would make a thorough survey of all German literature. For several days he worked hard, compiling many pages of notes and arranging them to form a syllabus. He attended lectures, visited occasionally with such learned professors as Gervinus, Bertrand, and Mittermaier—and studied in the cold University library until he nearly froze to death. But the effort failed.

That failure was closely related to the deep change taking place in Longfellow. The tragedy of Mary's death was a turning point in his life: the end of youth and the beginning of manhood. Although twenty-eight when he had set out for Europe on this second trip, he had shown no sign of deep intellectual or emotional development. Not until the intense anguish had torn down the pretty veil of sentiment, had he looked squarely at the unpleasant side of life. But keener perceptions and insight had prompted the writing of his first Heidelberg letter to Greene.

Pitilessly confronted by the implications of Mary's death, he had slowly been taking account of stock. What was literary ambition worth? Was the purpose of dusty research merely a bid for eminence? Did he really want to follow Ticknor along the paths of scientific German scholarship? Something more fundamental than the deep but transient heartbreak of that winter in Heidelberg lay beneath his inability to accept Ticknor's advice. Although he had a flair for foreign languages and a pilgrimlike reverence for the antique, the strange, the grotesque in foreign lands and literatures, Longfellow could do better with his gifts than spend them in the superficial kind of fact-hunting and borrowings from literary histories, which had gone into the *North American Review* articles.

This he began to learn in Heidelberg. His love of the German romantic poets taught him to shift the emphasis in his life to the language of sentiment and the emotions, where his real strength lay, rather than to emulate the intellectual feats of Ticknor. He could not yet guess that this change which was brought about by the German poets would lead him back to his boyhood zest for writing songs; that the sweet cadences of his long-silent voice would carry so far and touch many hearts throughout the world. But the foundation for this rise to fame as a singer was laid during this winter. Here was the rich soil from which conviction and confidence would grow slowly. In Heidelberg he was still too close to sorrow.

Werther's solution of his troubles was too pagan and terrible to satisfy Longfellow. Goethe's hero seemed to act from reasons and motives that were too weak. Yet he found much in the strange book which made him eager to defend it against the sneers of his countrymen. As he put it in his journal, there was a simple explanation of Werther's actions:

"To a man placed in a similar situation with Werther, and like him without a fixed Christian rule of conduct—they might seem powerful. His reflections are demons grim and terrible—like those that of old in bodily shape beset the saints—and like them they vanish at the sign of the cross." [8]

Goethe's *Wilhelm Meister* had an entirely different effect. Although he made little comment on *Wilhelm Meister* until after his return home, his letter to Greene was a confession of faith in a new course of action not unlike Meister's. Longfellow was serving an apprenticeship in living; trying to work out a pattern of conduct worthy of a beautiful soul—and Goethe said much to him that he could not have understood a year earlier.

The winter was not all gloomy and solitary. Frau Himmelhahn, the landlady, was always ready to amuse him with her gossipy stories. Clara Crowninshield and Julie Hepp were near at hand to entertain him with evenings of card playing or spirited arguments on the relative merits of Goethe and Schiller.[9] He went frequently to the Hepps for friendly visits. Furthermore, he made the acquaintance of William Cullen Bryant, who was spending the winter in Heidelberg with his family. No other man's poetry had exercised stronger influence on Longfellow during his early student days at Bowdoin. And he was quick to acknowledge it to Bryant when they met. "Let me say what a stanch friend and admirer of yours I have been from the beginning," he told him, "and acknowledge how much I owe to you, not only of delight, but of culture. When I look back upon my earlier years I cannot but smile to see how much in them is really yours." [10] Thus meeting his countryman for the first time, Longfellow was pleased with the calm and thoughtful repose of Bryant's face—and his expressive blue eyes. Bryant was fond of walking, and the two American poets made frequent trips together up into the hills or along the valley roads near the old town, until unexpected business difficulties on the *New York Evening Post* required Bryant's departure.

Neither friendships nor scholarship prevented the recurrence of depression. Into his journal notes on reading crept repeated cries of anguish:

"I cannot study. One thought occupies me night and day. She is dead—she is dead!—All day I am weary and sad—and at night I cry myself to sleep like a child. Not a page can I read without my thoughts wandering from it.

"To-night came a letter from Boston for Mary. She is not here. My heart aches for her family and friends at home. They do not yet know that she is dead; but will know it soon." [11]

His sorrow was increased in Heidelberg when he learned from America that his close friend and brother-in-law, George Pierce, had died. In this brief absence from home it seemed as though his world were breaking up. Pierce had been dear to him since Academy days because of his noble character, generous, frank, manly—gentle. ". . . in his death something was taken from my life which could never be replaced." [12] A new sense of loneliness settled down over him until his longing for sympathy and friendship broke through all reserve in his letter to Greene: "O, my dear George; what have I not suffered during these last three months! I am completely crushed to the earth; and I have no friend with me, to cheer and console me." [13]

A cousin of Greene came to Heidelberg during the winter—a young man, about Longfellow's age, and an American traveler, named Sam Ward. Fresh from his gay wandering about the courts of Europe, and sparkling with quick wit, Ward fascinated Longfellow with his anecdotes and conversation. After an evening with the Bryant family, the two young men adjourned to Ward's hotel room to continue their animated talk until four o'clock the following morning. The next evening they increased their friendship with a continuation of "desultory tattle of men and things." [14] Two days later, when Ward left Heidelberg, Longfellow accompanied him a short distance on his journey before bidding him an affectionate farewell.

Returning, he wrote to Greene an account of this meeting and expressed his belief that Ward had much ability; had managed to survive the misfortune of being "completely dunged with flattery," as Ward had inelegantly characterized himself. But it was truly distressing to think of Ward devoting his life to the treadmill of teaching. "One thing seems quite evident to me," Longfellow wrote, "and that is, that after four years roving through France and Germany with *carte blanche* as to his expenses—and a *temperament* of at least sixty-horse-power—he is wholly unfitted for going through the drudgery of a Professor's life." [15] The quondam Bowdoin professor had not revised his estimate of what he had described in Brunswick as a dog's life, and had already begun to dread the prospect of returning to the daily round of classes. But there remained a summer of freedom.

Spring brought uneasiness of mind and body which ended all work. "My mind has lost its sensibility and does not feel the spur," he wrote. "I cannot study; and therefore think I had better go home." [16] But, because Greene was still in Italy, he decided to travel through Austria and Switzerland and over the Alps. On July 8 he reached Innsbruck, where he was obliged to change his plans because the police office was unwilling to visé his passport, which was originally intended for the Tyrol only. Angry and disappointed, he felt so tired of solitary travel that he wished he had not undertaken it:

"My journey through the Tyrol and parts of Switzerland was very lonely, having no companions but those, whom I picked up one day, and was glad to drop the next. And then those grand and solitary regions made a most melancholy impression upon my sick soul; and at times when I stood all alone on the tops of the great mountains, and saw around me only barren cliffs, and icebergs, whose breath was like the breath of the grave,— cold and appalling—I thought I should have gone mad forever. Such a journey, under such circumstances, proved to me, that travelling is not always a cure for sadness. So far from dissipating my thoughts it concentrated them; so that in this experiment of moral alchemy,—this search after the philosopher's stone, this turning of lead into gold—the crucible was near being burst asunder." [17]

In the little town of Thun, he met a stranger from Boston, a prosperous merchant named Nathan Appleton who was traveling with his family to Interlaken. "How unlucky I am in not having met them there!" Longfellow complained. "I had but a few moments' conversation and we were off for Berne, this curious old city. . . . Good God! what a solitary, lonely being I am! Why do I travel? Every hour my heart aches with sadness. Tonight I am almost crazy. I wish I were at home once more!" [18] Apparently the Appletons were only slightly acquainted with the name of Henry W. Longfellow, for the younger daughter, Frances, wrote in her journal, that same day: "Prof. Longfellow sends up his card to

Father. Hope the venerable gentleman won't pop in upon us, tho' I did like his Outre Mer." [19] Eleven days later, after he had traveled to Geneva and back to Interlaken, Frances Appleton was quite surprised to meet an attractive, fashionably dressed young man, with fair complexion and chestnut-colored hair. "Called down to meet Mr. Motley & Prof. L—a young man after all," she wrote; then added cautiously, "or else the son of the poet." [20]

To Longfellow, the beginning of his acquaintance with the lovely daughters of Nathan Appleton brought the first sunlight into his dark loneliness. So gracious and charming in manner, so delightful and vivacious in conversation, these young ladies fascinated him. His brief visits with the Doane and Wells families on Beacon Hill had never brought him into the jealously guarded inner circle of Boston society. If he had been so fortunate, he could not have found two more talented and beautiful girls than Frances and Mary Appleton. In Interlaken, their friendliness was a cup of clear water to his thirst—and quite sensibly he decided to go no further in search of elusive alchemy.

As day followed day, he walked with the sisters about the rural paths of the town, compared notes with them concerning travel, told stories of his experiences in the Tyrol, or watched them as they made delicate pencil sketches of picturesque scenes, until his bitter loneliness, dissolving in this sweet companionship, was temporarily forgotten. After only three days, his journal entry revealed a new peace:

"August 2. A cold and cloudy day. No excursion made. The ladies writing letters and finishing sketches. Read Uhland and Count Auersberg, till dinner. After dinner walked with Miss Fanny. She sketched the cloister and a cottage on the Aar. After tea talked incessantly to M. A. She entered with spirit into the conversation. It was delightful. Since I have joined these two families from America, the time passes pleasantly. I now for the first time enjoy Switzerland." [21]

The following day Longfellow accepted an invitation to join the Motleys and the Appletons in a week of travel to Lake Lucerne, Zurich, and Schaffhausen. On the second day he wrote a particularly happy account of his good fortune and joy:

"4th. A day of true, and quiet enjoyment; travelling from

Thun to Entlebuch on our way to Lucerne. We have two carriages for the party; and my propitious star placed me in Mr. A's
travelling carriage with the two young ladies, who are all intellect
and feeling. I cannot say what kind of a country we have passed
through, for I hardly looked from the carriage window. The
time glided too swiftly away; for our conversation was of all that
is gentle and fair; and we read the Genevieve of Coleridge, and
the Christabel; and many other scraps of song; and little German
ballads by Uhland, simple and strange. And all this to me is a
passion;—a delight, strong and unchanging. At noon we stopped
at Langnau, and I walked into the fields with my fair and youthful
companions, and sat down by a stream of pure water that turned
a mill; and a little girl came out of the mill and brought us cher-
ries, and we feasted thereon, and the shadow of the trees was
pleasant, and my soul was filled with peace and gladness." [22]

Each day brought new joys. Tom Appleton, younger brother
of the sisters, was waiting to greet the party at Zurich. Longfellow liked his "slouched hat and merry heart." [23] In the heat of
the summer days the two young men rowed far out on the lake,
and swam with great zest. "Brother Tom is a mighty swimmer;
and my element is cold water," Longfellow wrote.[24] They inspired each other to new feats of merriment. The expenses at the
Hôtel du Corbeau seemed so enormous to them all that Longfellow left this warning in the guest book for other travelers to
read:

> Beware of the Raven of Zurich,
>   'Tis a bird of omen ill;
> A noisy and an unclean bird,
>   With a very, *very* long bill.[25]

One day, as he sat beside Frances Appleton in the great traveling carriage while they drove along the lake at Zurich, he read
her poems from the original German of Uhland. "The Castle
by the Sea" pleased them both so much that they decided to translate it. The joint enterprise was delightful to him. Together
they tested possible English words and phrases which would
capture Uhland's elusive mood, while she held the little book in

her hands. That evening, after they had walked down to the lake from the Hôtel du Corbeau and had taken a boat ride on the placid lake, they came back to finish the translation. How gracefully she turned her carefully chosen phrases! "Some of the best lines are yours," he reminded her later.[26]

Frances Appleton's youthful beauty fascinated Longfellow. There was almost a regal dignity and charm in her every motion. Although a girl of only seventeen years, her restraint and self-possession reflected qualities of mature control. And the sound of her voice, so rich and vibrant, was "musical and full of soul." When he watched her cross a room or walk ahead of him along the cool fields at Zurich, he was reminded of the stately Spanish maidens whom he had worshipped in his romantic younger days in Madrid. Indeed there was something Spanish about her very form and features. The full curves of her lips, the black wonder of her eyes—these "deep unutterable eyes," as he described them —matched so perfectly the rich melody of her voice. So calm, quiet, and at times almost sad, her eyes reminded him of the way the mountain lake caught and held the last serene glow of light from the evening sky.

Perhaps it was the power of her black eyes which made her dark auburn hair seem almost black to him—although the sunlight which caught in the slow waves of it shone golden-red. He summed up all he felt when he wrote: "Thus there was not one discordant thing in her; but a perfect harmony of figure, and face, and soul; in a word, of the whole being. And he who had a soul to comprehend hers, must of necessity love her, and, having once loved her, could love no other woman forevermore." [27] At Zurich, and after their return to Interlaken, his adoration grew so steadily that he could not bear to think of leaving.

After nearly three weeks, a sharp reminder of duty brought him down to earth. Faithful Clara Crowninshield wrote from Heidelberg that she was "out of patience waiting for an escort to America." [28] Reluctantly, but with direct speed, he returned to Heidelberg to make preparations for his voyage home. Within a week he left with Clara and the Bryant family for Paris; and the party sailed for New York from Havre on October 8, 1836.

Back at Interlaken, Frances Appleton continued her daily walks along the lake, and sketched in her album with deeper pleasure in remembrance. Two days following his departure she made almost no entry in her journal—only the briefest confession:

"Miss Mr. L. considerably." [29]

XXI

FLASHING SICKLE IN CAMBRIDGE

There is such a social spirit here and in Boston, that I seldom see a book by candlelight. Indeed, I pass half of my evenings at least in society: it being almost impossible to avoid it. All that I have done in the way of study is to prepare Lectures for the Summer. . . . So you perceive, I take things very easily. People here are too agreeable to let a man kill himself with study.[1]

CAMBRIDGE village was still an unspeculative, quiet community, with no enterprise other than the scholastic, when Longfellow took up his residence there in the fall of 1836. A mellow academic flavor, seeping from the Georgian brick buildings in the yard, permeated even the ample parlors of Tory Row on Brattle Street. The older members of the town were proud of their good fortune in having preserved a leisurely way of life. "It is generally conceded, that this town eminently combines the tranquillity of philosophic solitude, with the choicest pleasures and advantages of refined society," wrote a leading citizen, early in the century.[2] And nobody, from the stiffest, black-coated professor of Kirkland Street to the shiftless angler on the bridge to Brighton, watching his line as it floated out on the lazy current of the Charles River, had ever wished to question the validity of this proud boast. If any up-and-coming neighbor in Boston chid Cambridge citizens with provincialism, he would be obliged to confess that it was a refined provincialism. Tradition had long since made the town sacred for the Danas and Lowells and Holmeses. In those days, giants such as Judge Joseph Story, Abiel Holmes, and William Ellery Channing still walked the earth of Cambridge.

Longfellow found the town and college little changed in appearance since the times when he had come up from Brunswick to enjoy Folsom's hospitality or to sit before Felton's prized Franklin stove in Holworthy. Felton had been an astute proctor. He had discouraged the students from building bonfires in the yard, not by chasing the culprits but by removing the newly

239

ignited sticks from the blaze, thus putting out the fire—and then
by carrying the precious wood to his own room for proper burning.[3] But he was no longer an instructor and proctor living in a
dormitory. He had succeeded Professor Popkin as Eliot Professor
of Greek and had quarters at Dr. Stearns' in Professors' Row on
Kirkland Street. There was a vacant room there, if Longfellow
would like it. He would—for where was he likely to find a more
companionable friend than this learned humorist who was laughing himself fatter each year? "My chambers are very pleasant;
with great trees in front, whose branches almost touch my windows," he wrote to Greene, "so that I have a nest not unlike the
birds, being high up—in the third story." [4]

He was pleased to find that college duties would not begin immediately for him. The classes in French, Spanish, Italian, and
German were being taught competently by the experienced instructors, Sales, Bachi, Surault, and Bokum, foreigners all, who
had continued their duties in the department after Professor Ticknor's supervision had ceased. There was no pressing need for the
new Smith Professor's assistance—but would he prepare a course
of lectures on European literature for the spring term? Amazing
courtesy! How pleased Professor Ticknor would be to hear that
his long years of discouraging struggle were achieving results so
nearly in accordance with his ideal! Ticknor had urged that the
Smith Professor be relieved from all teaching: that he lecture
and supervise the department, while native instructors handled all
classroom drill and routine.

Quite naturally, Stephen Longfellow was very proud of his
son. The quiet paternal dominance had at last produced results
which seemed to satisfy both father and son. Although the conflict between them had always been subtle and unseen, each had
felt the tug of different points of view, different ideals concerning
the ultimate goal which the young man should seek. But the differences seemed smoothed out when Longfellow went to Harvard: at least, Stephen Longfellow hoped they were smoothed
out. He wrote the boy a letter in which he expressed his pleasure.
And just in case there might be any recurrence of Henry's original hankering for a merely literary life, he made passing reference to the value of combining two vocations:

"I rejoice, my dear son, that you are at length established in so very eligible a situation. With your literary tastes and habits, I can hardly conceive of a more pleasant location, and I most sincerely hope and pray it may remain permanent, and that no unfortunate circumstances may occur to mar your enjoyment or diminish your usefulness. I think your ambition must be satisfied, and your only object now will be to fill with eminence and distinction the office in which you are placed, and to become distinguished among the literary men of the age." [5]

Longfellow's assignment seemed like the complete fulfillment of his every wish—and incidentally, like an ideal position for a man of letters. "I have no classes to hear in College, and in all probability shall never be required to hear any," he wrote, not long after his arrival. "I am now occupied in preparing a course of Lectures in German Literature, to be delivered next summer. . . . From all this you will gather that my occupations are of the most delightful kind." [6] Later, he informed his father: "My first quarter's salary was paid without any ado. As yet, however, I have taken no active part in College instruction, there being no room for it. Therefore you need not be alarmed about my injuring myself with study." [7]

Pleasant, to have leisure for walking about the shaded streets of Cambridge, for calling on old friends and making new ones. And everybody was so cordial. Before he had completed his unpacking, Folsom had sent him a scrawled and hasty note: "I am impatient as a lover to see you. Don't fail to come to Club at my house tonight with Mr. Felton." [8] How grateful he felt to these men who had used their influence in his behalf! His father's classmate, Judge Story, as well as Simon Greenleaf, welcomed him warmly and invited him to visit them when he could. Story was interested in the literary pursuits of this young man. In his youth, the Judge had nursed similar ambitions and had even published a volume of poems.

A few of the professors who had taught his father at Harvard were still about town. Professors Hedge and Popkin, retired, lived side by side, and might be seen on the street frequently. Professor Popkin continued his traditional walk to the tobacconist's for the diurnal cigar which meant so much to him. He

was too fond of smoking, he thought, to trust himself with more
than one cigar in the house at a time. Rain or shine, he made the
daily trip to the village. His great black beaver was ample pro-
tection against weather, but his umbrella, opened, looked like a
portable tent. Another friend of Stephen Longfellow since the
days of their attendance at the Hartford Convention was old
Judge William Prescott of Boston, who invited young Longfellow over from Cambridge for Thanksgiving dinner. His son,
tall, slender, and sprightly, nearly ten years older than Longfellow, was also a man of letters who was keenly enthusiastic over
Spain. For ten years he had been working on a *History of Ferdinand and Isabella*, which was ready, at last, for publication.

Boston society opened quite casually to admit this new Harvard
professor, whose wine-colored waistcoats and light gloves gave a
not unfamiliar dash of European fashion to Beacon Street. His
inner grace of manner and warm smile were appealing even to
those who preferred black cloth for a gentleman's clothing. And
he came so well recommended. With the encouragement of
young Tom Appleton, still rambling about Europe, Longfellow
called on Mrs. William Appleton, whose son had but recently
died in Germany. The bereaved mother was cheered by talking
to this gracious youth who had seen William so shortly before
his death.

She introduced him to another of Tom's aunts: Mrs. Samuel
Appleton, who was so hospitable that her home became a frequent goal when Longfellow was in a mood for walking to Boston. One afternoon he found her preparing a packet of letters for
Nathan Appleton and his daughters. Would Longfellow care to
add notes? From his heart, he would. The memory of Frances
Appleton had been a flame tended with devotion since the moment of his departure from her in Switzerland. Only recently he
had recalled an incident which he hoped she had not forgotten:

"Jan. 8, 1837

"My dear Miss Fanny,
    "As I sat down a few evenings since to translate the piece I
here send you, I remembered the time when 'by the margin of
fair Zurich's waters' we translated together the little ballad of

Uhland. I remembered also, the delight you always felt in reading whatever was beautiful in his poems, and I thought it would
give you pleasure to see this Elegy of Matthisson, a writer celebrated for the elegance of his style, and the pleasing melancholy
of his thoughts. I therefore send it to you as a kind of Valentine;
with my warmest wishes of a Happy New Year to all of you. It
will serve you likewise as a German lesson, during the master's
absence. He hopes to resume hereafter his instructions in the
musical tongue.
    "With my best regards to your father and brother,
                "Very truly yours,
                        "HENRY W. LONGFELLOW." [9]

Because Nathan Appleton and his daughters did not plan to
return from Europe until the following fall, the impatient suitor
was glad there were so many distractions in Cambridge and
Boston. A few days later he wrote to Tom Appleton, on whose
sartorial taste he could rely with utmost confidence, to buy for
him "one dozen light-colored kid gloves at *Privat's*, Rue de la
Paix." There was little news or gossip to send with his request·
"And what shall I tell you of Boston? The inhabitants of the fair
city complain, that it is very dull:—that is that there are no
parties. Instead thereof, only Lectures. Waldo Emerson on
Transcendentalism—sufficiently obscure; Mr. Choate on the
'Poetry of the Sea':—in great demand, and much admired, tho'
to me tedious and *wishy-washy*, like the great sea itself." [10]
    Boston lectures could not compete with the amenities of friend-
ship, for Longfellow. Felton had introduced him to a group of
young friends, fellows of infinite jest, and all approximately Longfellow's age. One was Henry R. Cleveland, a cheerful, witty instructor who had been advised to retire because of illness. He
lived at Jamaica Plain, not far distant. George Hillard, whom
Longfellow had once hoped to secure as his coeditor for a new
periodical, was a frequent visitor in his room at Dr. Stearns'. But
his heart went out with warmest friendliness to dashing Charles
Sumner, who was lecturing in the Harvard Law School. As a
young man, he seemed much like Longfellow in tastes and
temperament: fond not only of literary pursuits but also of fash-

ionable attire, colored waistcoats and cravats. During his undergraduate days at Harvard he had been disciplined, ineffectually
but often, for appearing about the yard in buff-colored waistcoats, despite the official sanction of only black and white.[11]

Felton, Hillard, Cleveland, Sumner, and Longfellow banded
together as the "Five of Clubs," and any *gaudiolum* or *convivium*
held by this group was inevitably gay, witty, and memorable.
The carefree, hilarious spirit of the club revealed itself in such
notes as the following, from Cleveland to Longfellow, which was
smuggled into the midst of an august Harvard faculty gathering
at President Quincy's house:

"My dear Heinrich,

"Please to think and say now, von Herzen gern—I want you
to back out of the Faculty Meeting and come down and play
whist with us; make the receiving of this note a matter of the
last importance; Tell Mr. Quincy that your dearest friend is at
the last gasp—that an earthquake is swallowing up your house—
Or make a rush with some tragic shriek full of the bowl and
dagger department; at any rate get down here for a little nine
o'clock supper.

"Ever yrs.

"H. R. C."

"Monday evening" [12]

More dignified but always pleasant were visits with Felton to
the home of Professor Andrews Norton, who had retired from
academic cares to the arboreal luxury of Shady Hill, on the outskirts of the village; indeed, practically lost in the woods. Those
who had not made the acquaintance of Professor Norton, had not
been entertained with lettered hospitality in his home, and had
not played whist at one of his weekly parties or talked with him
on subjects other than religion, were in danger of considering
him a tight-laced reactionary who could not adapt himself to the
new ideas which had burst the confines of Calvinistic thinking.
The truth was that Andrews Norton had been in the vanguard of
Harvard men who had attacked and demolished the narrow limitations of an outgrown Congregationalism; that he had helped
smash these limitations with the precise trip-hammer of his logic.

But Professor Norton was out of patience with the slipshod German talk about intuitive philosophy and transcendental reason. There was Emerson, for instance, lost in the clouds. Whenever he continued to attack this new purveyor of German nonsense, his guest, the Smith Professor, nodded his head in agreement. It was dangerous to get Mr. Norton stirred up too much. But he would soon subside and become the genial, gracious host, happy to welcome to his hearth and board those who were particularly interested in modern literature. He had been so greatly pleased with the writings of Felicia Hemans that he had brought out two volumes of her poems in American editions not long ago. As an undergraduate at Harvard in 1804 he had been class poet; and he had continued to write poems in later years. One of his hymns, particularly precious to Longfellow, was that which had comforted Mary so often, during her last days in distant Rotterdam.

With so many interesting neighbors, Longfellow found little time for working on his notes for future lectures. Although there was no danger of his suffering a collapse from overwork, it was important, nevertheless, to show his ability in these first lectures; to convince the authorities, students, and townspeople that no mistake had been made in welcoming this outsider, this son of Maine, to the jealous confines of the Harvard Yard. He would begin with a survey of language development in both the southern and the northern countries of Europe. Then in later lectures he might advance to a consideration of German literature. Also, he was eager to display the new feather in his cap—his knowledge of Scandinavian literature, which seemed so important to him that he planned a series of lectures on it.[13] In connection with this plan he undertook to write an analysis of the Swedish "Frithiofs Saga" for the *North American*.[14] Dr. Palfrey, whom he met frequently on the streets of Cambridge, was now the editor of the *North American* and had invited him to resume contributions.

Another article which engaged his attention during his first year at Harvard was also sent to the *North American*. Early in March he received a letter and a book from a former Bowdoin classmate, Nathaniel Hawthorne. "We were not, it is true, so well acquainted at college," Hawthorne wrote, "that I can plead an absolute right to inflict my 'twice-told' tediousness upon you; but I have often regretted that we were not better known to each other." [15] In answer, Longfellow said that he liked *Twice-Told Tales*, and promised to write a review of it. With unrestrained enthusiasm he praised his classmate's first successful book:

"It comes from the hand of a man of genius. Everything about it has the freshness of morning and of May. These flowers and green leaves of poetry have not the dust of the highway upon them. They have been gathered fresh from the secret places of a peaceful and gentle heart. . . . This book, though in prose, is written nevertheless by a poet." [16]

Hawthorne was overjoyed. "Whether or no the public will agree to the praise which you bestow on me," he wrote, "there are at least five persons who think you the most sagacious critic on earth; viz., my mother and two sisters, my old maiden aunt, and finally, the sturdiest believer of the whole five, my own self." [17] This incident was the real beginning of their friendship.

Thus busily employed with diversions outside the college, Longfellow continued without participating in any professorial duties until the opening of the spring term, when he began teaching a small class in German. As at Bowdoin, he was eager to break down any barriers of formality between teacher and student; to meet on a common ground of interest. Circumstances were favorable for this beginning, since the Smith Professor was assigned temporarily to "Corporation Room No. 5." The young men were particularly flattered by one innovation: his courteous habit of addressing each as "Mister." One of his students, Edward Everett Hale, recorded a picture of Longfellow's first class:

"The regular recitation-rooms of the college were all in use, and we met him in a sort of parlor, carpeted, hung with pictures, and otherwise handsomely furnished . . . We sat round a mahogany table, which was reported to be meant for the dinners of the Fellows; and the whole affair had the aspect of a friendly gathering in a private house, in which the study of German was the amusement of the occasion." [18]

By reading and translating interesting passages, Longfellow hoped to hold the attention of his listeners. And this same method was a guiding principle which he intended to utilize in his lectures, which began on May 23. Again he was fortunate to have the Corporation room, and again one of the listeners was young Hale, who wrote in his journal:

"The lectures are to be extemporaneous translations of the German with explanations; as he called it, recitations in which he recites and we hear. He made a long introduction to the matter in hand, very flowery and bombastical indeed, which appeared to me very much out of taste. I believe, however, that it was entirely extemporaneous and that he was carried away by the current of his thoughts. In fact, he appeared to say just what came uppermost. The regular translation and explanation part of the lecture was very good." [19]

Hale did not mention that the Smith Professor was handicapped by a severe cold; that he gave only three lectures before succumbing to an attack of grippe or influenza which confined him to his room at Dr. Stearns' for more than two weeks.[20] Periods of illness seemed to be recurring with too much regularity to please Longfellow. In March he had written to his father that his heels had been tipped up by an annoying touch of influenza.

Inactivity brought a melancholy, at such times, which was nearly as difficult to shake off as the physical ailment. Although he rarely mentioned his loneliness, Longfellow could not avoid remembering the precious companionship of his brief married life, and the bitter hunger of his heart for the departed. These were intimate thoughts, not easily confided to anyone.[21] But George Greene, who had recently been appointed American Consul in Rome, had once shared his secrets in that same distant land of wonder, and could read between the lines of his letters. Early in February, Longfellow had written him:

"All would be well with me, were it not for the excited state of my nervous system, which grows no quieter, although I have entirely discontinued smoking. When the East-winds of Spring come, what shall I do? It is all delirium *now*—a pleasant excitement. *Then* it will be deep dejection, I fear. Think of me, when the next Sirocco blows! and imagine, that I feel as you do, tho' ruder blasts assail me, than will ever dare to breathe on the cheek of the *Roman Consul*, to whom all hail! . . .

"The Persianis you will take kindly by the hand, and say it is for me: and that I remember them all with much regard. Kiss the old lady; (on your own hook, though); and show them what I have to say of them and Rome in Outre Mer. Ah! this is a mad world, a mad world!

"I am very sorry to hear that your eyes are put out. You sit up too late o' nights, don't you? Hereafter be more exemplary and go to bed with your wife. And now rises up before me a picture of heaven under earth, which I met with a few days ago in Jean Paul Richter, the most magnificent of the German Prose Writers. Listen to his words! 'A look into a pure, loving eye; a word without falseness to a bride without falseness; and then under the coverlid a soft-breathing breast in which there is nothing but Paradise, a sermon, and an evening prayer. By heaven! with this I will satisfy a Mythic God, who has left his own Heaven and is seeking a new one among us here below!'—There, is not that beautiful?—My friend, learn to enjoy the present,—that little space of time between the great Past and the still greater Future." [22]

The warm sunshine of summer, bringing a return to health, drove away the "blue devils" and turned his thoughts to practical problems. He had been appointed, he discovered, to consult with a committee which would draw up a schedule of duties for the Smith Professor. The draft made by President Quincy was mailed to Longfellow soon after he reached Portland at the beginning of the summer vacation. To his dismay he found, on studying the lengthy document, that he was about to be harnessed into a far heavier load of cares and duties than he had ever pulled at Bowdoin. He was to superintend the four instructors; attend and hear recitations of the various classes of each instructor at least once a month; give instruction in two modern languages twice a week, "and thus in succession in all the languages taught"; conduct a senior recitation class during the summer term; also give at least two public lectures weekly on modern languages and literatures to the senior class in the summer term; and finally, give each student an individual oral examination, when a section had completed the study of a certain language. [23] Absurd and impossible! All of Professor Ticknor's work undone for his successor in a year. How wrong that successor's naïve assertion that he would probably never be asked to do any regular teaching! Suddenly he saw the entire scheme of leisure for literary pursuits obliterated under this landslide of pedagogical débris. He was so indignant that he refused to accept any such arrangement. Bluntly he expressed his criticism of the plan in a letter to President Quincy:

"PORTLAND, August 5, 1837

"Dear Sir,

"On reaching this place two days ago, I had the honor of receiving your letter of July 31, with the accompanying scheme of Duties, etc. As the plan has been matured by yourself and the other gentlemen of the Committee, I regret that I cannot give my full assent to it at once. But it requires of me more than I am willing to undertake. I therefore return the paper with such alterations as seem to me desirable.

"Allow me to suggest, also, that in your estimate of the number of hours employed and comparison of my duties with those of other Professors, you have given hardly weight enough to the consideration that the *kind* and *amount* of preparation necessary for an ordinary recitation, is different from that required by a Lecture—even the simplest oral lecture. Besides I seriously object to having my usefulness in the College computed by the number of hours occupied with the classes. From the nature of my studies, this would lead to very erroneous conclusions. As you are well aware, many days of hard study are often necessary for the preparation of a single lecture.

"I therefore take the liberty of suggesting several changes in your plan of duties, which I here inclose.

"Very respectfully yours,

"HENRY W. LONGFELLOW." 24

His arguments were convincing, his suggestions approved, and his wishes granted. After a revision of the schedule had been made, Longfellow's duties consisted of giving a lecture once a week, visiting each class once a month to supervise studies and instructors, and delivering two public lectures on literature weekly in the summer term. "Thus everything is settled to my entire satisfaction," Longfellow wrote, "and I shall commence the Term in great spirits, and lecture on the Faust of Göthe." 25

XXII

THE SUITOR REJECTED

. . . Even so heartfully give my greetings to the dear, dear Fanny, whom I shall always love as my own Soul. Oh! That little bit of reason which one may possess, can hardly be considered when passion sways us. How full my heart becomes. The last time, that we were together, we separated without understanding each other, for "in this world no one understands another easily." And this is very sad to me.[1]

"ALL THE Bostonians are at Nahant, coughing, shivering—and lying sick a-bed with rheumatism," Longfellow announced as he returned to the deserted town, late in the summer of 1837.[2] But his friends in Boston were not his immediate concern, for he had come up from Portland, well before the beginning of the Harvard team, in order to complete his moving from Dr. Stearns'. Tired of boarding-house fare, he was going to take rooms in Mrs. Andrew Craigie's stately and historic mansion on Brattle Street.

When he had called on the crotchety old lady in May, his first impression had not been cheering. Mrs. Craigie had come to her front door and had informed him curtly that she was taking no more students. Standing squarely in the open doorway, her head wound about with a white turban and her hands crossed in prim fashion behind her, she had stared down with an expression of utter finality. But he wasn't a student; he was the Smith Professor at the College. She continued to stare. How could a young man so fashionably dressed expect to be taken as a member of the Harvard faculty? But the Smith Professor! Was he, then, the author of *Outre-Mer?* Then he must come in. She had read the book with pleasure. As proof, she pointed to a side table. There was one of the first untrimmed parts, in its marbled paper cover.

Then, with a deference that was disconcerting, she invited him to inspect her famous house. Up the broad stairs they climbed to the second floor, and proceeded through the wide and airy halls. At each door Mrs. Craigie paused, pointed out the attractive or historical features of the room into which they were looking, then concluded abruptly, "But you can't have that." The ritual was repeated until they came to the room once occupied by George Washington. This should be his, if he wished. From the great windows he looked down on the southern lawns and gardens of the estate and noted the pleasant shade of the elms. How different from his third-story nest in Professors' Row! Elated, he thanked the turbaned lady and took his leave.[3]

Felton, at least, was not at Nahant. With his cheerful assistance, Longfellow transferred carpets, books, and furniture from Dr. Stearns' and arranged them according to his prejudices in the new quarters. An adjoining room, just vacated, afforded him a separate library, and from these windows he could look out across Brattle Street to the green meadows and the smooth waters of the Charles River. At meal times he was able to secure the ministrations of Mrs. Craigie's laconic and pious maid Miriam, who served him efficiently, if not elegantly, in his room. "The giantess," Longfellow decided to call her, despite Mrs. Craigie's deprecatory assurance, "Take her by and large, she is a good *crittur*." [4]

As soon as he was settled, Longfellow ceremoniously paid his respects to President Quincy to ascertain that his schedule of duties had been fixed satisfactorily—and came away more than pleased. It was almost too easy! With a slight feeling of guilt for having complained so strongly, he considered making amends by offering a public lecture course during the fall term, for any students who cared to attend. But as soon as recitations began, he found the responsibility of directing the foreign instructors no simple matter. Constantly distressed by the unruly attitude and conduct of their teasing students, the bewildered instructors carried so many petty problems to their young superior that he was perplexed by his "*four-in-hand* of outlandish animals, all pulling the wrong way, except one." [5] So he was well content to offer but one lecture course in the fall term, devoted to Goethe, and one in the winter term, on Dante.

There was still leisure for a variety of diversions, in Cambridge or in Boston. But he was always happy to return home, for he had taken a great liking for his Craigie House quarters. There was something appealing to him about the aristocratic dignity of the massive exterior of the house, flanked so securely with flowering shrubbery and the thick foliage of the elm trees. He liked to see it all in silhouette at night; then to walk up the gravel path to the ornamented archway of the great front door, so prettily set off with flower pots on the stone steps that led up to it. There was also a touch of elegance about the way in which Mrs. Craigie kept the large entryway lighted during the evening, so that one could ascend the carpeted stairs to the second floor without stumbling.

Longfellow's door was the first on the left at the top of the front stairs. Here was the kind of solitude he enjoyed. A few years later, Emerson's young hired man set out to find another kind of solitude; built himself a shack on the shore of Walden Pond in Concord, and settled down grimly but pleasantly to prove something and to write a book about it. The author of *Outre-Mer* would never have understood what to do with that kind of solitude. He preferred the snug warmth of rooms rich with traditions of the colonial days—and at the same time within easy reach of Boston society.

As for leisure, he had not yet made much use of it. The term was still too young. But, on a fall morning, it was pleasant to rise and make his toilet without haste, put on his striped calamanco morning gown and red slippers—then ring for the maid Miriam to bring breakfast. If the weather were fine, it was nice to have his tray put on a table near the one long window which caught the early morning sun and filled the room with light. Then, while he munched his toast, sipped his tea, and let the butter melt on the golden-brown waffles which Miriam made so well, he could study the way in which the lazy river Charles wrote across the green meadows a great silver letter—the last in Longfellow's name.

Breakfast over, he liked to stretch out on the sofa, book in hand, for a little desultory reading. Perhaps the persistent buzzing of the flies in the room annoyed him? Then he would rise, take a red silk handkerchief which he kept for the purpose, use it as a sling, and set about the massacre of the innocents. It reminded him of the way the Emperor Domitian had amused himself in ancient days. Before he went over to the Harvard Yard, he frequently took a turn about Mrs. Craigie's excellent gardens, alive with the brightness of many-colored blossoms.

At the close of the school day, he came back, rang once more for the giantess, took his favorite seat before the window, and as he ate his dinner, kept an eye on the evening strollers who were taking the popular walk along Brattle Street to historic Mount Auburn Cemetery in the cool of the evening. Some evenings, Felton dropped in for an hour before bedtime. Frequently, Longfellow would saunter out to call on Folsom and other friends. Then home for quiet reading by lamplight, before he undressed. He described all this to his sister Anne, in a playful letter—and concluded his account with the casual intelligence that the Appletons had come back from Europe.[6]

Anne, reading her brother's letter after it had made the journey in the mail stage from Boston to Portland, may have understood the implication of this offhand reference to the Appletons, for her brother confided in no other member of his family, apparently, with greater freedom. She may have known from past conversations that the return of Frances Appleton was cause for excitement—now that only the river Charles and not the inexorable Atlantic separated him from her.

Since they were at last in their home at Number 39 Beacon Street, Longfellow considered how to convey his sentiments best. Flowers, he decided, would be an appropriate reminder of Interlaken. One glorious fall day, he gathered a bouquet from the Craigie House gardens. Pondering a message to accompany them, he began a poem, "Flowers." As he wrote, he wove into the lines subtle reminders of those days when he had translated German poems with the help of the beautiful and talented Frances Appleton. Then, cautiously, he hinted at more intimate meanings:

> Spake full well, in language quaint and olden,
>   One who dwelleth by the castled Rhine,
> When he called the flowers, so bright and golden,
>   Stars, that in earth's firmament do shine.

Stars they are, wherein we read our history,
  As Astrologers and Seers of Eld,
Yet not wrapped about, with awful mystery
  Like the burning stars, which they beheld.

　　．　　．　　．　　．　　．　　．　　．

Gorgeous flowrets in the sun-light shining,
  Blossoms flaunting in the eye of day,
Tremulous leaves, with soft and silver lining,
  Buds that open only to decay:—

Brilliant hopes, all woven in gorgeous tissues,
  Flaunting gaily in the golden light;
Large desires, with most uncertain issues,
  Tender wishes, blossoming at night!

These in flowers and men are more than seeming;
  Workings are they of the self-same powers,
Which the Poet, in no idle dreaming,
  Seeth in himself and in the flowers.[7]

　　．　　．　　．　　．　　．　　．　　．

It was fortunate for Longfellow that he could not foresee his subsequent distress when he tucked this freshly written poem among the symbols of brilliant hopes—fortunate that he did not guess how uncertain was the issue on which he confessed his happiness depended. Nor did he find any disappointing moments during the following autumn days when he appeared frequently at the Appleton home, sat with Mary and Frances in their cheery parlor that looked out over Boston Common, and renewed the acquaintance made over a year earlier, in the land beyond the sea. The high-walled stronghold of Boston social tradition was honorably represented by the quiet culture and restrained luxury of the Appleton home. These two daughters of Nathan Appleton, educated by years of fashionable schooling and extensive European travel, had known far more advantages than most of their American friends. Whether their conversations with Longfellow veered from the literary gossip of Cambridge (Andrews Norton's scathing attack on Emerson) to reminiscences of Switzerland, or broke playfully into French dialogue, or led to a pleasant discussion of Goethe's *Faust*, he found them charming, vivacious, stimulating.

Having no morning duties at Harvard that fall, he developed the habit of walking to town through Cambridgeport (where Washington Allston's studio stood), over the bridge, and across Beacon Street to the Common. The bright colors of the flowers in gardens he passed, the glimpses through trees of red brick façades, trimmed with white, the soft blue skies of that Indian summer, all caught his attention, suddenly, with a new vividness. As in Interlaken, the dull pain left his heart and he was happy again.

He knew that, whenever weather permitted, Mary and Frances Appleton walked regularly about the shaded paths of the Common—it seemed a part of the Beacon Hill tradition. So the young Cambridge professor found no trouble in happening upon them casually, and with a touch of surprise, almost any morning when the warm fall sunlight came aslant through the leaves. Welcoming him graciously, they seemed happy to have him continue with them as they strolled down to the frog pond or up to the edge of Park Street before returning to their home. And each time Longfellow turned back toward Cambridge, he told himself that nowhere else in the world was there a woman who possessed the gifted loveliness of Frances Appleton.

With such thoughts in his head and with such uncontrollable excitement in his heart, he could not avoid an open revelation of love. His hopes had grown so steadily with the passage of many fall days that he was entirely unprepared for the cool rebuff with which Frances Appleton answered his expression of sentiment.[8] He was overcome with dejection. And the pain in his heart was not much more uncomfortable than the sting his pride had taken —for he had stumbled impetuously, clumsily, into an estrangement which might not be amended easily.

A short time after the catastrophe, Mary Appleton wrote a note to Longfellow, expressing her wish to see him, and reminded him of his plan for writing a Faust-in-New-England sort of play. In reply, Longfellow made a passing reference to his disappointment: "As to the Faustian episode of 'Belfagor in Beacon Street' I fear to undertake it now. I am too serious and sad. The devil would enter, as he does in the old Miracle Plays, shouting 'Ho! ho! ho!' And that is not the vein for your gentlemanly Belfagor; who as I had conceived the part, was to be nowise Satanic, but rather a soft and Pelham-devil, with french boots and *gants de beurre frais.*"

Then, after a paragraph in answer to some remarks which Mary Appleton had made on Goethe, he turned directly to the subject of his sadness:

"And what have you been doing in the bright parlor? Shall I sit there no more with you, and read in pleasant books! Are those bright autumnal mornings gone forever?

"Ach, du schöne Seele! Es wird mir gar traurig zu Muthe, wenn ich daran denke, und sehe, wie der schöne Traum dahin zieht,—wie die Wolke sich theilt, und in Thränen zerfliesst, und um mich wird alles so leer, und in meiner Seele eine dunkle Nacht —eine dunkle sternlose Nacht!—Und dass hab' ich Dir auf Deutsch sagen müssen, weil eine fremde Sprache ist eine Art von Däm- merung und Mondlicht, worin man den Frauenzimmern allerlei sagen kann—und so herzlich treu! Eben so herzlich grüsse mir die liebe, liebe Fanny, die ich immer liebe, wie meine eigene Seele. Ach! dass bisschen Verstand, das einer haben mag, kommt wenig oder gar nicht in Anschlag, wenn Leidenschaft wüthet. Wie wird mir das Herz so voll!—Das letzte Mal, das wir zusammen waren, gingen wir aus einander ohne einander verstanden zu haben: denn 'auf dieser Welt keiner leicht den andern versteht.' Und dass ist gar zu traurig.

"I pray you, thank her for remembering Victor Hugo's 'Songs of the Gloaming;' which came safely last evening, and which I have been reading to-day. Also do me the favor to send the ac- companying note to Mrs. W. A[ppleton] whose *fête* I shall not have the pleasure of attending.

"Good night, *liebes Fräulein,*
                    "Very sincerely yr. friend,
                                                   "H. W. L.
"Sunday eve,
"Dec. 10." [9]

In Cambridge, Longfellow's closest friends, Felton, Hillard, and Sumner, soon learned of his secret disappointment. Hillard quite bluntly expressed open skepticism as to the wisdom of continuing the abruptly terminated courtship and wished that his lovesick companion might abandon all thought of the matter. He could warn Longfellow that one hindrance to courtship was the jealous attitude of Nathan Appleton. But Hillard's remarks were ignored—he was even drafted into service as an accomplice in this amatory conflict, for Longfellow wrote him from Portland at the beginning of the winter vacation and enclosed a note for his beloved, with brief instruction for its delivery:

"PORTLAND. Dec. 21, 1837

"My dear St. George,

"It is so cold here that I cannot mend a pen; and my hand trembles like an old man's. Nevertheless I would fain write you a few words, begging you to send the inclosed without delay. I tell you, I shall succeed in this, O thou of little faith!

"It is awful cold to-day. They seem to keep all their 'cold snaps,' here for College Vacations. My mind is like a frozen inkstand. I believe there are some thoughts in it, but they wont flow out. There is no feeling in my fingers; under my nails are purple blood-spots. Circulation stops. Send me some news—a 'beaker full of the warm South' (say, Beacon Street) to give the currents of my veins full play. Give me some drink:—juices of Mandragora or Love-in-idleness. Touch my mind's eye therewithal.

"I left Boston in good spirits;

"And by the vision splendid
Was on my way attended

(Pen, do thy duty better). Coming events cast no shadows before them—only luminous outlines;—like the light of the rising moon, shining through the twilight. So shall it ever be; for with a soul within him and a heaven above him, why should man be sad.

"This is a dull town not-withstanding. My native place, too; a perfect hornet's-nest of early recollections, insects with stings. I have hardly been out of doors yet; but hear sundry reports about myself. They were brought from Boston by a dress-maker, a cousin of the Hammonds—who dwelling for a time at Russle's in Beacon Street, on her return to this place, says to her fair customers, that she saw me walking by at sundry times with Madonna Francesca,—*and describes our dress minutely!* Thus Boston gossip comes with Boston fashions;—both, by change of place assuming an aspect somewhat outré. . . ." [10]

Attesting true loyalty in friendship, Hillard doubly fulfilled his mission by sending the absent lover a bright picture of his "Madonna Francesca," to whom he delivered the note:

"BOSTON, Dec. 24, 1837

"Dear Henry
"The cold has not penetrated very deeply, for your letter is as warm and cordial as the ruddy drops that virile your friendly heart, and it flashed like a sunbeam over my path. The precious lining was in the hands of the 'dark ladye' within one hour after I took it out of the post office, which was this morning at 12. I saw the back of her bonnet (and there was expression even in that) at church today. So she is alive and well. I called there a day or two ago to lend Mary a book, and was chatting away very agreeably (I mean to myself) when Il Padre came in, and gave me a rather freezing reception, not knowing, I suppose that I was a married man, and above the troubled atmosphere of hope and fear, in which you lovers beat your wings. I felt a numbness stealing over my tongue, and soon took my leave. What an atmosphere of beauty and grace and tasteful luxury is diffused over the house. If you are ever its lord, I expect that poetry will ooze out of the pores of your skin. I delight to see you keeping up so stout a heart for the resolve to conquer is half the battle in love as well as war." [11]

After his return from Portland, Longfellow renewed attentions in Beacon Street with so little satisfaction that his vacation optimism yielded to gloom. Yet he was resolved to lay siege to the heart of the "dark ladye" until she yielded. At least she might encourage her ardent troubadour with some token of pitié. He liked to think of love in terms of the ancient game of medieval days. But this was no game; it was too deathly serious. Love had been sweet before, but never had he struggled with a passion such as this, that obliterated all other desire and ambition. And the well-meaning banter of his friends was like sand in the fresh wound.

Almost fiercely he turned for relief to George Greene, now in distant Italy, and opened his heart in a letter. He could be sure that this loyal friend, who had known him so well since those nights of shared aspirations in Naples, would not misunderstand and ridicule him. First of all, he flatly contradicted Felton's recent implication that Cambridge was full of merriment. Longfellow was in no mood for keeping company with the laughter-loving Greek professor. Instead, he wrote that a leaden melancholy hung over him—and that he was both nervously and physically upset by a feverish excitement which bordered on insanity. He even admitted that his despondency had caused him to miss some of his classes. But Greene would remember exactly how Longfellow had described similar symptoms during the previous summer, when he had left Heidelberg and had sought relief from sorrow by traveling through the Tyrol; an experiment of moral alchemy, he had described it, in which the crucible was nearly burst asunder. Now again the same danger arose. Only this time it was caused not by the remembrance of past loss but by the fresh pain of a new disappointment.

Nobody seemed to understand how serious soul-sickness could be. But he told Greene the truth: that the unsatisfied want was for a woman's love. Then he went on to give the brief story of his having met and fallen in love with Frances Appleton, and to swear that this glorious and beautiful being was a woman not of talent but of genius. That she should offer him only friendship in return for his love was the most bitter irony of all. But he had vowed to win her. And that one great thought was a flame that burned wildly in Longfellow's breast. To lose would be to die.

Greene must understand him here; this was no mere infatuation, no whim. The matter was truly earnest and serious. This passion was too strong to be quelled or forgotten. What the outcome would be, Longfellow dared not guess. But Charles Sumner, soon to visit Italy, would be able to give Greene further details about it. And when Longfellow next wrote, he hoped to be able to tell the story of how a miserable knight had won the love of the proud ladie of Beacon Street. There seemed to be so many reasons why they should be mutually drawn to each other that he would never be reconciled to her refusal.[12]

It was somewhat difficult to be faced with the duties of writing and giving lectures on the *Purgatorio* and *Paradiso* of Dante, when one was distracted with an aching heart and head. But soul-sickness, however serious, was a difficult explanation of absence from the Harvard lecture halls. So Longfellow managed to begin his class work as scheduled, on January 15. Throughout that winter he continued to labor under the shadow of this melancholy disappointment. Occasionally he ventured into Boston society, and almost always found the Appleton sisters—gay, lovely, popular—at whatever function he attended. Yet he had almost entirely given up his visits to their home on Beacon Street. Thus these brief social encounters only increased his unrest until he avoided the disordered state of mind by remaining in Cambridge. There was plenty to keep him busy now, for his lectures on Dante exacted much time for preparation. And his readings for the intended summer lectures also occupied hours which might otherwise have been gloomy.

This twofold preoccupation was not conducive to even the mildest display of interest or participation in the many-sided discussions of political and social reform incipient in New England at that time.[13] To Longfellow, sitting alone with his books and his dreams in the Craigie House chambers, the din of materialistic striving which came from the seaports and marketplaces of his country penetrated merely as meaningless sounds. The broken banks and broken heads strewn in the wake of the recent financial panic were insignificant and unreal to one who was learning to gaze abstractedly into his own soul for inspiration, and into the memories of the past for solace. Even the vital and significant message of Emerson, who had recently rocked the Harvard Divinity School with new ideas, touched him merely as a bundle of vague and harmless effusions. No sphere of interest could tempt him from his own narrow realm of sentiment.

When the Appleton family left Boston for the South, late in

March, he seemed relieved. With new eagerness he set to work immediately on literary projects which had been neglected. With Hawthorne he discussed a scheme for compiling a book of tales and legends to be called *The Wonder Horn*.[14] In Salem, one week-end, Longfellow visited his intended collaborator to discuss their plans.[15] But, as the details took shape, the two agreed that Longfellow should compile the book exactly as he wished, without the assistance of Hawthorne. "You see I have abundance of literary labor in prospect," Hawthorne wrote, shortly after Longfellow had visited him, "and this makes it more tolerable that you refuse to let me blow a blast upon the 'Wonder Horn.' Assuredly you have a right to make all the music on your own instrument; but I should serve you right were I to set up an opposition,—for instance, with a cornstalk fiddle or a pumpkin-vine trumpet." [16]

Another stint he had set for himself long ago was the writing of a survey sketch of Anglo-Saxon prose and poetry, to honor the appearance of Dr. Bosworth's finally completed *Dictionary*. After carefully studying many sources, he prepared his paper, which promised to guide the reader "among the dark chambers and mouldering walls of an old national literature, weather stained and in ruins." [17] He was still following his scheme of writing sketches of little known literatures, exactly as he had written sketches of strange lands. The same atmosphere of tradition, history, antiquity, and romance was made to shroud the two types of essay. The article concluded with an expression of hope that some scholar would soon undertake the writing of a history of Anglo-Saxon literature—a task which he confessed he had neither the inclination nor the ability to tackle.

In May, a few days after the Appleton sisters returned to Boston, Longfellow met them, quite by accident,[18] on the Common. Their cordiality and friendliness, so singularly gratifying to him, obliterated all past remorse and fear, and sent him back to the Craigie House that evening to begin his journal entry: "A day of Paradise." [19] Later, as he continued to enjoy the renewed friendship, doubts returned with his realization that even the warmest cordiality could never satisfy the peculiar loneliness of his heart. Glimpses into the homes of his married friends, serene in domestic joys, accentuated his discontent. After one evening of visiting, he cried out against the old pain which had begun afresh. Why could he not thrust these distracting thoughts out of his mind and be done with them? The answer was plain: the roots of this love ran down too deep within him.[20]

XXIII

A PSALM OF LIFE

*I kept it some time in manuscript, unwilling to show it to any
one, it being a voice from my inmost heart, and expressing my feelings at a time when I was rallying from the depression of disappointment.*[1]

SEARCHING for a course of action which might alleviate his suffering, Longfellow found a strangely confused sustenance in his readings for lectures. As he had explained to Mary Appleton, in one
of his letters, the religious faith diffused through the *Divina Commedia* was pleasant inspiration to him, after the strong pessimism
of *Faust*. While preparing his Goethe lectures a few weeks earlier, he had become particularly conscious of this contrast, he told
her: "I was imprudent enough to take up Dante the other day,
and he excites me more than any other poet. I hate to turn back
to Goethe." In the same letter he added: "Tell me, how can I
stop midway in an Introductory Lecture on Christian Dante to
take up Heathen Goethe?—So much for not being systematic." [2]

The literature of death and the life thereafter had frequently
occupied his thoughts, since Mary's going. Firm in his own Christian faith, he nevertheless continued to identify his own sorrow
with that of all writers, pagan or Christian. Obviously, his religious beliefs had been inherited, along with his mildly Federalist
views on politics, in diluted form from his mother and father.
Perhaps if Longfellow had been able to digest and assimilate the
meaty Unitarianism which Ichabod Nichols had preached in Portland, he might have made out of it something more than a pleasant belief in the fundamental goodness of man and the certainty
that all would be saved in an after life. But in religion, as in politics, Longfellow was content to fumble with a few ideas and never
bothered to get below the surface of them. That Unitarianism
was a dynamic, liberating creed to Channing, is certain; that it was
a convenience, acquired secondhand by Longfellow, is obvious.

Here again we approach from another angle Longfellow's fundamental weakness: an inability to work out ideas for himself and the consequent necessity for leaning on his parents and his favorite authors for support. Romantically steeped in the past, his vision of the problems that confronted him was always blurred by romantic preoccupation. Yet he disappoints us doubly by failing even to understand the past which he loved. Particularly fond of the Middle Ages, he nevertheless spent his time dallying with superficial aspects and outlines. For example, his study of Dante (which later became a means of escape from a tragedy which need not concern us here) did not get near the man or his age. Instead his early reading in the "Paradiso," as a part of his lecture preparation in 1838, led him by a new path back to the memory of the departed, rather than to an incisive understanding of Dante's life and work. The *Divina Commedia* blinded Longfellow to the essential spirit of Dante, his medieval realism. Dante reminded Longfellow primarily of the vague otherworldliness he had found in the poems of his favorite German authors. Thus, paradoxically, Dante's account of wandering through the world of the dead actually quickened Longfellow's sense of spiritual kinship with Novalis and Matthisson, who found the voice of night an emotional reality so vivid that the flesh-and-blood experiences of the day seemed like dreams.

In one of his moods of sadness, and sitting alone in his Craigie House study, on the evening of his thirty-first birthday, Longfellow revealed the persistence of this spiritual kinship by opening his journal and copying into it a poem which was inspired, not by his reading in Dante, but by his familiarity with Novalis. The pain of his new disappointment, accentuating the sorrowful memory of Mary's death, drove him back into the happiness of past days for consolation. The poem, which had been written probably more than a year earlier, was this:

EVENING SHADOWS

When the hours of day are number'd,
   And the soul-like voice of night
Wakes the better soul, that slumber'd,
   To a holy, calm delight.

Ere the evening lamps are lighted
  And like spectres grim and tall,
Shadows from the fitful firelight
  Dance upon the parlor wall,

Then the forms of the departed
  Enter at the open door,
The belov'd ones—the true-hearted,
  Come to sit with me once more.

And with them the Being Beauteous,
  Who unto my youth was given,
More than all things else to love me,
  And is now a Saint in Heaven.

With a slow and noiseless footstep
  Comes she, like a shape divine,
Takes the vacant chair beside me,
  Lays her gentle hand in mine.

And she sits and gazes at me
  With those deep and tender eyes,
Like the stars so still and Saint-like
  Looking downward from the skies.[3]

These lines are the first fruit of that maturing experience which he had known in Heidelberg. They represent the beginning of a new phase in Longfellow's literary career; the initial breaking away from the descriptive versification of his youth. Sorrow, which had taught him to look into his heart, had also driven him into a dream-world refuge. And guided by the mystical lines of the German romantics, he began to think of night as the time when the soul, unhampered by material distractions, is free to expand with the exotic beauty of flowers that bloom only in darkness.

Obviously, no dream-world philosophy could get along very comfortably with the teachings of Goethe. And Longfellow, reading widely in *Faust, Wilhelm Meister,* and *Dichtung und Wahrheit,* was tempted for a time to venture the sterner task of following this new master, out of the dream-world of night into

the bold activity of labor, as a means of finding peace. This he
revealed in his lectures at Harvard. On the second day of May,
1838, he began his new course on "Literature and the Literary
Life." After an introductory lecture characterizing the literature of Greece, Rome, and the Middle Ages, he advanced quickly,
in subsequent classes, to his favorite German prose authors, Richter, Hoffman, Tieck, and Engel. Then he came to Goethe. In
June, he finished his survey of the life of Goethe with some rhe-
torical questions and answers which showed that, in spite of his
own inconsistency, Longfellow was trying to learn Goethe's secret of growth through youthful passion to control and ultimate
peace:

"And now tell me, young gentlemen, what do you think of it?
From your own experience in the world—is it not best to take most
things coolly? even in the hot blood of youth? . . . Have you
never seen persons, who think the world in a desperate state; and
at war with everything, and enjoy nothing, because 'the time is
out of joint'? How calmly the philosopher stands amid all this
and says: that the best way to reform the world is to do one's
own duty, and not the duties of others. Let each one labor in his
sphere!

"This I conceive to be the amount of Goethe's indifferentism.
He has outlived the 'storm and pressure period' of indiscreet enthusiasm." [4]

He was struggling persistently to accept these very thoughts
as they applied to his own experience. He would not lose himself longer in weak surrender to sorrow, past or present. Novalis
had taught him a kind of escape, into the twilight of a world of
phantoms; Goethe was teaching him to face life boldly and coura-
geously, to accept the world not as a shadow but as a reality.
How sincerely Longfellow had exhorted Greene, a few months
earlier, "My friend, learn to enjoy the present,—that little space
of time between the great Past and the great Future." [5]

Although he found no difficulty in telling the Harvard students
how Goethe's practical gospel could heal the ailments of others,
Longfellow found his old wounds raked open afresh, as often as
he gave way to melancholy reflections about his past and future.

To be sure, few who met the cheerful Smith Professor on the streets of Cambridge guessed the unhappiness which rankled within. Yet, with impetuous regularity he tortured himself by returning frequently to Beacon Street. Schooled in flawless courtesy and gifted with innate charm, Frances Appleton met Longfellow with a serenity and ease which completely hid all trace of past annoyance. The less skillful professor did his best to equal her indifference—but made sorry work of it. Once, during the winter, he had met her unexpectedly at an exhibition of paintings in Boston. Like a troubadour in the old Court of Love, he felt himself grow flushed, then turn pale, and tremble like a leaf. It was amusing afterwards; at the time it was almost unbearable.[6] He would go, nevertheless, to lend the Appleton sisters books or to make brief calls, even though the "delicious deaths" sometimes resulted in hours of regret.

A few days after his last lecture on Goethe, and only a short time before he intended leaving Cambridge for the beginning of the summer vacation, a sparkling June morning tempted Longfellow out of doors and off across the country miles to Cambridgeport and Boston. And that night he wrote: "Passed the whole day in town. Went in soon after breakfast. The Common was lovely. Walked to and fro for an hour. Called at the Ap[s]. They were out. Met Fanny on the Common. Had I gone farther should have met her sooner. Afterwards saw Mary &c. &c. &c." [7]

The wheel of hope and disappointment had turned once more, and was followed by a day of restlessness. Having crowded his mind so recently with the simple rules of conduct offered by Goethe, he was not willing to give way to morbid brooding. He had been fighting for some time against such futile surrenders to unhappiness. One night shortly before the Appletons had returned from the South, Felton and Longfellow had spent a long evening together, "talking of matters, which lie near one's soul:— and how to bear one's self doughtily in Life's battle: and make the best of things." [8] And on the morning after his walk on the lovely Common, Longfellow sat alone in his Craigie House study, eager to put into poetry his new beliefs concerning the best way to bear one's self doughtily.

He had assimilated to his own needs some of Goethe's wisdom; had known experiences which qualified him as one who had completed an apprenticeship not unlike Wilhelm Meister's. In his recent suffering he had first inclined toward Novalis's creed that "the secret of Nature is nothing else than the fulfilled longing of a loving heart." [9] But since Frances Appleton disdained his love, Longfellow turned from Novalis to the practical teachings in *Wilhelm Meister:* "A man is never happy till his vague striving has itself marked out its proper limitation." [10] "It is not of yourself that you must think, but of what surrounds you." [11] "The safe plan is, always simply to do the task that lies nearest us." [12]

Furthermore, the indenture which had raised Meister from an apprentice in the art of living to the rank of a craftsman who had mastered a pragmatic and yet artistic plan of conduct had begun: "Art is long, life short, judgment difficult, opportunity transient—therefore, be doing." [13] Having learned to understand this much of Goethe's teaching, Longfellow was at last ready to construct his own liberating indenture. Another passage brought home from Germany in Longfellow's notebook offered additional, correlated suggestions: "Look not mournfully into the Past. It comes not back again. Wisely improve the Present. It is thine. Go forth to meet the shadowy Future, without fear, and with a manly heart." [14]

Saturated with these ideas, and conscious of his need for them, Longfellow turned against the dreamy sadness of the past, and tried to give up all vain hopes, by writing:

A PSALM OF LIFE

"Life that shall send
A challenge to its end,
And when it comes, say, 'Welcome, friend.' "

WHAT THE HEART OF THE YOUNG MAN SAID TO THE PSALMIST

Tell me not, in mournful numbers,
Life is but an empty dream!
For the soul is dead that slumbers,
And things are not what they seem.

Life is real—life is earnest—
  And the grave is not its goal:
Dust thou art, to dust returnest,
  Was not spoken of the soul.

Not enjoyment, and not sorrow,
  Is our destin'd end or way;
But to *act*, that each to-morrow
  Find us farther than to-day.

Art is long, and time is fleeting,
  And our hearts, though stout and brave,
Still, like muffled drums, are beating
  Funeral marches to the grave.

In the world's broad field of battle,
  In the bivouac of Life,
Be not like dumb, driven cattle!
  Be a hero in the strife!

Trust no Future, howe'er pleasant!
  Let the dead Past bury its dead!
Act—act in the glorious Present!
  Heart within, and God o'er head!

Lives of great men all remind us
  We can make *our* lives sublime,
And, departing, leave behind us
  Footsteps on the sands of time.

Footsteps, that, perhaps another,
  Sailing o'er life's solemn main,
A forlorn and shipwreck'd brother,
  Seeing, shall take heart again.

Let us then be up and doing,
  With a heart for any fate;
Still achieving, still pursuing,
  Learn to labor and to wait.

                              L.[15]

For the second time he had looked into his heart for inspiration. But the contrast between the thoughts in "Evening Shadows" and in "A Psalm of Life" was the contrast between Novalis and Goethe, between twilight and sunrise. That these two poems should have been written within a few months of each other was an indication of Longfellow's inner conflict at this time, for one emphasized the reality of dreams as completely as the other stressed the reality of life. And because each seemed too personal to be sent out casually, the two poems were not immediately offered for publication. One had been copied into his private journal; the other was a private outcry of longing for liberation from debilitating grief and indecision. This much Longfellow later confessed when he wrote of "A Psalm of Life," "I kept it some time in manuscript, unwilling to show it to any one, it being a voice from my inmost heart, and expressing my feelings at a time when I was rallying from the depression of disappointment." [16]

Yet there were further periods of storm and stress ahead—days when even the perception of release could not achieve release. The heart of a young man had to learn that resignation to the loss of Frances Appleton could not free his thoughts from loneliness; that he had fashioned a theory which he was not strong enough to test for long in actual experience. In spite of his frequent failures, he continued to try. Another expression of his sincerity of purpose and his resolve to build strength into his every thought and action was put into a poem entitled "The Light of Stars," also written in the summer of 1838 and published six months later as "A Second Psalm of Life." Again the idea was a tribute to the teachings of Goethe and a further denial of Novalis' dream-world philosophy:

.   .   .   .   .   .

> There is no light in earth or heaven,
>   But the cold light of stars;
> And the first watch of night is given
>   To the red planet Mars.
>
> Is it the tender star of love?
>   The star of love and dreams?

Oh no! from that blue tent above,
  A hero's armor gleams.

.   .   .   .   .   .

O star of strength! I see thee stand
  And smile upon my pain;
Thou beckonest with thy mailéd hand,
  And I am strong again.

.   .   .   .   .   .

Oh, fear not, in a world like this,
  And thou shalt know ere long;
Know, how sublime a thing it is,
  To suffer and be strong.[17]

His earnest intention to put the past behind him was also expressed at this time in a second long letter to his friend Greene, still in Italy. While spending the remainder of the summer vacation at his home in Portland, Longfellow wrote to his far-away friend that it was no use to hope longer; that he had written the *hic jacet* of that passion once and for all. There was resignation in his tone, but no bitterness. Once again he was repeating the firm belief which he had given voice to in "The Light of Stars": even suffering has its compensations.

But he added, before finishing the letter, that the winter had driven him to an increased amount of writing—enough to make volumes. And out of his thinking had come "a number of literary plans and projects, some of which will ripen before long and be made known to you." [18] But in the close of his letter, Longfellow lost his restraint and serenity in a few nervous sentences which implied the storm still going on beneath the surface: "I do not like this sedentary life. I want action. I want to travel. Am too excited, too tumultuous inwardly. And my health suffers from all this." [19]

XXIV

PAGEANT OF HIS BLEEDING HEART

The book is a reality; not a shadow, or ghostly semblance of a book. My heart has been put into the printing-press and stamped on the pages. Whatever the public may think of it, it will always be valuable to me, and to my friends because it is a part of me.[1]

IF LONGFELLOW could not be free for the kind of action which would clear his mind and heart of disappointment, one other way remained: he would write himself clear of it. This decision was already taking shape in his mind when he wrote to Greene of literary projects soon to be made known. He would write a prose romance modelled on the autobiographical German novels of Jean Paul and Goethe; one in which he could get out of his system the entire story of the past—and conclude by suggesting a course for the future which would take as its theme the central idea of action already expressed in "A Psalm of Life":

> Not enjoyment, and not sorrow,
> Is our destined end or way;
> But to *act*, that each to-morrow
> Find us farther than to-day.

The same strong conviction which had prompted the writing of that poem led to the writing of *Hyperion*. And each had been stimulated by Longfellow's unerring habit of identifying his own problem with those expressed in his favorite German writings. In the life of Goethe, Longfellow had noticed that there was a central idea similar to the theme of *Faust* and of *Wilhelm Meister*. In his lecture on Goethe, shortly before the summer vacation of 1838, he had impressed upon his students the interrelationship of these three phases of their study; had called attention to Goethe's passionate youth, his romantic yet strong manhood, and his serene, sublime old age. This threefold pattern of growth Longfellow

272

found in the characters of both Faust and Wilhelm Meister—a reflection from Goethe's own experience. In speaking of Goethe's old age he had said to his students at Harvard: "And upon this vantage ground of Truth the old man stood. Not grasping into the mysterious future, but self-possessed—resolved to make the best of the world as it was—looking with a benignant smile upon the indefinite aspirations of minds more enthusiastic than his own, but less clear-sighted." [2] When he lectured on *Wilhelm Meister*, Longfellow gave a brief explanation of the book, but chose Goethe's own commentary and interpretation: "It is the Life of a young man of middle walk in society, and his education by circumstances. The work had its origin, Goethe himself says, 'in the shadowy presentiment of the great Truth; that man oftentimes would fain make trial of that for which Nature has given him no talent; and undertake and follow out, that in which he can never acquire dexterity. . . . Thus do many waste the fairest portion of their lives and fall at last into strange sorrow. And yet it is possible that all these false steps lead to some invaluable good; a presentiment that in Wilhelm Meister is ever more and more developed. . . .' " [3]

But in his lecture on *Faust* Longfellow had tied the three parts neatly together. He had explained to his students:

"In the character and life of Faust, Goethe has exhibited doubtless many traits of his own character, and many passages of his own life: it is his own figure thrown back upon the Past in gigantic shadow. There is a desperate desire to know, what man can never know; to be more than man;—the same disappointment and despair. Then the lofty aspirations of the soul are quenched in sensuality; then the World of Art unfolds itself before the weary spirit;—and finally Faust ends where Goethe ended, in homely activity. Thus the threefold life is enacted; the threefold world lived through;—The Life and World of Passion;—The Life and World of ideal Art;—The Life and World of Practical Activity. The Intense—the Elegant—the Useful. . . . No matter how, and in what this Utility shows itself; so be, that it exist. The main point is to show, that different periods of life, with their different passions, frailties and endeavours, being lived through, the man comes out at last in useful activity, for as it said in Wilhelm Meister's Indenture, 'The spirit in which we act is the highest matter.' " [4]

This much, Longfellow's own experience had taught him to assimilate in his own way. Here was literary analysis thoroughly different from that perfunctory compilation of facts which he had made in his articles on foreign literature, written at Bowdoin. He had been so much younger then. During the past five years, his emotional and intellectual perceptions had matured and strengthened considerably. His approach to the writings of Goethe showed a new appreciation. True, indeed, that the essential arrangement of his material was lifted pretty directly from Goethe's autobiography, *Dichtung und Wahrheit*. Nevertheless, he understood what he took. In it he found a very simple and practicable solution to his own problems of vain striving.

While he spent the leisurely vacation days in Portland, he began to read more carefully in *Wilhelm Meister*, and found particular satisfaction in Goethe's emphasis on the ennobling power gained through suffering. At present, he was satisfied that he had risen above those bitter disappointments occasioned by Frances Appleton. His letter to Greene had expressed a firmness of purpose in putting that past behind him—an idea which was to find frequent iteration in *Hyperion*. And a few days after writing to Greene he wrote to Hillard from Portland, assuring his Boston friend that he had completely recovered, as he playfully put it, from his late serious accident on Beacon Street. But there was seriousness behind the remark, for he closed the letter to Hillard with a quotation from *Wilhelm Meister:*

> Who ne'er his bread in sorrow ate,
>   Who ne'er the mournful midnight hours,
> Weeping upon his bed has sat,
>   He knows you not, ye heavenly powers.[5]

The quatrain must have been closely related to his thinking about the plan for *Hyperion*, because it was later used as the motto of "Book the First." Perhaps he even started writing the first chapters in Portland. At least, there is evidence that the work on the romance had already begun, soon after he had resumed his duties at Harvard, for he wrote in his journal: "September 13th. Looked over my notes and papers for Hyperion. Long for leisure to begin once more." [6]

Why should he not write an elaborate account of his mental and spiritual apprenticeship, his own *Wanderjahre?* As Goethe and others had portrayed, with varying degrees of autobiographical truth, the progress of their souls through vain strivings to the firm ground of serenity, so Longfellow would depict his own wearisome journey. He would begin by describing the bewilderment and loneliness which had followed the death of Mary Potter Longfellow, and would continue with the story of his unhappy love for Frances Appleton. The purpose and climax of the romance were definitely fixed in his mind before he began to write, for he had already chosen the name of his hero, Hyperion, which would also serve as the title of the book. He would show how the soul of youth, lifted up by high-reaching aspirations, could surmount all suffering with a victory bolder than Werther's suicide. And this struggle toward a practical application of Goethe's utilitarian philosophy of action and labor was identical with that already expressed so simply in "A Psalm of Life." But most important of all was Longfellow's hope that the process of giving vent to his inner moods of morbid restlessness and grief would liberate his mind from them once and for all.

Carlyle's interpretation of *Wilhelm Meister* was closely associated with Longfellow's plan for writing a similar story of a hero whose aspirations and idealism saved him from the pitfalls of life. Longfellow had liked the passage so well that he had quoted Carlyle in his summer lecture on *Wilhelm Meister:* "As the English translator says; 'The book is called a Romance; but it treats not of Romance characters. It has less relation to Fielding's Tom Jones, than to Spenser's Faery Queen. The scene is not laid on this firm earth, but in a fair Utopia of Art and Science and free Activity; the figures, light and aeriform, come unlooked for, and melt away abruptly, like the pageants of Prospero in his enchanted Island.' " [7] In the same sense, Longfellow intended making a romance of *Hyperion*. And who could offer a better guide to cloud-land figures and prose adornments than the magnificent Jean

Paul? Thus he could apply to his own needs the content of Goethe and the form or prose style of Richter.

To give the outlines of his romance specific grounding in auto-biographical fact, Longfellow began his narrative when the hero, still blinded by the sorrow of death, was making his solitary way along the Rhine toward Heidelberg. The theme, recurring frequently, was introduced at the outset with an echo from Novalis, when the author told how "Death cut down the sweet, blue flower, that bloomed beside him." "Then the world seemed to him less beautiful, and life became earnest. It would have been well if he could have forgotten the past; that he might not so mournfully have lived in it, but might have enjoyed and improved the present. But this his heart refused to do . . ." [8] The phrases in each chapter sound like overtones from "A Psalm of Life."

As Longfellow continued, he grew dissatisfied with the name he had chosen for the hero and changed "Hyperion" to "Paul Flemming." Yet, he liked the Greek meaning of the original name so much that he kept it for the title of his romance. When the character of Frances Appleton appeared in the story after Flemming had met and fallen in love with her, he experimented with names until he finally decided to call her "Mary Ashburton."

Having found Jean Paul a master whose prose style he admired to the point of imitation, he had full justification for any number of sallies away from his main plot in search of decorative prose-poetry descriptions, ornamental travel stories, touching legends, anecdotes, and even extended conversations on literary topics.[9] Without any great effort he modified his earlier *Outre-Mer* method of alternating sketches of byways in foreign lands and in foreign literatures: he introduced long sections of his college lectures on German authors, presenting them as dialogues between his principal characters. He even managed to work in a number of translations of German poems made for use in his classes—and was particularly careful to quote in full the lines of Uhland's "Castle by the Sea" which he had put into English with Frances Appleton's help at Zurich.

As he wrote chapter after chapter of *Hyperion*, he was tempted by the curiously inconsistent illusion that, if he described his heroine in phrases sufficiently lyric, his words might create a magic mirror for Frances Appleton not unlike that in the fountain which had led Narcissus to become enamored of his own image. Possibly he recognized no inconsistency in wanting his romance to achieve the very end which he had bravely renounced; or if he saw the paradox, he did not have the power to correct it.

Regardless of his renunciation, expressed in letters, poems, and the rapidly growing *Hyperion*, all of his strong resolves vanished whenever he saw Frances Appleton. And there were times when Boston Common was a lodestone exerting irresistible attraction. Early in October, 1838, after they had met and talked distantly with each other on the Common, he confessed in his journal that the pleasure led to more pain and confusion of mind than he could master.[10] Learning discretion from bitter trials of this sort, he again made up his mind to avoid Beacon Street entirely. "I feel better to live in one place, and not like the baby in the Bible, be cut in two," he wrote in his journal. "The baby was not—nor will I be." [11]

But the battle had to be fought anew, day by day, with heart often winning over the will—and with the manuscript of *Hyperion* neglected until the fortunes of war again favored reason. In one of his protracted periods of surrender to love, he wrote a third letter to Greene, whose absence in Italy did not keep him in ignorance as to the reason why his friend's letters contradicted each other. This time he told Greene that Frances Appleton still held his reason captive; that he could not help hoping that their souls would eventually understand each other. Quite appropriately, he began his confession with a quotation from Coleridge: "And now open your heart and hold it open by the four corners while I pour into it 'all thoughts, all passions, all delights' which fill my own." [12] Then he went on with the assertion that even though the stately and sublimely beautiful being showed no sign of yielding, he likewise was determined to sail with flag nailed to the mast, grim in his determination to hold out as long as she did. In spite of this distraction, he added, he would soon put his mind stubbornly to work on a piece of writing that would have repercussions even in distant Italy.

Of course Longfellow had forgotten that Greene had been told this passion had been buried with a brave *hic jacet*. The stars over

Cambridge had brought a new mood into the ascendency, and
Mars was now the inspiration for battle, not with self, but with
one who might as well surrender. True to his word, he did not
abandon *Hyperion* for long. Instead, he transformed it from a
soul-purging remedy into a weapon aimed at the disdainful citadel
on Beacon Hill. There might be more than one way to effect
capitulation. In his first boldness, he even lost his fear of embar-
rassments in Boston society—and with rash confidence accepted
an invitation to attend a social gathering at the home of Frances
Appleton's aunt. His journal entries reveal his quick regret:

"Tuesday. Dec. 11. Made my first appearance at a party this
season. It was at Mrs. S. Appleton's. A very bright, beautiful
affair. My darling Fanny there. Tried to speak unconcernedly,
but made poor work of it. No matter.

"Wednesday. Dec. 12. Could not work this morning after the
unusual occurrences of last evening. Wrote a page in Hyperion,
and could go no farther. Alas! all my thoughts are scattered.
Walked to town and dined with Charles Amory—my usual reasons—on such occasions.

"Thursday. Dec. 13. College a little dull. Foolish to begin
parties again. Nonsense, when I had grown quiet here." [13]

Again convinced that even the loneliness of the Craigie House
offered more peace than the consequences of wounded pride, he
stayed at home and worked faithfully on new chapters of *Hyperion*. Although the winter term continued without further mishap, he became convinced, as the months passed, that isolation
and the cold persistence of reason had finally achieved permanent
control. He had become reconciled to his failure. At last he was
willing to test his strength by looking without emotion into
Frances Appleton's devastating eyes. To Beacon Street he went,
passed the day, and returned to record the triumph of indifference:

"March 23. A delightful day with the Appletons. Dined with
them; went to the new Green-House in the afternoon and back to
tea. We had most pleasant and animated conversations, as in the
olden time. They are dear children, notwithstanding they have
no talent for matrimony. Thus do I enjoy, what Richard Crashaw
calls:

"Delicious deaths, soft exhalations
Of soul; dear and divine annihilations;
A thousand unknown rites
Of joys, and rarified delights." [14]

The quietly sardonic tone of the jesting sentence about matrimony proved that he had gained a temporary respite from inner strife—had accepted with fresh resignation the apparently inevitable conclusion to this tale of lost love which he was living and writing at the same time. Now he was ready, he thought, to practice the bold affirmations which he had proclaimed in "A Psalm of Life." In such a mood he turned to the unhappy task of writing the climax to *Hyperion;* the pages which would stand as both colophon and epitaph to his love for Frances Appleton. On April 6 he recorded in his journal: "An exact counterpart and pendant of yesterday; and I at work on my Romance—changing and arranging and writing out various portions. Wrote the last chapter; though others remain to be written." [15]

These closing pages of *Hyperion* were concerned with Paul Flemming's final renunciation of hope. The climax to the narrative occurred just before the beginning of the last chapter, when Paul Flemming discovered the inscription which served as motto for the book: "Look not mournfully into the Past. It comes not back again. Wisely improve the Present. It is thine. Go forth to meet the shadowy Future, without fear, and with a manly heart." [16] The discovery of the inscription, so closely related to "A Psalm of Life," caused Paul Flemming to make two distinct resolves. He would be lost no longer in sorrow over the death of his "friend," and he would waste no more time over his hopeless love for Mary Ashburton. The sentences concerning the second resolve may have been parts of the interpolations or changes made on April 6, for they express a complete renunciation similar to that revealed in Longfellow's journal at this time:

"And, oh! how many disappointed hopes, how many bitter recollections, how much of wounded pride, and unrequited love, were in those tears through which he read . . . from that hour forth he resolved, that he would no longer veer with every shifting wind of circumstance; no longer be a child's plaything in the hands of Fate, which we ourselves do make or mar. He resolved henceforward not to lean on others; but to walk self-confident and self-possessed; no longer to waste his years in vain regrets; nor wait the fulfilment of boundless hopes and indiscreet desires; but to live in the Present wisely, alike forgetful of the Past, and careless of what the mysterious Future might bring. And from that moment he was calm, and strong; he was reconciled with himself!" [17]

In the concluding chapter, entitled "The Last Pang," Flemming continued from St. Gilgen to Stuttgart, where the dénouement occurred. The night before his departure, he heard the voice of a young woman in the room adjoining his at the inn, and knew that he was listening to Mary Ashburton, as she read the prayers of the Church of England:

"His heart could not be deceived; and all its wounds began to bleed afresh, like those of a murdered man, when the murderer approaches. His first impulse was of affection only, boundless, irrepressible, delirious, as of old in the green valley of Interlachen. He waited for her voice to cease that he might go to her, and behold her face once more. And then his pride rose up within him, and rebuked this weakness. He remembered his firm resolve; and blushed to find himself so feeble. And the voice ceased, and yet he did not go. Pride had so far gained the mastery over affection. He lay down upon his bed, like a child as he was. All about him was silence, and the silence was holy, for she was near; so near, that he could almost hear the beating of her heart. He knew now for the first time how weak he was, and how strong was his passion for that woman. His heart was like the altar of the Israelites of old; and though drenched with tears, as with rain, it was kindled at once by the holy fire from Heaven!

"Towards morning he fell asleep, exhausted with the strong excitement; and, in that hour when, sleep being 'nigh unto the soul,' visions are deemed prophetic, he dreamed. O blessed vision of the morning, stay! thou wast so fair! He stood again on the green sunny meadow, beneath the ruined towers; and she was by his side, with her pale speaking countenance and holy eyes; and he kissed her fair forehead; and she turned her face towards him beaming with affection and said, 'I confess it now; you are the

Magician!' and pressed him in a meek embrace, that he 'might rather feel than see the swelling of her heart.' And then she faded away from his arms, and her face became transfigured, and her voice like the voice of an angel in heaven;—and he awoke, and was alone!

"It was broad daylight; and he heard the postilion, and the stamping of horses' hoofs on the pavement at the door. At the same moment his servant came in, with coffee, and told him all was ready. He did not dare to stay. But, throwing himself into the carriage, he cast one look towards the window of the Dark Ladie, and a moment afterwards had left her forever! He had drunk the last drop of the bitter cup, and now laid the golden goblet gently down, knowing that he should behold it no more!

"No more! O how majestically mournful are those words. They sound like the roar of the wind through a forest of pines!" [18]

No more? Deep in his heart, Longfellow felt that he could never reconcile himself to those majestically mournful words. As has been pointed out, his maturity since the death of Mary Longfellow had shown itself most prominently in his emotional growth; in his new power to feel deeply and to be moved deeply. Herein lay his strength. Offsetting this was his inability to reason himself out of any passionate longing for an ideal. Throughout this trying courtship, there was never any doubt about what he must have to secure happiness. Always he was impelled inexorably to yearn for one hope—that she would reward love with love.

He could not forge from Goethe's teaching, or his own thinking, any chains strong enough to hold him to a course of action that shut this one glowing hope out of sight. He could not build a wall of rationalizations strong enough to withstand the battering of his stubborn passion. And stubbornness was a subtle power in Longfellow—a kind of spoiled-child way he had, of setting his heart on something and refusing to be denied. But possibly this same trait had kept him within sight of the boyhood ambition. He had once written to his sister from Germany that his poetic career was over; that he would never again write poetry. But in his journal, later, he had written, "I wonder." [19]

So now he wondered. Was it still possible that his portrayal in the pages of *Hyperion*, those word pictures of his beloved as she was reflected in his eyes, might move the lady to understand, when she read the book, how tender and deep was his love for her? In a fourth letter to Greene, on the familiar subject, he admitted that such a hope persisted. There were two mighty wills at work here, he wrote, and he would not concede, quite yet, that victory was hopeless. "I am as much in love as ever. . . . The lady says she *will not!* I say she *shall!*" In fact, he told how he was about to make one last desperate gamble with *Hyperion*. In his earlier letters, he had not told Greene what secret literary work he had been preparing for so many months. But now, with the book done and almost through the press, he could not resist a complete revelation of his hopes:

". . . next week I shall fire off a rocket which I trust will make a commotion in that citadel. Perhaps the garrison will capitulate; —perhaps the rocket may burst and kill me. You will know soon. I mean to say that I have written a Romance during this last year, into which I have put my feelings,—my hopes and sufferings for the last *three* years. Things are shadowed forth with distinctness enough to be understood; and yet so mingled with fiction in the events set down as to raise doubt, and perplexity. The *Feelings* of the book are true;—the *events* of the story mostly fictitious. The heroine, of course, bears a resemblance to *the lady*, without being an exact portrait; so that the reader will say 'It is!—no, it is not! And yet it must be!' Don't misunderstand me. There is no betrayal of confidence; no real scenes described;—and the lady so painted (unless I much deceive myself) as to make her fall in love with her own sweet image in the book. Now I hardly need to tell you that I look forward with intense interest to next week.

"The publication of the book will probably call down upon my head tremendous censure; and I trust also equal applause. As a literary work it far surpasses anything I have before written. How could it be otherwise, when you remember the circumstances of its origin." [20]

Although Sumner, then traveling in Italy, had met Greene as Longfellow had hoped, he had not been inclined to take this courtship too seriously. After hearing various details of Longfellow's letters sent to Greene, Sumner wrote a teasing letter from Rome, in which he called Longfellow's attention to the excellent advice of Sir John Suckling. But his words came to hand far too late to have any influence. The remarks of Boston newspapers were of far more concern to Longfellow, just then, than the advice of either Sir John or Charles Sumner. And even though Greene had been promised a full account of what happened when this strange German "rocket" landed in the "garrison" on Beacon Hill, he had to wait. Probably there was no immediate reaction from that camp; nothing to tell. The Appletons remained at their summer home in Stockbridge until late in the fall and were thus spared the first wave of gossip which scampered and splashed about Boston as soon as the book was out. Felton wrote two indignant answers to the most insulting reviews—entitling one, "Hyperion to a Satyr." [21] But the noise and vituperation continued in print and by word of mouth. Beacon Hill had not relished such a tempest in a teapot for many years. On October 1, Longfellow told Greene about it:

"Sumner's letter from the Convent gave me a glimpse of you the other day. It revived the past rather too vividly. Likewise a Miss Hinkley has lately returned from Italy and brought the story of my romantic passion for Madame Julia in days gone by. This, too, revives the past rather too vividly. I sometimes wish myself in Italy again. You have so much freedom there. I have been rending asunder some of the Boston cobwebs of prejudice and narrow-minded criticism by publishing a strange kind of a book, which I have the audacity to call a *Romance*. Most people think it is not because there is no bloody hatchet in it. You will like it *notwithstanding*. The Boston papers are very *savage*, and abuse me *shockingly;* for all which I am very glad; inasmuch as it proves to me, that the book is *good*. I take all such things very calmly. If you were here you would be very angry; and would jump out of your skin, like the Danish ghost. I shall send you a copy of the book as soon as I can find an opportunity. It has had a fine run; and a large edition sold in a few weeks. I have now in press a volume of poems, under title 'Voices of the Night'—containing all I have written since my residence here—some of my earlier pieces, and some translations. This, too, you shall have by first opportunity. But, hang it, there are no opportunities here in Camb. *Hyperion* is as much a Romance, as Childe Harold or the *Roman de la Rose*. And now, Geordie, you can do me a *very* great favor;—namely by getting these books noticed in the foreign journals; in Paris for instance, in the *Revue de Deux Mondes* &c. You know what *cursed sharps* [sheep?] our countrymen are, and how they follow everything that comes from the other side of the sea. The fact that these books had been noticed in Italy, Germany, or France would do me great good. I dont know that I shall need this, but I may; as the *opposition* seems to be *savage & strong*." [22]

No word came from the most important critic. Although Frances Appleton was thoroughly indignant to find herself figuring so prominently in such a narrative, discretion and reserve kept her from making any immediate comments. Of course, nobody was deceived by the thinly veiled anonymity. And even the European setting could not easily mystify the Beacon Street spinsters who, behind close-drawn shutters, had watched the whole affair with wide eyes, during the past year.

But Longfellow had other cares. Colman, the publisher in New York, failed because of the effects of the current financial panic, after only half the edition had been distributed. Commenting on this unfortunate mishap, Longfellow wrote to Greene:

"No matter; I had the glorious satisfaction of writing it; and thereby gained a great victory, *not* over the 'dark Ladie' but over myself. I now once more rejoice in my freedom; and am no longer the thrall of anyone. I have great faith in one's writing himself clear from a passion—giving vent to pent up fire. But George, George! It was a horrible thing; as my former letters must testify. I have an indistinct idea of raving on paper to a large amount. But it was all sincere. My mind was morbid. I have portrayed it all in the book; and how a man is to come out of it; not by shooting himself like Werther; but in a better way. In the present North American Felton has given a fine vindication of it as a Romance; though he does not touch this point, which is *the* point. If I had called the book 'Heart's Ease, or the Cure of a morbid mind' it would have been better understood. I called it *Hyperion* because it *moves on high* among clouds and stars, and expresses the various aspirations of the soul of man. It is all modeled on this idea; style and all. In fine it contains my cherished thoughts for

FRANCES APPLETON
Courtesy of Houghton Mifflin Company.

three years. Pardon my saying so much. In offset, I will send you the '*horrible dispraise*' I spoke of; though the papers that uttered it have since nearly come round; and have even praised some parts of it. *How victorious is Silence!*" [23]

Ahead of him was one silence not likely to be interpreted as victorious. Several months after the publication of *Hyperion*, Longfellow succumbed to a prophetic mood of restlessness, and set out on foot as of old, one spring day, through Cambridgeport, over the Charles River to Boston. As he walked along the familiar street, his heart must have turned completely over. He saw coming toward him, the graceful, the stately, the unmistakable dark Ladie. Probably his inner turmoil was caused in part by his uncertainty as to how a hero should act out the sequel of a romance in which he had recently published his resolve to look no more on the face of his beloved. But the self-possessed heroine, undoubtedly smarting still because of the unexpected impertinence of *Hyperion*, solved his dilemma for him. As she came nearer, one may easily imagine how he searched her face for signs of friendliness or hostility—at least for a glance of recognition.

That night, heavy at heart, he traversed the weary miles to Cambridge, climbed to his room, opened his journal, and left us only this brief record of the incident: "Met the stately dark ladie in the street. I *looked* and *passed*, as Dante prescribes." He concluded the account of this meeting with one final, despairing sentence:

"It is ended." [24]

XXV

NEW LONGING FOR FREEDOM

*I am weary and sick to-night. College duties called me from my
bed before day-light. My nature rebels at this. I hate such over-
early rising. The apperition of a tall negro with a lantern in my
bed-room at such a holy hour disturbs the golden morning vision.
Breakfast at six is intolerable. . . . A benediction on such early
rising. It needs one. Shall I have no more glorious midnights? Shall
I creep to bed at nine, stuffed with day-light, like a drowsy peasant
"stuffed with distressful bread"?* [1]

No AMOUNT of scandalous innuendo or harsh criticism from reviewers shook Longfellow's faith in *Hyperion*. Never a penetrating critic of his own writings, he was satisfied to find that he had
created a minor sensation in Boston and Cambridge. And he had
been told that the book had sold rapidly. If many readers were
angry with him for having kneaded his romance into a concealing
hash of travel essays and college lectures on German literature,
their indignant fault-findings did not worry him. "I do not like
the book," wrote one reviewer. "It is such a journal as a man who
reads a great deal makes from the scraps in his table drawer. Yet
it has not the sincerity or quiet touches which give interest to the
real journals of very common persons." [2]

Protected by the comfortable adulation of his friends, Longfellow pretended not to feel these rude gusts of criticism. Somewhat fantastically he claimed that an abundance of attacks proved
the merit of *Hyperion*. "But I have the approbation of those whose
approbation I most desire," he concluded, "and, of course, do not
much care how others curse and abuse." [3]

He did care. Public recognition and praise were still his strongest incentives to writing, even though he had rejected this unpleasant fact in Heidelberg and had protested that henceforth, at
least, a brighter light than fame should guide him. Naturally, this
resolve was weakened by such extravagant praise as that which
had greeted his "Psalms" when first they caught attention in the

Knickerbocker; for this kind of recognition was closely related to his longing to write something permanent and lasting. Heretofore all his aspirations for literary attainment had been hindered not only by the consequences of his father's early hostility to his plans and the resultant diverting of his talent, but also by the very meagre competence of that talent. Nevertheless, the ardent hope, mistakenly watered with scholarly activity at Brunswick, trampled down by the demands of classroom routine, and ignored for long periods of time during the excitement of foreign travel, had survived and grown. Then Longfellow had fashioned a challenging hymn to courage—an exhortation to living in the present. And with the success of that single poem, his hope blossomed into faith.

At first he had been surprised to watch the working of his words on other people's minds. The newspapers in New York copied the poem from the *Knickerbocker,* and the newspapers in Boston copied it again, until the lines became familiar, like a glorified popular song that had caught more than the fancy of the young nation. "A Psalm of Life" was quoted, discussed, and eulogized with more enthusiasm and fervor than any other poem that had ever been published in America. And the poet in Cambridge, standing with renewed vigor in the Harvard lecture hall as he unfolded the beauties of German prose, or walking down familiar streets in Boston, carefully dressed as always, from his colored tie to his polished boots, vibrated to this popular response and derived from it new faith in his own exhortations.

Thus stimulated, he returned to the peace of his Craigie House study to write more poems that would speak from his heart to the hearts of the people; psalms of life and psalms of death. Editors in Boston, New York, and Philadelphia began to solicit his contributions with flattering persistence. No wonder that he lost interest in compiling laborious articles for the *North American,* for that path to eminence had been a tedious one, at best. Only the demands of friendship had led him to dig out some old notes made at Bowdoin, and to fix them into an article on Anglo-Saxon poetry as an American introduction to Dr. Bosworth's *Dictionary.*[4] He had taken no pleasure in writing it.

In the spring of 1839, he had put aside another learned study, when the ideas for a third "Psalm" came to him. Two days later, he descended to the dusty plains of scholarship: "Have been at work upon a paper for N. A. R. on the French language in England, till my head aches. I had rather write Psalms." [5] Week followed week, and the paper remained unfinished. Over a year later he made reference to it again in his journal: "Worked at an article on the French Language in England for the N. A. Revue. I have lost my love of labor and dry research into dusty books." [6] When the tedious compilation was published, his father's praise elicited a further confession: "I am glad you found anything interesting in the French article. To most people it must be very dull. It is the result of some studies I made formerly in Brunswick; and which probably at the present moment I should not have either time or inclination to make. Having the materials at hand, I thought it worth while to work them up." [7]

The old hunger for unhampered devotion to the life of a man of letters had been adding to his discontent. In the back of his mind was the favorite dream of going abroad to live indefinitely. Soon after the publication of *Hyperion*, he wrote in his journal: "I have been thinking of Spain; and have a presentiment that one day or another I shall go there in a Diplomatic character. That would be pleasant; Secretary of Legation for instance." [8] Wistfully, he looked over into the greener fields of endeavor where such friends as Jared Sparks, Prescott, Willis, Clark, and Cogswell were laboring. Cogswell had shown an amazing courage in breaking away from one position after another, because he had not liked them. From Europe he had returned to teach at Harvard; dissatisfied, he had set up his own school at Round Hill; and now he was in New York, no longer a teacher but the editor of the *New York Review*, which was rapidly becoming a worthy rival of the *North American*.

Cogswell's acceptance of this editorial position had been a disappointment, indirectly, to Longfellow, who had been dreaming again of establishing a literary newspaper. While visiting Sam Ward (his friend whom he had met in Heidelberg), during a recent vacation spent in New York, Longfellow had talked about the plan with such enthusiasm that Ward had enlisted Cogswell's support. Everybody seemed agreed that the idea was sound.

With never-failing impulsiveness, Longfellow had announced the project to Greene, in Italy:

"You desire a newspaper and shall have one soon. Mr. Cogswell, Sam Ward, Mr. Sparks and myself think of starting a new one in New York. The plan, however, is not yet ripe, and may come to nought; particularly as Cogswell will doubtless go to Europe again, on the following most agreeable footing. Old Mr. Astor has given the city of New York 350 thousand dollars for a public Library; and Cogswell has the management of the matter, I believe, and will doubtless be librarian and go forth to buy books. This may break up the plan, as he was to be editor. We shall see. Librarian and Editor both he cannot be; as I will not, for one, engage in any paper, the editor of which will not devote himself solely to it. Then y^r cousin Sam is *so* flighty! However, more of this when I know more." [9]

In the summer vacation of 1838, Cogswell had visited Longfellow at his home in Portland, where there was ample time for leisurely discussions of the newspaper project. A mellowing peace and serenity filled the rooms of the Longfellow house, now that the children had grown up and departed. Longfellow's gentle sister Anne, who had been married to George Pierce so shortly before his death, was still living at home. Zilpah and Stephen, both showing traces of infirmity and age, were always happy to give proud welcome to their son and his guests. Behind the square brick house, flower gardens and the shade of fruit trees invited visitors. For sentiment's sake, one of the old pews, salvaged from the destruction of the first Parish Church, had been set up against a fruit tree. To this secluded retirement, Longfellow brought his guests, in the cool of a summer evening, to enjoy after-dinner coffee and cigars.

Cogswell had not yet been appointed librarian, so perhaps the plan could be carried out. If not, Longfellow considered establishing such an enterprise in Boston. After his return to Cambridge he talked about it with Felton, already much at home with his buxom bride in his newly built cottage, and blissfully happy —"just like a child with both hands full of flowers," as Longfellow had described him to Greene.[10] Always cautious, Felton listened and made suggestions. Longfellow, returning to the

Craigie House, recorded the effect. "The newspaper prints itself in my imagination," he wrote in his journal, a little later. "I have already published several No's. and have a large subscription list. Ha! cheating fancy! I know your old tricks, and this time you shall not catch me." [11] Hawthorne liked the idea: "I saw Mr. Sparks some time since," wrote the custom-house official, "and he said that you were thinking of a literary paper. Why not? Your name would go a great way toward insuring its success; and it is intolerable that there should not be a single belles-lettres journal in New England. Whatever aid a custom-house officer could afford should always be forthcoming." [12] But the scheme was finally abandoned because it required too many risks.

Longfellow found Hawthorne's warm loyalty the same at all times. Since George Bancroft's political influence had brought Hawthorne out of his Salem owl's nest into the custom-house and into Boston lodgings, the Bowdoin classmates managed to convene more frequently for a quiet supper-for-two at the Coffee House or the Tremont, with a bottle of wine between them and a long evening of conversation. This shy man from Salem was destined to go far, Longfellow knew, even though he failed to understand Hawthorne's reticences. His clean-cut features and great shock of black hair were striking; but the true nature of the spirit was revealed in the naïve, childlike smile and in the lambent glow of his eyes.

Other friendships helped crowd out Longfellow's disappointments. The literary circles of Boston had begun to pay him a slightly greater deference. Apparently his writings had hung new weights on the clock of his reputation, in the eyes of all. Dinners in Boston were more the rule than the exception with him, during certain parts of the school year. Invitations came constantly from his friends there. William Hickling Prescott, handsome, gay, and forty, still a bit surprised at his own rise to fame after the publication of his first book, was fond of society and entertainment. And following a brisk dinner-table conversation (always enlivened with a seasoning of his host's inevitable gossip), it was pleasant to adjourn to the rich library of Spanish books; to exchange comments and opinions on the history and literature of Castile.

Surprising that Prescott should be so widely read, with those weak eyes of his. To look at him one would believe him more a social lion than a scholar. Yet nobody could ever accuse him of being a bookworm. Early in the morning, perhaps before Longfellow had finished his breakfast of tea and toast in his study, Prescott was likely to interrupt him by pausing, in his horseback ride, to bid the Craigie House poet good morning. Although he enjoyed a strong horse and a stiff gallop, he would need to take more care. His friends were troubled at the way he limped about Boston after he had been thrown so hard from his horse on Winter Street. Down he had come on the paved sidewalk, "all bent up, like a Hindoo god." [13] It was a wonder he hadn't broken every bone in his body.

Although Longfellow still enjoyed riding, he had given it up because of the expense. Cambridge was a costly place to live in, he had found. And frequent walks to Boston were all the exercise he needed. Then too, there were so many diversions on the way, friends who stopped to talk, or landscape scenes that painted themselves in his memory. Occasionally he drank a cup of tea with the white-headed Cambridgeport painter, Washington Allston, still exacting, self-critical, and secretly perplexed over his canvas of *Belshazzar's Feast*. Even though the artist could never satisfy himself with it, he gave his best to his friends as unreservedly as he did to his painting, until his studio became a meeting place for those who liked to explore the realms of aesthetics in discussions of painting or poetry—for Allston was also an author. But the old man's garrulity and frequent repetition of the same stories made Longfellow a bit impatient. On mornings after such occasions, if he passed Allston's studio and knocked at the door, he found that the old man was still sleeping in his home near by. The reek of stale cigar-smoke was proof that a symposium had almost outlasted the night.

At times, the town of Cambridge held stronger attractions for Longfellow than Boston. Emerson's lectures, for example, were social events which he did not like to miss. In the winter of 1838, Emerson had given a series of lectures in Cambridge on a variety of subjects: "On the Affections," "On Being and Seeming," and "Holiness." [14] To be sure, Longfellow was not always certain that he grasped what Emerson was trying to say, but some people weren't sure that Emerson did, either. Jeremiah Mason said a sharp thing when asked if he could understand this nebulous and flowery oracle: "No, *I* can't, but my daughters can." [15] If he had become resigned to giving up preaching, some thought it might be well for him to give up controversial subjects which roused the ire of Cambridge theologians. Referring to his attendance at the lecture on "Holiness," Longfellow had written: "This lecture is a great bug-bear to many pious feeble souls. Not exactly comprehending it, (and who does?) they seem to be sitting in the shadow of some awful Atheism or Deism or other *ism*." [16] Several months later, Longfellow wrote to Sam Ward: "Don't fail to hear Emerson's lectures. The difference between him and most other lecturers is this: From Emerson you go away and remember nothing, save that you have been much delighted; you have had a pleasant dream in which angelic voices spake. From most other lecturers you go away and remember nothing, save that you have been lamentably *bored*, you have had the *nightmare*, and have heard her colt neigh." [17]

The doctrine of transcendentalism was spreading about Boston and Concord like a disease from which Cambridge was fairly immune. But Longfellow found the supporters and followers of Emerson wherever he went. One day at George Hillard's home in Boston, where he had stopped for tea, he met two particular exponents of German thought: Rev. Frederic Henry Hedge, on a visit from Bangor, and Miss Elizabeth Peabody, who had opened a bookstore for the distribution of foreign literature.

There had been some attempt to pitch Longfellow into the camp of transcendentalism after he had published *Hyperion*. One reviewer had accused him of writing "in that Germanico-metaphorical style in which small ideas are now-a-days clothed and magnified, just as small-waisted boys are stuffed out with cushions and pillows, when they would enact Falstaff." [18] Felton had put that rascal into his place. If his friends wished to discuss the poetic merits of Jean Paul, or the novels of Goethe or the poems of Novalis, Longfellow was glad to join them, but he did not know the doctrines of Schleiermacher and Vatke and Baur and De Wette; furthermore he was not interested. He had even refused George Ripley, who had asked Longfellow to contribute German translations to his *Specimens of Foreign Literature;* had expressed his regrets even after his name had been printed as a prospective contributor with Felton and O. B. Frothingham, to John S. Dwight's volume from Goethe and Schiller.

Everyone seemed suddenly to have joined the fad of importing foreign literature. Even Emerson had taken a hand in the business by bringing out an edition of Carlyle's *Sartor Resartus*, a book certainly more German than English. And in the spring of 1838, Emerson suggested a different importation—had urged a Boston publisher to print an edition of poems by a young Englishman not so old as Longfellow. "Mr. Emerson is desirous that we should publish an edition of Tennyson's Poems," write C. C. Little & Co. to Longfellow, "& says that his volume is in your hands. . . . We have Mr. Emerson's consent to print from his volume." [19]

All this activity, social and literary, was interesting to Longfellow, so long as he could escape from it to the green-walled solitude of his library on the second floor of the Craigie House. The great house beneath the greater elms was beginning to assume the aspect of a private hotel, since Mrs. Craigie had rented rooms to Dr. Joseph Worcester, who had come from Salem to work on his American Dictionary, and to little old Aunt Sally Lowell, familiar to all Cambridge folk. Longfellow liked the genteel manners of this cheerful lady who, in spite of her seventy-odd years, was a sprightly little creature, as brisk and buzzy as a fly. After he had visited her in her rooms a few times and had received her in his own part of the house, he ventured a suggestion. Perhaps she would be willing to arrange his meals for him, so that he should dine with her? She was delighted. And Longfellow, tired of eating in solitary dignity, was equally happy over the new order of things.[20]

Aunt Sally, flattered beyond words by so much attention, made good use of this chance to confide her family troubles. The Lowells seemed to be coming to a bad end, after all these years. A nephew of hers—a senior at Harvard, named James Russell Lowell—had recently disgraced himself by inattention to his studies and had been rusticated to Concord shortly before commencement in 1838. And this, after he had been chosen to write the class poem, which he was unable to deliver! More recently, a brother of hers had become involved in moral and financial delinquencies which were likely to cost Aunt Sally a great deal of pride—and possibly some money. "This is the first stain on the escutcheon of the Lowells!" she bemoaned to Longfellow.[21]

Even the entertaining company of Aunt Sally could not eliminate the gloomy hours when Longfellow, securely hidden in his own rooms, gave way to the sorrow of his failure to win Frances Appleton. He concealed his sadness from most of his friends, and continued as though nothing had happened. But, try as he would, he could not forget. In Portland, his sister Anne kept the secret, and expressed her love and sympathy in tender ways, such as that which prompted her spring greetings:

"In the box which accompanies this you will find a bunch of sweet May-flowers which I hope will reach you in some decent state of freshness and beauty.

"I think they will revive in you recollections of the days of yr. childhood, Deerings woods & the Wind Mill pasture—but if they only call forth the exclamation, beautiful & sweet, & remind you of the love of yr. Sister Anne they will have fulfilled their mission."[22]

This very tenderness of love was what his heart cried to find. But Frances Appleton had never shown him the slightest encouragement—a burning thought that smouldered always within him. When his days were filled with the cares of his lecture classes or with the joys of friendly intercourse in Cambridge and Boston, he could find pleasure in the conviction that life was not an empty dream. "Act,—act in the living present" he had said. But his continued attempts to follow such a command failed so often that he seemed to be losing ground. Even his health suffered—and more was needed to explain his debility than long hours, early rising, and occasional overindulgence in his favorite Schloss Johannisberger. Yet work brought some relief:

"I feel better these College work-days, when I can let my electricity off among my pupils; and like Eugene Aram, with a great sorrow at my heart 'sit among the urchins in the school.'

Activity—constant—ceaseless activity! That is what I need. My heart breaks when I sit alone here so much!" [23]

Here was a paradoxical situation: debility restraining him from the activity which he welcomed. For three years he had been suffering from a chronic condition of varied ills. Colds, grippe, and influenza had confined him to his room at Dr. Stearns' during several weeks of his first year at Harvard. And at the beginning of the fall term, 1838, he had written:

"A new month,—a new College year, and a new book in my Journal begins today. I am neither in good health nor good spirits; being foolishly inclined to indigestion and the most unpleasant melancholy. It is a kind of sleepiness of the soul, in which I feel a general indifference to all things." [24]

Thus a variety of ailments, physical and mental, were conspiring to increase his dissatisfaction with his position as Smith Professor at Harvard College. The future had seemed so promising, when he had begun with the expectation of filling a supervisory capacity; occasional lectures and no teaching. But the burden had increased until it irked him: "Perhaps the worst thing in a College Life is this having your mind constantly a play-mate for boys," he had written in September, 1838, "constantly adapting itself to them; instead of stretching out, and grappling with men's minds." [25] Again the cycle of hope, trial, and disappointment had been completed, and he had returned to the same discontent which he had fought to escape at Bowdoin.

Once more he longed to find a larger audience, to devote himself entirely to literature, his first love. Writing was not easily sandwiched between afternoons of lecturing and mornings of classroom preparation, particularly when ailments tormented him. In the fall and winter of 1838 he had been plagued with serious toothaches which finally required professional attention in Boston. "The dentist tugged merrily at my tooth for five minutes," he recorded. "At length it came out. He said he never knew one come so hard." [26] The following day he was assailed with a motley squad of remorses and pains:

"Oct. 17. Face sore and swollen. Look like King Henry VIII. A working day in College. Have I been wise to give up three

whole days to College classes? I think I have; for thus I make my
presence felt here; and have no idle time, to mope and grieve over
that most sad and sorrowful thought, which haunts me, *Forever!*" [27]

Nevertheless, a series of incidents had caused Longfellow so
much dissatisfaction with decrees of the Harvard Corporation
that he offered to resign the Smith Professorship. The beginnings of an unpleasant situation came one day when President
Quincy called at Longfellow's room to talk about a delicate
matter. He wished Longfellow to request the resignation of
venerable Francis Sales, who had served faithfully as French instructor at Harvard since the department of modern languages
had been created.[28] In 1803, when George Ticknor was preparing to enter Dartmouth, Sales had tutored him in Boston; sixteen
years later, when Ticknor returned to begin his work as Smith
Professor at Harvard, Sales had begun teaching as Ticknor's subordinate. He had continued faithfully ever since. Now, an old
and useless man, he was being cut adrift. Could nothing be done
for him? Would it not be possible to secure retirement for him
with half-pay? President Quincy regretted that he could not
secure it.

"Thus one of these days," wrote Longfellow, "if I grow old
in the service of these men, shall I likewise be remorselessly set
free." [29] The anticipation was unpleasant. To increase his uneasiness, he had previously been obliged to request the resignation
of Instructors Saurault and Bokum. Bernard Rölker was soon appointed to replace Bokum, but Longfellow was prevailed upon
to take over the duties in the French department with additional
wages as recompense. The year passed without any consideration of relief for this temporary arrangement.

Here was a violation of the schedule of the Smith Professor's
duties which Professor Ticknor had worked so assiduously to
secure; moreover, a violation of the written agreement which
Longfellow had made with the authorities at the beginning of
his second year. In recommending a Frenchman to fill this vacancy, Longfellow wrote to the President and the Corporation
a very blunt statement of the matter:

"Harvard University

"Gentlemen,

"Feeling it important, that before commencement of another term, the place of French Instructor should be filled, I take the liberty of recommending Mr. Chas. Hutet of New York, as a person qualified to fill the station. In accordance with your wishes I took charge of the French instruction during the past year; but am unwilling to do so longer. It seems to me of great importance that the French should be taught by a Frenchman, as the other modern languages are by natives of the countries where spoken; and I therefore respectfully request, that Mr. Hutet may be appointed.

"Henry W. Longfellow

"Cambridge, August 17, 1839." [30]

While this matter was still being considered, a glittering door to freedom seemed to open before Longfellow's eyes. John Jacob Astor, the hard-headed German adventurer who had come to America with seven flutes, to open a music store, and had already become the richest man in America, wanted to send his young son to Germany for six years of fashionable education—a curious throw-back. But would Longfellow like to accompany the boy as a companion and tutor? Sam Ward, his friend in New York, thought he could arrange it. Certainly Ward, who had married one of Astor's daughters, was in position to speak an influential word or two. It would be a pleasant change from teaching, Ward suggested.[31] Pleasant, indeed! Longfellow was jubilant. Here was exactly the kind of escape he had looked for these many years. Hastily he wrote begging Ward to use strongest persuasion; then began dreaming of what he should do in Europe.

A harsh note of unpleasant command to duty broke into his dreaming, for the President and Fellows of Harvard College replied with disconcerting candor that they found it inexpedient to increase the number of instructors in the foreign language department, and that the Smith Professor would be expected to continue giving instruction to the French students. Indignantly, Longfellow communicated this decision to his father, and added:

"Now the Smith Professor does not wish nor intend to do any such thing, if he can help it. At all events, if I stay I shall hit upon some way of shortening the time devoted to instruction in languages; or the labor will finish me before winter. In all probability I shall have a letter from New York tomorrow; and if the proposals of Mr. Astor are as good as I expect they will be, I shall feel very much inclined to accept them. No doubt, if I could bring myself to give up all my time to the College, and not pursue any other study, I could get along very comfortably. But the idea of standing still, or of going backward is not to be entertained by such an ardent temper as mine." [32]

He decided to make no reply to the President until he had heard from New York. Of course, there was no reason to feel certain as he did about the European trip. Yet, such a prospect was so attractive that nothing must spoil it for him now. It was what his destiny seemed to call for. After a few days he wrote his father again to say that Mr. Astor had taken a temporary notion into his head to keep the boy at home. Since everyone thought it was a passing whim, Longfellow was undismayed:

"However I have faith, that it will all come right at last; and that I shall go, and devote myself wholly to literature without any breaks or interruptions. I shall then produce something which will live. Meanwhile, I have organized my classes, and the term begins under very favorable circumstances, save the one you are aware of, namely no French Instructor." [33]

When the news came, about a week later, that other arrangements had been made by Mr. Astor, Longfellow turned the full blast of his resentment against the unhappy situation at Harvard, which immediately seemed far worse than ever before. In communicating this unpleasant news to his father, he concluded:

"I am very sorry; but as there is no remedy, I must forget it as soon as possible. But my work here grows quite intolerable; and unless they make some change, I will leave them, with or without anything to do. I will not consent to have my life crushed out of me so. I had rather live awhile on bread and water. I feel all the time, that I am doing wrong to stay here under such circumstances; though I know this is not *prudent*. . . .

"This week I have written two more Psalms. One of them you will have in the next Knickerbocker; and the other, I know not where. Moreover I am going to put to press a volume of Poems without delay. All my last pieces; and a selection from the earlier ones; together with Translations." [34]

Forced to make a decision that would guard his time from too great a number of encroachments, he considered the possibility of resigning from the Smith Professorship. But could he earn a living with his pen? The problem was the old one which he had debated so many times after his father had refused to let him risk financial security by setting out boldly as an independent man of letters. Since that time, he had probed all possibilities of escape. Now, with the promise of continued solicitations from various magazine and newspaper editors, Longfellow could be sure of enough income from his writing to make at least a part of his college salary unnecessary. His friend and neighbor, Jared Sparks, had recently effected an ideal arrangement with the college. Although appointed McLean Professor of History, he lectured only during the fall term, taught no classes, and received a small but regular salary. Such an arrangement would exactly fit Longfellow's needs, for he would enjoy giving a few lectures each year, provided his other duties were removed. He would resign the Smith Professorship. With great care he presented his plan to the President and the Corporation, in a detailed letter:

"Gentlemen:

"I respectfully beg leave to call your attention once more to the subject of my duties as Smith Professor in the University. You will recollect that when I entered upon my labors in the Department of Modern Languages, the special duties, which devolved upon me as Head of the Department, and Professor of Belles Lettres, were agreed upon by a Committee of the Corporation and myself. Native teachers having always been employed to instruct in the elements and pronunciation of the Modern Languages, the general supervision of the Department, instruction in some of the higher works of modern foreign literature, and certain courses of Lectures were assigned to me. This arrangement, so far as I know, proved satisfactory to all the parties concerned.

"You will also recollect, that in the Summer of 1838, two gentlemen, namely the French and the German Instructors, for reasons which it is unnecessary to specify, resigned. Another German teacher was immediately appointed, but as no suitable person occured at the moment to fill the place of French Instructor, the appointment of one was postponed for a season, and I consented to take charge of the classes in that language. I would respectfully remind you of the distinct understanding at the time, that this arrangement was to be only a temporary one, and to be given up as soon as a suitable appointment could be made. It happened, however, that I continued to instruct French during the whole year.

"At the commencement of the present academic year, I proposed the name of a French gentleman: and this nomination was laid by the President before your honorable body. No appointment, however, was made; but on the contrary a vote was passed, requiring the Smith Professor to instruct all French classes for the future.

"I do not, of course, Gentlemen, call in question your right to modify the duties of my Professorship; and I have proceeded to organize the classes, and commenced the instruction in the elements of the French language, agreeably to your vote. But I still entertain the hope that a different arrangement, and one more in harmony with the intent of a Professorship of Belles Lettres, and more advantageous to the University, may yet be made. The symmetry and completeness of the Department are at present destroyed. The organization introduced by Mr. Ticknor, and continued successfully, to the great honor of the University, is broken up. The French language has no native teacher. And I submit to you, Gentlemen, whether depriving the Department of the services of such a teacher will not justly be regarded by the public as lessening the advantages of a residence at the University.

"I have now under my charge 115 students in French, and 30 in German. Of course, with so many pupils my time is fully occupied. I can exercise very little superintendence over the Department; and have no leisure for the prosecution of those studies, which are absolutely requisite for the proper discharge of the duties originally prescribed to me. When the labor of mastering the Literature of even a single nation is considered, the utter impossibility of accomplishing anything, under the present arrangement,—in the various fields of Foreign Literature, over which my Professorship ranges, will be at once apparent. An object of greater importance is clearly sacrificed to one of less. I am required to withdraw from those literary studies and instructions, which had been originally marked out for me, and to devote my time to elementary Instruction. Now if my labors are of any importance to the College it is to the former class of duties, that the importance belongs. The latter can be performed as well, perhaps better, by an instructor, employed and paid in the usual way. In point of fact, my office as Professor of Belles Lettres is almost annihilated, and I have become merely a teacher of French. To remedy this, Gentlemen, I make you the following propositions:

"I. That I should be wholly separated from the Department of Modern Languages, and be only Professor of Belles Lettres.

"II. That I should reside, as now, in Cambridge.

"III. That I should not be a member of the Faculty.

"IV. That my duties be confined to lecturing during the Autumn Term; and the rest of the year be at my own disposal, as in the case of the Professor of History.

"V. In consideration of which I relinquish one half of my present income from the College, and receive one thousand dollars per annum.

"Respectfully submitted, etc. etc.

"HENRY W. LONGFELLOW." [35]

Such a weighty matter took weeks of discussion, explanation, argument, elaboration. The plan was too radical for the Corporation to consider—too far removed from their own thoughts and past arrangements. So when all the tumult had subsided, the two parties were exactly where they had started: the President notified the Smith Professor that the former vote of the Corporation had been rescinded; that the Smith Professor might hire a French instructor to fill the vacancy which the Smith Professor had been filling. All the other matters were settled in a quiet but negative fashion.

Again there was the sound of doors closing—quietly this time—as Longfellow turned back to the monotony which he had so nearly escaped.

XXVI

LITERARY SHOP TALK

Since my last letter I have published another book;—a volume of poems, with the title of "Voices of the Night." It contains the Psalms;—Manrique, and some of the Earlier Poems. Its success has been signal. It has not been out three weeks; and the publisher has not more than fifty copies left, out of nine hundred. This he told me four days ago. A copy is in the binder's hands for Maria, and will be sent with Hyperion & Outre Mer. Every one praises the book. Even the Boston papers which so abused Hyperion, praise this highly. Hyperion they could not understand. This they feel more. So that I come out of my last six-months' literary campaign with flying colors.[1]

At last, Longfellow decided, he had written enough poems to make a book. The "Psalms," which had continued to excite adulation, were so few in number, however, that they needed buttressing with translations and earlier poems. First place would be given to the new ones, including "Floral Astrology," "A Psalm of Life," "The Light of Stars," "Evening Shadows" (which had appeared in the *Knickerbocker* as "Voices of the Night" and was entitled "Footsteps of Angels" in the book) and "Midnight Mass for the Dying Year." He had another new poem, not yet published in any magazine, which reflected his gradual return to the healing twilight world of dreams and meditation. He still found himself returning wearily to the consoling night voices after the trials and burdens of the day:

Night

I heard the trailing garments of the Night
    Sweep through her marble halls!
I saw her sable skirts all fringed with light
    From the celestial walls.

I felt her presence, by its spell of might,
    Stoop o'er me from above;

The calm, majestic presence of the Night,
  As of the one I love.

I heard the sounds of sorrow and delight,
  The manifold, soft chimes,
That fill the haunted chambers of the Night,
  Like some old poet's rhymes.

From the cool cisterns of the midnight air,
  My spirit drank relief;
This saved me from the frenzy of despair,
  The apathy of grief.

O holy Night! from thee I learn to bear
  What man has borne before!
Thou layest thy finger on the lip of care,
  And it complains no more.

Peace! Peace! Orestes-like I breathe this prayer!
  Come in thy broad-wing'd flight!
Aspasia! the thrice-prayed for! the most fair!
  My best beloved Night! [2]

In choosing *Voices of the Night* as his title, Longfellow ignored the seven earlier poems and the translations selected from *Outre-Mer*, *Coplas*, and *Hyperion*. To give unification to these three separate groups which comprised the book, he enclosed them in a specially written framework of "Prelude" and "L'Envoi," the first being a sketch of his own growth from boyish joy in nature and descriptive writing to a more mature appreciation of nature in its relation to life. These are the last six stanzas of the "Prelude":

Visions of childhood! Stay, oh stay!
  Ye were so sweet and wild!
And distant voices seemed to say,
It cannot be! They pass away!
Other themes demand thy lay;
  Thou art no more a child!

The land of Song within thee lies,
  Watered by living springs;

The lids of Fancy's sleepless eyes
Are gates unto that Paradise;
Holy thoughts, like stars, arise;
    Its clouds are angels' wings.

Learn, that henceforth thy song shall be,
    Not mountains capped with snow,
Nor forests sounding like the sea,
Nor rivers flowing ceaselessly,
Where the woodlands bend to see
    The bending heavens below.

There is a forest where the din
    Of iron branches sounds!
A mighty river roars between,
And whosoever looks therein
Sees the heavens all black with sin,
    Sees not its depths, nor bounds.

Athwart the swinging branches cast,
    Soft rays of sunshine gleam;
Then comes the fearful wintry blast;
Our hopes, like withered leaves, fall fast;
Pallid lips say, It is past!
    This Life is not a Dream!

Then look into thine heart, and write!
    Yes, into Life's deep stream!
All solemn Voices of the Night,
All forms of sorrow and delight,
That can soothe thee, or affright,
    Be these thenceforth thy theme.[3]

Thus he pointed out his growth without seeming to realize that the last stanza of the "Prelude" contained exhortations which contradicted each other. If Longfellow were to continue looking into his heart he might find their inspiration for a poem such as his first "Psalm," which accepted the reality of life, or he might find there inspiration for a poem such as "Evening Shadows," which accepted the reality of a dream world. And so the "Prelude" could not point out unity in these poems because there was no unity. By printing the first two "Psalms" in a book bearing a title so contradictory in implication as *Voices of the Night*, the author revealed the confused state of his own feeling and thinking. Despite his vague groping, he had not yet worked out any practical way of living which answered his needs; instead, he wavered between a longing to live bravely in the present and a longing to live peacefully in a sweet realm of visions.

But he offered the American nation songs already popular, and the success of *Voices of the Night* was far greater than Longfellow, in his moments of greatest optimism, had anticipated. Within a month the first edition of nine hundred copies was exhausted, and within a year the book had gone into its fourth printing. One discord jangled in the harmony of praise. An anonymous reviewer in the Philadelphia *Gentleman's Magazine* for February, 1840, accused Longfellow of plagiarism, pointing in particular to Tennyson's "The Death of the Old Year" as the source of "Midnight Mass for the Dying Year." This, he said, belonged to the "most barbarous class of literary robbery; that class in which, while the words of the wronged author are avoided, his most intangible, and therefore least defensible and least reclaimable property is purloined." [4]

The charge and the bitterness of the review produced a mild furor in Philadelphia and New York papers. Longfellow, curious to get behind the scenes, wrote to his friend Willis Gaylord Clark, the twin brother of Lewis, and an editor of the daily *Philadelphia Gazette:* "Pray who is it that is attacking me so furiously in Philadelphia. I have never seen the attacks, but occasionally I receive a newspaper with a defense of my writings, from which I learn there has been an attack. I thank you for what you have done for me; for your good thoughts and good words." [5] Willis Clark did not know who had written the review, but he was not averse to firing a blast in the dark, particularly since he could aim in the general direction of William E. Burton, the successful English actor who had turned editor. With a malice and disregard for truth quite in keeping with the vituperative editorial policies of the time, Clark replied:

"You ask me who attacks you here. The only ones I have seen

against you, have been in *Burton's Magazine*—a vagrant from England, who has left a wife and offspring behind him there, and plays the bigamist in *this* with another wife, and his whore besides; one who cannot write a paragraph in English to save his life. I have answered thoroughly, any attack upon you—and shall continue to do so, whenever they appear." [6]

The attack in *Burton's* was written by Edgar Allan Poe, an obscure writer whom Burton had assisted with an offer of work at $10 a week. But this critical sally against the successful New England poet was merely one of Poe's introductory greetings, followed by even more condemnatory remarks in the next few years.

The *Gentleman's Magazine* was in no way essential to Longfellow's success. His name, already solicited by enterprising magazine and newspaper editors, began to take a prominent position in lists of contributors. Conscious that his thin stream of originality could not meet heavy demands, yet eager to take advantage of generous offers, he sent translations of poems from the German, translations from the prose of Jean Paul Richter, excerpts from his notes on German literature, and occasional book notices. Because New York periodicals offered far more opportunities for the author than those in Boston, he sent most of his pieces to the *New World, Colman's Monthly Miscellany,* the *New York Mirror,* the *Ladies Companion,* and the *Knickerbocker.*

Remuneration was growing better since Louis A. Godey and George Rex Graham had begun to find that there was profit for the editor in offering a generous honorarium to the best writers. George Pope Morris seemed to be making Longfellow a liberal offer when he set a price of $25 for two columns in his paper. Although he stipulated that such a contribution should be original, Longfellow managed to secure his acceptance of several manuscript pages of translations chosen from Jean Paul. But what an astonishing number of words the *Mirror* could absorb! His article occupied only three-quarters of a column.

Judged by their promises, the editors of the *Knickerbocker* also made liberal payments. Lewis Gaylord Clark was an industrious man, attractive and quite handsome, in his well tailored clothes and neatly trimmed black beard. He seemed to have money for sartorial needs, at least. Liking him so much, Longfellow was not immediately troubled by Clark's chronic habit of making excuses, and for three years continued to send him poems—among them "A Psalm of Life," "Floral Astrology," "The Reaper and the Flowers," and "Footsteps of Angels." Always sorry that he could not pay immediately, Clark pleaded hard times, talked of the unfortunate effect of the 1837 financial panic, and then forgot. Longfellow never received a cent from him for any of these poems.[7]

Undoubtedly the credulous author might have continued to accept these protestations without questioning the good faith behind them, had not the newspapers announced that the *Knickerbocker* had arranged to pay Washington Irving $2,000 a year for his regular contributions.[8] Somewhat annoyed, he had sent Clark the manuscript of "The Fifth Psalm," in the fall of 1839, with a little note written along the margin:

"My dear Clark, I here send you the best poem I ever wrote— It is wild and weird, and like the approaching season, which it sings. May you like it! . . . By the way, when Mr. Edson makes out his back accounts he must 'remember me.' In your admiration for new friends, you must not forget the old, who have been with you from the first." [9]

Sam Ward, whose growing friendship with Longfellow brought him into the thick of many negotiations of a literary nature, thought Clark deserved all the indulgence which his friends could give, when he learned that Clement E. Edson, Clark's partner, was "a great scamp" who had been pocketing all the proceeds. But there were several editors who were eager for an excuse to steal Longfellow from the old "*Knick.*" Park Benjamin, the lively cripple who had already survived editorial hardships on nearly a half-dozen periodicals, seldom made a trip to Boston without limping up the gravel path of the Craigie House to call. Benjamin, who liked to think of himself as the Professor's literary agent, continued angling until he had managed to secure some very good pieces, including "The Wreck of the Hesperus."

The writing of the Hesperus ballad was a complete turning away from the mood of *Voices of the Night.* Longfellow was not forgetting his assertion that poetry sprang primarily from the heart; he was merely conscious of a desire to branch out, as he had told Greene:

"Since the poems [*Voices*] I have broken ground in a new field; namely *Ballads;* beginning with the '*Wreck of the Schooner Hesperus on the Reef of Norman's Woe*,' in the great storm a fortnight ago. It will be printed in a few days, and I shall send it in some newspaper. I think I shall write more. *The National Ballad* is a virgin soil here in New England; and there are great materials. Besides I have a great notion of *working upon people's feelings.* I am going to have this printed on a sheet, and sold like *Varses*, with a coarse picture on it. I desire a new sensation, and a new set of critics. I wish you were sitting in the red arm-chair before me, that I might inflict it on you. Nat Hawthorne is tickled to death with the idea. Felton laughs, and says, 'I wouldn't.' " [10]

Hawthorne wanted a great pile of broadside copies of the "Hesperus" ballad, so that he might distribute one to each skipper of each craft he boarded at the customhouse. He promised to listen to their remarks, and report to Longfellow.[11] Splendid! But in the end, the quiet voice of Felton prevailed.

The desire to write ballads had been in Longfellow's mind for some time, perhaps since the day in Heidelberg when he discovered the German ballads in the *Boy's Wonder-Horn* of Arnim and Bretano. In speaking of it in *Hyperion*, he had written: "I know the book almost by heart. Of all your German books, it is the one which produces upon my imagination the most wild and magic influence. I have a passion for ballads! . . . They are the gypsy-children of song, born under green hedgerows, in the leafy lanes and by-paths of literature,—in the genial summer-time." [12] He had even considered incorporating a long Scandinavian ballad as a part of *Hyperion*. The idea had come to him after he wrote in his journal, "I have been looking at the old northern sagas, and thinking of a series of ballads or a romantic poem on the deeds of the first bold Viking who crossed to this western world, with storm spirits and devil machinery under water." [13] The translation for *Hyperion* was never made, but the Viking ballad later became "The Skeleton in Armor."

Longfellow was encouraged by the praise given his first ballad. Theophilus Parsons, his severe friend who had once warned him against the dangers of seeking to escape from the hard path of life's duty, wrote a note of thanks for his complimentary copy of *Voices:* "I think your residence abroad, & your thorough acquaintance with foreign literature, has affected your style, sometimes injuriously. But you are now one of us, I hope for good—& every year & every new effort will make you more entirely our own. Your ballad about the Fisherman's Daughter, which is now going the rounds of the papers, is the best thing of its kind our country has produced." [14]

To express his delight in being allowed to dispose of the "Hesperus" ballad, Park Benjamin had turned a few verbal somersaults:

"Your ballad 'The Wreck of the Hesperus' is grand. Enclosed are $25 (the sum you mentioned) for it, *paid by the proprietors of the New World,* in which glorious paper it will resplendently coruscate on Saturday next.

" 'The Mirror' quotha! the Mirror cant pay for its printing. 'The Ladies Companion!' Unworthy of *such* a poem;—though, by your promise you must *very soon* send *to me* some new stanzas for that truly feminine publication. 'A special edict, obey!' But only to think of Harry Longfellow's most magnificent Ballad keeping company with 'Stanzas' by Miss Snooks and 'Lines on an Infant' by Sarah Smirk. No! of all American journals, the New World is alone worthy to contain 'The Wreck of the Hesperus.'

"Your good and beautiful letter about Allston's poems appears in the Signal of today. You will also see it in the New World, of which I shall send you half a dozen copies. Do you wish to do a favor to a brother poet? Richard H. Dana is in town, and about to commence a course of literary lectures at the Stuyvesant Institute. Write me something in praise of his fine powers and his reputation in New England. Hillard told Sargent that he should send me a notice of Voices of the Night. When are you coming to New York? You ought to remain here long enough to repeat your lectures 'on your own hook.' " [15]

Such a generous flow of shop talk implied that Park Benjamin had achieved his coveted wish to have Longfellow in tow. The series of lectures to which he referred was to be delivered under the auspices of the New York Mercantile Library Association, in the winter of 1840, by such notables as Charles Francis Adams, Horace Mann, and Ralph Waldo Emerson.

For more than a decade, lyceum courses had increased in fashion and popularity throughout the country; for exactly a decade, Longfellow had been harboring definite ambitions to take part in lyceum programs, to draw great crowds while he sang his eloquent and poetic praise of favorite foreign writers. His interest in lecturing had begun in Göttingen, early in 1829, when he had written a long letter to his father, with the proposition that father and son should offer courses of lectures on law and literature in Portland.[16] This was more than a boy's dream, for the heart of the plan was not abandoned by Longfellow when he accepted the position at Bowdoin. He had subsequently proposed a course which he wished to deliver in Portland.[17] And although there is no evidence which indicates the inducements Longfellow suggested, when he offered, through Ichabod Nichols, to teach at Harvard, he may have wished to give a course of free lectures, subsidized by the college, in anticipation of the Lowell lectures which began in the old Federal Street Theatre, Boston, late in December, 1839.[18] This hypothesis seems less fantastic in the light of his later decision to give free public lectures in Cambridge, open to those outside the College.[19] And when the demands of his duties made this extra work impossible, he persisted by taking a specific plan to President Quincy and the Corporation for them to decide: if the College would give Longfellow the use of the Chapel during the summer vacations, he would deliver a series of lectures to the townspeople on a variety of currently popular subjects such as German authors and their writings. ("Every body talks about German literature and German Philosophy," he told Greene, "as if they knew something of them." [20]) But he had returned from a faculty meeting one night, to write in his journal:

"President told me, that the Corporation would not allow me the use of the Chapel for Public Lectures in the Summer. They do not approve my plan. So it ends. Human life is made up mostly of a series of little disappointments or of little pleasures.

The great wonder-flowers bloom but once a life-time; as marriage, and death." [21]

At that time, he had not given up the general idea. In a letter to his sister he wrote: "How do you all flourish in Portland? I shall pass next summer vacation with you. I have made up my mind on that point. I am going to Lecture there. Don't you think I can get an Audience for a course of Literary matters? . . . My own opinion is, that I can." [22] He continued to hold this belief until June, when an even better opening presented itself. The Society for the Diffusion of Useful Knowledge wished him to give several lectures in Boston during the winter of 1839. Telling his father of this offer he added: "I am not sure that I shall not accept. I have almost given up the Portland plan. It does not promise much; and I fear would look like *spunging*, in these hard times." [23] But he finally refused the Boston invitation also, because it did not promise well. When he was invited to give three lectures in the program of the New York Mercantile Library Association, however, in company with several distinguished speakers, he accepted with haste. Permitted to select his own subjects, he decided to speak on "The Life and Writings of Dante" for his first two lectures, and for his third "The Life and Writings of Jean Paul F. Richter," on the evenings of January 24, 27, and 29, 1840.

The visit to New York was a respite from college labors at Cambridge. There was a cosmopolitan atmosphere about Manhattan that contrasted pleasantly with the New England provincialism of Boston. Then, too, Longfellow moved in the best circles there, for he was a guest in Sam Ward's elegant home on Bond Street, where three attractive sisters entertained him graciously. Worthy of the constant attention given them, these young ladies were known throughout fashionable New York as the "graces of Bond Street." Felton, who had met them all, grew ecstatic in his praises. Trying to make his brooding friend surrender his morbid habit of dwelling on past failure he later wrote:

"Longfellow, you are the most insensible block in existence not to fall in love with one of those incomparable sisters—and Charles is as bad. Julia is the most remarkable person I ever knew. Every time I see her, some new power of attraction strikes me; and I am astounded that all the unmarried men are not piled up at her feet. If the three destinies could bring matters into such a train as to divide that band of graces between you and Charles [Sumner] and [S. G.] Howe, I should piously exclaim, 'nunc dimittis domine.' " [24]

Although Longfellow had failed to uproot the old love, Frances Appleton's perpetual coldness had resulted in such complete despair that he was willing to pay earnest suit to the youngest Ward sister, Anna, still in her teens. And before he left New York, he had quite thoroughly convinced himself that he was in love with her, although she obviously found the Harvard Professor much too middle-aged! [25]

The journey home was a miserable experience, in perfect keeping with his mood. In spite of the time of year, and the frozen Sound, which made passage by boat impossible, the stagecoach set out for New Haven on wheels, lurching through the drifts half the night, and finally toppling over into a ditch. Although nobody was hurt, the episode was extremely undignified for the gentleman who had recently given three very successful lectures before large crowds in New York.[26] From Portland, where he went to spend the remainder of the winter vacation, Longfellow began his thank-you letter to Ward:

"I write you from the extreme Down East, from the fair city, which gave birth to John Neal, Nat Willis and myself, and into which I entered triumphantly last evening, just as the town sexton was ringing nine. . . .

"How suddenly I have passed from New York into the retirement of a provincial Capital. The cries and carriage wheels of Broadway are still ringing in my ears. I can see the smoky light come through the window curtains in the attic. I can hear your boots on the stairs, and hear you say '*Well, old gentleman!*' and have almost the filial impiety to wish I were still with you, and that we were to sit with Mersch this evening and drink Johannisberg. These things pass away; but they are the *aroma* in the enameled goblet of *Life*, whose rich perfume we perceive *before* and *after*, but not *while* drinking the strong reality then overpowering with anticipation and remembrance." [27]

XXVII

INNER CONFLICT

These days, wholly devoted to others, seem taken entirely out of my existence. I did not intend to study very hard this term, on account of health, but I had no idea of doing so little. Hang it—I get vexed to think of it some times. My whole existence is consumed in obtaining the means to support respectability. *Then I grow philosophical—and things go on the old train.*[1]

RETURNING to Cambridge at the end of the winter vacation, Longfellow found that visiting and lecturing in New York had not relieved the monotony of school days. Although his hours were not heavy, they were so irksome that he could not resist frequent outbursts of this nature: "With what coarse contrast the constantly recurring Three Days (*Les Trois Jours*) comes crashing in! Poetic dreams shaded by French Irregular verbs! Hang it! I wish I were a freeman!" [2]

Yet, he would not pay too high a price for escape. Regardless of what he might say or write in moments of annoyance, he was unwilling to win his freedom by surrendering his quarterly salary. Poetry meant more to him than French irregular verbs, but not more than respectability and social standing. He could be an artist only in so far as his art did not interfere with his jealously preserved reputation for being smartly dressed and his gracious cordiality as host to friends who came for suppers at the Craigie House.

Although called upon to rationalize, Longfellow found little difficulty there. He was becoming an expert at it. In the face of increasing inner conflicts, however, he found that his health continued to suffer; that his nerves were constantly on edge. The most insidious cause of these disorders was a long-standing and uncontrollable remorse. Visits to New York, attempts to fall in love with some one else, hours of absorbing literary endeavor, evenings of social gaiety, nights of convivial pleasure—none of these arrested heartache. Idle hours had annoyed him since the

publication of *Hyperion* and *Voices of the Night*. His complaints
of impatience, to Ward, drew forth an immediate letter of solicitous encouragement: "The tranquillity that weighs upon you is
a slumber of all passions. With an object, a direction before you,
more energy than you could ever boast of before would astonish
you and second your effort." Ward continued: "It is the crouch
of the Tiger who committed a debauch upon flesh & blood not
long ago and now lies in a secluded jungle little frequented by
prey—and himself indifferent whether a victim approaches or not.
Yes! even a Tiger can feel *rassasié* without having eaten—by the
sole effects of his last repast and a Poet with the sweetest and most
precious gifts can look upon the World—its censure & its applause
—with indifference—provided he lie in a jungle like the Craigie
House." [3]

Although Ward knew the actual ailment, he was careful to
avoid spilling any salt in the never-healed wound. Longfellow's
friends in Cambridge and Boston were not always so successful,
because they found more difficulty in protecting him. Try as he
might, he could never control the exasperations which surged in
him whenever he went into Boston society. Not long before he
had written to Ward of his unhappiness, he had suffered from one
such accident. He had gone to Boston and had enjoyed a tête-à-
tête dinner with Hillard. Then, after they had parted, he had
taken a turn about the Common. What fantastic devil had
prompted him to decide to call on the Ticknors that evening, he
would never be able to guess. He had been an ass, he told himself afterwards, for having gone at all. For he blundered into a
room full of ladies. And there in the midst of them sat lovely
Fanny, with some assiduous gentleman paying court. To make
matters worse, the gentleman was none other than Hillard! He
left almost immediately, feeling more like a baited bull than an ass.
Furious, he had stamped back to Cambridge. Mrs. Norton,
motherly in her understanding, was frequently of comfort on
such occasions. So on this evening he had gone out to Shady Hill.
He concluded his journal entry for the evening thus: "There I
beheld what perfect happiness may exist on this earth, and felt
how I stood alone in life, cut off for a while from those dearest
sympathies for which I long." [4]

And Mrs. Norton, recognizing the symptoms, welcomed him to her home, showed her sympathy, and won his confidence. She knew the Appleton family well, for she was a daughter of Samuel Eliot, and very familiar with the ways of Beacon Hill. Yet there was little she could do, for the present.

As the spring grew into summer, Longfellow sank deeper into despondency. Having gone to Portland for the vacation, he wrote to Ward again, complaining of his senseless attempt to ride two horses at once. Couldn't he make a living at some more pleasing occupation in New York? Ward quickly smothered this old question under practical arguments and illustrations:

"The only remedy I can see for the depression which appears to visit you in Portland would be to consider yourself a little less miserable & unhappy than most of your fellow mortals. To a poet it is useless to talk of positive happiness. His good fortune must be his unluck compared with that of other Bards. Think of Halleck toiling at Mr. Astor's books—carrying forward million after million to page after page, and this another's wealth. Think of him receiving such pittance as two thousand a year chained to the oar, and such an oar! until he drop from the galley bench into the Sea of Death! Think of him living in this bustling city where Gold is worshipped and genius neglected—always poor among the stupid rich—He one of the Victors in the great Tournament of this age, toiling up and down Broadway until his hair turns grey —amidst the blind and shallow crowds that know him not! Then reflect upon the peaceful spot in which you are fulfilling your destiny—surrounded by poor scholars whose riches resemble your own—leading a life of toil not unenlivened by Romance. I am sure the Comparison is in y^r favor & if you place y^r case a moment beside the existence of a miserable scribbler in this Gotham—a Hoffman, a Benjamin, a Sargent, a Clark, *et hoc omne genus*— you can but feel happy that their lot is not yours. I do not asperse those gentry—but I mean to say that it is because they made a trade of letters that their existence is miserable." [5]

These arguments were much the same that his father and Theophilus Parsons had used, fifteen years earlier. And they were much the same that made him break forth in bitter denunciation, six years later: "In truth it must be spoken and recorded—this is a dreadful country for a poet to live in. Lethal, deadly influences hang over him, the very 'Deadly Nightshade' of song. Many poetic souls there are here, and many lovers of song; but life and its ways and ends are prosaic in this country to the last degree." [6] But the practical Sam Ward brought Longfellow out of his summer despondency by stirring up new literary enthusiasm. Since the spring term, Longfellow had done some intensive reading in Spanish drama as preparation for a series of class lectures, and had thus been led to consider writing a play: "A good idea! Yes, I will write a comedy,—'The Spanish Student.' " [7] He could easily construct a composite plot to serve as a vehicle for expressing some of the choicest Spanish proverbs and lyrics, in translation, and could thus offer his readers or his audience a unique glimpse into Spanish lands and literature. But how should he make his plot entertaining enough to sustain the scraps of translation which he wished to use? After he had decided to adapt the familiar theme of love between a Spanish youth of noble family and a pretty gpysy girl, his interest lagged. He had no enthusiasm for the project until he received, while in Portland, Sam Ward's account of the fascinating European dancer, Fanny Elssler, who was causing a sensation in New York and Philadelphia:

"She is a charming dancer, the ideal of a fascinating mistress. Her eyes charm the Pit & boxes—by a mightier spell than the boa-constrictor's. But he who yields to her influence must from that moment become a voluptuary. Her influence is sensual, her *ensemble* the incarnation of seductive attraction. She has been as often bought & sold as absolution from & by priests. She retains the shadow of love—the substance hath long since departed—perhaps it was buried with the Duke of Reichstadt. . . . Such a Woman is dangerous to her sex and to Humanity. . . . These danseuses personify the creatures of our dreams—appearing angels to the sentimental and Sultanas to the sensual beholder." [8]

Stimulated by Ward's reference to the paradoxical elements of beauty and ugliness, good and evil, in the character of Fanny Elssler, Longfellow set to work on his comedy. He made his heroine, Preciosa, a dancer of innocent character whose reputation had suffered because of her sensual appearance on the stage. Two contrasting speeches in the first act indicated the conflict and motivation for the plot of "The Spanish Student":

> And would you persuade me
> That a mere dancing-girl, who shows herself,
> Nightly, half naked, on the stage for money,
> And with voluptuous motions fires the blood
> Of inconsiderate youth, is to be held
> A model for her virtue?

> I believe
> That woman, in her deepest degradation,
> Holds something sacred, something undefiled,
> Some pledge and keepsake of her higher nature,
> And, like the diamond in the dark, retains
> Some quenchless gleam of the celestial light! [9]

Here was a subject racy enough to set all Boston by the ears! It might cause an even greater sensation than *Hyperion*. With joy and excitement, Longfellow worked so hard on his comedy that he had finished the first draft before he returned to Cambridge in the fall of 1840. Nobody should know about it until Longfellow could show it to Ward, to whom he wrote:

"Why can't you come here for a day or two? I want to see you very much, and have a great many things to show you in the literary way. I will read you the 'Skeleton in Armor,' which is too long to copy; and something still longer, which as yet no eye but mine has seen, and which I wish to read to you first. . . . At present, my dear friend, my soul is wrapped up in poetry. The scales fell from my eyes suddenly, and I behold before me a beautiful landscape, with figures, which I have transferred to paper almost without an effort, and with a celerity of which I did not think myself capable. Since my return from Portland I am almost afraid to look at it, for fear its colors should have faded out. And this is the reason why I do not describe the work to you more particularly. I am not sure it is worth it. You shall yourself see and judge before long." [10]

With characteristic loyalty, Ward appeared at the Craigie

House the following week-end, and gave his friend sincere but reserved praise. Certainly, Preciosa was not a very exact picture of Fanny Elssler! Longfellow, who had already seen her in Boston, since his return, could appreciate that. But the play had parts in it which Ward thought highly of; he even hoped there might be some way of helping to find a producer in New York.

All that Ward had said about the actual "Preciosa" was confirmed when Longfellow watched her dance. To his father in Portland he wrote, "We have nothing new here, save Fanny Elssler the dancing girl, who is a beauty, and an admirable dancer. She has excited great enthusiasm among the Bostonians. Her Spanish dances are exquisite; and remind me strongly of days gone by. She has five hundred dollars a night; consequently makes with her heels in one week just what I make with my head in one year." [11] And Ward, back in New York, found a statuette of this exquisite "Preciosa" (even Emerson said that her dancing was pure poetry) which he sent to Longfellow.

Ward had found Longfellow's ballad of "The Skeleton in Armor" far more exciting than the play. For a year he had heard his friend talk about experimenting with ballads, and had been greatly pleased with the "Hesperus" poem. Also, his sister Julia Ward and his friend Cogswell had been with Longfellow at Newport one summer day in 1838, when they discussed the origin of the round tower there, mistakenly supposed to have been built by the Northmen. Later, he had learned of Longfellow's stopping at Fall River, on the return trip, to view the strange skeleton dug up within an encasing coffin of iron armor. His interest in the poem which Longfellow had built around these two incidents was colored by sentiment so great that he had insisted on taking a copy of the ballad back to New York, where he was sure he could get $25 for it. And who could appreciate it more than Halleck? At Astor's countinghouse, Ward read it aloud to the author of "Marco Bozzaris." "His bright eyes glistened like diamonds," Ward wrote to Longfellow, "and he read it through aloud himself with delight. . . . It will spread like wildfire over the country, and richly reward you. Halleck remarked there was nothing like it in the Language!" [12] Unfortunately, from a remunerative point of view, the poem was given to Clark, who joyfully published it in the *Knickerbocker*, with Longfellow's marginal notes, after the fashion of Coleridge's "Ancient Mariner." Again Clark gave liberal promises instead of payment.

After this brief splurge of writing, Longfellow lapsed into a period of comparative quiet. The weary round of class work required too much of his listless energy, for he was not feeling very well. Shortly after Christmas, Charles Sumner (who had returned from his European travels less than a twelvemonth earlier) carried him off to Philadelphia for visits there during the Christmas vacation. The whirl of balls, dinners, parties, and entertainments, the glamour of society, and the warmth of hospitality wherever they went, made a strange contrast to the phlegmatic ways of Boston. Sumner, glad to have diverted his friend from concealed broodings, wrote a note to Hillard, with characteristic gusto:

"We are in successful experiment here. Three or four engagements for every evening; beautiful virgins and wives, beautiful women, who have made the vow. We had determined to leave today; but could we resist the polite requests & invitations of the most beautiful, gracious and distinguished here? Longfellow actually lost his appetite by sitting by the side of a most beautiful girl at dinner—the belle of Philad^a. What will come of it I know not. I have met the most fascinating woman I have ever seen in America—beautiful as morning, with the esprit of France, the dark hair and eyes of Mrs. Norton & the glowing soul of the South—But alas! she is married—to a Senator in Congress!" [13]

Although Longfellow's account of the visit, written to his father after he had returned to Cambridge, was curbed by filial restraint, it implied that the pace of Boston society was picking up so rapidly that it might even surpass that of Philadelphia:

"We were received with the utmost cordiality and kindness;—dined and breakfasted and supped;—and seldom went to less than three parties in an evening. All this is very agreeable for a while; but a week satiated me, and have come back to this place in hope of being a little more quiet. But, alas! fallacious hope! I have already received six invitations to dinner, and I know not how many to parties and concerts &c. In fine, for the sake of change, I have turned my habits of life upside down; and do nothing but run to and fro from morning till night and from night till morning. It grows very tiresome, and the effect is to make me cling more closely to Cambridge and the life of a student." [14]

The winter passed pleasantly as an interim of peace. Sumner came over from Boston frequently to pass a quiet week-end—to stretch his majestic length on the sofa and entertain himself with reading while Longfellow worked. Felton was never absent for long. On March 7, Longfellow wrote in his journal, "Felton dined with me, on fried oysters, porter and Hock. This is pleasant:— a fine suite of rooms in the old castle here, a good servant—a table of my own to sit down at—and the face of a friend opposite." Four days later he wrote, "Felton came up at nine at night in his dressing gown. We tried the Capri wine—a bottle of red—and a bottle of white. Delicious wine—mild and laughing. The white is best. Why blame Tiberius for liking Capri?" This fondness was indulged with too much abandon, apparently, for his entry on the following day contained the observation, "Drinking wine at night is not good." And the day after that: "Unwell-ish. Have not yet recovered from the Capri." [15]

As spring came on, he confessed to his father that soft evening air and open windows stirred his blood; "I cannot possibly sit still. Change of place seems almost indispensable; yet, being chained I can only move in thought." [16] He would have enjoyed more frequent visits to his friends in New York. Instead, Ward or Halleck or Cogswell came up at irregular intervals, for a night or two. There was an intimate warmth about Longfellow's friendship which endeared him to these men, for he gave far more of sympathy and understanding than he asked. In spite of the inner moods of discontent and uneasiness he was constantly cheerful in the presence of others. Only a few guessed that he was not completely happy.[17] His letters to Ward were generally bright, playful, and full of color, or nonsense, as the mood dictated:

"It is a rainy Sunday. I am writing on the small round table near the window. Behind me sits Charles Sumner, reading the 'Sketch Book,' and exclaiming 'I wish I knew Irving! How shall I get acquainted with him?' I reply, 'By means of Sam Ward.'

Then he asks, 'When is Ward coming here?' I ask the same question. Let the answer come soon—and you with it, old *gentleman*.
Sumner is *bivouacking* with me for a day or two. Another exclamation from him, 'What a beautiful writer Irving is!'—Felton
is also sitting by the stove, reading an article on Greece in the
Democratic Review. What would I not give if I could now hear
the tramp of your boots on the stairs, and your inspiriting voice
singing, 'Was kommt dort von der Höhe?' The truth is, you
must come here for a few days. We have been separated too
long; and though passage of letters—though the mail keeps the
grass from growing on the road between us, yet the railroad of
speech would do it more effectually. I shall return the visit with
interest this winter.

"Shall you lecture this winter? I shall not. I have refused all
invitations to that effect—three in number. I mean to hold my vacation sacred, and free from ordinary cares. They are my recon-
ciliations with the world after long seclusion. The next one I
hope to enjoy much; and partly in your society, though that horrible winter passage on the sound terrifies me in advance. Kindest
regards to your wife,

"Most truly yours,

"H. W. L." 18

After the spring and summer passed without any sustained literary activity, Longfellow felt refreshed and eager for work.
"I have never commenced a Term in better health and spirits,"
he wrote to his father in the fall of 1841, "and I think everything
will go on vigorously and harmoniously." 19 With his schedule
of lectures arranged for afternoons, he was free much of the time.
Two projects were in his mind. He believed that he had enough
ballads and other poems to make a small book. Then, there was
the manuscript of "The Spanish Student," for which he held
great expectations. Perhaps the success of the comedy would be
assisted if he could prepare the way with the little book of ballads.
He explained the plan to Ward:

"I have two or three literary projects, foremost among which
are the *Student* and the *Skeleton*. I have been thinking this morning, which I shall bring out first. The Skeleton, with the few

other pieces I have on hand, will it is true, make but a meagre volume. But what then? It is important to bring all my guns to bear now; and though they are small ones, the shot may take effect. Through the breach thus made, the Student may enter the citadel in triumph." [20]

His confidence was founded on his belief that the comedy, the most sustained poetic composition he had yet undertaken, had unusual possibilities. It could be published in a magazine, brought out later as a separate book, included in a collection of his poems, and even produced on the stage. Undoubtedly his knowledge that N. P. Willis was reaping a small fortune from plays had influenced Longfellow to consider this literary form. While still at work on the first draft of "The Spanish Student" he had written to Greene: "Nat Willis . . . says he has made ten thousand dollars the last year by his writings. I wish I had made ten hundred. He has just published, or rather *re*-published three plays in London." [21] If Willis could succeed, why should Longfellow fail? The little book of *Ballads* was published by John Owen in December, 1841, and was well received. The breach had been made; the time was at hand for marching triumphantly into the citadel of larger public esteem. But certain doubts arose to hinder the working of his plan, most important of all being his sudden loss of faith in the play.

Perhaps this unexpected development was caused by illness. Although the fall term had begun well, Longfellow soon found that his strength gave out quickly under even the light requirements of his schedule. Only about six weeks had passed before he confided to Ward that he could not continue much longer before taking a long rest—possibly a German water cure. Ward was a bit skeptical, at first, as to the value of these fashionable institutions. On October 24, 1841, Longfellow wrote him, "I am glad you think better of the *Wasser-Cur* (Water-*dog*). That will be my pool of Bethesda. I shall never get well till my good Angel troubles the water for me." [22] He wanted, if possible, to obtain a leave of six months and sail for Europe in the spring. On November 14, he sent a good-natured but accurate description of his condition to Ward, who had expressed his concern:

"In answer to your kind inquiries after my health, what shall

I say? I think there is no immediate danger of my entering 'the Green Gate of Paradise';—but I am all unstrung, eating only bread and meat,—which, all things considered, one may content one's self withal. Not a glass of wine—not a drop of coffee—not a whiff of tobacco. No agile limbs like yours,—no slapping stalwart health, like Sumner, but a meek, Moses-like state of being, not without its charms. That reminds me that Dr. Palfrey had discovered that the Hebrew word usually translated *meek* in connection with Moses, does not mean *meek*, but miserable; and so we should read 'Now Moses was the most miserable of men';—which makes much better sense than the old reading." [23]

Recalling Longfellow's buoyant enthusiasm over the first draft of the Spanish play, Ward urged him to complete it. Longfellow answered dejectedly: "As to the *Student of Alcalá*, I have no longer any courage to look at it. Neither you, nor Sumner, nor Ticknor, nor Felton likes it; and I am so weary that I cannot nerve my mind to the task of correcting it. I shall probably throw it into the fire." [24]

Although the prospect of leaving for Europe became much more interesting than "The Spanish Student," he made a few half-hearted attempts to find a publisher. Colman was no longer in the running. Even John Owen was on the verge of bankruptcy. The continued aftermath of uneasiness following the panic of 1837 still made all publication an uncertain risk for author and agent alike. Consulting with Park Benjamin on the problem, Longfellow suggested that George Rex Graham might be willing to publish "The Spanish Student" in his popular magazine. Graham had already secured two contributions from Longfellow, and had expressed his eagerness, through Benjamin, to have Longfellow's name on his list of regular contributors. "Your plan of publishing The Student of Alcala in Graham's Magazine is good," Benjamin responded. "Send me the first Act as soon as you please." [25] Unwilling to continue such an important transaction through Benjamin, Longfellow wrote direct to Graham, who answered that he should like to publish the play, provided a satisfactory arrangement could be made:

"But in regard to the play, at what rate would you dispose of it? Of its worth we cannot judge as well as yourself—though I would gladly give $150—which you will probably deem 'no consideration'—If so, say the word, and we will see if we can do better, though candidly, everything really good, is pilfered by the weekly papers so soon after the magazine is out, that the original publisher may well doubt, whether his labours are rewarded." [26]

Graham's letter made Longfellow wary. Would he lose the copyright if he risked such publication and subsequent piracy? In spite of the handsome offer, he was tempted to avoid the danger of pilfering by continuing his search for a book publisher. Ward, when consulted on this point, reassured him: "Reserving to yourself the copy-right I would undoubtedly let Graham publish The Student of Alcala for $150—a very snug sum in these hard times—provided you get the money. I should lose no time in closing with Graham. Let him publish in two Nos.—or 3. Owen can get an Edition out in the summer." [27] Still, Longfellow felt need for caution. Graham was a comparative newcomer in the periodical field. His eager expressions of liberality sounded dangerously like the *Knickerbocker* promises. There was, to be sure, some excuse for delayed payments at this time, since no business had suffered more severely from the depression than publishing. Largely as a consequence of these unsettled times, William Cullen Bryant had encountered trouble in finding a publisher for the younger Dana's *Two Years Before the Mast.* And a few months later, young James Russell Lowell, disillusioned by the failure of his *Pioneer* magazine, warned Poe: "Be very watchful of your publishers & agents. They must be driven as men drive swine,—take your eyes off them for an instant & they bolt between your legs & leave you in the mire." [28]

Longfellow knew that such conditions existed. Trying to secure a publisher for a volume of travel letters written in Italy by George Greene, he had sought the influential aid of Epes Sargent, on the *Mirror,* and had regretfully informed Greene of his failure: "After some delay I got an answer from Sargent showing that nobody pays now-a-days. He writes; *'the fact is, that all our publishers, whether of books or periodicals, are desperately poor at present. Money is not to be had.'* And this is very true; you have no idea of the state of things." [29] For reasons such as these, Longfellow was naturally reluctant to surrender to Graham this very important manuscript in exchange for nothing more than the promise to pay $150—the very size of the amount aroused new suspicion. But when Longfellow indirectly voiced his desire for proof of Graham's good faith, the editor was indignant. The eager solicitations ceased, and the matter was not discussed further.

Annoyed and discouraged, he prepared to go abroad without seeing his triumphant creation enter the waiting citadel. President Quincy had secured permission for the Smith Professor to be absent from his duties from late April to the fall, with the understanding that he should return in time to begin classes. Weary in mind and body, he gave up all hope of success for "The Spanish Student," deciding that he had been wrong in his earlier anticipations. With at least a show of indifference he left the manuscript and the arrangements for publication in the hands of Sumner and Hillard, his legal advisers, and set out for the water-cure in Germany late in April, 1842. In the fall, immediately after the play began to appear serially in *Graham's Magazine*, Felton did his best to avoid serious criticism in this pleasant fashion, when he wrote to Longfellow:

"The first act of the Spanish Student is out and has made some considerable sensation here. Sally Lowell was at first a good deal troubled and shut herself up several days. Since then she has emerged into day-light, and is now doing as well as can be expected. Several old women have laid it under ban and forbidden their daughters to read it. This only makes the daughters the more earnest to get hold of it, and they have been not a little disappointed to find it no worse." [30]

XXVIII

PEACE

Everybody is delighted with this engagement, and I more than everybody. Life was too lonely—and sad; with little to soothe and calm me. Now the Future opens its long closed gates into pleasant fields and lands of quiet. The strife and struggle are over, for a season, at least, and the troubled spirit findeth its perfect rest.[1]

HE KNEW he was running away. Germany would do, almost anywhere would do, provided there were long, long miles between him and Cambridge, between him and Frances Appleton. Like his own Paul Flemming in *Hyperion*, he had vowed to be strong, but had finally confessed how weak he was beneath the compelling burden of love. Four years he had fought toward self-mastery, always with the sound of her voice in his ears, as though she were in the next room. At last, he dared stay no longer; the pain in his heart and the irritating routine of his labors had sapped courage until he dared nothing but retreat.

His closest friends understood. "Yours is a strange malady," Ward wrote to him shortly before he sailed, "and you must not wonder if I look for its seat and origin in the heart and not in the stomach. . . . I know by experience that friendship, fame, the wine cup and literary pursuits are insufficient to fill up the place of a passion that cannot be exaucée." [2] Like devoted brothers, Sumner and Hillard had arranged the final details of his departure. Only their protests of danger had restrained him from taking passage for Europe earlier in the spring. Finally, Sumner had arranged passage on the ship *Ville de Lyon*. And the last letter delivered to Longfellow before he embarked had been a tender farewell from this fiery young lawyer who, hiding his own secret sorrow, had grown to depend on his Craigie House friend:

"Dear Henry,

"Will this parting word reach you? I write, not knowing; but the chance of again uttering a word to your soul, before you descend upon the sea, is enough. We are all sad at your going; but I am more sad than the rest; for I lose more than they do. I am desolate. It was to me a source of pleasure and strength untold, to see you, & when I did not see you, to feel that you were near, with your swift sympathy & kindly words. I must try to go alone, hard necessity in this rude world of ours! For our souls always in this life need support, & gentle beckonings, as the little child when first trying to move away from its mother's knee. God bless you! my dearest friend, from my heart of hearts. You know the depth of my gratitude to you. My eyes overflow as I now trace these lines. . . . May you clutch the treasure of health; but, above all, may you be happy!" [3]

If activity could have spelled happiness, Sumner's solicitous wish might have been realized. After four or five days in Paris, Longfellow traveled in leisurely fashion through Belgium, visiting Bruges, Ghent, and Antwerp, then continued up the Rhine to Marienberg, where he was to take the water-cure. Although his desire for travel was satisfied, travel did not bring peace. Most of his letters concerning his stay at Marienberg were outwardly cheerful, concealing the persistent loneliness which he had hoped to shake off. Yet he confessed to his sister Anne that he had not escaped inner sadness by putting an ocean between himself and those he loved. He continued:

"I need not tell you . . . that no new friends can make good the absence of the old; and that I often grow impatient of restraint; and long for motion and change of place. I want to see you all again, though I have been so short a time absent; and should like to take a run through Italy and Spain; and then come home. You may rely upon it; I shall be very glad to get back." [4]

One other friend he dared trust with his intimate thoughts: Mrs. Andrews Norton in Cambridge. How consoling the serenity of her home had been to him, and how conducive to soul-revealing confession, her longing to help! She knew all that was written between the lines of Longfellow's letter from Marienberg, which concluded a description of the Rhine valley thus:

"I cannot tell you how often we walk together through these

HENRY WADSWORTH LONGFELLOW, *aet.* 35
From the painting (1842) by G. P. A. Healy.

scenes, and how I long to see you again. There are so many things to recall the absent,—the fragrance of a flower, a strain of music, a casual resemblance in voice, manner, or feature; in fine, a thousand little things without a name, which suddenly startle me from my dream and make my pulses beat quicker." [5]

Although the fad of hydropathy was recommended to cure many ailments, no doctor would have promised to correct Longfellow's trouble with water. In fact, the treatment required that he have a fairly healthy constitution to begin with. No tottering invalid could have survived the punishment of being plunged from the warm folds of steaming blankets under the chilling falls of a mountain stream. The pummelling of *masseurs* and the rigorous exercises that accompanied them were not intended for the puny. "I have had a 'crisis,' " he wrote to his father—and not without reason, after undergoing several weeks of such treatment. "It lasted about a fortnight. Since then I am better. I am sorry to say, however, that I am not yet perfectly well. Begging your pardon for the insult, I do not believe that any one can be *perfectly* well who has a brain and heart." [6]

Wisely, he did not spend the entire summer moping about the quondam nunnery of Marienberg. To those who met him during his stay there, he seemed quite healthy and good-natured. Through the courtesy of one acquaintance, Herr Landrat Heuberger, with whom he took an occasional *Spaziergang* about the countryside, he met Heuberger's friend, the young poet Ferdinand Freiligrath, living in the near-by town of St. Goar. Immediately the two young authors became fast friends. Each admired the other's writings, and each tried his hand at translating favorite poems. In expressing his first enthusiasm over Freiligrath's verses, Longfellow wrote:

"There is great vigor and freshness, and abundance of expression in them. His imagination is powerful; and revels in distant and almost unknown scenes;—the desert, the jungle, the lonely caravan—the negro, the lion. His subjects are almost invariably striking if not strange; and his metre and rhymes equally so." [7]

Unable to visit each other often during the first month of their acquaintance, the two poets began a correspondence which was to continue for many years. The four-day *Ausflug* down the Rhine which Longfellow made with Freiligrath and his friends late in July enabled him to appreciate for the first time the vitality, wit, and enthusiasm of this spirited German. Playfully, Freiligrath and his friends adopted the American visitor into their circle with ceremony. The owner of Freiligrath's apartment, Ihl by name, furnished an excuse for the group to consider themselves inhabitants of "Ihlium": Freiligrath, of course, was "Hector"; Fräulein Louise von Gall, a beautiful and talented young woman visiting at St. Goar during the summer, became "Helena"; and Longfellow was "Nestor," although a later attempt to create a romance led his match-making friends to consider "Paris" more suitable.[8]

With these merry friends Longfellow spent many summer hours, either at Freiligrath's home or on subsequent trips up and down the Rhine—diversions which filled the days with the desired activity. Carried away by his enthusiasm and loathing the thought of returning to the classroom, he wrote to President Quincy at Harvard, explaining that his water-cure had not been entirely satisfactory, and asking for another six months of absence. The President's reply was kindly but blunt. He reminded the Smith Professor that the original petition had been granted with reluctance and concluded with the regret that any further absence must be arranged with discontinuance of Longfellow's salary. No more was said on the subject.

In the middle of September, he took leave of his friends at Marienberg and, after one last trip up the Rhine, made his way slowly down the river, across Belgium to the Channel, and to London to visit Charles Dickens. His brief meeting with Dickens in America, not many weeks before his departure for the water-cure, had been pleasant. While all Boston clamored to entertain the popular and attractive young author of *Pickwick Papers*, Felton and Longfellow had smuggled him over the Charles River to Cambridge and the Craigie House for a quiet breakfast at which Andrews Norton, a true Anglophile, made the fourth member of the party.[9] Before Dickens returned to England, he had sent Longfellow a warm note of invitation: "My dear Longfellow,—You are coming to England, you know. Now listen to me. . . . Have no home but mine." [10] In answer to Longfellow's letter from Germany, Dickens had written:

"My dear Longfellow,—

"How stands it about your visit do you say? Thus: your bed is waiting to be slept in; the door is gaping hospitably to receive you. I am ready to spring towards it with open arms at the first indication of a Longfellow knock or ring. And the door, the bed, I, and everybody else who is in on the secret, have been expecting you for the last month." [11]

True to his word, Dickens entertained his American friend with zest, although many of the *literati* were absent from the city. Samuel Rogers, the banker-poet and patron, was on hand to entertain Dickens and his guest with excellent food and Schloss Johannisberger. And in the mornings, before social amenities began, some time was given to sartorial intricacies of measurement and fitting, by some of London's best haberdashers, for Longfellow was particularly fond of English styles. Dickens playfully chid him for his fastidious demands, in a letter written soon after his return to Cambridge: "McDowall the bootmaker, Beale the hosier, Laffin the trowsers-maker, and Blackmore the coat-cutter have all been at the point of death; but have slowly recovered. The medical gentlemen agreed that it was exhaustion, occasioned by early rising,—to wait upon you at those unholy hours!" [12]

Sailing for home from Bristol aboard the *Great Western* on October 22, 1842, Longfellow had an extremely rough passage which gave him little incentive for leaving his berth. During the hours of protracted idleness his mind was occupied with thoughts probably inspired by the chapter on "Slavery" which he had read in Dickens's manuscript *American Notes*. Although Charles Sumner had previously urged him to bring his talent to the aid of the antislavery cause, he was not fond of writing occasional poems. Yet Freiligrath's romantic poems about negroes, wild animals, and little-known regions of the earth showed him how he could turn antislavery sentiments to some account by combining them with romantic word-pictures. In his first letter to Freiligrath after his return to America, Longfellow wrote:

"We had a very boisterous passage. I was not out of my berth more than twelve hours for the first twelve days. I was in the forward part of the vessel, where all the great waves struck, and broke with voices of thunder. In the next room to mine, a man died. I was afraid that they might throw me overboard instead of him in the night, but they did not. Well, there, 'cribbed, cabined, and confined,' I passed fifteen days. During this time I wrote seven poems on Slavery; I meditated upon them in the stormy, sleepless nights, and wrote them down with a pencil in the morning. A small window in the side of the vessel admitted light into my berth, and there I lay on my back and soothed my soul with songs. I send you some copies. In the 'Slave's Dream' I have borrowed one or two wild animals from your menagerie!" [13]

Once he had reached New York, Longfellow was obliged to forget his slavery poems temporarily, for Sumner and Felton had made a special trip from Boston to greet their friend; to celebrate his arrival in convivial fashion, and to accompany him back to Cambridge with rejoicing. As soon as possible, however, he arranged with his friend John Owen to print the slavery poems, which appeared in December, 1842. Curiously, the best propaganda poem in the yellow-covered pamphlet was not written aboard the vessel, but was revamped from a portion of the ten-year-old Phi Beta Kappa poem.[14]

The response was varied. Hawthorne wrote: "I never was more surprised than at your writing poems about Slavery. . . . You have never poetized a practical subject hitherto." [15] A writer in the *Dial*, dissatisfied with the gentle tone of moralizing which tried to redeem these poems from a purely romantic treatment, called the pamphlet "the thinnest of all Mr. Longfellow's thin books; spirited and polished like its forerunners; but the topic would warrant a deeper tone." [16] Henry Ware, Jr., in his letter of praise, assured the author that these slavery poems were "all one could wish them to be,—poetry, simple, graceful, strong; without any taint of coarseness, harshness, or passion." [17] Ware wrote better than he knew, for he gave here a perfect summary of criteria for all poetry acceptable to mid-nineteenth century taste. And Longfellow, schooled in elegance and refinement, was helping to formulate and establish those literary prejudices which were to become so thoroughly Victorian.

A half-year of absence from duties at Harvard enabled him to step back into the round of labor with renewed interest. The winter season of social activity helped break the solitude of his beloved Castle Craigie with the diversions of parties and concerts in Cambridge and Boston. Occasionally he even ventured to call on the Appleton family in their home on Beacon Street. Tom, still a fellow of infinite jest, was preparing to go to Europe in the spring, and Longfellow was happy to write several letters of introduction. Mary Appleton, recently married, was no longer within the family circle. Frances Appleton remained at home, quiet, cool, reserved as of old—and even more beautiful. Longfellow, profiting by the memory of his earlier mistakes, did not try to break down the proud and lonely estrangement which had grown between them.

He could appreciate now, that the ways of Beacon Hill were quite contrary to the less delicate bluntness of Portland and Brunswick. Perhaps if he had not been so hasty in his importunate wooing, he might have fared better; possibly his ardent courtship had thrown the stately Dark Ladie on the defensive because his appearance in Boston society was clouded in the obscurity of his social standing. Having come to Cambridge as a widower and an outsider, he could not easily attain recognition within the stringent social structure of Beacon Hill. No laws hindered one from wandering interminably along the shaded walks of Boston Common, but one crossed Beacon Street and entered the bright parlors there only on invitation. This was snobbishness only to those who did not understand.

Yet, there were many who refused to understand, even in the city itself. One young man, a scion of the Otis family, expressed the matter well to a friend. Writing from Boston in the winter of 1840, he had referred to Frances Appleton thus:

"Fanny is neither more nor less charming than before her trip to Washington. When I see her come into a room in the ev'g, in full dress, I am on the point of falling in love with her—at any rate with her distingué air & fine eyes. But the d—l of it is I never can get any farther—but on the contrary find the effect too soon evaporates.

"To be serious, if I were ever so desirous of marrying, I be d—d if I think I ever would fall in love with a Boston woman. They are, & always were, wet blankets to me." [18]

Nevertheless, the reticence in Frances Appleton was ingrained, inherent; not a mere Boston mannerism. Her seeming diffidence was a part of her nature, as her immediate family knew. They accepted her as one who dwelt apart even from them, on a higher plane of thought and aspiration. Longfellow had seen this difference, had felt it, and had been captivated by it. "A woman not of talent but of genius," he had described her, to Greene. That friend far away in Italy had been the only one to whom Longfellow dared reveal his passion unreservedly, because he was removed from it all. Yet, strangely, Greene had encouraged Longfellow with constant assurance of ultimate success. At the very time when hope had been so nearly dead that Longfellow was trying to fall in love with one of the bland graces of Bond Street, Greene had written from Rome:

"Miss Maria Sedgewick has passed several weeks here this winter & I have seen as much of her as I could. She is a delightful woman . . . But what interested me most was that she is the intimate friend of Miss A. & of her own accord, told me that she was every day expecting to hear of your success. She talked a great deal about this & I am the more confident in my belief that you cannot fail—tho' some cause or other has thus far been acting against you." [19]

Ah! but did Miss Sedgwick know, at that time, how Longfellow had offended Miss A. by making public the story of his love for her: by putting it in plain print and offering it for sale, between the covers of a book, in Cambridge, Boston, and New York? Even if Frances Appleton had been at the point of forgiving this ardent and impetuous lover for the rashness of his premature courtship, could she ever put out of her mind the cold anger and scorn which she must have felt while Boston gossips bandied her name about as they gloated over the pages of *Hyperion?* Had his conduct seemed to her a supreme instance of poor taste and boorish back-country ignorance? If only he could know! Blindly he had dreamed that she would fall in love with Mary Ashburton; that Paul Flemming would finally hear her say, "You are the magician."

Although he did not know the depth of her resentment, Longfellow knew that Frances Appleton was still offended. She rarely discussed the matter, even with her intimate friends. But she had made one pointed confession of annoyance, in writing to a cousin, about three months after the publication of *Hyperion*. Having encouraged her cousin to continue his literary efforts, she cautioned: "By the way, don't make me patroness of any of your 'thought-children' as you call 'em. I consider myself too juvenile to enact the role of godmother & have already been hoisted into such a public notoriety by a certain impertinent friend of mine you wot of, that I am entirely disgusted with the honor." [20] Over three years had passed since the publication of *Hyperion*. The disgust had softened, but the resentment had not enabled Frances Appleton to forgive Longfellow. Even her ability to converse politely with him in Boston drawing rooms did not encourage him to venture past commonplace remarks.

In Cambridge, motherly Mrs. Norton continued to carry Longfellow's unhappiness close to her heart. Had she not drawn from him those obliquely revealing letters, written from Marienberg? She knew Beacon Street and she knew young Frances Appleton. She may even have noticed that Frances Appleton, for all her pride, was growing tired of her stubborn isolation.[21] Perhaps Mrs. Norton deliberately tried to bring these two lonely children past the barrier which separated them; perhaps there was no element of chance in their both being invited to Shady Hill, one evening in April, 1843. Before the end of that evening, the estranged pair found themselves isolated, briefly, in the great window nook, where talking might be a bit more private than at one of the Nortons' inevitable whist tables. Although he had taught himself a wearisome lesson in restraint, Longfellow could not fail to notice that the stately, dark lady seemed slightly to encourage his friendliness. No matter that they made only a beginning. The wind had definitely changed, and there was promise of blue skies again. The hour was commemorated in his journal.[22]

Less than a week later, he ventured to call at familiar 39 Beacon

Street. If friendship were ever to be reëstablished, there was the necessity for cleaning away the clutter of unpleasant memories; the difficult task of finding works which might offer reassurance and win forgiveness. The old mistakes would not be made again. That was a promise. After this torturing visit, Longfellow reiterated what he had said, by writing a note to her. And Frances Appleton's answer, warm and sensitive as her own dark eyes, was as welcome as the April showers:

"Dear friend:

"I have just received your note & I cannot forbear telling you that it has comforted me greatly. I trust with all my heart that it is—& will be as you say—that a better dawn has exorcised the phantoms for aye, that its cheering, healthy beams will rest there as in a perpetual home within those once-haunted walls you speak of.

"I could not well disguise, I own, how much some of your words troubled me. I should never have ventured to speak so frankly to you had I not believed the dead Past *had* buried its dead, & that we might safely walk over their graves, thanking God that at last we could live to give each other only happy thoughts. I rejoiced to see how calmly you met me, until Saturday when I trembled a little, as we are apt to do for a long cherished hope. But I will put aside all anxiety & fear, trusting upon your *promise*. . . .

"What a sultry April shower this is—but how the grass is brightening under it!

"Very sincerely yrs,

"Fanny E. A.

"Beacon St. Monday p. m. [April 17]" [23]

To be admitted once again into the joy of friendly companionship with the one he loved—and yet to be restrained by promises from revealing the pent-up torrents of that joy and love—was nothing short of Herculean labor. Apparently his visits to Beacon Street were limited by order, to one a week. But only four Saturdays came and went before Longfellow was relieved of this restriction. Frances Appleton needed no words spoken; she knew his heart as well as she knew her own. And he, after seven years of studying patience, had learned to labor and to wait. The fifth week had not passed before her love broke down the old wall of pride. At last she yielded—and her humble surrender was sent impetuously in a brief note dated May 10.[24]

No sooner had the note been delivered at the door of the Craigie House than Longfellow, scanning the words, was off for Boston, on foot. "I walked with the speed of an arrow," he wrote later, in his journal, "—too restless to sit in a carriage—too impatient and fearful of encouraging anyone!" The old familiar road through Cambridgeport and across the river was transformed, that May day, even more vividly than when he had first begun to make such walks, in the Indian summer of 1837. "I received Fanny's note, and walked to town," he wrote, "amid the blossoms and sunshine and song of birds, with my heart full of gladness and my eyes full of tears!—Oh, Day forever blessed; that ushered in this *Vita Nova* of happiness!" [25]

The first joyful note of announcement was sent to Portland:

"My dearest mother,

"I write you one line, and only one—to tell of the good fortune which has just come to me—namely that I am engaged. Yes, engaged to a very lovely woman—Fanny Appleton—for whom I have many years cherished a feeling of affection. . . . Alex will tell you the rest. I hate to *write* of such things." [26]

Perhaps his mother has not been taken into his confidence as fully as his public had. One letter of announcement, written in collaboration with Frances Appleton, made direct reference, however, to the public attitude, and to Longfellow's own regret concerning that error in taste:

"My dear Jewett,

"I have been long, very long your debtor for a most friendly and interesting letter; but the news I now send you is so precious, that it will amply repay you for any delay or seeming neglect.

"I am engaged to your beloved and beautiful cousin—Fanny,— *the* Fanny! What powers have brought this to pass—by what hitherto invisible, golden threads of sympathy the Fates have woven this glorious '*Yes!*' into the dark warp of my life,—by what magic the mist has fallen, and we find ourselves standing hand in hand in the mystic circle—I cannot venture to tell you. Suffice, that it is so; and think with what a jubilant spirit I sit me down to write you this letter!

"Were you here you would be touched and amused likewise with the interest everybody takes in the matter. There has been, from the beginning, a spice of romance in it, which has taken hold of several exciteable imaginations and thanks to my heedless imprudence, the public has been a kind of confidant in the whole affair. But now, thank God, this imprudence is forgiven and forgotten by the only one of whom I had to ask forgiveness and oblivion of the past;—and reconciliation falls like peaceful sunshine upon the present. . . ." [27]

In such a tumult of excitement he managed to see *The Spanish Student* through the press (published by John Owen in June), to continue his college work, to notify other friends, to call daily at the home of his beloved, and to make arrangements with her for a wedding that should take place as soon as the summer vacation began. There should be no waiting, even to fulfill the proprieties of Beacon Hill. But amid the excitement, there was the sobering duty of writing to the Potter family in Portland. To Mary Potter's oldest sister he wrote:

"Yes, my dear Eliza, I am to be married again . . . and I have chosen a person for my wife who possesses in a high degree those virtues and excellent traits of character, which so distinguished my dear Mary. Think not, that in this new engagement, I do any wrong to her memory. I still retain, and ever shall preserve with sacred care all my cherished recollections of her truth, affection and beautiful nature. And I feel, that could she speak to me, she would approve of what I am doing. I hope also for your approval and for your father's." [28]

From Mary Appleton Mackintosh in London, Longfellow received congratulations written in a slightly minor key. She had accompanied her husband to England with some reluctant misgivings, and expressed in this letter not only her pain of being separated from her family but also her understanding of Frances Appleton's unusual character:

"Accept my congratulations, not the coldest though the last among the thronging ones of your many friends. That theirs are so ardent & so frequent is the more reason perhaps that mine should like Hamlet outdoing Laertes, heap Pelion on Ossa.

"But across the dreary solitude of Sea, a single cheer is lost, and the strange and new scenes you are enacting on the other side, seem so aloof from my quiet formula of existence as to have an alien air. . . .

"All this is however the natural sting of absence from the Happiness of those we love, and how I love Fanny even you can never know. All beside this is warm hopefulness for a most happy Future for you both, with matched oars to sweep the summer Sea of Life with your Prow true to the Great Haven and its welcoming shores. God's speed to you both. God must speed so fearfully important an undertaking, which without that would be the maddest of Human adventures after the Eldorado. I have no heart to talk to you of Fanny; if you really know her it is of no use, and if you do not it is too late. I certainly almost feared she was too aloof in her goodness and deep directness of Soul from us poor ones to ever find a fitting mate, and I need not say how noble a compliment I pay you in saying that I rejoice that Heaven has given her one fitted to be her husband." [29]

The quiet wedding took place in Frances Appleton's home on Beacon Street on July 13, 1843—about three months after the meeting at Shady Hill. Although only the most intimate friends had been invited, the evening gathering which filled the spacious rooms included over fifty persons, brightly dressed in formal attire. Longfellow's closest friends were there: Charles Sumner to serve as groomsman; Hillard; Sam Ward; Pitt Fessenden; and Felton, whose pleasant duty it was to be escort for shy Anne Longfellow, up from Portland to represent her family.

Such finery and splendor almost frightened Anne. But she would never forget the picture made by the bride and groom standing with Ezra S. Gannett, the minister, before the hushed guests. Frances Appleton, who had won Anne's heart immediately, looked more lovely than ever, in her simple white muslin dress and her bridal veil, adorned with natural orange blossoms. "Oh, it was a beautiful scene," Anne wrote to a friend shortly afterward. "My darling brother never looked one half so handsome in all his life before, and Fanny was in all respects the perfection of all brides—the soul which shone so expressively in both their faces brightened and beautified the picture indescribably." And the wedding supper which followed the ceremony, the white linen cloths laden with flowers, fruit, cakes, and ices, the two tables covered with the bride's "magnificent presents," added festive refinements. As Anne said, "The joy of the occasion seemed to affect every heart—and then all was so quiet and homeish—no fuss or parade." [30]

And Longfellow, receiving with his bride the felicitations of many friends, knew the unhappy pilgrimage was ended, the long period of restlessness over, the victory truly won. The unspeakable joy of that evening was a symbol of consummation, a fulfilment of those confused longings for happiness which had been his quest. He could look back at all his stumblings, errors, failures, and pains without regret, for he had come through to peace. No longer could he be troubled by unrealized ambitions and impatient gropings after eminence. He had set out with ardent determination to establish himself as a man of letters, without guessing the hindrances, the digressions, the pains which he must face. And there had been times when the road he had followed seemed so far from that which he had sought that faith crumbled. Now faith had been so completely restored that he knew he could go on to even greater accomplishment than he had dreamed.

In spite of his earlier dissatisfaction, Longfellow had already won high praise from his countrymen. Although he did not know it, Charles Sumner had written a letter, that very wedding morning, which expressed the general attitude of all who had found comfort in *Hyperion* and *Voices of the Night:*

"I do not think it is essential that the first poets of an age should write *war odes.* Our period has a higher calling, and it is Longfellow's chief virtue to have apprehended it. His poetry does not rally to battle; but it affords succor and strength to bear the ills of life. There are six or seven pieces of his far superior, as it seems to me, to any thing I know of Uhland or Körner; calculated to do more good, to touch the soul to finer issues; pieces that will live to be worn near the hearts of men when the thrilling war-notes of Campbell and Körner will be forgotten. You and I admire the poetry of Gray. . . . But I had rather be the author of 'Psalm of Life,' 'The Light of Stars,' 'The Reaper and the Flowers,' and 'Excelsior,' than those rich pieces of Gray. I think Longfellow without rival near his throne in America. I might go further: I doubt if there is any poet now alive, and not older than he, who has written so much and so well." [31]

And the poet had just begun his career. What songs and stories, legends and romances might yet come from his pen to raise him even higher in the estimate of his countrymen? But for the present he cared only for the victory and honor of love. If there had been many waverings of direction in his spiritual journey, there had been no change of heart during the seven years since he had met Frances Appleton in Interlaken. The gossip whispered behind the hand on Beacon Hill might be as critical as that of one woman who complained, "Fanny Appleton's engagement was communicated to me in her own handwriting, otherwise I should have been tempted to doubt the fact! I confess I am more than surprised. I will tell you the truth. I like the Professor very much, and it may be that he will suit her perfectly; but I do not like her marrying a man whom she has already refused. I say this to you in confidence." [32] But such talk could not touch the two who knew their own hearts. In announcing her engagement to her brother Tom, Frances Appleton had written:

"The heart does not reveal even to itself the gradual filling of its fountains, but a time arrives at last when the stone must be thrust aside which has sealed them up & they gush forth wondering at their own abundance. To speak more plainly, tho' not more naturally, it is only to be marvelled at that this blessing did not manifest itself to me long ago. And we have both come to the comforting conclusion that it is best as it is, that our characters have been ripened to appreciate it & receive it with fuller gratitude than if the past experience had been spared us." [33]

Finally, as though she would make complete surrender of any

reproach harbored since the publication of *Hyperion*, she gave to her husband, for a wedding present, the sketch book made in Switzerland with Longfellow during the days which had seen the beginning of their love. The little book, bound in green Levant morocco, was simply inscribed:

"Mary Ashburton to Paul Flemming." [34]

NOTES

The reader is hereby cautioned to remember that there are several editions of the *Life* and *Works* with distinct pagination differences; that confusion will arise if an attempt is made to check my references in any edition other than that specified here:

Samuel Longfellow, *Life of Henry Wadsworth Longfellow, with Extracts from His Journals and Correspondence*, Boston, 1886, 2 vols.

Horace E. Scudder (editor), *The Complete Writings of Henry Wadsworth Longfellow, Craigie Edition*, Boston and New York, Houghton, Mifflin and Company [1904], 11 vols.

Chapter I: From These Roots

Throughout Chapter I, background information frequently used without documentation has been drawn from four main sources:

W. Willis, *History of Portland*, Portland, 1833.

George Lowell Austin, *Henry Wadsworth Longfellow*, Boston, 1882.

W. Willis (editor), *Journals of the Rev. Thomas Smith, and the Rev. Samuel Deane*, Portland, 1849.

Because many excellent studies of the Longfellow and Wadsworth genealogy are available, none is given here. A compact and convenient outline may be found in the Appendix to Samuel Longfellow's *Life*. Further genealogical background information in this first chapter has been drawn from two detailed studies in *Henry Wadsworth Longfellow, Seventy-fifth Birthday, Proc. Maine Hist. Soc.*, Portland, 1882 (edited by Henry S. Burrage).

1. Longfellow, "My Lost Youth."
2. W. Willis (editor), *Journals*, 49.

Chapter II: A Boy's Will

1. Samuel Longfellow, *Life of Henry Wadsworth Longfellow*, I, 15; hereafter designated "*Life*."
2. *Life*, I, 6–7.
3. MS, Craigie House Papers (hereafter designated "CHP"). See also *Life*, I, 7. In editing this letter, Samuel Longfellow corrected a slight colloquialism in the second sentence, made by his six-year-old

brother. In the *Life*, the unnecessary "to" is omitted from "Will you please to buy." Unimportant as this change is, it conveniently represents the beginning of Samuel Longfellow's deliberate changes made to satisfy his own prejudices, regardless of the inevitable danger of distorting the actual character of the original.

4. MS, dated Portland, Jan. 16, 1814, Mary King Longfellow Papers (hereafter designated "MKLP"). The correspondence between Zilpah and Stephen Longfellow from 1807 to 1825 is now (1938) in the possession of Miss Mary King Longfellow (a daughter of the poet's brother Alexander) in Portland, Maine.

5. MS, CHP; also *Life*, I, 7–8.

6. MS, dated Portland, Jan. 20, 1814, MKLP. A compressed passage from this letter occurs in the *Life*, I, 8–9.

7. MS, dated Boston, Feb. 6, 1814, MKLP.

8. MS, dated Feb. 13, MKLP.

9. MS, dated Portland, Feb. 14, 1814, MKLP.

10. Samuel Longfellow is almost certainly wrong in his statement (*Life*, I, 13–14): "It is believed that it was at his [Stephen's] instance that the old church covenant of the First Parish was modified in its doctrinal statement, before he could conscientiously assent to it in becoming a 'church member.' "

The Portland controversy over church doctrine began fiercely when Ichabod Nichols was ordained in 1809, and the direction and attitude of the First Parish Church was determined long before Stephen Longfellow joined. That he was an important figure in the church life as well as in the civil life, one may gather plainly, however, from a letter dated Gorham, Oct. 15, 1814 (MS, MKLP), and written by Zilpah to Stephen:

"We had a very pleasant visit from Mr. Nichols the other day, and I had a little ride with him before dinner, which was quite agreeable to me. He appears much gratified that you have concluded to join *us*, it will not only be fulfilling a duty on your part, but it will have a very happy influence on the minds of others, indeed it has, he thinks, had a good effect already. He added, 'People of small capacity who are not in the habit of thinking for themselves, when they see such a step taken by one who is competent to decide, and who usually does nothing without deliberation, are led to conclude that it is a duty which cannot be passed by. There is a satisfaction in having those make a profession, the correctness of whose past lives gives assurance that there will be nothing in their conduct in future to disgrace the cause they espouse, who are able to give a reason of the hope that is in them, and to silence gain sayers. It is happy, as it respects the church, to have those join it who have respectable talents, who are persons of good judgment, to whom its ministers may safely apply for council. . . .' "

11. MS (billet), dated June, 1814, CHP.
12. MS, dated Portland, Dec. 24, 1814, MKLP.
13. *Seventy-fifth Birthday Proceedings*, 79–80.
14. MS, MKLP.
15. MS, dated Aug. 10, 1815, MKLP.
16. *Ibid.*
17. *Robinson Crusoe* inspired Longfellow in one of his earliest attempts at versification. In an essay entitled "My School Boy Days" (published in the "Brazen Nose College" series, in the *Portland Advertiser*, Nov. 15, 1825), Longfellow referred to it: "Then came my romantic days. . . . I began to write poetry. . . . The first attempt in which I put forth the vigour of my young mind, was a paraphrase of the wild romance of Robinson Crusoe. One of the most remarkable features of this performance, was the genealogy of the Crusoe family, carried back into the dark ages of their history, and brought down to that notable period, in the time of my hero's father, when, according to my version,

> 'His eldest boy
> Was killed at Fontenoy.' "

(For correlated reference to this couplet, see *Life*, I, 92.)
18. Of the three, Scott exerted by far the greatest influence. No other poet was so important to Longfellow during the apprentice years. Although Bryant's influence on the college poems, written from 1824 to 1825, is obvious, Longfellow had learned to pattern his verses after the ballad stanzas of Scott from 1819 to 1824.

An obvious illustration of Scott's early influence may be found in the lyric "To the Novice of the Convent of the Visitation," which recalls the novice Clare in the "Convent" canto of *Marmion*. Furthermore, since Longfellow copied a passage from Scott's *Lady of the Lake* on the first page of his Portland Academy notebook on Oct. 4, 1819, it seems probable that Longfellow's opening references in "Youthful Years" to "the harp that hung so long unstrung," was prompted by Scott's opening line of Canto I:

"Harp of the North! that mouldering long hast hung."

Scott left his impress in a variety of ways. His use of quaint words and archaic phrases appealed to Longfellow so strongly that he never outgrew his early fondness for them. A more subtle influence of Scott was the stimulation in Longfellow of a very strong interest in medieval lore and chivalry; in knights, monks, fair ladies, and heroic deeds. It is quite safe to assume that Longfellow's entire interest in Europe sprang originally from his fascinated wanderings through the romantic world of far-off lands and ancient times in Scott's poetry and prose.

19. *Life*, I, 14. The lyrics of Thomas Moore were probably familiar to Longfellow through some American edition of *Irish Melodies*, the first such edition having been published in Philadelphia in 1815, with others quickly following. One particular lyric of Moore, "Oh! breathe not his name," may have influenced Longfellow in the "Lovell's Pond" lines. Even as Moore had wished to enshrine and preserve the memory of Robert Emmet, so Longfellow was eager to keep green the name of Captain John Lovewell.

20. President Appleton would appeal to Longfellow as a subject for elegy, because the learned divine had been a prominent figure in both Brunswick and Portland. He had frequently preached in the First Parish Church during Longfellow's boyhood.

21. The Longfellow family has refused me permission to quote, from this unpublished source, samples of the young apprentice's early and amusing lines. The copy book bears an inscription inside the front cover, in Longfellow's boyish hand: "Begun this book October 4, 1819, Finished it November 23, 1819. Portland Academy." MS, CHP.

22. Longfellow's own copy of Upham's *American Sketches*, New York, 1819, is now in the Harvard College Library. In that copy, containing his early autograph, there are several marked passages and a few pencilled notations. Although there is no comment written beside the poem entitled "Lovellspond," there is a criticism of Upham's knowledge of the historical facts concerning this battle. A second poem refers to the same encounter, and is entitled, "The Birchen Canoe." In a footnote on page 116 of *American Sketches*, Upham explains that the incident referred to the death of one of Lovewell's men, who was drowned while trying to escape from the battle in a canoe. After the note, Longfellow has written in pencil:

"Great mistake—soldier did not perish thus. He reached the shore badly but not mortally wounded & lived on many years."

23. The two poems are here given entire. Upham's:

Lovellspond

The scene in 1725, of a desperate encounter with the savages

In the earth's verdant bosom, still crumbling, and cold,
Sleep the soldiers who mingled in battle of old;
They rush'd to the slaughter, they struggled and fell
And the clarion of glory was heard in their knell.

Those brave men have long been unconscious and dead,
The pines murmur sadly above their green bed,
And the owl and the raven chant loudly and drear
When the moon-beam o'er Lovellspond shines on their bier.

The light of the sun has just sunk in the wave,
Oh, in billows of blood set the sun of the the brave;
The waters complain as they roll o'er the stones,
And the rank grass encircles a few scatter'd bones.

The eye that was sparkling no longer is bright,
The arm of the mighty death conquer'd its might;
The bosoms that once for their country beat high,
To those bosoms the sods of the valley are nigh.

The shout of the hunter is loud on the hill,
And the sounds softly echo o'er forest and rill;
But the jangling of arms shall be heard of no more,
Where the heroes of Lovellspond slumber'd in gore.

Longfellow's:

THE BATTLE OF LOVELL'S POND

Cold, cold is the north wind and rude is the blast
That sweeps like a hurricane loudly and fast,
As it moans through the tall waving pines lone and drear,
Sighs a requiem sad o'er the warrior's bier.

The war-whoop is still, and the savage's yell
Has sunk into silence along the wild dell;
The din of the battle, the tumult, is o'er
And the war-clarion's voice is now heard no more.

The warriors that fought for their country—and bled,
Have sunk to their rest; the damp earth is their bed;
No stone tells the place where their ashes repose,
Nor points out the spot from the graves of their foes.

They died in their glory, surrounded by fame,
And Victory's loud trump their death did proclaim;
They are dead; but they live in each Patriot's breast,
And their names are engraven on honor's bright crest.

—HENRY.

24. "The Battle of Lovell's Pond" appeared in the *Portland Gazette* for Nov. 17, 1820. I have given a detailed account of Longfellow's indebtedness to, and later friendship with, Upham in "Longfellow's Original Sin of Imitation," *The Colophon:* New Series, I, 97–106 (Autumn, 1935).

25. The complete story of Longfellow's first printed poem exists in several versions. The first account was written in some detail by

Longfellow and published only five years after the event. It forms a part of the "Brazen Nose College" essay mentioned in note 17 of this chapter. Although Samuel Longfellow made no mention of this account, the version in the *Life* (I, 22–3) follows it closely and even uses certain phrases directly from it.

A different version, published four years before the *Life* appeared, and purporting to have Longfellow's authentication, may be found in F. H. Underwood, *The Life of Henry Wadsworth Longfellow*, Boston, 1882, 39–40. This account adds two distinct variations, one of which suggests that William G. Browne may have been instrumental in persuading Longfellow to publish the poem: "The young author had never yet seen aught of his compositions in type . . . but the persuasion of one of his schoolfellows overcame his modesty." The second variation is this: "He waited patiently for the next issue of the paper, and was not a little chagrined to find, that, when it did appear, —the poem was left out. The weeks flew by, and still the poem remained unpublished. In a fit of disgust, the young author repaired to the editorial sanctum, and demanded the return of the manuscript. The request was granted; and Longfellow then carried it to the editor of the rival newspaper, . . . by whom it was accepted and published."

This last variation has an apocryphal flavor; yet, if error crept into Underwood's account, the fault was probably due to the failing memory of Longfellow, for Underwood wrote the larger part of his biography under the poet's supervision, shortly before his death.

26. Reprinted in George Thomas Little, *Longfellow's Boyhood Poems*, edited by Ray W. Pettengill, Saratoga Springs, 1925, p. 22.

27. Quoted from a "Notice" dated "Bowdoin College, August 23, 1821" and signed "William Allen, President of Bowdoin College." Published in the *Portland Gazette* for Sept. 11, 1821.

For calling this "Notice" to my attention—and for many other similar courtesies—I am indebted and grateful to Mr. Manning Hawthorne.

28. *Life*, I, 17.

29. One other incident concerning Longfellow's Academy days was written into and with a "Sonnet to H. W. Longfellow: A Reminiscence" by Elizabeth Oakes Smith and dated April 2, 1882:

> A little onward tend thy feet, sweet friend:
> > How brief the space since, side by side, were we,
> > Weird children, in that "city by the sea,"—
> Each golden-haired,—whose mystic visions tend
> To nobler heights than youthful fancy kenned!
> > Then Cushman's classic mind enthuséd thee,
> > And Martin's stately grace coercéd me.
> Thy retrospective eye a moment bend:
> > I was thy Dian then, Endymion thou,—

A timid boy, a thoughtful girl,—nor knew
The bond that linked, and yet estranged, us two.
I see the glory of thy youth but now,
As, rolling back, the golden gateway threw
Its flash of light athwart thy entering brow.

The authoress added, in a footnote: "The young gentlemen of the Academy were assiduous in their respectful attentions to Miss Penelope Martin's scholars, which amounted to little more than lifting the hat as they passed. There was an old post at the corner of Middle and King Streets into which time had deftly wrought a pigeon-hole, which served us as a post-office; and into this aperture the young gentlemen of the Academy deposited harmless missives addressed to heathen deities of the feminine order." (W. Sloane Kennedy, *Henry W. Longfellow, Biography, Anecdote, Letters, Criticism*, Cambridge, Mass., 1882, p. 332.)

CHAPTER III: BOWDOIN FRESHMAN

The background information in this chapter, concerning Bowdoin College, its history, appearance, and faculty, has been drawn mainly from five sources:

Egbert C. Smith, *Three Discourses upon the Religious History of Bowdoin College During the Administrations of Presidents M'Keen, Appleton, & Allen*, Brunswick, 1858.

Nehemiah Cleaveland and Alpheus S. Packard, *History of Bowdoin College with Biographical Sketches of Its Graduates from 1806 to 1879, Inclusive*, Boston, 1882.

Leonard Woods, *Address on the Life and Character of Parker Cleaveland*, Brunswick, 1860.

Horatio Bridge, *Personal Recollections of Nathaniel Hawthorne*, New York, 1893.

Louis C. Hatch, *The History of Bowdoin College*, Portland, 1927.

1. See note 6 of this chapter.

2. This very obvious reason was a butt for a Longfellow jest two years after his graduation from Bowdoin. While traveling from France to Spain he was reminded of Brunswick and wrote to his family:

"I can give you no better idea of that province of France called Landes of Gascony, than by telling you that it resembles precisely the pine plains which surround the village of Brunswick,—which makes one wonder that the French do not place a college there; it would 'keep the students out of temptation'!" (*Life*, I, 103–4.)

3. MS, MKLP.

4. MS, dated Portland, Feb. 16, 1822, CHP. Although there is no

definite proof that Longfellow, his brother, and Preble studied their freshman subjects under the supervision of Cushman at the Portland Academy, there is much circumstantial evidence. Professor A. S. Packard of Bowdoin believed this possibility to be true. (See his paper, "Longfellow as a Student and Professor at Bowdoin College," in *Seventy-fifth Birthday Proceedings*, 99.) Longfellow made frequent references, in his letters to Pierce, to activities of friends and teachers at the Academy. Under date of June 28, 1822, he wrote to Pierce:

"For the particulars of our 'Scrape' at the Academy, you must apply to Greenleaf—Preble has written him particularly upon that subject." His later comments on this "scrape" imply that he was at the Academy with his brother and Preble at this time. MS, CHP.

5. MS, dated June 2, 1822, CHP.

6. One of these letters (MS, Zilpah Longfellow to Lucia Wadsworth, dated New York, June 22, 1822, MKLP) is quoted in part as motto for this chapter.

7. MS, dated Albany, June 30, 1822, MKLP.

CHAPTER IV: COLLEGE LIFE

1. MS, Longfellow to his mother, dated Bowdoin, Dec. 7, 1822, CHP.

2. See particularly Cleaveland and Packard for instances.

3. Bridge, 39.

4. MS, CHP.

5. MS, dated Oct. 3, 1822, CHP.

6. MS, dated Oct. 5, 1822, CHP.

7. MS, dated Oct. 13, 1822, MKLP.

8. MS, dated Nov. 26, 1822, CHP. Two sentences from this letter are quoted in the *Life*, I, 27 n. Believing that Longfellow contributed a "Carrier's Address" to the *Portland Gazette* for Jan. 1, 1822, Little (p. 16) writes:

"He was a competitor, at the age of fourteen, for the prize offered by the *Portland Gazette* for the best New Year's Address for 1822. . . . It speaks well for the literary atmosphere of Portland that on this occasion the editor of the *Gazette* found himself not only fully supplied with poems, but also in great perplexity as to which should be awarded the premium. As a compromise he awarded the prize to one, printed another for the carrier, and gave his readers three of them in successive issues of his journal. They are unsigned . . . all are upwards of one hundred lines."

I have studied these unsigned pieces and can discover no basis for conclusive identification of any one as by Longfellow.

9. MS, dated Dec. 8, 1822, CHP.

10. MS, dated Bowdoin, Dec. 7, 1822, CHP.

11. Charles Nolcini may have helped to stimulate Longfellow's interest in foreign lands. The boy's friendship with Nolcini probably began while Longfellow was taking piano and flute lessons from him during Academy days. Under date of Dec. 26, 1822, Preble wrote from Portland to Longfellow, who was still at Brunswick: "Next week I attend the French school at Nolcini's. . . . I advise you to study French with me this vacation, prithee do." A later indication that the plan was carried out is contained in a letter from Zilpah to Henry, dated April 6, 1823; "Nolcini says he wishes you young gentlemen, his pupils, would write him in French. Do make the attempt."

There are constant references to Nolcini in the family correspondence. Apparently he set one of Longfellow's early poems to music, for Longfellow wrote to his sister Anne in October, 1824: "Has Nolcini finished my song yet? If he has brought it over to you, pray let me know how it sounds, and whether it's worth having . . . though I presume it will be." MSS, CHP.

12. MS, to his father, dated Feb. 18, 1823, CHP.

13. MS, dated March 1, 1823, CHP.

14. MS, dated March 29, 1823, CHP.

15. Hatch, 306. Details concerning the evening program drawn from the manuscript records of the Peucinian Society, Bowdoin College Library.

16. MS, dated April, 1823, CHP.

17. MS, dated April 23, 1823, CHP. Quoted in more detail, but with editorial tinkering, in the *Life*, I, 30.

18. MS, dated May 9, 1823, CHP. Also in *Life*, I, 30–31, with minor changes.

19. MS, dated April 5, 1823, CHP. This letter contains a detailed account of the scrape.

20. I have been interested in this scrape, not merely because it was a moment of excitement in Longfellow's college life but because it succinctly reveals the background of antagonism, the bitter dislike of Allen, felt by members of the class of 1825 (which registered its final protest at the 1825 commencement, when half the class refused to attend the president's reception), and narrow religious attitudes which Longfellow complained of, throughout his undergraduate years and during his years of teaching at Bowdoin. Material concerning the scrape has been drawn in part from the MS "Records of the College Government of Bowdoin College," Bowdoin College Library.

21. MS, dated May 11, 1823, CHP.

22. MS, dated June 22, 1823, CHP.

CHAPTER V: NEW HORIZONS

1. See note 5 of this chapter.
2. *Life*, I, 28 n.
3. MS "Records of the Peucinian Society," Bowdoin College Library. A twenty-six-page pamphlet was published: *Catalogue of the Library of the Peucinian Society*, Brunswick, 1823.
4. *North American Review*, IX, 64 (July, 1819). The reviewer was Gulian C. Verplanck.
5. MS, dated Oct. 19, 1823, CHP.
6. A quotation from Longfellow's remarks made in presenting resolutions upon the death of Irving at a meeting of the Massachusetts Historical Society on Dec. 15, 1859. *Proc. Mass. Hist. Soc.*, Boston, 1860, 393.
7. *The Sketch Book* was first published in seven parts from May, 1819, to September, 1820. There is absolutely no evidence that Longfellow was familiar with *The Sketch Book* before the summer or fall of 1823; until after he had become a member of the Peucinian Society.

Because there was no book-form edition of *The Sketch Book* published in America until 1824, and because the second and third editions were issued in parts from 1820 to 1823, it is fairly certain that Longfellow could have known only the parts-edition, even if he did not discover it until the fall of 1823. See W. R. Langfeld and P. C. Blackburn, *Washington Irving: A Bibliography*, New York, 1933, 15–23.

8. MS, to his sister Anne, dated Oct. 26, 1823, CHP.
9. MS, dated Oct. 19, 1823, CHP.
10. MS, dated Dec. 4, 1823, CHP.
11. MS, dated Oct. 26, 1823, CHP.
12. *Idem*.
13. "Philip of Pokanoket" and "Traits of Indian Character" were not included in the first American edition, but were included in the first English edition, 1820. Thus, this supposition isn't much good, unless Longfellow knew the English edition.
14. The first American edition was in *Transactions of the Historical and Literary Committee of the American Philosophical Society*, Philadelphia, 1819, Vol. I.

In a letter to his mother, dated Bowdoin, Nov. 9, 1823, Longfellow described his reaction to this book:

"Since I wrote you last I have read but one volume. That is Heckewelder's 'Account of the History, Manners and Customs of the Indian Nations of Pennsylvania and the neighbouring states.' This is a very interesting volume, and exhibits in a new and more agreeable light the character of this reviled and persecuted race. It appears from this account of them and of their customs, (and I see no reason why he should not be relied upon as correct, since he passed the greater part of a long life amongst the Indians) that they are a race possessing magnanimity, generosity, benevolence, and pure religion without hypocrisy. This may seem a paradox, but nevertheless I believe it true. They have been most barbarously maltreated by the whites, both in word and deed. We have heard them branded as a very scandal upon humanity,—cruel, malicious, wicked and without natural affection. Their outrages!—what ear has not heard of them a thousand times? whilst the white people, who rendered their cruelty more cruel, their barbarity more vindictive, publish abroad the crimes and thank heaven in their hypocrisy, that they are not like these persecuted heathen. I wish you could read this volume. I do not know whether it is in the Portland Library or not, though I am rather inclined to think it is. Get it as soon as you can and read it and see what a noble race have been almost entirely cut off and exterminated from the face of the earth, by the coming of the whites." MS, CHP.

15. These two paragraphs from the "Dialogue" were printed (probably for the first time) in an anonymous article, "Longfellow's First Wife and Early Friends," *Every Other Saturday*, Vol. I, No. 2, pp. 20–21 (Jan. 19, 1884).

16. MS, dated Dec. 11, 1823, CHP. See also *Life*, I. 34–35.

17. MS, dated Nov. 9, 1823, CHP.

18. MS, dated Dec. 1, 1823, CHP.

19. *Idem.*

20. MSS, dated Dec. 29, 1823, and Jan. 1, 1824, CHP.

21. MS, dated Nov. 4, 1823, CHP.

22. MS, CHP.

23. MS, dated Jan. 22, 1824, CHP.

24. MS, dated March 2, 1824, CHP. See also *Life*, I, 37–38.

25. Was Longfellow's contribution published? I believe it was, anonymously. This subject will be discussed at some length in my forthcoming Longfellow bibliography.

26. MS, dated April 4, 1824. MKLP.

27. Although the Doane and Wells families were old friends, and possibly distant relatives, of the Wadsworth family, Longfellow had made the acquaintance of Dr. John Doane Wells in Brunswick, for he was Professor of Anatomy and Surgery in the newly founded Bowdoin Medical School.

Longfellow's interest in Europe and his desire to travel may have been quickened by Dr. Wells, who had gone to France to study medicine in 1820, two years after his graduation from Harvard. He remained there until 1822, when he returned to teach at Brunswick. (Cleaveland and Packard, 100.)

28. MS, dated Feb. 22, 1824, MKLP.

CHAPTER VI: SELF-DISCOVERY

1. MS letter, Longfellow to his father, dated Dec. 5, 1824, CHP. See also *Life*, I, 53.

2. MS, dated March 21, 1824, CHP.

3. *Portland Advertiser*, Jan. 14, 1824; reprinted in Little, 23–24.

4. MS, dated March 13, 1824, CHP.

5. *Idem.*

6. A. S. Packard, "Longfellow as a Student," 102.

7. MS, dated Dec. 5, 1824, CHP. Obviously, if Longfellow's father had expressed himself concerning the law, the boy had not wished to take him seriously. See the *Life*, I, 52.

8. MS, dated Dec. 31, 1824, CHP. Also in more detail in *Life*, I, 55–56.

9. MS, dated Dec. 26, 1824, CHP. Also in *Life*, I, 56. Notice that this letter was not received by Longfellow until after he had written the letter dated Dec. 31, 1824.

10. MS, dated Jan. 24, 1825, CHP. Compressed in *Life*, I, 57–58.

11. MS, dated March 7, 1824. CHP.

12. Three poems: "To Ianthe," *Advertiser*, Aug. 28, 1824, forty-eight lines; "Jepthah's Daughter," *Advertiser*, Sept. 22, 1824, forty lines; "Old Parish Church," *Advertiser*, Sept. 25, 1824, sixty-four lines.

13. McHenry proved to be something of a scoundrel. After a series of strange maneuvers, he managed to back out of all his promises without paying Longfellow anything for at least three, and probably four, generous contributions.

14. MS, dated Nov. 1, 1824, CHP. See also *Life*, I, 46. For the actual amount paid Longfellow for his contributions to the *Gazette*, see note 13 of chap. VII.

15. The first poem published in the *Gazette* was "Thanksgiving," dated "Sunday evening, October, 1824." An anecdote concerning the writing of "Thanksgiving" was related by John Owen, a native of Portland who attended the Portland Academy with Longfellow, was graduated from Bowdoin two years after him, became a publisher and bookseller in Cambridge, and subsequently published six of Longfellow's books. In late life he recalled the following story, which undoubtedly has embroidery about the edges:

"I shall never forget one of the visits which I paid to my old school-friend just after the opening of my sophomore year. It was in the month of October, and on a sabbath evening. After some hours spent over my books, I called at his room late in the evening. I found him in an old arm-chair with a copy of Shakspeare . . . an English copy, if I remember rightly . . . lying on his lap, and over that a sheet of paper, on which he had been writing, in a clear, legible, and neat hand, some inspiration of the moment. The object of my visit was twofold: first, to obtain some information with regard to one of the instructors; and secondly, to renew our friendship. He received me most cordially, and at once told me he was jotting down some verses. We went over again, in pleasant talk, the experience of the ballad on 'Lovewell's Fight'; and I suggested that perhaps poesy was not his forte. 'Let me read you something,' he remarked, without directly responding to my playful jest. And he began with the lines, 'When first in ancient time, from Jubal's tongue.' 'You see, I have a cold,' he added, 'and could not go to devotional exercises. But I must do something in keeping with the day.'" G. L. Austin, *Henry Wadsworth Longfellow*, Boston, 1883 (1882), 70–71.

16. MS, dated Nov. 17, 1824, CHP. See also *Life*, I, 46.

17. MS, dated Jan. 18, 1825, CHP. See also *Life*, I, 60.

The review of *Highways and Byways*, First Series, 1823, seems to have found no place in print. After the *Gazette* and the *Review* had refused it, Longfellow thought to dress it up in new clothes to accompany a review of the Second Series (1824) and wrote to Parsons in February, 1825:

"I see that a Second Series of High Ways and By Ways has been published. If I can get the work in good season, however singular you may think my conduct to be after a failure, I intend to write a review of the volumes just issued and to publish the article, in connection with the former one, in the New York 'Atlantic Magazine'—if the Editor will take the writings. A review of the second series would be a good pretence for bringing forward the first at so late a period."

Parsons, who had just relinquished the editorship of the *Gazette* to J. G. Carter, replied on Feb. 25, 1825:

"As to your review of Grattan's new book, why do you not send it to Mr. Carter? He will be as glad to print it as any one."

Under date of March 30, 1825, Carter answered Longfellow's question thus:

"I think you had better review the 'New Series' of Highways & Byways independently of the first series, the review of which is in my hands. If that review had been received in season I think Mr. P. would without doubt have inserted it."

On May 2, Carter wrote:

"I have received your review of High Ways & By Ways; . . . Your review is in type for our number for 15 May." It appeared unsigned, as the first article in the issue for May 15, 1825, and was nine pages long. It was never collected; has never been reprinted, and seems to have escaped the notice of Longfellow students.

(Quotations are all from MS, CHP, except for the first letter, Longfellow to Parsons, MS, James T. Fields Papers, Huntington Library, San Marino, California.)

18. MS, dated Oct., 1824, CHP.

19. Longfellow's only reference to this poem seems to be in a fragment of a letter sent to Parsons some time in January, 1825:

"With regard to my poem before the Peucinian Society, I think it will not do for the Gazette. It is too long for such a work— amounting to about 400 lines. The subject is 'The Poetry of the Dark Ages'—which perhaps you will say is better subject for a dissertation than a poem." (MS, Huntington Library.)

There is strong reason for believing that this long poem formed the basis for Longfellow's "Phi Beta Kappa Poem" delivered at Bowdoin in September, 1832. A detailed consideration of this relationship will be included in my forthcoming Longfellow bibliography.

20. MS, dated Jan. 10, 1824, MKLP.

21. MS, dated March 7, 1824, CHP.

22. MS "Records of the College Government of Bowdoin College," Bowdoin College Library. The action was taken on Dec. 28, 1824. When Stephen returned at the end of April he was immediately rusticated again, because he had brought back no satisfactory "testimonial of good conduct." When he returned to take examinations in June, after a second period of rustication (at home, under his father's strict supervision) his marks were exceptionally good. Remaining a member in good standing, he was graduated with his class in the fall of 1825.

23. MS, dated April 6, 1825.

24. *American Sketches*, 11–12.

25. A subsequent cause for Longfellow's early interest in Indian subjects may be found in an encouraging letter written to him on July 11, 1825, by J. G. Carter:

"You have a happy style for the *Essay*, and a talent for *description* which, if you are fortunate in your subjects, will make your writings very popular. I should think some story might be found or at least the facts of it, in the early history of our country which properly wrought up and described would be very interesting. Have you studied the Indian character enough to take some story involving some of the peculiar traits which distinguish the race? There are many effecting stories to be found in the Indian histories or histories of Indians. These are only hints hastily thrown out for your consideration. I think you would succeed in the kind of writing of which

I am speaking. The story of the 'Broken Heart' in the Sketch Book is of the kind to which I allude. And there are others of the same class in the Sketch Book." MS, CHP.

Perhaps this letter helped to divert Longfellow's interest from poetry writing, for he wrote very little after his graduation—and when he returned to any sustained plan for original writing (it was in Dresden, in January, 1829), his intention was to write a "Sketch Book of New England" in which there were to be at least three stories based on Indian legend and history.

26. *The Illustrated Fryeburg Webster Memorial*, Fryeburg, Maine, 1882, 30. The record of the visit to the Wadsworth farm is preserved in a MS diary of Peleg Wadsworth, Jr., in the Wadsworth House, Hiram, Maine.

The "Ode Written for the Commemoration at Fryeburg, Maine, of Lovewell's Fight" was first printed in the *Portland Advertiser*, May 24, 1825. It was reprinted in book form in *Seventy-fifth Birthday Proceedings*, 152–54.

27. MS, dated June 29, 1825, CHP.

28. MS, dated April, 1825, CHP. See *Life*, I, 62.

29. It appeared in the *Portland Advertiser* for May 27, 1825. On April 23, 1825, Browne had written to Longfellow:

"Will you upon occasion, contribute a No. to my 'Walking Gentleman'; he would be grateful for the favor, & I should esteem it another mark of friendship added to the many you have already shown me." MS, CHP.

30. MS, dated July 22, 1825, CHP. See also *Life*, I, 65.

31. MS, dated July 31, 1825, CHP. See also *Life*, I, 66.

32. A. S. Packard, "Longfellow as a Student," 103. The Chatterton essay was sent to Jared Sparks, editor of the *North American Review*. Under date of Sept. 15, 1825, Sparks wrote to Longfellow (MS, CHP):

"Your letter & the article on Chatterton have been received. It is now twenty two years since Chatterton's works were published, and considering they were fully handled in the Edinburgh Review, & have been from time to time touched upon in the Quarterly, both of which circulate in this country, it appears to me that any formal notice at the present time will not have sufficient interest for the American public.

"With the first part of the article I am particularly pleased, as a specimen of chaste and agreeable writing, nor do I see any faults, unless it be the length of the quotations, and perhaps the diffuseness in the remarks, which follow. Did the subject appear to me as one of particular interest, I should gladly insert the article in the Review.

"You know we try to be as much *American* as possible, & for that reason it is desirable to seek topics, which have some immediate relation to this country, and to passing events. As you express a willingness to contribute to the North American Review, I hope you will find it convenient at some time to take up a work of this description."

Carter next refused the Chatterton article, concluding his excuses: "Besides I do not like to have the impression get abroad that the Gazette is made up of what the North American has refused." MS, CHP.

33. "Our Native Writers," *Every Other Saturday*, I, 116 (April 12, 1884).

34. *Life*, I, 254.

CHAPTER VII: ESCAPE FROM THE LAW

I have drawn heavily on two main sources for the background material in Chapter VII:

George S. Hillard (editor), *The Life, Letters, and Journals of George Ticknor*, Boston, 1887.

Orie William Long, *Literary Pioneers: Early American Explorers of European Culture*, Cambridge, 1935.

Professor Long deals with George Ticknor, Edward Everett, Joseph Green Cogswell, George Bancroft, John Lothrop Motley, and Longfellow.

1. MS, Longfellow to his father, dated Jan. 24, 1825, CHP.

2. MS, Chamberlain Collection, Boston Public Library.

3. MS, dated Aug. 16, 1825, CHP.

4. In the next four months, Longfellow published exactly four poems; in the next four years, he wrote almost no poetry, according to his own confession. Many factors contributed to this sudden decline of interest and activity. Certainly, such words as those in Parsons' letter helped to discourage him. Then too, the boy's father had unwittingly contributed to his discouragement. On Jan. 28, 1825, Stephen had written:

"I think you publish your productions too soon after they are written . . . without allowing time for reflection and examination. And if you reëxamine them, you will probably find some defects, which would have been corrected if you had adopted the course I recommend. I hope you will not be bounded by these observations, they proceed from the purest motives and the kindest feelings, and I hope will produce beneficial effects." (MS, CHP.)

In answer, Longfellow wrote, "Your good advice I shall hereafter follow." But he had been stimulated to rapid writing by his pleasure in selling and publishing his verses—the joy of seeing them quickly in print. During this period, he never owned any large sheaf of unpublished poems on which he worked. Almost as soon as he finished a poem, he sent it off to an editor. His father was right on this point. Yet the voluntary sacrifice of this publishing incentive was soon followed by a loss of interest in, or of persistent devotion to, his writing.

Here is another important contributing factor. Longfellow stopped writing when he left Bowdoin. The classroom influence of Professor Newman, and the requirement of compositions for class work undoubtedly spurred this student on, with many others. Away from Newman, away from the requirement, interest lagged.

Defensively, Longfellow turned to criticize other poets for the same fault which his father had pointed out in his verses. The subject became a mild obsession. Felicia Hemans' poetry, during the period when she had been writing only a little, "bore the marks of much care: she wrote admirably then, but of late, by her own carelessness, she has fallen short of her own excellence." In another letter, Longfellow praised the poetry of "L. E. L." but qualified his remarks: "I think she writes and publishes with a haste that would prove fatal to most any poet." (MSS, Longfellow to Caroline Doane, dated Dec. 4, 1825, and Dec. 31, 1825, CHP.)

5. He could not have hoped for more genuine praise than that which was paid him unknowingly by his own master, William Cullen Bryant, who wrote in the *New York Review* for July, 1825 (one month before Parsons wrote to him):

"We do not know of all the numerous English periodicals, any one which has furnished within the same time, so much really beautiful poetry as may be found and still continues to be found in the columns of this *United States Gazette*. We might cite in proof of what we advance, the 'April Day,' the 'Hymn of the Moravian Nuns,' and the 'Sunrise on the Hills,' all by H. W. L., we know not who he is . . ."

6. Parke Godwin, *Life of William Cullen Bryant*, New York, 1883, I, 295.

7. "The Lay Monastery," *United States Literary Gazette*, II, 24 (April 1, 1825).

8. Parsons had written on August 16; the commencement took place on September 7—less than a month later.

9. Irving's "Account" is a valuable mirror for the times, because it reflects the tone and mood of romantic sentiment which was spreading through America at this time. For an understanding of Longfellow's attitude toward European lands and literature, one may interpret the implications of Irving's almost-closing words:

"It has been either my good or evil lot to have my roving passion gratified. I have wandered through different countries, and witnessed many of the shifting scenes of life. I cannot say that I have studied them with the eye of a philosopher; but rather with the sauntering gaze with which humble lovers of the picturesque stroll from the window of one print-shop to another; caught, sometimes by the delineations of beauty, sometimes by the distortions of caricature, and sometimes by the loveliness of landscape."

Indeed, Irving and Longfellow may be seen to have in common far more than an elegant prose style!

10. A more detailed treatment of the "Brazen Nose College" essays will be found in my forthcoming bibliography.

11. "Youthful Years," *Portland Advertiser*, Dec. 30, 1825. The proof of authorship and of Browne's ownership of the manuscript is found in a letter, Browne to Longfellow, dated Oct. 16, 1824 (MS, CHP):

". . . my gratification was great in reading your 'Youthful Years.' I have read it over three or four times . . . There is in the last verse, an idea, that I was much pleased with & yet it was not so much the idea as the expression—it rings in my ears, it is never out of my mouth—it is this—

" 'Sorrow is for the sons of men
        And weeping for earth's daughters.' "

12. MS, dated March 13, 1826, CHP. See also *Life*, I, 69.

13. Published April 1, 1826. For his contributions to the *Gazette*, Longfellow was paid the equivalent of $43.67. According to a letter to him from Cummings, Hilliard & Co., the publishers of the *Gazette*, dated July 28, 1825, the rate of payment was one dollar a column for prose and two dollars a column for poetry. For contributions to Vol. I of the *Gazette*, Longfellow was paid $17; to Vol. II, $19.67; to Vol. III, $7.00. Very little of this money was actually paid in cash to Longfellow. Instead, it was used by him for book purchases and magazine subscription payments.

14. Charles Hart Handschin, *The Teaching of Modern Languages in the United States* (U. S. Bureau of Ed. Bul., 1913, No. 13, Washington, 1913), 17 ff.

15. MS, dated May 2, 1826, CHP. The letter begins: "I have been too constantly engaged since my arrival here to write you, until this last hour of my stay, when I am expecting every moment to hear the stage, which is to carry me to Northampton, drive up to the door."

16. *Idem.*

17. *Idem.*

18. Long, 88.

19. Long, 140.

20. MS, dated May 5, 1826, CHP.

21. MS, dated May 14, 1826, CHP.

22. MS, dated March 17, 1826, CHP.

23. According to a letter to his sister Anne, Longfellow left four poems: "I forgot to tell you that the pieces I wrote for it [*Atlantic Souvenir*] were entitled 'The Spirit of Poetry'— 'The Burial of the Minnisink'—'Song of the Birds'—and 'The Dead Bird, A Ballad.'" (MS, dated May 14, 1826, CHP.)

Of these, "The Song of the Birds" and "The Burial of the Minnisink" appeared in *The Atlantic Souvenir*, Philadelphia, 1827 (1826), 113–14, 200–201; "The Spirit of Poetry" appeared in *The Atlantic Souvenir*, 1828 (1827), 38–39; "The Dead Bird, A Ballad" was not published there under that title—and probably it was never published. No record of it has been found. In the "Book of Vanity," an autobiographical notebook concerning poems, written by Longfellow in 1846, he said, ". . . the 'Spirit of Poetry' and the 'Burial of the Minnisink' were written immediately after leaving College, in the autumn of 1825." CHP.

24. MS, dated May 7, 1826, CHP. See also *Life*, I, 71–72.

25. MS, CHP. Samuel Longfellow, not satisfied with the ending of this letter, rearranged the sentences to satisfy his own prejudices. See *Life*, I, 72.

26. *Life*, I, 113.

27. MS, dated June 15, 1826, CHP. See also *Life*, I, 77.

28. *Outre-Mer, Complete Writings*, VII, 18–19; quoted from the introduction entitled "The Pilgrim of Outre-Mer," which offers enlightening comparison with "The Author's Account of Himself" in *The Sketch Book*.

CHAPTER VIII: THE PILGRIM DISAPPOINTED

Although I have drawn much background material for Chapter VIII from the sources used in the *Life*, I, 76–101, my purpose has been quite distinct from the purpose of Samuel Longfellow. He emphasized the externals, by means of editorial manipulation, omission, and deletion. He allowed the reader to know what Longfellow saw and did, but concealed much evidence which revealed Longfellow as a boy, immature in thoughts and emotions.

Furthermore, Samuel Longfellow's editorial method, as revealed in his treatment of Longfellow's first European journey, completely kept from sight the conflict between Longfellow and his parents during the absence from home; concealed the father's growing dissatisfaction with which he greeted the son's accounts of dallying in picturesque regions instead of settling down to long and arduous study.

By way of contrast, I am *primarily* concerned with evidence which was omitted by Samuel Longfellow—evidence which reveals that

Longfellow was the romantic pilgrim; and that he was not a scholar such as Ticknor or Bancroft or Cogswell. I have also been concerned with the conflict of wishes between father and son, for a specific reason: this conflict proves that the impulsive romantic was not qualified, either by experience or by inclination, to become the remarkable scholar and linguist, *on this first trip,* as so many biographers and literary historians have implied he was. I am particularly dissatisfied with Samuel Longfellow's handling of this period, not because he omitted, but because he concealed, in such a way as to distort the plain truth.

James Taft Hatfield, in *New Light on Longfellow* (Boston, 1933, 8–23), helps to perpetuate a false impression of this first European trip, by shifting the emphasis in an attempt to prove that Longfellow's one increasing purpose was to get to Germany. Like Samuel Longfellow (whom he praises), Professor Hatfield misrepresents the facts by choosing only such excerpts as serve his purpose. The story is indeed one so filled with conflicting motives and impulses that one would prefer to avoid the pilgrim's inconsistencies by some such convenient simplification. But this first trip is the foundation on which Longfellow's entire life as a scholar and poet rests. To distort that foundation is to distort our understanding of all that was built upon it.

1. MS, dated Oct. 2, 1826, CHP.
2. MS, dated June 15, 1826, CHP.
3. *Idem.*
4. *Outre-Mer,* VII 23.
5. *Outre-Mer,* VII 24.
6. *Outre-Mer,* VII 30–31.
7. In the *Life* (I, 79) the facts concerning this trivial incident are twisted by giving telescoped passages and sentences from Longfellow's letter, in this abbreviated form:

"I went immediately to Madame Potet's, No. 49 *Rue Monsieur le Prince,* where I intend to reside whilst I remain in Paris."

This conceals any suggestion as to how Longfellow had the wisdom to go directly there. Compare such complete mastery of the situation with the impression given in the original passage, which reads:

"As my first object was to find Eben Storer I went immediately to Madame Potet's—'No. 49—Rue Monsieur le Prince Faux—St. Germ.' —The family were all from home, but knowing French enough to make myself understood by the servants I got my baggage taken from the cabriolet and awaited their return. They arrived about midnight, which by the way is not a very late hour here. I was received with the greatest kindness—for Cousin Eben it seems had told Madame of my coming to Paris and had procured a room for me here, where I intend to reside whilst I remain in Paris." MS, dated Paris, June 20, 1826, CHP.

8. MS, dated Paris, June 20, 1826, CHP.

9. MS, to his father, dated Oct. 19, 1826, CHP. D'Eon was probably a private tutor in either Portland or Brunswick. This is the only reference to him which I have found.

10. MS, to his sisters, dated July 10, 1826, CHP.

11. *Idem.*

12. MS, dated July 23, 1826, CHP. Compare *Life,* I, 83.

13. MS, dated July 11, 1826, CHP.

14. MS, dated July 23, 1826, CHP. Samuel Longfellow, apparently reluctant to reveal the implication that Longfellow leaned so heavily on the aid of Madame Potet for French instruction, edited this sentence thus:

"[In my French] I am coming on famously, I assure you." *Life,* I, 84.

There is no indication that Longfellow received any other instruction during the summer of 1826. His letters during this period contain no reference to his study of the language, and later they contain no mention of reading in French literature or work in French libraries. He kept no notebook at this time. But see note 15 of Chapter IX.

15. The chapter is entitled "The Village of Auteuil."

16. MS, to his father, dated Aug. 12, 1826, CHP.

17. MS, dated Aug. 17, 1826, CHP. See also *Life,* I, 86. A few of the opening sentences from this letter may be worth adding here:

"I have been residing for the last fortnight at this pleasant village of Auteuil. . . . As to the village itself, there is nothing remarkable about it—at least nothing further, than that it was formerly the residence of Benjamin Franklin, and the famous tragic poet Racine. This may have sanctified the place, by making it classic ground, but after all, a French village, in its best estate, can be little to the taste of Brother Jonathan."

18. *Idem.* Omitted without indication in the edited version in the *Life,* I, 86–87.

19. *Idem.*

CHAPTER IX: PATERNAL GUIDANCE

1. See note 4 of this chapter.

2. MS, dated Portland, Aug. 11, 1826, CHP. This is apparently the first letter Longfellow received from his father after reaching France, although it contains this sentence: "I wrote you by the first Packet after you left New York on the subject of your visit to Göttingen."

Longfellow made no mention of that letter, and it is not among the letters to Longfellow now in the Craigie House. Probably it never reached him.

Stephen was willing to coöperate with his son, when he wrote this letter. He gave an elastic itinerary which he was willing to have his son discuss and modify. A part of the letter, containing the sentence quoted in the text, reads:

"My impression is very strong that your advantages for acquiring a knowledge of the French language are greater at Paris than they can be at any other place. Will it not be better for you to remain where you are till you have accomplished that object? It has occurred to me that it will then be best to go to Spain & spend the winter, then to Italy & then to Göttingen, if it should be thought advisable to visit that place, & then you might pass over to England if circumstances should permit. These are suggestions on which I wish to know your views. . . .

"August 27. Having lost the opportunity of sending the above letter as was intended, I avail myself of the occasion . . . I had supposed that by diligence & close application to your studies you would be able to acquire competent knowledge of the French so as to visit Spain early this winter or this autumn; and in the Spring go to Italy & after remaining there a few months spend the summer & succeeding winter in Göttingen."

Since Stephen Longfellow contradicted himself here by referring to Göttingen as a place which seemed hardly worth visiting, and then as a place important enough to spend a summer and winter, perhaps we should not blame the son too much for being confused.

3. MS, dated Portland, Aug. 11, 1826, CHP.

4. MS, dated Oct. 2, 1826, CHP. Quoted with brief but significant omissions in the *Life*, I, 87–88. This is the only letter quoted in this chapter of the *Life* which indicates any conflict between father and son.

5. MS, dated Oct. 2, 1826, CHP.

6. *Idem.*

7. MS journal, CHP. This journal, devoted solely to the account of Longfellow's trip through the Loire valley, is the only known journal kept by him in France. It begins: "October 3, 1826. Left Paris in the Diligence for Orleans at 6 o'clock in the morning. . . ." The entry quoted in the text is recorded under the date, Oct. 5, and begins:

"This day I was to start on my foot excursion along the banks of the Loire. A very dull—disheartening kind of a morning—no doubt that in Sewall's almanack it is marked quite down the page 'Expect—much—rain—about—this—time!' 'Very—miscellaneous—kind —of weather—for—sundry—purposes—' but not for a journey on foot. Determined, however, that nothing but a downright storm should stop me. Crossed over to Orleans, found my knapsack at the Diligence office. Forgot to mention in the proper place, that the said knapsack contained all my clothing for my journey—and that I had left it behind me at Paris—not carelessly—but unfortunately."

The quotation from Irving in the beginning of his first European notebook suggests that Longfellow may have been considering the probability of using this experience for literary purposes later. It was used; the material expanded to form the chapter in *Outre-Mer* entitled, "The Valley of the Loire." (The entry was also used in writing a subsequent letter to his brother. See *Life*, I, 90.)

8. MS, to his brother Stephen, dated Oct. 26, 1826, CHP.

9. MS, dated Paris, Oct. 19, 1826, CHP. In the letter which Longfellow wrote to his father on the same day, he made no mention of the trip.

10. MS, dated Oct. 19, 1826, CHP.

11. *Idem.*

12. *Idem.*

13. *Idem.*

14. MS, dated Dec. 3, 1826.

15. *Idem.* This letter probably reached Longfellow around Feb. 15, 1827. In a letter dated Paris, Feb. 19, 1827, he answered and protested that there had been a misunderstanding about his having taken no instructor. "And indeed I always presumed that it was taken for granted. At Auteuil—one month—I was without one—because there were none there—but immediately after my return I commenced anew my lessons—and continued them as long as I thought necessary." This answer would apply perfectly, if one interpreted it as meaning that his instructor was Madame Potet. Under any circumstance, the reply is mildly evasive and is not strong enough to convince me that he had any instructor in French, other than some such well-meaning friend as Madame Potet.

16. Nathaniel Hazeltine Carter, Longfellow's school teacher in the early days of the Portland Academy. He became editor of the *New York Statesman*, to which Longfellow subscribed, in 1819; went abroad in 1825, and wrote letters which were published regularly in the *Statesman;* in book form in 1827.

17. MS, dated Dec. 23, 1826, CHP. See also *Life*, I, 97–98.

18. MS, dated Feb. 13, 1827, CHP.

CHAPTER X: SPAIN AND A NEW BEGINNING

Background material for Chapter X has been drawn from Iris Lilian Whitman, *Longfellow and Spain*, New York, 1927, a study which furnishes valuable supplement to the *Life* (I, 102–34) not only because of a more exhaustive treatment but also because the letters and journal entries are quoted from the originals in more complete form than in the *Life*. Because of such thorough treatment, any detailed reprinting of letters and journals here would be superfluous.

I have concentrated on two aspects of Longfellow's visit in Spain: the social pleasures enjoyed in Madrid, and the romantic experiences. Such emphasis clarifies a point which may be deduced in part from the evidence in *Longfellow and Spain:* that Longfellow's knowledge of Spanish literature did not begin until after he had completed his eight months of residence in Spain; that in all his journal passages and scores of letter-pages, written from Spain, Longfellow made no reference to any Spanish author except Cervantes and no reference to any Spanish literature except ballads which he had found translated by Byron or Lockhart. This is important, in that it reveals a point zealously concealed by Samuel Longfellow: during this first European visit, Longfellow was *not* primarily interested in study and scholarship.

1. MS, dated Bordeaux, Feb. 26, 1827, CHP. See also *Life*, I, 100.
2. MS, dated Madrid, March 20, 1827, CHP. See also *Life*, I, 106.
3. MS, dated Aug. 11, 1826, CHP.
4. MS, dated March 20, 1827, CHP. See also *Life*, I, 107.
5. In Whitman, 25, is this statement: "Lieutenant Slidell and Longfellow doubtless lived in the same house while in Madrid, for Slidell refers to *Calle Montera* as his residence while there; he mentions Florencia and Don Valentín."

In a letter to Longfellow dated Feb. 15, 1829 (MS, CHP), Slidell makes a passing reference to Florencia and adds:

"Tell me if in all your wanderings you have anywhere met with a damsel whether of high or low degree so gentle, so kind, so unaffectedly amiable as that same Florencia?"

The probability is that if Slidell had rooms in the home of Don Valentín, he moved out when, or soon after, Longfellow moved in. For Longfellow wrote, not long after the return from the Guadarrama trip, that Slidell had left Madrid for Gibraltar. See *Life*, I, 110.

6. MS, to his sister Elizabeth, dated Madrid, May 15, 1827, CHP. See also *Life*, I, 115.
7. MS, dated Madrid, March 20, 1827, CHP. See also *Life*, I, 103.
8. MS, dated May 15, 1827, CHP. See also *Life*, I, 116.
9. MS, dated March 20, 1827, CHP. See also *Life*, I, 109.
10. Whitman, 8.
11. MS, dated March 20, 1827, CHP.
12. *Idem.*
13. *Proc., Mass. Hist. Soc.*, Boston, 1860, 394.
14. *Ibid.*
15. S. Austin Allibone, *A Critical Dictionary of English Literature and British and American Authors*, Philadelphia, 1871, 3 vols.,

II, 1788. (This passage is contained in a letter written by Irving to Allibone.)

16. *Life*, I, 117.

17. MS, dated March 20, 1827, CHP. Compressed in *Life*, I, 108.

18. MS, Longfellow to his father, dated Dec. 29, 1839, CHP. See also *Life*, I, 338.

19. MS, dated July 16, 1827, CHP. See also *Life*, I, 123.

20. Whitman, 37. Of course, the obvious explanation of this insensibility was not that Longfellow had turned Spanish but that he was protected by a chronic limitation which kept him from recognizing reality when he was confronted with it. The best commentary on this phase of Longfellow's character is that of Professor Odell Shepard, in his excellent "Introduction" to the Longfellow volume in the American Writers Series (New York, 1934, p. xxvii):

". . . Self-indulgently romantic, he uses imagination rather for escape from reality than for penetration of it. . . . In an early story called 'The Baptism of Fire,' published in *Outre-Mer*, he writes a cool description of an execution by fire and hanging which gives, at first, the effect of a callous brutality. One soon realizes, of course, that the writer is half asleep, that he has failed to bring the terrible experience home to himself as a thing that once actually happened—as a thing the like of which was happening in his own country in his time as in ours. Had he keenly realized this, either he would not have written the story at all or else he would have written it with an anguish of mind that would have made it live. But it remained for him, as it does for us, merely something in a book, distant in time and place, a faintly lurid spot in the light and shade of history."

Professor Shepard's critical essay on Longfellow is throughout incisive and shrewd. It is by all odds the best short treatment of Longfellow that I know.

21. MS, dated July 16, 1827, CHP.

22. *Idem.*

23. *Idem.* This passage occurs in a letter to his mother. A diary entry describes the same incident:

"Another dance at night in the hall:—join in it—my first motion with my hands in the air knocked off the manager's hat:—my second——"

A comparison of these two descriptions reveals the method in which Longfellow assembled much of the material later used in writing *Outre-Mer*. Often his first notations were sketches, incomplete fragments of sentences, which were expanded with care and with increasingly self-conscious, archaic, and ornate phrasings, in the long letter-journals which he sent home from Spain. These letters, carefully preserved by his parents at his request, later grew very simply into the chapters on Spain when *Outre-Mer* was compiled. Entire passages will be found in the letters which are identical with sentences in *Outre-Mer*, except for changes of a few words.

24. Whitman, 40.

25. MS, to his mother, dated May 13, 1827, CHP. This passage is omitted, without indication, from the letter as printed in the *Life*, I, 110–12.

26. MS, letter dated Portland, July 17, 1827, CHP.

27. MS, letter dated Madrid, July 16, 1827. In the *Life*, I, 120–21, the edited version of this passage contains several trivial corrections which improve on the original.

28. MS journal entry, quoted in Whitman, 52. Notice the imitation of Irving in this passage. It recalls the sentence with which "Rip Van Winkle" begins:

"Whoever has made a voyage up the Hudson must remember the Kaatskill mountains."

Furthermore, the paragraph immediately following the one quoted in the text is equally revealing. Mrs. Everett had suggested that Longfellow write a book about Spain, and here is the self-conscious beginning of Longfellow's introduction of elegance into journal passages. Undoubtedly the plan of writing a "Spanish Sketch Book" had taken definite shape in his mind, by this time. The second paragraph continues:

"In the early autumn of the year I made a tour through La Mancha. The withered leaves were already dropping—and the immense plains around me, as far as the eye could reach, looked brown barren and sunburnt. I have never seen a country that wore so desolate a look. You trace the road stretching for miles before you—with neither cottage nor green tree beside it: and in some parts of the country, when you start on your journey in the morning, you may see in a direct line before you the village in which you will pass the night. As I dislike to be hurried through a country, however sad and solitary it may be, without seeing its peculiarities, I took a seat in the wagon of a carrier from Castile to Andalusia. I found but few objects to interest me on the road: and when a stage-coach swept by—with its guard galloping beside it—and cheerful faces at the windows—I could not help envying the little world within, and feeling somewhat heartsick that I should be lingering so long behind." (MS, CHP. See also Whitman, 52–53.)

Possibly the self-consciously literary beginning of this journal troubled Samuel Longfellow, who omitted the opening paragraph and the first sentence of the second paragraph, here quoted. See *Life*, I, 125.

29. Whitman, 57. The last sentence, so honest and provincial, was omitted in the *Life*, I, 127.

30. Whitman, 65. Compare *Life*, I, 131.

31. Whitman, 65–66. Compare the passage in *Outre-Mer* (VII, 262) beginning: "Is this reality and not a dream? Am I indeed in Granada? Am I indeed within the walls of that earthly paradise of the Moorish Kings?"

32. MS journal; see also *Life*, I, 132. Notice on the same page: "There are moments in our lives to which we feel that romance could add nothing, and which poetry itself could not beautify. Such were those I passed in lingering about the Alhambra and dreaming over the warlike deeds of other days."

33. *Life*, I, 134.

CHAPTER XI: ROMANCE IN ITALY

Although several studies have been made on the general subject of Longfellow and Italy, none is of value here, because there is so little evidence available concerning the extent or quality of Longfellow's literary accomplishment during his first visit to Italy.

Outre-Mer, containing nearly four full chapters relating to Italy, was written after Longfellow had done considerable research at Göttingen, and after he had spent months compiling his inaugural address on the languages and literatures of southern Europe. Yet, there are only four references, scattered and superficial, to Italian authors and their writings. The reference to " 'Bandello's laughing tale' " suggests greater familiarity with Sir Walter Scott than with Bandello. The phrase occurs in Scott's "Search After Happiness."

The chapters in *Outre-Mer* and the letters describing his wanderings in Italy or about Rome are convincing proofs that his primary interest in Italy was romantic rather than scholarly.

1. MS, Longfellow to his mother, Florence, Jan. 18, 1828, CHP. Compare with *Life*, I, 140.

2. MS, dated Portland, Aug. 25, 1827, CHP. No mention of this significant change in plan is made in the *Life*. The expenses of this trip did consume all of Henry's patrimony—and more. At the time of his father's death, Longfellow made cash payments to his brothers and sisters, individually, to compensate them for shrinkage in their inheritance caused by the amount of money spent by Longfellow during his first and second European trips.

3. MS, dated Portland, Sept. 10, 1827, CHP. The letter begins: "On the 25th of August I wrote you in answer to your letter of the 20th of May, and advised you not to relinquish the idea of visiting Italy as you would pass so near it, & it would probably be the only opportunity you would have of visiting that country. If you go to Germany it will not be much out of your way to go by the way of Italy, and I should be sorry for you not to visit that country. . . . I consider it much less important to learn to speak the Italian language

than the French or Spanish, but if you can conveniently learn it, you had better do it, as you may hereafter regret that you did not improve the opportunity."

4. MS, dated Marseilles, Dec. 14, 1827, CHP. A different excerpt from this same letter is given in the *Life*, I, 135.

5. "Italian Scenery" was published in the *United States Literary Gazette*, I, 267 (Dec. 15, 1824).

6. Longfellow's interest in Byron has never been sufficiently explored. There are many indications that he carried "Childe Harold's Pilgrimage" through Spain and Italy with him, as a guidebook. An early clue showing his familiarity with it may be found in the opening sentence of a letter written shortly after his arrival in Spain: "It is just a year to-day since I said, 'My Native Land, Goodnight!'" (*Life*, I, 112.) Byron's lyric containing the quoted line, occurs in Canto I of "Childe Harold's Pilgrimage."

Later, while travelling through southern Spain, Longfellow began his journal entry concerning Seville by quoting Byron's brief description in the eighth stanza of "Don Juan," Canto I:

> a pleasant city,
> Famous for oranges and women.

Quite in the Byronic mood, to have Longfellow like this line! Other lines from Byron are similarly quoted in the journal entries concerning Cadiz. (See Whitman, 58, 60–62.) But notice also that in describing the city of Alhama, Longfellow quoted a passage from an old ballad having the refrain,

> Ay de mi Alhama!

and added, "You will find the whole of the ballad and its translation in Byron." (Whitman, 64.) Final proof that Longfellow used Byron as a guide-book may be found in a letter written by him to Greene from Venice, over a year later:

"I am very sorry I left Childe Harold in Rome. Mr. Hooper has it; you must get it from him; it will serve you when you come here." (*Life*, I, 154–55.)

7. MS, documented in note 1 of this chapter. Professor Hatfield gives a quaint twist to this passage by quoting it as an indication that Longfellow was impatient to get to Germany. (Hatfield, 13; compare with *Life*, I, 141–42.)

8. MS, dated Rome, March 26, 1828; compare with *Life*, I, 143.

9. *Outre-Mer*, VII, 280–81.

10. MS, documented in note 8 of this chapter.

11. Samuel Longfellow is misleading in his failure to show that Longfellow's immature and erroneous actions, as a student and budding scholar, threw him on the defensive almost as soon as he began

his European study. The result has been that many literary historians, basing their conclusions on the *Life* by Samuel Longfellow, have falsely claimed that Longfellow, setting out for Europe at the age of nineteen, and returning with a complete mastery of the French, Spanish, Italian, and German languages, was a brilliant student and one of America's great linguistic scholars. The truth is that he was a mere boy who was not yet ready to accept fully the meaning of the responsibilities which he had shouldered when he accepted the Bowdoin offer. As for his scholarship, he could never be compared with Ticknor, Bancroft, or Cogswell, for he simply did not have the ability or the inclination to drive himself to persistent, twelve-hours-a-day study. He could skim more surface, granted. Barrett Wendell was fond of saying that Longfellow was too much a poet to be a great scholar—and too much a scholar to be a great poet.

12. MS, dated March 26, 1828, CHP. This passage is quoted with editorial assistance in the *Life*, I, 144.

13. In a notebook entitled "Rome During the Carnival," Longfellow made the following entry, probably written in April, 1828:

"How these gaieties of the Carnival have banished from my thoughts the memory of ancient days and ancient deeds! But now as I sit in the solitude of my chamber—in the silence of night—they come crowding upon my recollection!

> "Eternal City!—O'er whose walls
> Night, like the cloud of ages falls!
> Strange memories of thine infant state
> And dreams of ancient deed and date,
> O'er which so beautiful and long
> Has glowed the holy light of Song—
> Crowd on me—as my eye descries
> The steps of ancient centuries!

"Alas! my muse has caught no inspiration from the 'clear blue sky of Italy'—perhaps this may be attributed to the misfortune under which I suffer—of thus far having caught but very seldom a glimpse of that 'clear blue'— We have had rather too much of that 'rain—rain—ceaseless—pitiless rain!' " (MS, CHP.)

14. This passage occurs in the lengthy "Dedication" to Longfellow in the beginning of Greene's three-volume *Life of General Nathanael Greene* (New York, 1867). Longfellow had earned Greene's especial gratitude in connection with this book, by sharing equally with him the heavy expense of having the *magnum opus* published.

15. *Idem.*

16. MS, dated Rome, June 28, 1828. See also *Life*, I, 147–48.

17. *Idem.* Since the pilgrim deliberately evaded the scholarly plan

of hurrying on to Göttingen to pursue his studies, the entire passage from this letter deserves consideration here:

"There is so much in this city to delay the stranger—the villages in the environs are so beautiful—and there is such a quiet and stillness about everything, that were it in my power I should be induced to remain the whole year round. You can imagine nothing equal to the ruins of Rome. The Foro Romano and the Coloseum are beyond all I had ever fancied them:—and the ruined temples—the mausoleums —and the old mouldering acqueducts which are scattered in every direction over the immense plain which surrounds the city—give you an idea of the ancient grandeur of the Romans, and produce in your mind ideas, which cannot be easily defined, nor communicated." (CHP; compare with *Life*, I, 147–48.)

18. MS, dated July 11, 1828, CHP.

19. Longfellow covered his tracks so carefully, by avoiding references to his interest in Julia Persiani, that the evidence is slight—and confusing. Consider the circumstantial evidence first. His letters from Rome began with unrestrained encomiums of a general nature, concerning these pretty and talented daughters, with no mention that one was married. Then no mention of them was made until he wrote to give an account of his illness. Why did he stop writing about them, unless he feared that his family might associate (quite obviously) his tarrying in Rome with his fondness for the Persiani sisters?

Now for direct evidence. Greene shared the secret, which was so much of an event that Longfellow mentioned it in a letter to Greene, twelve years later. At the time when the unsuccessful wooing of Frances Appleton seemed to make Longfellow dwell with consoling pride on the memory of better days, he wrote:

"Why don't you write me some of the gossip and scandal of Rome? How are the Persiani's? Where is Fabio? Lorenzano? The Lante's, the mother, and that *hot* daughter, with the pale sister?—and old Magrini, who amuses every American he can get hold of with my amour with Julia. No one returns now from Rome without *that* story. I am glad of it. How is Julia, do you hear?" (MS, dated Jan. 2, 1840, CHP.) See also pp. 247–48, 283.

20. Was Julia Persiàni married at this time, or was this use of the word "Mrs." a blind to set suspicions at rest? I am inclined to think that she was a young widow. There are no references, except this, to Julia as a married woman. In fact, Greene, Longfellow, and George Cooke (an American artist in Rome) referred to her always in their letters as simply "Julia." And if she were married and her husband living, Longfellow would naturally have referred to it in his earlier letters. Why should she be living with her parents if she had a husband, living? In a much later letter, Longfellow implied that there

was some tragedy in her life. Nine years after his departure from Rome, he wrote to Greene, who was again in Italy:

"Remember me cordially to the Persiani's. Don't forget it. I am very glad that Julia is married. Whom did she marry? Poor soul!" (MS, dated Jan. 6, 1838, CHP.) Another sentence concerning this matter of marriage occurs in the letter quoted in note 19 of this chapter.

"How is Julia, do you hear? What did you say her name was?"

21. MS, CHP. Longfellow was not averse to twisting the facts a bit, whenever it was expedient. The entire Persiani episode shows that. In the present instance, this letter stated that he was taken ill "in the beginning of July." But such a statement is either deliberately twisted or a miscalculation, for in the letter written to his mother on July 11, Longfellow mentioned that he had just returned from a visit to L'Ariccia, and implied that he was in excellent health and spirits.

This trivial point assumes importance when it is added to the accumulation of evidence which shows that Longfellow did his best to stretch the facts to conceal the actual reason for his remaining in Rome. He pretended that the illness was more serious than it really was. By implication, we know that he was perfectly well on July 11. On July 31, according to his letter, he was well enough to travel from Rome to the village of L'Ariccia.

The argument concerning the letters of credit is not too satisfactory, because Longfellow knew so many Americans in Rome, by the time he had been there over six months, that he could certainly have made temporary arrangements through one of them for letters of credit to use in Germany. Furthermore, Preble was in Germany to help him when he arrived at Göttingen. He also argued that he had waited until he might learn the paternal wish as to plans for going on, in the face of increasing expenses. But he had earlier acknowledged his father's decision on the subject; had received the letter in Marseilles, just previous to his departure for Italy.

In fact, Longfellow makes the reader suspicious, by finding too many excuses. And finally, this letter concerning his illness was written on August 4. He did not leave Italy until fifteen weeks later although he was well enough to return to Rome early in September. And the cause of his departure was plainly the unpleasant news that Bowdoin had retracted the offer of the professorship!

22. See note 19 of this chapter. Furthermore, George Cooke, writing from Rome shortly after Longfellow had left, defended his delinquency as a correspondent by saying that he knew Longfellow would be reading in letters from Julia all that could possibly interest him concerning Rome. (MS, dated Jan. 6, 1829, CHP.) Although Longfellow carefully saved letters written to him, and although the letters

saved may still be found carefully bound in the Craigie House, the letter books for this period contain no letters from Julia Persiani.

23. MS, dated Venice, Dec. 19, 1828, CHP. This excerpt is omitted in the edited version of this letter in *Life*, I, 155–56.

24. *Idem.*

25. The additional note is dated Trieste, Dec. 27. See note 2 of Chapter XII.

26. MS, dated Portland, April 9, 1828, CHP. Explaining the reason for the refusal of the professorship, Longfellow's father wrote in this letter:

"There was perfect unanimity in the Board of Trustees in favor of appointing you a Professor in the first instance & they so voted, but unfortunately none of your particular friends attended the meeting of the Overseers, and being unacquainted with you, they thought it most prudent to pursue the course they adopted. I have no doubt but they intend to give you the Professorship at the end of a year from next Commencement if you should be acceptable as an instructor— Indeed I think they will be likely to do it next commencement, if you should return qualified for the station and they find you will not accept a subordinate position."

Stephen Longfellow was a shrewd man. The last sentence of his letter quoted above was calculated to find its mark, and it did. Probably the father was not too keenly upset by this ruling, since he realized that the disappointment would stimulate his son to more energetic preparation in Europe. That last sentence became Longfellow's governing motive during the remainder of his stay in Europe. There were occasional, but only minor lapses. Probably his concentration, while in Germany, on the language and literature of France and Spain was an indirect confession of his own realization that he had not prepared himself to sufficient advantage in these two primary languages which he would be expected to teach.

Compare this quotation from Stephen Longfellow's letter with the statement in the *Life*, I, 156 fn.

Chapter XII: With Preble in Germany

1. See note 13 of this chapter.

2. MS, dated Trieste, Dec. 27, 1828, CHP. The letter begins: "I reached this city yesterday on my way to Dresden, and shall leave it tomorrow to pursue my journey. Inclosed are letters from Venice. In reading over what I have written you I feel much disposed to destroy the letter; but not having time to write another—nor indeed wishing to write again on so painful a theme I think it best to send you what I have written. If my language is too violent, excuse . . ."

(Compare this with the edited version of the same letter in the *Life*, I, 159–60.)

3. As above, Trieste, Dec. 27, 1828.

4. A representative list of titles from his notebook, made at this time, may be found in the *Life*, I, 165.

5. See my article, "Longfellow's Projected Sketch Book of New England," *The Colophon*, New York, IV, Part 15, n.p. (Autumn, 1934). Of these titles, two were later used:

"The Indian Summer," in *The Token*, Boston, 1832 (1831), 24–35;

"The Bald Eagle," in *The Token and Atlantic Souvenir*, 1833 (1832), 74–89.

There is one indication that Longfellow had been working on an idea similar to the story of the Bald Eagle Tavern for some time. In a letter to his friend Patrick Greenleaf in Portland, Longfellow had written from Paris:

"I wish you to rummage about amongst all the old American papers that you can lay your hands on, and when you come across a file of those published when Fayette was in America I wish you to cut out all the ridiculous pieces of poetry touching him—all accounts of country celebrations—all toasts &c &c. All, in fine, which is the least peculiar. Make them up in a package and direct it to me . . ." (MS, dated Oct. 23, 1826, Bowdoin College Library.) Later, he wrote that he had received the package.

6. In Dresden he began gathering material and a bibliography for the study which was later presented in his inaugural address at Bowdoin. The introductory paragraph of the address was written in first draft on the boat, while Longfellow was making his return voyage to America. See note 2 of Chapter XIV.

7. MS journal, dated Jan. 28, 29, CHP.

8. Longfellow's amusingly realistic and mildly inelegant thumbnail sketch of this Dresden tutor occurs in his MS journal under date of Feb. 9, 1829. I regret that the Longfellow family has refused me permission to quote it.

9. Longfellow's detailed description of the room, and the drawing made by him, were included in the first issue of the *Old Dominion Zeitung;* reproduced in Hatfield, 15–16.

10. MS, undated, but probably June, 1828, CHP. See *Life*, I, 146. Longfellow and Preble followed this suggested formula for making a news sheet. They kept a day-book in which they both made entries whenever they felt inclined. The book quickly degenerated into a hodge-podge of nonsense, sketches, jokes, quotations, and miscellaneous remarks. It is entitled "Journal of O. V. I.: Scrawls of a broken neck." MS, CHP.

11. The context of the line is amusing, in its present connotation. It occurs in "The Castle of Indolence":

> Full oft by holy feet our ground was trod,—
> Of clerks good plenty here you mote espy;
> A little, round, fat, oily man of God
> Was one I chiefly marked among the fry;
> He had a roguish twinkle in his eye,
> Which shone all glittering with ungodly dew,
> When a tight damsel chanced to trippen by;
> But when observed, he shrunk into his mew,
> And straight would recollect his piety anew.

Quoted in *Outre-Mer*, VII, 294.

12. The six numbers of this manuscript newspaper are among the CHP, intact except for the third number, which has been mutilated. From it has been cut a drawing by Longfellow, which showed himself seated at a table, a long-stemmed pipe at his mouth, a stein of beer on the table, a volume of Goethe in one hand, and clouds of smoke ascending from his pipe. This drawing is entitled, in Longfellow's autograph, "H. W. L. 'in the clouds' at Göttingen." The original is now in the Speck Collection of Goethe material, Yale University Library.

The drawing is reproduced as a frontispiece in Hatfield's *New Light on Longfellow*, but is thus a bit misleading, because Longfellow paid more attention to the *Old Dominion Zeitung* than to Goethe, while in Göttingen. As Professor Long has pointed out, "There is no evidence that Longfellow, during this Göttingen period, had any particular interest in Goethe." See "Goethe and Longfellow," *The Germanic Review*, VII, 145–75 (April, 1932).

13. MS, dated Feb. 27, 1829. The concealing method of Samuel Longfellow is excellently revealed by comparing this quotation with the emasculated version printed in the *Life*, I, 166–67.

14. The skeptic is invited to compare Longfellow's training and preparation with that of George Ticknor, as revealed in his letters and journals during his residence in Göttingen, preparatory to opening a department of modern languages at Harvard. (See *Life, Letters, and Journals of George Ticknor*, I, 70–120.)

15. MS, dated May 15, 1829; see also *Life*, I, 169–70.

16. MS, dated March 28, 1829, CHP.

17. MS, dated May 15, 1829; see also *Life*, I, 171. The excerpt quoted in the *Life* begins, "I am now very much occupied with my studies." A very revealing letter, filled with shifting emotions of hope and fear.

18. MS notebook. When the American students at Göttingen in 1890 held a celebration on July 4 to pay tribute to earlier American

students at Göttingen, they placed a memorial tablet on the house where Longfellow stayed: Rothestrasse 25. But Professor Alois Brandl, who made an address on Longfellow at Göttingen, admitted that of the books—about twenty in all—which Longfellow drew from the University library during his stay, almost every one dealt with the literature of France, Spain, and Italy. (See *Festreden bei der Erinnerungsfeier an Everett, Bancroft, Longfellow und Motley*, Göttingen, 1890.)

19. MS, documented in note 17; see also *Life*, I, 171.

20. MS, documented in note 15; see also *Life*, I, 170.

21. MS journal entry dated Cassel, May 13. These last six lines were used in a poem entitled "To a Mountain Brook," published over the signature "L." in the *New-England Magazine*, I, 164 (August, 1831). The poem, fifty lines, in blank verse, has never been identified as Longfellow's, heretofore. But compare these lines, from "To a Mountain Brook," with those quoted in the text:

> When Spring first parts the snowy hair of Winter,
> And lays his hoary temples on her breast,
> Like the fair Roman girl, that history boasts,
> Who on her gentle bosom warmed and nursed
> The second childhood of her poor old father.

22. MS, documented in note 16; see also *Life*, I, 167–68.

23. MS, documented in note 17; see also *Life*, I, 171–72.

CHAPTER XIII: PROFESSOR AT BOWDOIN

The background material for this chapter and the next two has been drawn from those sources concerning the history of Bowdoin College which are listed at the beginning of the notes for Chapter III. Although there is an abundance of literature concerning the litigation between Bowdoin College and President Allen, the fundamental issues were those already settled in the famous "Dartmouth College Case," with which Allen had been closely associated. My brief summary of the matter touches only the parts which interested and affected Longfellow as a member of the faculty.

1. MS, Longfellow to James Berdan, dated Bowdoin College, Aug. 14, 1830, CHP.

2. MS, to his father, dated Aug. 17, 1829, CHP.

3. MS, Bowdoin College Library.

4. Under date of Sept. 5, 1829, Ebenezer Everett, secretary of the Bowdoin trustees, sent to Longfellow copies of the votes of the board concerning the professorship:

"In the Board of Trustees of Bowdoin College, Sept. 1, 1829:

"Mr. Henry W. Longfellow having declined to accept the office of Instructer in Modern Languages,

"Voted, that we now proceed to the choice of a Professor of Modern Languages, and Mr. Henry W. Longfellow was chosen.

"Voted, that the Salary of said Professor be established at eight hundred dollars annually, until the further order of the Boards, to commence, when he shall enter upon the duties of his office at the College.

"Voted, that so much of the vote passed Sept. 7, 1825, as restricted instruction in Modern Languages to the Senior and Junior Classes, be repealed.

"Board of Trustees, Sept. 2, 1829

"Voted, that the Executive Government may at their discretion for the ensuing year, provide, that instruction be given to the Sophomore and Freshman Classes, as well as to the other Students.

"Voted, that Henry Longfellow be appointed Librarian for one year with a Salary of one hundred Dollars.

"Voted, that the induction of Professor Longfellow into office be made in such manner, and at such time, as the Executive Government may prescribe. . . ." (MS, CHP; compare with *Life*, I, 174–75.)

5. Longfellow described his daily duties in a letter to Greene, documented in note 6 of Chapter XIV. See *Life*, I, 183–84.

6. MS, CHP. In this letter, Longfellow's comments concerning his "dreamy sensations, and vague recollections of a sunny land" support my interpretation of his first trip to Europe as more a romantic pilgrimage than a scholarly enterprise.

7. F. Sales edited a French grammar in 1821, and also a Spanish grammar; Charles Follen edited a German grammar which was printed in Boston in 1825; Bachi edited an Italian grammar for his classes. (Information compiled from the Textbook Collection, Harvard College Library.)

8. Professors Cleaveland, Newman, Smyth, and Upham had compiled elementary treatises for their students, on subjects as diverse as mineralogy, rhetoric, mathematics, and mental philosophy.

9. MS, Longfellow to his father, dated Oct. 24, 1829, CHP.

10. Griffin, who had been encouraged by the Bowdoin faculty to established a press in Brunswick twenty years earlier, was an exceptionally competent printer, although Longfellow did not fully appreciate him at first. The young professor's knowledge of printers' methods was rudely increased when the neatly sewn manuscript of his French grammar was returned to him as a pile of separate sheets, which had been cut apart for distribution to the compositors. Returning the mangled manuscript with the proof sheets, Longfellow wrote in a conspicuous place on the first galley:

Mr. Griffin, Mr. Griffin,
If your devil Theodore

> Cuts my copy any more
> I will lick him in a jiffin.

In retaliation, the compositor set up these four lines in an equally conspicuous place and printed them as a part of the corrected proofs. (Little, 55.)

11. MS, dated April 10, 1830, CHP.

12. MS, dated Dec. 20, 1829, CHP.

13. Since Longfellow was not yet inducted, these texts are compiled "By an Instructer." A second edition of these was published in 1831, and of the *Proverbes Dramatiques* in 1832, all by Gray and Bowen of Boston.

14. *Life*, I, 184. For some reason which is not apparent, Longfellow concealed from Greene the dissatisfaction which found such vehement expression in his other letters. Later, he avoided making disparaging remarks to Greene about Bowdoin because he had promised Greene that if it were possible, Greene should be brought in to take the vacancy caused by Longfellow's departure.

15. MS, April 14, 1830, CHP.

16. In a letter to Cleaveland, dated Cambridge, Oct. 3, 1837, Longfellow mentioned these happy evenings:

"And how is Mrs. Cleaveland?—and Martha Anne, and Elizabeth & Mary? Does music flourish as of old? Are those pleasant Autumn evenings as they used to be—with cheerful fire-light—and lamps, and songs? And in the midst of all, does any well known, old, familiar tune ever recall the memory of one, who still cherishes a most lively and grateful remembrance of that kindness which in other days made your house a home to him?" (MS, owned by H. W. L. Dana, on deposit in CHP.) See also Longfellow's sonnet, "Parker Cleaveland," written much later.

17. MS, dated April 6, 1830, CHP.

18. Mary Thacher Higginson, "New Longfellow Letters," *Harper's Monthly*, CVI, 779 (April, 1903). Mary Thacher, a niece of Mary Potter, married Thomas Wentworth Higginson. Through this Potter relationship, Mrs. Higginson inherited some letters written by Longfellow and his wife to the Potter family in Portland. After T. W. Higginson had used many of the letters in his study of Longfellow (American Men of Letters Series), selections from the remaining letters were published by Mrs. Higginson in *Harper's*.

19. MS, dated April 14, 1830, CHP.

20. MS, dated July 13, 1830, CHP.

21. "New Longfellow Letters," 779. In apologizing to Berdan, some months later, for having failed to fulfill his promise to invite Berdan to Portland during the summer, Longfellow made excuses before he came to the point:

"The few letters, which I have written during this period, are limited to those which bore the superscription of a young lady of Portland, to whom I have sworn fealty. You saw the same lady in New York, last Summer—Miss Mary S. Potter. Please communicate the news—if news it be—to all Mr. Storer's family. Surely this is quite as succinct and categorical a statement of the case, as could well be made out." (MS, dated Jan. 4, 1831; owned by Carroll A. Wilson, New York City.)

Such a timid announcement implied that Longfellow was fearful of exactly such good-natured banter as Pierre Irving wrote when he heard the news:

"I had given up all thought of hearing from you . . . as one too deeply infested with the tender passion to be able to make good your engagement. You will understand from this that I was not so wholly ignorant of the sentimental relation you hold to a certain Miss P. . . . as you seem to suppose. . . . Write as soon as you can succeed in diverting your thoughts a few moments from that picture of connubial bliss with which you are feeding your imagination." (MS, dated June 24, 1831, CHP.)

CHAPTER XIV: POET TURNS SCHOLAR

1. See letter documented in note 6 of this chapter.

2. The *Inaugural Address*, edited with a "Prefatory Note" by George T. Little, was published by the Bowdoin College Library in 1907. The subject of the address was decided upon by Longfellow, after his intensive period of study in Göttingen—and before his return to America. In a notebook (MS, CHP) Longfellow wrote, apparently while on the homeward voyage from Europe in 1829, a few trial sentences:

"Mr. President and Gentlemen. I have looked forward to this day with feelings of pleasure and solicitude. To the desire I have long felt of revisiting once more the scenes of collegiate life, and of rendering friendly by long-interrupted intercourse . . . In selecting a theme for the discourse, which according to established custom on similar occasions, should occupy the remainder of the time allotted to us this morning, I have deemed it of importance to choose one, which should bear a near relation to the charge with which I have just been intrusted. Actuated by this feeling, I have selected as not irrelevant to the occasion, the Origin of the Languages and Literature of the South of Europe. I am sensible that it is a subject too vast to be thoroughly treated in a discourse . . ."

3. MS, dated March 10, 1829, CHP.

4. MS, dated May 25, 1829, CHP.

5. See the closing sentences of Longfellow's letter quoted on p. 154.

A further elaboration of the plan is contained in a letter written to his brother Stephen on Dec. 23, 1829:

"I am now engaged in two grand designs, which with their subordinate branches and ramifications keep my imagination active and serve as a catholicon for ennuie, etc. The first is in aiding and abetting the establishment of a grand High School for Young Ladies, at Portland: in which Furbish is to teach the usual English studies; Geradot, the French; Señor Correa, (a Spaniard, friend of Geradot) the Spanish; and Nolcini, Italian and Music. Such is a rough outline of the plan which I leave it to your own imagination to fill up." (MS, CHP.)

6. In a letter to George Greene, dated June 27, 1830, he wrote:

"This term I am writing a course of lectures on Modern Literature —or rather on French, Spanish, and Italian Literature which I am to deliver in Portland next winter. It will also be my college course and I shall commence lecturing in a few days to the two upper classes." (MS, Williams College Library. Notice how carefully this scheme was expunged in the garbled version of this letter printed in the *Life*, I, 184.)

7. The Augusta lecture was given on Oct. 6, 1830. In the (Augusta) *Kennebec Journal* for Friday morning, Oct. 8, 1830, an account of the convention included the following reference:

"The lecture of Professor Longfellow in the evening, on female education, was very interesting and was heard by a large audience. Many of his figures and illustrations were very apt and striking; the whole written in a finished style, and evincing much reflection and correct observation of things."

8. MS, documented in note 6; omitted when this letter was edited for the *Life*, I, 183–84.

9. MS, dated July 8, 1830, CHP.

10. *Life*, I, 185.

11. Longfellow described his plan for this series in a letter to Greene, dated Oct. 7, 1832:

"If you can find time to read a long article on the Italian Language and its dialects, have the goodness to look into the last No. of the *North American Review* (October No.). You will there find a paper upon the subject which I took considerable pains to write, and to have correctly printed. As I corrected the proofs myself I am answerable for all inaccuracies. Please read, and criticise. You will see that of two or three Dialects I had no specimens. Can you supply the lacune?—and have you any specimens of those dialects in which I have nothing but the Lord's Prayer?—If so please communicate them to me. I am going on to complete the series of papers for Mr. Everett of the N. A. R. taking up next the Spanish and Portuguese Languages, afterwards the German and English. The French was treated of before. If you have any *specimens* of these languages which are rare or

curious, you will do me a great favour by informing me thereof."
(MS, CHP.)

There were at least six articles in this series: (1) "Origin and
Progress of the French Language," *North American Review,* XXXII,
277–317 (April, 1831); (2) "Spanish Devotional and Moral Poetry,"
N.A.R., XXXIV, 277–315 (April, 1832); (3) "History of the Italian
Language and Dialects," *N.A.R.,* XXXV, 283–343 (Oct., 1832); (4)
"Spanish Language and Literature," *N.A.R.,* XXXVI, 316–44 (April,
1833); (5) "Anglo-Saxon Literature," *N.A.R.,* XLVII, 90–134 (July,
1838); (6) "The French Language in England," *N.A.R.,* LI, 285–308
(Oct., 1840).

12. MS, documented in note 6.

13. *Life,* I, 150.

14. MS, dated Philadelphia, July 19, 1830, CHP.

15. Although Everett may be accused of having tempted Longfellow away from original writing by welcoming his hackwork sum-
maries from literary histories of Spain, France, and Italy, he urged
Longfellow to place original writing ahead of translations, in importance. Accepting Longfellow's first suggestion for an article on
foreign languages, Everett wrote:

"Allow me to ask if you do not mean to publish anything in the
way of travels. Slidell has done himself great credit by his book on
Spain, and you would probably write a much better one. . . . Have
you ever published any collection of your poems?" (*Life,* I, 185.)

On Jan. 30, 1831, Everett wrote: "I am glad to learn that you think
of publishing some sketches of your travels in Europe. The sooner
you set about it the better; and the freshness and distinctness of your
recollections, which you will want to give life to your notes, will
begin to pale very soon." (MS, CHP.)

When a year passed without the appearance of Longfellow's travel-
book, Everett wrote, on April 27, 1832:

"Our friend Irving is coming out with a new Sketch Book from
which I expect great things. Cannot you give us something in the
form of travels and sketches in prose and verse about Spain? The
subject is excellent and almost new." (MS, CHP.)

One year later, April 3, 1833, he wrote that he was happy to learn
that *Outre-Mer* was to be published, and promised to aid the book
with a review in the *North American Review.*

16. Here is a list of the first appearances of the "Schoolmaster"
series:

(1) "The Schoolmaster," *New-England Magazine,* I, 27–30 (July 1,
1831). Only one paragraph from this essay was printed in *Outre-Mer.*

(2) "The Schoolmaster," *N.-E.M.,* I, 185–89 (Sept. 1, 1831). This
essay, revised, became the chapter of *Outre-Mer* entitled "The Norman Diligence."

(3) "The Schoolmaster," with subtitle "The Village of Auteuil," *N.-E.M.*, II, 283–87 (April, 1832). Reprinted, with alterations in the first paragraph, as the chapter of *Outre-Mer* entitled, "The Village of Auteuil."

(4) "The Schoolmaster," with subtitle "Recollections of the Metropolis," *N.-E.M.*, III, 9–13 (July, 1832). Here is the *Sketch Book* method, which Longfellow was developing in his own fashion, and still in its crudest form: descriptions of Paris, and snatches of history or legend, largely translated, with slight modifications, from G. F. P. de Saint-Foix, *Essais Historiques sur Paris*, six volumes, London, Paris, 1763. This essay was discarded—not used in *Outre-Mer*.

(5) "The Schoolmaster," *N.-E.M.*, III, 284–89 (Oct., 1832). A story translated from Saint-Foix and not used in *Outre-Mer*.

(6) "The Schoolmaster," with subtitle "The Walk Continued," *N.-E.M.*, IV, 131–33 (Feb., 1833). The concluding paragraph of this essay formed the nucleus for the sketch in *Outre-Mer* entitled "Père La Chaise."

17. MS, dated Jan. 4, 1831, owned by Carroll A. Wilson.

CHAPTER XV: SCHOLAR ATTACKS AMERICA

1. See note 11 of this chapter.

2. MS, dated Aug. 21, 1831, CHP. A part of this same letter to Anne Longfellow is quoted as the motto for Chapter XVI. She had been spending several weeks in Fryeburg, Maine, where she was recuperating slowly from a nervous breakdown caused in part by the death of her older sister Elizabeth in 1829.

3. The most complete account of Mary Storer Potter's life, from which a part of my material is taken, may be found in Thomas Wentworth Higginson, *Henry Wadsworth Longfellow* (American Men of Letters Series), Boston and New York, 1902, 59–64.

4. In a letter to his sister Anne, dated July 10, 1831 (MS, CHP), Longfellow wrote: "I have concluded to remain at least one term more with Mrs. Fales. I should prefer house-keeping were it possible, but I cannot procure a tenement. I do not think that Mary will like to board out: but I do not tell her so, since there is no remedy." (MS, CHP.)

The "Fales House," as it was formerly called, was a one-story wooden house built in 1820. At the time when Longfellow took his bride there, it faced on what is now Potter Street, at the corner of Maine. When Joshua L. Chamberlain, a later owner of the house, returned from the Civil War with the stars of a major general on his shoulders, he remodelled the house by raising it into the air and building another story beneath it, with the front door on Maine Street. It is still standing, at 226 Maine Street.

Longfellow spent his first year as Professor of Modern Languages as a dormitory resident; his second year, from 1830 to 1831, he boarded and roomed at Mrs. Fales's; at the beginning of his third year, late in September, 1831, he brought his bride to Mrs. Fales's; in October, 1832, the Longfellows moved into the house on Federal Street known as the Robert Dunlap House, still standing but now much changed by remodelling.

For details of information concerning Longfellow's various living quarters in Brunswick and for numerous other courtesies, I am particularly indebted and grateful to Miss Elizabeth F. Riley, Assistant Alumni Secretary at Bowdoin.

5. MS, dated Oct. 5, 1831, CHP.

6. Here are three of the Spanish translations listed as they appeared:

(1) "The Death of Agrican the Moor," *New-England Magazine*, II, 332–33 (April, 1832). This is a new addition to the Longfellow canon. Although published here unsigned, an identical quatrain from this translation may be found in the *Inaugural Address*, 95.

(2) "Sonnet: Art and Nature," *N.-E.M.*, III, 304 (Nov., 1832). Also unsigned, but identified as a Longfellow translation because he reprinted it in *Coplas*.

(3) "The Ballad of the Five Farthings," *N.-E.M.*, IV, 406 (May, 1833). Another addition to the Longfellow canon. Of the twenty-eight lines, ten occur in the *Inaugural Address*, 92–93.

7. "The Indian Summer," *The Token*, Boston, 1832 (1831), 24–35; "La Doncella," *The Token*, Boston, 1832 (1831), 280. This lyric was later reprinted in the chapter of *Outre-Mer* entitled "A Tailor's Drawer." Longfellow copied his first translation of this poem into his journal at Göttingen on May 17, 1829. Later, at Bowdoin, he made another translation of the same piece and copied it into the same journal over the date June 18, 1831. This second version is here used.

8. *Inaugural Address*, 6–8.

9. "Report B, Harvard College, Nov. 6, 1846." Quoted in Whitman, 107.

10. *Life*, I, 201.

11. *North American Review*, XXXIV, 59 ff. (Jan., 1832).

12. The record of Longfellow's friendship with Charles Folsom is partially preserved in a series of twenty-five letters from Longfellow to Folsom from 1832 to 1839, now among the Folsom Papers in the Boston Public Library. The first letter, written immediately after Longfellow's return from the first visit, begins:

"I am once more 'entre mes Lares.' We left Boston on Tuesday evening, as was my intention when I last saw you, and after passing a cold and doleful night in the stage-coach, were finally ushered into Portland by the sound of the 11 o'clock bell." (MS, dated Portland,

Feb. 12, 1832, BPL.) Most of the letters concern the printing of the textbooks.

13. MS, dated Paris, July 11, 1826, CHP.

14. MS, dated March 25, 1832, CHP.

15. MS, dated April 27, 1832, CHP.

16. A detailed account of this period may be found in Hatch.

17. MSS, dated Jan. 28, 1833, and April 3, 1833, CHP.

18. MS, to Messrs. Gray & Bowen, dated March 29, 1832, BPL.

19. MS Memorandum Book, Bowdoin, 1830–33, CHP.

20. *Life*, I, 178.

21. MS, George C. Shattuck, Jr., to Miss E. F. Prentiss, dated April 14, 1832, Massachusetts Historical Society Library, Boston.

22. MS, dated June 2, 1832, CHP.

Before the close of this third year, Longfellow undertook a rather ambitious literary task of translating the long Spanish "Coplas de Don Jorge Manrique." In August, 1832, he asked Folsom to borrow a volume containing it, from the Harvard College Library, and concluded:

"I am slowly preparing some Spanish Translations for the press, so that you and the Colonel Metcalf need not forget me."

After commencement, he set to work and had completed the translation before the end of the fall vacation. When his attempt to find a publisher for his book of Spanish translations failed, Longfellow sent the entire translation of "Coplas" to the ever cordial Buckingham, who printed it in the *New-England Magazine*, III, 454–57 (Dec., 1832).

CHAPTER XVI: RESTLESSNESS

The background material for this chapter has been drawn largely from unpublished letters which are not directly quoted. Although I have drawn directly from only a few of the letters in the Folsom Papers, I have found them of much value. Furthermore, the bound volumes of letters written to Longfellow, and still kept among the Craigie House Papers, are of much importance in that they reflect many of Longfellow's interests, thoughts, and activities, in lines written as answers to his questions, suggestions, and observations.

1. MS, Longfellow to his sister Anne, dated Aug. 21, 1831. CHP.

2. MS, dated Sept. 18, 1832, CHP. Alexander Everett added his commendation: "I hear golden reports of your Poem."

Longfellow was elected to the Bowdoin chapter of the Phi Beta Kappa society on September 7, 1826—while he was in Europe. The chapter was at that time less than a year old. (In passing, it might be worth mentioning that Longfellow was also awarded a Master of Arts degree, automatically, after the English custom, at Commencement in 1826.) He was initiated to Phi Beta Kappa on September 3, 1829—and at the same meeting was chosen as poet for the following annual meeting. This honor he did not, for some unknown reason, fulfill.

3. MS, dated Oct. 24, 1832, CHP.

4. MS, dated Nov. 27, 1832, CHP.

5. MS, dated Oct. 11, 1832, BPL.

6. MS, dated Oct. 31, 1832, BPL.

7. The enterprising S. G. ("Peter Parley") Goodrich purchased *The Atlantic Souvenir* from Carey and Lea and combined it with *The Token* for 1833. Longfellow's two contributions were:

"The Bald Eagle" (see note 5 to Chapter XII); and "An Evening in Autumn," *The Token and Atlantic Souvenir*, Boston, 1833 (1832), 150–52.

This original poem, twelve six-line stanzas, was chopped from the "Phi Beta Kappa poem." It seems to have been sent to Goodrich in the summer of 1832, before the "Phi Beta Kappa poem" was delivered at Bowdoin. Six poems were thus taken from this long, unpublished poem, and published separately over a period of ten years. A detailed account of this curious quarrying is given in my forthcoming bibliography.

8. MS, dated Oct. 1, 1832, CHP.

9. This article was entitled "Spanish Language and Literature." See note 11 of Chapter XIV.

On Jan. 8, 1833, Longfellow wrote to Folsom:

"I have the article on Spanish language nearly completed. It will probably be in the next No. of the N. A. unless Mr. Everett finds it too stupid. The Italian article in the October No. was found to be *"dull and learned"*—so I understand. Such disquisitions do not seem to suit the taste of periodical readers. I shall try another key soon. Is there in the Cambridge Library a Dictionary of the old Langue d'Oc in which the Troubadours wrote? I want to study their poetry more thoroughly—and have great quantities of it before me—but I have no dictionary, and, moreover, no faculty of guessing out meanings. . . . I will send back all the books I have from Cambridge Library, together with those from yours, which I have kept so long." (MS, BPL.)

10. MS, dated Nov. 14, 1832, BPL.

11. An outline analysis of compilation methods used by Longfellow is given in my forthcoming bibliography. It reveals the following: in compiling *Outre-Mer*, Longfellow made use of nine articles previously published by him in magazines; he introduced excerpts and translations from twelve French poets or prose writers; he introduced sixteen translations from Spanish authors—including several translated sonnets which had already appeared not only in

magazine form but also in book form in *Coplas;* he introduced four translations from the Italian and Latin; and twenty-eight quotations from English authors.

12. Luther S. Livingston, *A Bibliography of the First Editions in Book Form of the Writings of Henry Wadsworth Longfellow,* New York, 1908, 16. The letter is dated March 9, 1833.

Livingston was perhaps the first to call attention to Samuel Longfellow's unfortunate omissions and alterations of letters in the *Life,* and to correct alterations by printing from the original letters such passages as concerned bibliographical matters, in his compilation of the Chamberlain bibliography.

Referring to this letter of March 9, Livingston mentioned that it was printed in the *Life* (I, 192–93) and added, "but portions were omitted or altered, and therefore the list, with portions of the letter, is printed here as written."

Livingston's presentation, on page 12, of Longfellow's list of activities and publications was made to prove the authorship of "The Bald Eagle." He pointed out, also, that Higginson, thrown off the trail by Samuel Longfellow's omissions, wrote, after making some good guesses, "Perhaps no solution of this conundrum will ever be given."

Obviously, there never was a conundrum here, until the original letter was garbled by Samuel Longfellow.

13. MS, dated April 8, 1833, CHP.

14. *Complete Writings,* VII, 18.

15. MS, dated Boston, May 14, 1833. Two other letters have bearing on *Coplas.* The first, written by Longfellow to Hilliard, Gray & Co., on Oct. 17, 1832, reveals his Yankee practicality concerning business details. Offering them *Coplas* for publication, he wrote:

"The book will be small—about 150 or 200 pages 12mo. I offer it to you on the following terms:

"1. That the book be printed on as good paper, and in the same form and style as the 'Syllabus de la Grammaire Italienne' published by Gray and Bowen last spring.

"2. That this work be done at the University Press, Cambridge.

"3. That the proofs be sent to me for correction after they have been read by Mr. Folsom—and

"4. That I shall have 25 copies of this work for distribution and half the profits arising from the sales, after the expenses have been paid.

"My wish is to make rather an elegant book than a large one and as the number of pages is rather small it will be a matter of some importance to have the paper thick." (Livingston, 18–19.)

The second letter concerning *Coplas* was written to Greene on July 16, 1833:

"I have also another little book in the press. A translation of the

'Coplas de Don Jorge Manrique a la Muerte de su Padre,'—the original to be printed with the translation—*le texte en regard*, as we say in France. There is also an Introductory Essay, and a few additional Specimens of the Moral & Devotional Poetry of Spain. I know not when it will be finished for at the rate the printer creeps along I should think it would take him two years. Is it printed in Boston.

"Well—and what do you suppose the profits of this writing, and printing to be?—A mere nothing. I do maintain, that the publishers of our country are as niggardly a set as ever snapped fingers at a poor devil author. If the whole edition of Outre Mer No. 1 sells I shall make *fifty dollars!* Of the other book, I am to have half the *profits* if there are any—in books from the publisher's store! Prodigiously encouraging?" (Livingston, 19.)

16. MS, owned by W. T. H. Howe, Freelands, Covington, Kentucky. *Outre-Mer* was probably published early in July. On July 16, Longfellow wrote to Greene:

"Last week I sent you by mail, the first No. of 'Outre-Mer.' I do not yet know how the book will succeed with the public, as it is just published, and I have not heard from my booksellers. No. 2 will be put forth sometime in autumn." (Livingston, 16.)

Notice that the letter to Hilliard, Gray & Company plainly states that the book was already printed before a publisher had been found. Since the publisher's name appears on the title page, obviously the title page signature was printed last, after the publisher had been secured: some time between June 30 and July 16.

17. MS, dated Portland, June 6, 1833, CHP.

18. MS, dated July 16, 1833; postscript dated July 17, CHP. The same day, Longfellow wrote to his brother-in-law, George Pierce:

"My dear George, you must help me now or never. I see by the Boston papers of today, that Mr. Walsh, Secretary of Legation at Madrid, is dead; and I mean to apply for the situation. In this you can be of the greatest service to me. You are personally acquainted with Secretery Woodbury, and very intimate with Mr. Olney; who, if he were willing, could doubtless, do much in gaining me the good will of Mr. Woodbury. If I can obtain his interest at *court*, it will be a great point gained; for it is generally believed, and I suppose upon good grounds, that he has much influence with the President." (CHP.)

19. MS, dated July 20, 1833, CHP.

20. MS, dated July 7, 1833, BPL. From the date of this letter, it is plain that the establishing of a female school had been planned before Longfellow learned of the vacancy in the Spanish legation.

21. MS, first draft, dated Cambridge, Aug. 18, 1833, BPL. Final draft in New York Public Library.

CHAPTER XVII: VAIN PROJECTS

1. See notes 5, 9, and 13 of this chapter.

2. *Life*, I, 191. Describing the occasion, a writer in the next day's *Boston Daily Advertiser* commented:

"The Poem was delivered by Professor Longfellow, of Bowdoin College, and was distinguished by a judicious union of the lively and serious. Its measure was somewhat less adapted than the heroic for the purpose of declamation. It is, in fact, difficult for an audience on such an occasion to follow any other; but notwithstanding this disadvantage, the poem was eminently successful in fixing the attention of those who heard him, as well as in conveying a strong impression of his power. After giving a rapid and brilliant sketch of the intellectual characteristics of what are called the dark ages, he entered upon a still more interesting one of the peculiarities of our own. The prevailing modes of education afforded him opportunities for satire, which were not lost, and he concluded with a fine poetical display of the great moral objects, which all intellectual education is intended to subserve. The performance was throughout calculated to raise the reputation which has been previously acquired by its author, and if it should be laid before the public in permanent form, will be read with pleasure, as combining a strain of good-humored satire with passages of unusual power and beauty."

3. In *The Token and Atlantic Souvenir*, 1834 (1833), 79–98. Circumstantial evidence gathered to prove that Longfellow was the author of this Spanish tale signed "L" may be found in Ralph Thompson, "Additions to Longfellow Bibliography," *American Literature*, III, 305–8 (Nov., 1931). A trivial addition to that evidence may be of interest: one of the two characters in the tale is named "González"—the surname of the family with whom Longfellow lived in Madrid.

4. Long, *Literary Pioneers*, 101. Letter dated Jan. 15, 1834.

5. MS, dated Feb. 14, 1834, CHP.

6. "New Longfellow Letters," 781.

7. *Idem.* Letter dated April 6, 1834. Part of the friction over the revivals was caused by the renewed attempts to superimpose a rigid Congregational orthodoxy after the return of Rev. William Allen as reinstated president in July, 1833. Judge Story's ruling in the Circuit Court at Portland, in May, 1833, was that the act of 1831, by which Allen had been ousted, was unconstitutional—and therefore void. Furthermore, he ruled that the state legislature had overstepped its power in trying to control the policy of a corporate institution. (Hatch, 83–84.)

In a letter to Alexander Everett, dated July 16, 1833, Longfellow had written:

"You will see by the papers that Pres. Allen was received with some glee by the students; I suspect it was only for *the fun of it*. I was not present at his *entrée*, being then on a visit at Portland. Things have taken their old course; and matters move on smoothly. We are all very glad to be beyond the reach of farther Legislative interference, though some of us would not be sorry to have Dr. Allen resign." (MS, CHP.)

Allen continued to lose favor with the faculty, students, and trustees until he found it advisable to resign, six years later. To celebrate the occasion, the students spent the eve of his departure in perpetrating an ingenious variety of wild pranks. From the dormitories, cornets blared and hand bells were kept ringing, while candles burned in every window. The following morning, when one of President Allen's hymns was announced (Allen was exceedingly proud of having written a book of hymns—most of which are pretty bad) the choir brazenly got up and walked out of the chapel. That evening, after Allen had gone, a mysterious and efficient fire burned his vacated house to the ground. Since then, the president of Bowdoin has occupied a house off campus.

8. MS, to Greene, dated July 20, 1834, CHP.

9. *Mass. Hist. Soc. Proc.*, LVI (1923), 160. Letter dated Feb. 23, 1834; original in the Library of Congress.

10. John Neal's attitude was indicative of the general feeling that Longfellow leaned too heavily on others. In a letter dated Portland, Aug. 6, 1833, Neal wrote to thank Longfellow for a copy of *Outre-Mer*, No. I:

"I had purchased and read your new work before I received the copy from you, for which please accept my hearty thanks; and I have been hoping to see you or at least to have time to write a few words to you on the subject. But there is no hope—and briefly therefore, till I see you, let me say that much as I like the stories, I am provoked with you to find you so indifferent on the subject of breaking your own pathway.—Why be like anybody? I do not say as others will, why *imitate* anybody, for I don't believe you capable of sacrificing so much for so little purpose. But why not be yourself—and yourself only?

"Your reflections on Père la Chaise are really eloquent and impressive, or rather impressive and eloquent, for example—why choose a subject which compels everybody to think of Addison's reflections on Westminster Abbey?—So too in another of the papers, full of beautiful writing, and one touch of pleasantry worthy of acceptation, why happen to follow in the track of George Colman, the younger in his Duke of Lincoln, who, by the way, followed hard after the hunchback of the Arabian Knights. But enough—give us yourself as you see, think and talk—and your book will be received with cordiality. But woe to you if you *resemble* anybody!—such is the judgment of the people. And for once the people are right." (MS dissertation, Irving T. Richards, *John Neal*, Harvard, 1934, Appendix A. Harvard College Library.)

When Neal reviewed the Harper edition of *Outre-Mer* in the *New England Galaxy* for June 6, 1835, he began:

"If Washington Irving had never appeared, Henry W. Longfellow would occupy about the place now in literature which the author of the *Sketch Book* does—not the author of the *Knickerbocker* mind ye, that's another affair—but since, owing to no fault of Longfellow, he happened to be the day after, he labors under a great disadvantage. In the first place there is a general resemblance in the character of the two men—they are alike in their unobtrusive gentleness—alike in their sly humor—alike in their pleasantry—they are acquainted, have associated together, and perhaps travelled together,—at any rate they were in Old Spain together for a long while. Now, under these circumstances, how would it be possible for Longfellow the youth, not to catch something of the peculiar tints that were always playing about the countenance of that mind, so much older, so much admired by himself in common with millions, and so renowned."

11. MS, dated July 20, 1834, CHP.

12. The account of this entire transaction is given in several letters from the firm of Harper to Longfellow, CHP.

13. Quoted from the catalogue of sale, American Art Association, Anderson Galleries, New York, Feb. 13–14, 1924, Lot No. 490. The date of the letter is given as Aug. 18, 1834. Present location of the original unknown to me.

CHAPTER XVIII: GOOD-BYE TO BRUNSWICK

1. See note 16 of this chapter.

2. "The Wondrous Tale of a Little Man in Gosling Green," by Charles F. Brown, *The New-Yorker*, I, n.p. (Nov. 1, 1834).

3. *Idem.*

4. MS, dated Nov. 2, 1834. In the century since the appearance of "The Wondrous Tale," a number of well-meaning people have trotted proudly into print with the "discovery" that Longfellow wrote it. Within one week after its appearance in the *New-Yorker*, it was pirated in Isaac Clark Pray's *Boston Pearl and Literary Gazette* for Nov. 8, 1834. It reached home shortly after, when it appeared in the Brunswick *Literary Pioneer and Juvenile Key* for January 17, 1835. (The *Literary Pioneer* was published by Joseph Griffin.) It was reprinted in the *Brunswick Telegraph* for January 12, 1863.

In the *Boston Transcript* for March 2, 1912, the entire story was reprinted, with a long account of the "discovery" of authorship. The *Transcript* article was signed by Justin Jones, a former printer's devil in Griffin's shop, who had begun work for Pray in Boston shortly before the story was printed in the *Pearl*. Jones claimed he had known both Longfellow and John Schwartkins in Brunswick.

The story was last reprinted as "An Unknown Prose Tale by Longfellow," by J. T. Hatfield, in *American Literature*, III, 136–48 (May, 1931).

5. Bibliographical summary:

(1) "The Blank Book of a Country Schoolmaster," *Knickerbocker*, III, 370–73 (May 1, 1834). The fourth excerpt, entitled "The Happy Man and the Lucky Dog" (pp. 371–72) was later patched into *Hyperion* without any good excuse (Book 4, Chapter II, pages 252–54). The excerpt was clipped from the *Knickerbocker* and pasted into the original manuscript of *Hyperion*, CHP. This misled Hatfield (p. 76) to describe it as "part of an unnoticed prose article which Longfellow had already published."

(2) "The Blank Book of a Country Schoolmaster," *Knickerbocker*, IV, 214–19 (Sept., 1834).

(3) "The Blank Book of a Country Schoolmaster," *Knickerbocker*, V, 33–34 (Jan., 1835).

These are reprinted entire in *Complete Writings*, VI, 488–505.

Clark had approached Longfellow through a mutual friend, George Cooke, whom Longfellow had met in Rome. In this way, Clark had solicited contributions in April, 1834.

6. MS journal, CHP.

7. MS journal, CHP.

8. "The Warning," in *Poems on Slavery*, Cambridge, 1842.

Although the detailed treatment of these excerpts seems to fit more appropriately into my forthcoming bibliography of Longfellow, it may be of interest to mention here two other poems taken from the "Phi Beta Kappa poem":

(1) "Sunset After Rain," in Roscoe Goddard Greene's *A Practical Grammar of the English Language*, Portland, 1835. These three six-line stanzas are the opening lines of the "Phi Beta Kappa poem."

(2) "Eternity," in *The Christian Family Annual* (place?), 1846, p. 219.

9. MS, dated Oct. 14, 1834, CHP.

10. Harvard College Papers, Harvard College Library.

Simon Greenleaf also wrote to Joseph McKeen in Brunswick. McKeen, the treasurer of Bowdoin, wrote an answer which is here given because it is of importance in throwing light on our picture of Longfellow at Bowdoin:

BRUNSWICK, Oct. 20, 1834.

Dʳ Sir,

I have this moment received yours of the 17th–I have been aware that Mr. Longfellow has been considered a candidate for some more eligible & lucrative situation & have not for a moment doubted that he would soon leave us.

From the first he has been popular as an instructor, very much so, & took great pains to gain the affections of the students. As a disciplinarian he did not promise well. Indeed I suppose his notions about such things were very lax. He was young—some of the students had been his fellows, & the officers his instructors. Under these circumstances it is not strange that he was not decided as an officer.

As he has grown older & acquired more experience, he has improved & is now I think a very good officer. If he differs, in a meeting of the Govt from his colleagues he will let *them* know it, & give his reasons for it, but the *students* will never know it from *him*.

There is no skulking nor slinking from responsibility but he is always so far as I know, strictly honorable with the Government. There is a good deal in this—possibly more than you are aware.

There is more "nerve," more of decision, more of the *man* about him than some casual observers might expect. He stands high here with officers & students. In looking over what I had written to see what it amounts to, I have some fear that my remarks upon his anxiety to gain the affection of the students, might not be construed correctly. It was in him a laudable ambition and I think it becomes a young officer of a college by all fair and honorable means to acquire the affections of his pupils; for by it he may exert & influence which will do away with the necessity of discipline. I should like to see more of it.

Yours &c,

Jos. McKeen.

11. MS journal entry, dated Dec. 3, CHP.

12. MS, dated Cambridge, Dec. 1, 1834, CHP.
Ticknor had received a salary of $500 a year, but did not live in Cambridge and was not a member of the faculty, technically speaking.

13. MS, dated Dec. 6, 1834, CHP. To understand Longfellow's subsequent bitter remorse over the death of Mary Longfellow, one must take special notice of the persistence with which his friends and relatives tried to dissuade him from making the trip. His father opposed it from the first, on financial grounds; Ichabod Nichols had disparaged the thought of such needless "exile" as soon as Longfellow had suggested it, several months earlier; President Quincy was obviously giving permission, as Longfellow pointed out to his father, but did not give any encouragement by offering the financial support which Harvard had given Ticknor when he had prepared for the position in Europe; and finally, Mary was not pleased by the prospect.

14. MS, dated Dec. 8, 1834, CHP.

15. MS, dated Feb. 2, 1835, CHP.

16. MS, to Charles Folsom, dated Feb. 26, 1835, BPL.

Greene's interest in purchasing some of Longfellow's books on foreign literature was due to the misfortune of his having lost his own library aboard a ship that foundered before it reached home. But apparently Longfellow's prices were too high for Greene, since Greene did not buy many.

17. MS, dated Portland, March 21, 1835, CHP.

Longfellow's place at Bowdoin was taken by Charles Goodwin, who had studied foreign languages under Longfellow and had been graduated from Bowdoin at the head of his class in 1832. He was given only a tutorship as Longfellow's successor. But he went abroad to study languages, from 1835 to 1837. In writing to his father a few days after returning to Brunswick early in February (the letter is dated "Sunday evening") Longfellow talked about his successor:

"I suppose that Prof. Cleaveland gave you an account of the doings of the Executive Government after the receipt of my letter. They are in negociation with Mr. Goodwin—a student of Andover, who graduated here about three years ago. He wants higher wages than were first offered him, and I think it probable, that he will accede to the last proposition made him; which is to give him four hundred dollars for the remainder of the College year. They do not seem to have taken a fancy to Mr. Greene and are fearful, that he would not get along very well with the students. Under such circumstances it would be useless to urge his claims. The favorite project at present is to let some graduate of the institution go abroad, as I did, and appoint him Professor on his return.

"We advertised our furniture yesterday—and made some sales forthwith. . . ." (MS, CHP.)

CHAPTER XIX: EUROPE AND TRAGEDY

The material in this chapter is drawn almost entirely from manuscript sources. The journal which Longfellow kept during his stay in England is one of the most complete records kept by him. It may be found, with a few omissions, in Irving T. Richards, "Longfellow in England: Unpublished Extracts from His Journal," *Publications of the Modern Language Association*, LI, 1127–39 (Dec., 1936).

1. MS journal entry for Dec. 31, 1835, CHP. The passage begins:

"Thursday 31. Thus closes another year—every way the most important year of my life. I pause to look back, like one awaking from a sorrowful dream. How strangely it moves before me—and how dark. Far back stands the peaceful home . . ."

2. MS, to his father, dated London, May 14–17, 1835, CHP.

3. Journal entry for May 21, 1835.

4. Journal entry for May 31, 1835. In this section of the chapter, I have given very close paraphrases of the detailed accounts Longfellow wrote daily. But all direct quotations are Longfellow's own.

5. Journal entry for May 31, 1835.

6. Journal entry for June 3, 1835. The beginning: "Breakfasted at Mr. Carlyle's, in a quiet, friendly way. He spoke of the interesting spots in the old city of London—the surprise with which in treading some of the bye-lanes he came out upon little green squares—'and saw great trees growing in the heart of a brick and mortar wilderness.' "

7. Journal entry for June 3, 1835.

8. Journal entry for June 3, 1835.

9. Journal entry for May 21, 1835.

10. Journal entry for May 22, 1835.

11. From a letter written by Mary Potter Longfellow to one of her sisters, May 24, 1835. ("New Longfellow Letters," 782.)

12. MS, dated Stockholm, Aug. 10, 1835, CHP.

13. "New Longfellow Letters," 784.

In one of Mary's letters: "Henry is a much better traveller than you would imagine. He always makes *his bargain*, as we Yankees say, beforehand, wherever we go; and the moment he pays for anything it is entered in his account-book. We have not lost anything yet, although he has so much baggage to look after. Then he has books to buy for the College, which has occupied much of his time, as he must look over their catalogue of five volumes to see if they have the book already—then all those accounts are kept separately."

Longfellow was authorized by the Harvard Corporation to spend the sum of two hundred pounds sterling in purchasing books for the college library, according to a statement in a letter from Longfellow to T. W. Ward, dated Stockholm, July 23, 1835. MS, Harvard College Papers.

14. Journal entry for June 2, 1835.

15. Journal entry for June 6, 1835.

16. MS, dated Stockholm, Aug. 10, 1835, CHP. There were no profits.

17. Journal entry for June 9, 1835.

18. Journal entry for June 10, 1835.

19. Journal entry for July 8, 1835.

20. MS, dated Stockholm, Aug. 10, 1835, CHP.

21. Journal entry for Sept. 2, 1835.

22. Journal entry for Sept. 7, 1835.

23. MS, dated Copenhagen, Sept. 20, 1835, CHP.

24. Journal entry for Sept. 21, 1835.

25. Journal entry for Nov. 17, 1835.

26. Journal entry for Nov. 29, 1835.

27. Higginson, 107–11.

28. In his journal Longfellow wrote, on Dec. 4, 1835:
"The body of my wife has been embalmed and sent to America, that hereafter we may lie side by side in the peaceful shades of Mount Auburn. It is incredible how much consolation I draw from this thought."

In his Heidelberg journal, under date of March 16, 1836, he wrote:
"A letter from Mary Goddard informs me that vessel carrying the body of my dear Mary has reached Boston; and that the coffin would be deposited in the Tomb at Mount Auburn, Feb. 15. O that I could have been there." MSS, CHP.

CHAPTER XX: WINTER IN HEIDELBERG

Because of the careful analysis of Longfellow's reading and studies in Heidelberg given in Hatfield's *New Light* (in the text, 37–43; in the appendix, 164–77), I have made no attempt to give a complete account here. Instead, I have been interested, not so much in the extent of his scholarly accomplishment, as in the maturing attempt Longfellow made to assimilate various aspects of German romanticism in particular and German literature in general, to his specific needs, immediately after his wife's death.

1. MS, from Longfellow to Greene, dated Heidelberg, March 25, 1836, CHP.

2. MS, dated Jan. 22, 1836, CHP.

3. Journal entry for Jan. 22, 1836, CHP.

4. See note 11 of Chapter XV.

5. Her last words, recorded in his journal.

6. Journal entry for Dec. 17, 1835, CHP.

7. *Life*, I, 216.

8. Journal entry for Dec. 29, 1835, CHP.

9. Hatfield, 39.

10. *Life*, I, 43. Mrs. Bryant and her two daughters remained in Heidelberg after Mr. Bryant's departure late in January. They travelled with Longfellow and Clara Crowninshield to Paris at the end of the summer, and returned to America on the same boat.

11. Journal entry for Jan. 20, 1836, CHP.

12. *Life*, I, 216 fn.

13. MS, documented in note 2 of this chapter.

14. Samuel Ward, "Reminiscences of Henry Wadsworth Longfellow," *North American Review*, LXVIII, 457 (May, 1882).

15. MS, documented in note 1 of this chapter. The inelegant self-characterization is also quoted in this letter.

16. Journal entry for June 20, 1836, CHP.

17. MS, Longfellow to Greene, dated Paris, Sept. 12, 1836.

18. Journal entry for July 20, 1836, CHP.
19. Journal entry of Frances Appleton for July 20, 1836, CHP.
20. Journal entry for July 31, 1836, CHP.
21. Journal entry for August 2, 1836, CHP.
22. Journal, CHP.
Samuel Longfellow (*Life*, I, 235) omits so little in editing this passage—and yet modifies the original implication so much!
23. Journal entry for August 8, 1836, CHP.
24. Journal entry for August 10, 1836, CHP.
25. Journal entry for August 11, 1836, CHP.
26. Longfellow later wrote:
"That which has the most delightful association of all is 'The Castle by the Sea.' It was written at Zurich, August 9, 1836. You will remember it, dearest Fanny; the lovely drive along the lake, down the hill-side to the town. You held the little volume of Uhland in your hand, and we put a stanza or two into verse as we drove along in the spacious travelling carriage. Some of the best lines are yours." (Entry in a MS written by Longfellow for Frances Appleton Longfellow, at her request. In it he gives accounts of the writing of certain of his early poems. Longfellow playfully entitled the notebook: "Book of Vanity." CHP.)
The original manuscript of "The Castle by the Sea," with lines written in the hand of each, is in the Craigie House. On the back is Longfellow's later inscription: "A Heart-Treasure—July 4, 1839." This was shortly before the publication of *Hyperion*.
27. This quotation, and the entire description of Frances Appleton is taken from *Hyperion*, the third and fourth chapters of "Book the Third."
28. Journal entry of Frances Appleton for August 17, 1836, CHP.
29. Entry for August 19, 1836, CHP.

CHAPTER XXI: FLASHING SICKLE IN CAMBRIDGE

The background material for my sketch of Cambridge village and its inhabitants in 1836 has been drawn from three main sources:
(1) James Russell Lowell's famous essay, "Cambridge Thirty Years Ago."
(2) T. W. Higginson, *Old Cambridge*, New York, 1899.
(3) A. F. Peabody, *Harvard Reminiscences*, Boston, 1888.
Many of the letters written by Longfellow during this period and included in the *Life* give much insight. Of particular importance concerning Longfellow's relations with Harvard College is the correspondence between Longfellow and President Quincy, in the Harvard College Library.

1. MS, dated March 22, 1837, CHP. For source of title for this chapter see page 193. See also *Life,* I, 191fn.
2. Abiel Holmes, *The History of Cambridge,* Boston, 1801, 6.
3. Peabody, 208.
4. MS, dated Feb. 1, 1837, CHP.
5. MS, dated Feb. 26, 1837, CHP.

This is a significant letter. It marks the end of the conflict between father and son—a conflict which had been carried on with great politeness, ever since Bowdoin undergraduate days. Never, during these years of dominance, did Stephen Longfellow permit his son to stray off into fields of "merely literary" endeavor. And now, with the young man established at Harvard, the father could write praising him for having attained a position that was "very eligible" and conducive to "usefulness." But there is a certain element of uncertainty between the lines—a fear that Henry may yet be seduced into merely literary activities. The father knew that the original ambition and yearning had by no means been extinguished.

6. MS, dated Feb. 1, 1837, CHP. See note 4.
7. MS, dated March 22, 1837, CHP. This passage is omitted in the *Life.*
8. MS note, undated, but addressed to Longfellow at Dr. Stearns', CHP.
9. MS, CHP. See the note immediately following.
10. MS, dated Jan. 23, 1837. In this letter, Longfellow told how Tom Appleton's aunt had invited him to write "a Valentine for your sisters." He added: "I contributed some Translations from the German for Miss Fanny, and a copy of the 'Hymn to the Flowers' for Miss M. This letter will probably reach you sooner than the package."

Longfellow actually sent two poems, now preserved in CHP. The "Elegy Written in the Ruins of an Old Castle" was published in the *Knickerbocker,* XIV, 211–12 (Sept., 1839). The second poem, "The Wave," was originally translated from the German of Tiedge by Longfellow for use in connection with the Harvard winter lectures which he was preparing. It was not published until *Voices of the Night,* Cambridge, 1839.

Another passage from the letter to Tom Appleton is too good to pass over. Writing of Boston doings, Longfellow added:

"And then there is an Oratorio, where the part of David is sung by a very fat man, and the part of Goliah by a very small one; and when the pebble hits Goliah on the head it is represented by a great blow on a bass-drum, and for fear there should be any mistake, *explained in the bill!*"

11. A. S. Pier, *The Story of Harvard,* Boston, 1913, 125.
12. MS note undated, CHP. Referring to the Harvard faculty

meetings in a letter to Parker Cleaveland, dated Oct. 3, 1837, Long-fellow wrote:

"Did the President tell you he met me in Washington Street two or three days ago? I was glad to see him. It brought back to me the Government Meetings where we had so much fun. They are dull enough here as you remember, probably. All business—no merry quirks, and discussions *de omnibus rebus*. Remember me next Monday night; and be merciful in the administration of justice. We are very savage here, in that particular. Almost too severe." (MS, owned by H. W. L. Dana, on deposit in CHP.)

13. Writing to his father on May 12, 1837, Longfellow gave a sketch of his course of lectures:

"1. Introduction. History of the French Language.
2. The other Languages of the South of Europe.
3. History of the Northern, or Gothic, Languages.
4. Anglo-Saxon Literature.
5 and 6. Swedish Literature.
7. Sketch of German Literature.
8, 9, 10. Life and Writings of Goethe.
11 and 12. Life and Writings of Jean Paul Richter."

(*Life*, I, 251.) This list grows less impressive when it is remembered that each topic number received only one hour of classroom elaboration.

14. "Tegnér's Frithiofs Saga," *North American Review*, XLV, 149–85 (July, 1837).

A part of the introductory description, dealing with rural life in Sweden, was reprinted as "Life in Sweden" in *The Boston Book*, 1841 (1840), 193–201. It was later reprinted in a slightly revised form as the prose Preface to Tegnér's "The Children of the Lord's Supper" in *Ballads*.

15. MS, dated Salem, March 7, 1837, CHP. See also *Life*, I, 250.

16. "Hawthorne's Twice-Told Tales," *North American Review*, XLV, 59–73 (July, 1837).

17. MS, dated Salem, June 19, 1837, CHP. See also *Life*, I, 255.

18. Hatfield, 52–53.

19. Hatfield, 55.

20. MS, Longfellow to his father, dated June 10, 1837: "Since I last wrote you I have been quite unwell; in fact I was not well when I wrote. Three weeks ago I was attacked violently with Influenza, I supposed. Unfortunately it was the day before my Lectures commenced. I had announced the Lectures, and expecting to get over my cold, every day, I began to lecture, and fought against bad weather, and influenza, and blue devils, till finally I got the worst of it, and after three Lectures was obliged to give up. That was ten

days ago. Since then I have kept pretty closely to the house . . . I am, however, nearly well and hope next week to begin again with College duties." (CHP.)

21. To Eliza Potter, his wife's sister, Longfellow wrote in December, 1836 (Higginson, 113–15):

"My Dear Eliza,

By tomorrow's steam-boat I shall send you two trunks, containing the clothes which once belonged to your sister. What I have suffered in getting them ready to send to you, I cannot describe. It is not necessary, that I should. Cheerful as I may have seemed to you at times, there are other times, when it seems to me that my heart would break. The world considers grief unmanly, and is suspicious of that sorrow, which is expressed by words and outward signs. Hence we strive to be gay and put a cheerful courage on, when our souls are very sad. But there are hours, when the world is shut out, and we can no longer hear the voices, that cheer and encourage us. To me such hours come daily.

I was so happy with my dear Mary, that it is very hard to be alone. The sympathies of friendship are doubtless something—but after all how little, how unsatisfying they are to one who has been so loved as I have been! This is a selfish sorrow, I know: but neither reason nor reflection can still it. Affliction makes us childish. A grieved and wounded heart is hard to be persuaded. We do not wish to have our sorrow lessened. There are wounds, which are never entirely healed. A thousand associations call up the past, with all its gloom and shadow. Often a mere look or sound—a voice—the odor of a flower—the merest trifle is enough to awaken within me deep and unutterable emotions. Hardly a day passes, that some face, or familiar object, or some passage in the book I am reading does not call up the image of my beloved wife so vividly, that I pause and burst into tears,—and sometimes cannot rally again for hours.

And yet, my dear Eliza, in a few days, and we shall all be gone, and others sorrowing and rejoicing as we now do, will have taken our places: and we shall say, how childish it was for us to mourn for things so transitory. There may be some consolation in this; but we are nevertheless children. Our feelings overcome us."

22. MS, dated Feb. 1, 1837, CHP. Mangled in *Life*, I, 248–49.

23. MS, containing a digest of the "Scheme of Duties for Modern Language Department," dated July 31, 1837, which was sent to Longfellow and returned. Harvard College Library.

24. *Idem.*

25. MS, dated Cambridge, Aug. 23, 1837, CHP. Longfellow's success in achieving a modification of the plans was due in part to a strong feeling among certain members of the Corporation that too

much time was being spent on modern languages in the Harvard curriculum. Writing to President Quincy about this matter on Aug. 10, 1837, James Walker gave his opinion:

"Indeed I cannot but fear that the attention now paid to modern languages in the College is disproportionate, & I should not, for one, be so well reconciled as I am, to the present arrangement, if we were in a better condition to give instruction in Political Economy, Natural History, Civil History, Engineering, & other branches of teaching which have more to do with practical life." (MS, Harvard College Papers, Harvard College Library.)

CHAPTER XXII: THE SUITOR REJECTED

The notes for the next three chapters are extremely important. They help to show how closely the various "Psalms" are related to *Hyperion*—how this poetry and prose were unified subjective expressions of the most important crisis in Longfellow's life.

By sheer coincidence, he faced this crisis at the very time when he felt the sway of German romanticism, particularly of the *Sturm und Drang* writers. Fascinated, and pulled off his guard for a brief period, Longfellow indiscreetly dared play the part of a pale American Byron, bearing "the pageant of his bleeding heart" across Europe, in the pages of *Hyperion*.

Soon after the book was written and published, he came to his Yankee senses—and behaved himself properly for the rest of his life. It was a curious interlude. The loss of his wife, just before the winter in Heidelberg, and then the falling in love, desperately, with a woman who spurned him—these were accidents which forced him out of his ingrained reticences temporarily, and induced him to reveal heart and soul clearer than at any other time.

1. See note 9 of this chapter.
2. MS, to his father, dated Aug. 23, 1837, CHP.
3. This anecdote, often repeated, was first given in some detail by Longfellow himself. See the quotation in the *Life*, I, 263–64.
4. MS, documented in note 2, above.
5. MS, to his father, dated Oct. 29, 1837.
6. MS, dated Sept. 21, 1837, CHP. The Longfellow family has refused me permission to publish this letter in its original form.
7. Quoted from the MS (CHP) which Longfellow sent to Frances Appleton with this brief note: "With many thanks and a few flowers." Another MS version, apparently the first, is dated "October 3, 1837." A third MS version, sent by Longfellow to the *Knickerbocker*, is owned by Carroll A. Wilson. "Floral Astrology" was first published in the *Knickerbocker*, X, 498 (Dec., 1837). In the "Book of Vanity," Longfellow explained:

"Flowers. I wrote this poem on the 3rd of October 1837; to send to Fanny with a bouquet of Autumnal flowers. I still remember the great delight I took in its composition; and the bright sunshine that streamed in at the southern windows, as I walked to and fro, pausing ever and anon to note down my thoughts. The poem will always carry me back to that golden, beautiful Autumn of Fanny's return from Europe. Whenever I read it I live over again that season of love and restlessness, of hope and fear."

With great caution, Samuel Longfellow paraphrased a single sentence of this entry. "Fanny" becomes "a friend," etc. See *Life*, I, 270. Apparently believing this love story too intimate for the purposes of biography, he applied the same cautious editing principle to all references to Frances Appleton, in the journals and letters—regardless of the fact that such deletions frequently rendered the printed context misleading or unintelligible.

8. "Longfellow's correspondence, however, contains hints that his first proposal met with rejection . . ." (Henry Marion Hall, "Longfellow's Letters to Samuel Ward," *Putnam's Monthly Magazine*, III, 40 (Oct., 1907). There are various letters in the Craigie House which contain Longfellow's reference to this fact. I have been refused permission to publish them.

9. Hatfield, 50–52. The German passage may be translated thus:
"Ah, thou beautiful soul! It makes me very sad at heart, when I think of it, and see how the lovely dream there is ended—how the clouds dissolve, and merge into tears, and about me everything becomes so empty, and in my soul a dark night—a dark, starless night!— And this I was forced to say to you in German because a foreign speech is a sort of twilight and moonlight, wherein one may say all sorts of things to womenfolk—and so heartfully sincere. Even so heartfully give my greetings to the dear, dear Fanny, whom I shall always love as my own Soul. Oh! That little bit of reason which one may possess, can hardly be considered when passion sways us. How full my heart becomes! The last time that we were together, we separated without understanding each other, for 'in this world no one understands another easily.' And this is very sad to me."

Professor Hatfield's attempt to explain the "Belfagor" remark as a reference to La Fontaine is far-fetched and unnecessary, in the light of what is known. Longfellow had discussed with Mary Appleton his plan to write a play which would combine Faust legends and Belfagor themes, with a New England setting. (He had already quoted a section of Machiavelli's "Novella" entitled *Belfagor* in his Bowdoin text, *Novellieri Italiani*, 1832, pp. 48–62.) And a few days before Longfellow wrote on this subject to Mary Appleton, she had written him a letter concerning his projected play. I have removed this letter at the request of the Longfellow family.

10. MS, CHP.

11. MS, dated Boston, Dec. 24, 1837, CHP.

12. This closely written four-page quarto letter is one of the most self-revealing and therefore important autobiographical documents which Longfellow wrote. I deeply regret that the Longfellow family refused me permission to quote it. It is dated Jan. 6, 1838, CHP.

13. A very good illustration of this is contained in a characteristic entry in his journal for March 2, 1838. I regret that the Longfellow family refused me permission to quote it.

14. What relation this book would have had to the Arnim and Brentano *Boys' Wonder-Horn,* which Longfellow had read in Germany with so much pleasure two years earlier, we may only guess. Under date of March 21, 1838, Hawthorne wrote to Longfellow from Salem:

"I was sorry that you did not come to dinner on Sunday, for I wanted to have a talk with you about that book of Fairy Tales which you spoke of. I think it is a good idea, and am well inclined to do my part toward the execution of it. . . . You shall be editor, and I will figure merely as a contributor; for as the conception and system of the work will be yours, I really should not think it honest to take an equal share of the fame which is to accrue." (*Life,* I, 280–81.) The invitation to visit Hawthorne was accepted on the following week-end. See the following note.

15. Samuel Longfellow's misrepresentation of the truth through prudish editing is best illustrated by comparing his version of Longfellow's visit to Salem at this time (see *Life,* I, 281–82) with the original passage in the journal (CHP). I intended to print the two passages here. Unfortunately, however, the Longfellow family has refused my request to quote the original two-hundred-and-eighty-six-word passage which Samuel Longfellow compresses, without any indication of omission, into a dull, colorless, and emasculated passage of fifty words—containing mistakes which, for Longfellow's sake, ought to be corrected.

16. *Life,* I, 281.

17. For full title and documentation, see note 11 of Chapter XIV.

18. These accidental meetings became more or less of a habit. In this particular case, Longfellow knew they had returned, for he had written in his journal, one week earlier:

"May 5. The Appletons have returned. I saw their lights last night, as I passed down Beacon street on my way home." (MS, CHP.)

19. MS journal entry, dated May 12, CHP. Only a fragment of the original entry now remains, since Longfellow cut from this journal, not many years before he died, several pages which he destroyed. The remaining part of the passage is:

"A day of Paradise. Walked to town at noon; for I could not sit still. Half way, Mrs. Eliot, my excellent, much-esteemed friend took me up in the Pope's carriage. A delightful drive over the bridge— with the warm sunshine and cool sea-breeze.

"Saw the Appletons walking on the Common. Jumped from the carriage and ran in pursuit. I was indeed rejoiced to see them. Tom, Fanny, Wright and Mary were walking together. Gave [   ]."

20. See MS journal, May 16, CHP. The Longfellow family has refused me permission to quote it. Another related entry, under date of May 19, which is carefully edited in the *Life* (I, 287), reads in the original thus:

"Met Lady Fanny, with a pretty young friend in black. Why don't all ladies wear black, like the Spanish! Nothing so sets off a woman, as black. Well: I took a turn with Lady Fanny; she was as cool as an East wind. Left her at her father's door; being obliged to decline her invitation to tea; which, to tell the truth, seemed to me, to be given reluctantly."

Chapter XXIII: A Psalm of Life

1. See note 16 of this chapter.

2. MS, documented in note 9 of Chapter XXII.

3. "Evening Shadows" was later revised and lengthened before its publication: "Voices of the Night: A Third Psalm of Life," *Knickerbocker*, XIII, 376 (May, 1839). Here quoted from MS journal, CHP.

4. MS lecture notes, dated June 13, 1838, CHP.

In *Hyperion* (VIII, 76–77), the chapter "On Literary Fame" makes an interesting bridge of thought between this college lecture and the writing of "A Psalm of Life."

" 'And after all,' continued Flemming, 'perhaps the greatest lesson which the lives of literary men teach us is told in a single word: Wait! Every man must patiently bide his time.' "

And again (*Hyperion*, VIII, 67):

"It is better, therefore, that men should soon make up their minds to be forgotten, and look about them, or within them, for some higher motive . . . that they should be constantly and quietly at work, each in his sphere . . ."

This thought, taken from Goethe, is the ultimate goal toward which Paul Flemming gropes in action. Held in morbid sorrow by his double burden of woe, he continues to reach out after a release, a higher course of action, and finally gains the inspiration from the inscription on a marble tablet in the chapel at St. Gilgen. Thus, the climax to *Hyperion* is the firm resolve of the hero (VIII, 318–19):

" 'Thither will I turn my wandering footsteps,' said he, 'and be a man among men, and no longer a dreamer among shadows. Henceforth be mine a life of action and reality! I will work in my own sphere, nor wish it other than it is. This alone is health and happiness. This alone is Life:

> Life that shall send
> A challenge to its end,
> And when it comes, say, Welcome, friend!' "

The ideas here and in "A Psalm of Life" are seen to be interlocked. Furthermore, this quotation of three lines from Crashaw was first used as a motto for "A Psalm of Life," when it was originally published in the *Knickerbocker*.

5. MS, Feb. 1, 1837, CHP.

This exhortation to Greene (quoted on p. 248) follows immediately after a quotation from Jean Paul Richter's *Quintus Fixlein*. Curiously, Longfellow blended the ideas of Richter with the ideas of Goethe. One might almost be convinced that Longfellow's original inspiration for the theme implied in the title of *Hyperion* was derived from Richter's introductory remarks in *Quintus Fixlein*, about finding how to enjoy pleasure by soaring above the clouds of life—and that he was led to modify this initial idea by his reading and teaching Goethe. I am convinced that Longfellow borrowed his motivation and general outline and prose style of *Hyperion* from Jean Paul; that he borrowed only the action-philosophy and conclusion based upon it, from Goethe.

6. MS journal entry for Feb. 28, 1838, CHP. The Longfellow family has refused me permission to quote this passage.

7. MS journal entry for June 26, 1838, CHP. The first draft of "A Psalm of Life" was written, according to the date in Longfellow's own hand on the manuscript, the following day—June 27, 1838.

8. MS journal entry for April 28, 1838, CHP.

9. Compare this quotation from Novalis's *Die Lehrlinge zu Sais* (copied into Longfellow's journal) with his assertion to Greene:

"The truth is this. My nature craves sympathy—not of friendship but of Love. This want of my nature is unsatisfied. And the love of some good being is as necessary to my existence as the air I breathe."

10. *Wilhelm Meister's Apprenticeship and Travels*, translated from the German of Goethe by Thomas Carlyle, London, 1899, 2 vols., I, 17.

11. *Ibid.*, II, 132.

12. *Ibid.*, II, 2. These passages are very similar to many in *Hyperion*. Compare just one:

"Believe me, the talent of success is nothing more than doing what you can do well; and doing well whatever you do—without a thought of fame. If it comes at all, it will come because it is deserved, not because it is sought after. And, moreover, there will be no misgivings, no disappointment, no hasty, feverish, exhausting excitement." (VIII, 78.)

13. *Wilhelm Meister*, II, 75. Hippocrates's famous phrase was familiar to Longfellow, quite naturally, long before he found it here or in Goethe's *Faust;* he had even quoted it in *Outre-Mer* (VII, 277). It is here given from Meister's indenture because its use in "A Psalm of Life" seems to me so closely allied to the indenture in purpose and in implication.

14. Although this quotation was first used by Longfellow as the motto for *Hyperion*, its relation to "A Psalm of Life" is obvious, when it is considered in connection with the sixth quatrain of the version of "A Psalm of Life" quoted in the text.

15. Quoted from the *Knickerbocker*, XII, 189 (Sept., 1838). The original manuscript in the Craigie House is a confusing text because it contains so many deletions, revisions and suggested rearrangements of stanzas. The manuscript is dated twice: the earlier date (June 27, 1838) indicates the time when stanzas 1, 2, 3, 4, 7, 8, and 9 were written; the later date (July 26, 1838) indicates final completion. See also note 16 of this chapter.

Much light is thrown on the significance of "A Psalm of Life" as an autobiographical document, if one approaches it through the notations in Longfellow's various notebooks, journals, college lectures, and miscellaneous manuscripts. Many scholars have made learned guesses as to the sources of "A Psalm of Life"—and particularly as to Longfellow's source for the idea that "Life is but an empty dream." The diversity of their ingenious findings has clarified, however, the essential fact: that the ideas in this poem had passed current for so many centuries that the only important question that needs answering is: How long had Longfellow thought of life as a dream, and what made him turn against that thought with such flat denials?

That is the question which I wish to consider here.

During his undergraduate years at Brunswick, Longfellow must have brought a romantic interpretation to the religious teachings of life as an unimportant journey to that better land of Heaven. It had colored the moralizings of his "Phi Beta Kappa poem," delivered at Bowdoin. The last stanza of that poem contains a reference to life as a dream:

> "Oft in that silent hour when day has fled,
>   The spirit of some dear departed friend
> Has watched above me and in whispers said,
>   That when life's transient dream was at an end
> They that have loved in life shall meet again
> Where there is neither sorrow, tears, nor pain."

Except for the verse form, this quotation is so closely related in spirit to "Evening Shadows" that it might be mistakenly supposed to belong to it. The same thought was the central theme of Manrique's "Coplas," which Longfellow had liked so much that he had translated it, printed it in a magazine, reprinted it in book form, printed it again in *Outre-Mer*, and finally included it in *Voices*. A poem used so frequently must have contained thoughts which satisfied Longfellow thoroughly. And one verse is enough to show that the interpretation of life as a dream was already a part of Longfellow's romanticism:

> "Even could the hand of avarice save
> Its gilded baubles, till the grave
> Reclaimed its prey,
> Let none on such poor hopes rely;
> Life, like an empty dream, flits by,
> And where are they?"

Thus Longfellow was prepared by sentiment, reading, and religious teaching to find in the mournful numbers of Matthisson, Salis, Novalis, and Vaughan a satisfying escape from life by projecting his thoughts into the past of memories and into the future, where hopes would be fulfilled and loved ones united. And after the death of his wife, how much more strongly such a concept must have appealed to him. Did he not confess it anew, in the first long letter which he wrote after Mary's death (see p. 226): ". . . and I say to myself,—

> " 'Peace! Peace! she is not dead, she does not sleep!
> She has awakened from the dream of life.' "

But the reading of Carlyle and Goethe—and his own constant dissatisfaction with regrets and longings—made him turn away, at times, from the thought of life as a dream. In his review of *The Great Metropolis*, published in the *North American* in April, 1837, Longfellow had found Grant's picture of London so solid and practical that he had written:

"We have an affection for a great city. . . . We feel that life is not a dream, but an earnest reality."

This phrase comes very near to the later assertion that life is not an empty dream, and very near to the affirmation:

> "Life is real! Life is earnest!"

But there was no strength in Longfellow for meeting life as an earnest reality—at least, no strength for very long. Nothing shows this more clearly than his mildly mystical and romantic kinship with Matthisson, Salis, and Novalis, which had found such perfect expression in "Evening Shadows."

Yet this was exactly the vague dreaminess which Longfellow found shattered by the clear voice of Goethe, preaching a doctrine of action, in the bright sunlight of morning. Undoubtedly the most important single factor in Longfellow's growth of understanding at this time was the necessity for *teaching* Goethe at Harvard. By the time he had completed his lectures in June, 1838, his own imitative thoughts, saturated with classroom materials, could not help reflecting Goethe. And so he turned his back on the mystic in him and in other poets who had sung in mournful numbers: he wrote his protest and his denials in "A Psalm of Life."

Again he showed that he was not constituted to accept the challenge of life as a reality. In a very short time he was writing psalms of death, and had returned to an optimistic but mystical communion with the voices of night. Thus, "A Psalm of Life" was betrayed by the inevitable inconsistency of Longfellow's character—perfectly symbolized in the contradictory appearance of that morning-light poem in a volume entitled *Voices of the Night*.

16. MS notebook entry—in the "Book of Vanity." He recorded the completion of the poem in his journal on July 26—one month after he had written the first six verses:

"Wrote 'Psalm of Life,' which, I suppose will soon go into the Knickerbocker, or some other Magazine."

The three-line motto, unattributed, at the beginning of the poem in this first printed form is a passage inaccurately quoted from Crashaw's "Wishes to His Supposed Mistress."

These lines, already mentioned, were also quoted as a motto to the chapter in *Hyperion* entitled "Footprints of Angels." See also note 4, above.

As an instance of Longfellow's consideration of this poem as being very personal and subjective, it is worthy of note that he did not permit his name to be attached to "A Psalm of Life" in the *Knickerbocker*. It was merely signed "L." On the other hand, he had published "Floral Astrology" there over the signature, "Prof. H. W. Longfellow, Cambridge University." In all fairness, it should be stated that this title and ascription were almost certainly pinned on by Clark, the editor of the *Knickerbocker*.

17. This poem was published in the same issue of the *Knickerbocker* with another poem:

"A Second Psalm of Life: the Light of Stars" (signed "L."), *Knickerbocker*, XIII, 77 (Jan., 1839).

"A Psalm of Death: the Reaper and the Flowers," *Knickerbocker*, XIII, 13 (Jan., 1839).

An instance of Longfellow's inconsistency of thought in the matter of denying that life is a dream may be found implied in his having used as a motto to "A Psalm of Death" these lines from Vaughan's "Friends Departed":

> "Dear, beauteous Death! the jewel of the just,
>   Shining nowhere, but in the dark;
>   What mysteries do lie beyond thy dust,
>   Could man outlook that mark."

"The Light of Stars" also has a strikingly close relationship to *Hyperion:*

"Flemming looked at the evening sky, and a shade of sadness stole over his countenance. He told not to his friend the sorrow with which his heart was heavy, but kept it for himself alone. He knew that the time, which comes to all men,—the time to suffer and be silent,—had come to him likewise, and he spake not a word. Oh, well has it been said that there is no grief like the grief which does not speak!" (*Hyperion*, VIII, 87–88).

"Oh, there is something sublime in calm endurance, something sublime in the resolute, fixed purpose of suffering without complaining, which makes disappointment oftentimes better than success! . . . He did not rail at Providence and call it fate, but suffered and was silent." (*Hyperion*, VIII, 248–49.)

18. *Life*, I, 293. Probably most of the writing was done in his journals. But, as I have already said, these journal pages which contained so many revelations of an intimate nature, were cut out— nearly one hundred pages in all—and destroyed by Longfellow. The mutilated journals, still showing the stubs of pages gone, are preserved in the Craigie House.

19. *Life*, I, 294. Samuel Longfellow cut the heart out of this long and exceedingly important letter, with his reticent editing. Unfortunately, however, I have been given no alternative but to quote him —even to quote his mistakes—because the Longfellow family has refused my request to quote direct from the original letter. In the original, the passage expressing his dislike of sedentary life is written in short, choppy phrases, separated by dashes. It conveys perfectly the uneasy nervousness of this period. I wish I might have quoted it without Samuel's additions. This letter is dated August 6, 1838, CHP.

CHAPTER XXIV: PAGEANT OF HIS BLEEDING HEART

1. MS, Longfellow to Greene, dated July 23, 1839, CHP.
2. MS lecture notes, June, 1838, CHP.
3. *Idem.*
4. *Idem.*
5. MS, dated Portland, Aug. 16, 1838. Mass. Hist. Soc. There

were other parts of this letter which I wished to quote, but the Longfellow family refused me permission.

6. MS, CHP.

7. Quoted from Carlyle by Longfellow in his MS lecture notes,
June, 1838, CHP.

8. *Hyperion*, VIII, 31.

9. Compare Longfellow's remarks in *Hyperion*, concerning Jean
Paul's prose style with Longfellow's characterization of *Hyperion*:

"It is his nature,—it is Jean Paul. And the figures and ornaments of
his style, wild, fantastic, and ofttimes startling, like those in Gothic
cathedrals, are not merely what they seem, but massive coignes and
buttresses which support the fabric. Remove them, and the roof
and walls fall in. And through these gargoyles, these wild faces,
these images of beasts and men carved upon spouts and gutters, flow
out, like gathered rain, the bright, abundant thoughts that have fallen
from heaven. And all he does is done with a kind of serious playful-
ness." (*Hyperion*, VIII, 43.)

"This book [*Hyperion*] does somewhat resemble a minster, in the
Romanesque style, with pinnacles, and flying buttresses, and roofs,

> Gargoyled with greyhounds, and with many lions
> Made of fine gold, with divers sundry dragons.

You step into its shade and coolness out of the hot streets of life;
a mysterious light streams through the painted glass of the marigold
windows, staining the cusps and crumpled leaves of the window-
shafts, and the cherubs and holy-water stoups below. . . . Have you
not heard the sound of church-bells, as I promised,—mysterious
sounds from the Past and Future, as from the belfries outside the
cathedral,—even such a mournful, mellow, watery peal of bells as is
heard sometimes at sea, from cities afar off below the horizon?"
(*Hyperion*, VIII, 243–44.)

10. MS journal entry, dated Oct. 2, 1838, CHP. The Longfellow
family has refused me permission to quote it.

Longfellow was conscious of his inconsistency and his weakness, as
he revealed so many times in *Hyperion*. Consider one instance,
in which the Baron laughs at him for saying that he has no hope:

" 'But are you sure the case is utterly hopeless?'

" 'Utterly! utterly!'

" 'And yet I perceive you have not laid aside all hope. You still
flatter yourself that the lady's heart may change. The great secret
of happiness consists not in enjoying, but in renouncing. But it is
hard, very hard. Hope has as many lives as a cat or a king.' "
(*Hyperion*, VIII, 240.)

11. MS journal entry, dated Oct. 6, 1838, CHP.

How thoroughly he understood himself, one may determine in this case by consulting *Hyperion* again:

"Do not think you have gained the mastery yet. You are only riding at anchor here in an eddy of the stream; you will soon be swept away again in the mighty current and whirl of accident. Do not trust this momentary calm. I know you better than you know yourself. There is something Faust-like in you; you would fain grasp the highest and the deepest, and reel from desire to enjoyment, and in enjoyment languish for desire. When a momentary change of feeling comes over you, you think the change permanent, and thus live in constant self-deception." (*Hyperion*, VIII, 160–61.)

12. As I have already pointed out in the "Introduction," this passage which I here quote from the *Life* (I, 300) is inaccurately quoted, from Longfellow's original. Samuel Longfellow very thoughtfully corrected his brother's incorrect remembrance of Coleridge's line. Because the family has required me to remove the original letter from my text, and has only reluctantly given me permission to paraphrase it, I am obliged thus to relinquish the use of this extremely important and self-revealing letter to Greene, dated Oct. 22, 1838. The two and one-half printed pages drawn from this letter in the *Life* (I, 300–302) illustrate my statement in the "Introduction" concerning the harm which may be done to a letter when passages are omitted to such an extent that the original tone of the letter is vitiated. Furthermore, the text as quoted in the *Life* contains many undesignated omissions and telescoped sentences.

13. MS journal entries, CHP.

14. *Idem.*

15. *Idem.* During the entire writing of *Hyperion*, loyal Felton had frequently served as critic and editor. Even after the manuscript was in the hands of the printer, final changes were made at Felton's suggestion. In leaving one new change at the press, Longfellow left a note for Folsom, chief editor of the University Press:

"July 1. Felton says we shall want hereafter a Bowdler to publish a *family* Edition of the work. As to the *blind* beggars on p. 106 he thinks they ought to be prosecuted for indecent exposures of their persons. I have thrown a cloak upon them." (Folsom Papers, BPL.)

In truth, Felton's greatest fear was that the author's bold indiscretions might lead Longfellow himself to make indecent self-exposure!

16. *Hyperion*, VIII, 316.

17. *Ibid.*, 316, 318.

18. *Ibid.*, 326–28.

19. See page 223.

20. MS, dated July 23, 1839. Notice how this passage of the letter is toned down and telescoped in the *Life*, I, 327. I have quoted one

brief passage from Hatfield, 70; other passages which I had intended
to quote have been removed at the request of the Longfellow family.

21. In the Boston *Mercantile Journal* for Sept. 27, 1839, a long
review opened the way for slander with this beginning:

"The hero is young, he has lost 'the friend of his youth,' whose
death is declared in the curious assertion, 'the bough had broken
"under the burden of unripe fruit;" '—whether his wife or his lady-
love, does not yet appear."

Felton's spirited reply, "Hyperion to a Satyr," was published in
another newspaper, the *Boston Courier*, for Oct. 2, 1839.

22. Livingston, 24–25.

23. MS, dated Jan. 2, 1840, CHP. Notice how neatly Samuel Longfellow robs this letter of its intended value in the *Life*, I, 342.

24. Hatfield, 70. This printed quotation from the journal entry is
incomplete; but I have been unable to quote from the original journal
entry (dated April 24, 1840), because the Longfellow family has refused me permission. The Dante reference is to the *Inferno*, Canto
III, line 51: "Let us not speak of them, but look, and pass."

CHAPTER XXV: NEW LONGING FOR FREEDOM

To keep a unified narrative in the preceding chapter, I omitted
many references to matters not directly concerned with the story of
Paul Flemming and Mary Ashburton. This chapter, considering those
omitted matters of literary interests, friendships, and college problems, from the fall of 1838 to the fall of 1839, runs parallel in time
to the preceding chapter—adds substance to the picture without
advancing the narrative.

1. MS journal entry, dated March 6, 1839, CHP.

2. Orestes A. Brownson, in the *Boston Quarterly Review* for January, 1840. The review contains specific criticism of the love story
in *Hyperion:*

"Then to me the direct relation in which we are brought to the
author is unpleasing. Had he but idealized his tale, or put on the veil
of poetry! But as it is, we are embarrassed by his extreme com-
municativeness, and wonder that a man, who seems in other respects
to have a mind of delicate texture, could write a letter about his
private life to a public on which he has as yet established no claim.
. . . Indeed this book will not add to the reputation of its author,
which stood so fair before its publication."

3. MS, undated, but written in September, 1839, CHP.

4. In a MS letter to his father, dated April 30, 1838 (CHP), Longfellow wrote:

"The Article on Anglo-Saxon Literature was finished last week.
It is long and elaborate; and I think will interest and amuse you. I do

not give a dry review of the Dictionary; but after mentioning it with due praise, go on to show what there is in the Literature of the language to induce people to study it, and consequently buy the Dictionary. . . . Well for me, was it that I was prepared for the task by previous study of some years ago." See also page 261.

5. MS journal entry, dated March 28, 1839, CHP.

6. MS journal entry, dated June 27, 1840, CHP.

7. MS, dated Oct. 25, 1840, CHP.

8. MS journal entry, dated April 1, 1840.

9. MS, dated Portland, Aug. 6, 1838, CHP. Compare with the *Life*, I, 292–93.

10. MS, dated Aug. 6, 1838, CHP.

11. MS journal entry, dated Oct. 31, 1838, CHP.

12. MS, dated Jan. 12, 1839, CHP.

13. MS, Longfellow to his father, dated April 30, 1838, CHP.

14. These titles are given in Longfellow's journal. See the *Life*, I, 277, 278, 282. In a letter to Clara Crowninshield, dated July 28, 1838, Longfellow wrote:

"Emerson continues to make a stir. Not long ago he preached a most extraordinary sermon here; concerning which the Reverend Dean Palfrey said that 'what in it was not folly was impiety!'—oh! After all, it was only a stout *humanitarian* discourse: in which Christ and Göthe were mentioned together as great philosophers." (MS, owned by Carroll A. Wilson, New York City.)

15. MS journal entry, March 8, 1838, CHP. See also *Life*, *I*, 277–78.

16. MS, journal entry, dated March 28, 1838.

17. Hall, "Longfellow's Letters," *Putnam's*, III, 42 (Oct., 1907).

18. Anonymous review of *Hyperion*, in the Boston *Mercantile Journal* for Sept. 27, 1839.

19. MS, C. C. Little & Co. to Longfellow, dated April 27, 1838, CHP.

Longfellow's early interest in Tennyson may be gathered from an undated letter from him to Frances Appleton, MS, CHP. It must have been written in 1837–38.

"Madonna Francesca,

"Fearing I may not find you at home this bright morning I take the liberty of writing this, to tell you what a delightful day I passed with you on Monday; and to say how much I wish these scraps of antiquated song may please you.

"The Ballad of Agincourt is old. The other piece, though somewhat 'masked like hoar antiquity,' is modern. Yet how quaint and sweet.

"Did you ever read Tennison's Poems? He too is quaint, and at times so wondrously beautiful in his expressions, that even the nicest ear can ask no richer melody:—and the most lively imagination no lovlier picture, nor more true. For instance, what words could better describe the falling of those silver streams in the Lauterbrünnen Valley, than these two lines from page 109.

> A land of streams; some like a downward smoke,
> Slow-dropping veils of thinnest lawn, did go.

Or the description of Rosalind on p. 121.

> To whom the slope and stream of life,
> The life before, the life behind,
> In the ear, from far and near,
> Shineth musically clear.

Did not the cold night-air after the play, give you a cold?
"Most sincerely yʳˢ,

"H. W. LONGFELLOW."

20. Information drawn from unpublished letters and journal entries which the Longfellow family has refused me permission to quote.

21. A direct quotation, given in a letter from Longfellow to his father, dated March 8, 1840, MS, CHP.

Sarah Champney Lowell (1771–1851) was a half-sister to the father of James Russell Lowell.

22. MS, Anne Pierce to Longfellow, dated May 8, 1840, CHP.

Anne Pierce's loneliness after the early death of her husband was a bond which drew brother and sister even closer together. On August 4, 1841, Longfellow wrote in his journal (CHP):

"I sit mornings in Annie's chamber. She is out of town. But here in this chamber she has gathered the wrecks of her first great venture on Life's ocean. Returned again to harbor:—all lost, save hope and heart. Around me are George's books in their cases;—the busts of Milton and Byron:—and a little cast of a child folding a lap-dog to its bosom. On the table where I write are books of devotion, and Commentaries on the Gospel; and the Life of our Saviour. Before me the bed, on which so many weary nights have been passed in tears for the departed—in dreams of that happiness which can return no more on earth. O thou pious and afflicted soul!—It shall not be long!"

23. MS journal entry, dated Nov. 5, 1838, CHP. A journal entry for Sept. 4, 1838, sums the matter up:

"I think I was never more dejected, than now in this bright beginning of the glorious Autumn. The main-spring of Life seems to be broken, or so weak within me that it does not recover itself after that cruel pressure. It is just a year since the Appletons returned. What a difference between my feelings *now* and *then*."

24. MS journal entry, dated Sept. 1, 1838, CHP.
25. MS journal entry, dated Sept. 10, 1838, CHP.
26. MS journal entry, dated Oct. 16, 1838, CHP.
27. MS journal entry, dated Oct. 17, 1838, CHP.
28. MS journal entry, dated Oct. 19, 1838, CHP.
29. *Idem.*
30. Harvard College Papers.
31. MS, dated Aug. 21, 1839, CHP.
32. MS, dated Sept. 1, 1839, CHP. Quoted with confusing omissions, but with the verbatim vote of the Corporation, in the *Life*, I, 330.
33. MS, dated Sept., 1839, CHP. Although the day of the month is not given, internal evidence suggests that the letter was written just before Sept. 10—the day he wrote in his diary this attempt to be casual:

"A letter from Sam Ward; says that Cogswell is going to Europe with young Astor, and not I. Well, that is cruel, after asking me! No matter." (MS, CHP.)

34. MS, dated Sept. 21, 1839, CHP.
35. MS, Harvard College Papers.

Chapter XXVI: Literary Shop Talk

In this chapter, I have been able to concentrate on Longfellow's mental and spiritual conflicts by omitting references to certain aspects (such as the writing of individual poems like "Excelsior" and "The Village Blacksmith") which have already received adequate treatment in the *Life* or in the notes to the *Complete Writings*. When nothing new could be drawn from a repetition of material already presented, I have consistently avoided it.

1. MS, Longfellow to Greene, dated Jan. 2, 1840, CHP.
2. MS, CHP. The autobiographical significance of this version is clarified by a comparison of these two early lines:

"This saved me from the frenzy of despair,
   The apathy of grief."

with the lines which displaced them in the final, printed version (*Complete Writings*, I, 17–18):

"The fountain of perpetual peace flows there,—
   From those deep cisterns flows."

3. Original MS, CHP.
Compare the ideas in the "Prelude" with those in the climactic pages of *Hyperion* (VIII, 319):

"Why have I not made these sage reflections, this wise resolve sooner? Can such a simple result spring only from long and intricate process of experience! Alas! it is not till Time, with reckless hand, has torn out half the leaves from the Book of Human Life, to light the fires of passion with, from day to day, that man begins to see that the leaves which remain are few in number, and to remember, faintly at first, and then more clearly, that upon the earlier pages of that book was written a story of happy innocence, which he would fain read over again. Then comes listless irresolution, and the inevitable inaction of despair; or else the firm resolve to record upon the leaves that still remain a more noble history than the child's story with which the book began."

Yet notice that Longfellow's idealized and romantic autobiographical sketch in the "Prelude" is quite at odds with the facts. He could never live for long in that kind of real world "where the din of iron branches sounds." Even as a poet, he soon ceased drawing his materials out of his own heart—out of his own sorrows and joys. Almost immediately after the publication of *Voices*, and throughout his life, he was hunting for subject matter. And more and more he found his themes outside himself—in the historical records of his own country or of Europe. Consider how few of his poems after the "Psalms" are subjective lyrics.

Thus, the delineations of autobiographical value in the "Prelude" are most accurate when most contradictory. Specifically, the last verse might be stated thus: "As a poet, you and I must sing of how to pursue life—and of how to escape it"!

4. Quoted from Edgar Allan Poe's review of *Voices*, which appeared in *Burton's Gentleman's Magazine* for Feb., 1840. (Poe had previously reviewed *Hyperion* in *Burton's Magazine* for Oct., 1839.) Longfellow protested that the criticism was unfair, in a letter to Ward, written some time between Feb. 10 and 27, 1840: "My brother told me yesterday that some paragraphs had appeared in some New York paper saying I stole the idea of the 'Midnight Mass' from Tennyson. Absurd. I did not even know that he had written a piece on this subject." (Hall, "Longfellow's Letters to Samuel Ward," *Putnam's*, III, 42 (Oct., 1907).) The evidence is somewhat against Longfellow, however, on this score, for we have proof that he had in his possession a copy of Tennyson's *Poems*, London, 1833, which contains "The Death of the Old Year." See note 19 of Chapter XXV.

5. MS, dated July 5, 1840. Owned by W. T. H. Howe.

6. MS, dated July 18, 1840, CHP.

7. The first poem for which there is record of Clark's payment ($15) is "The Village Blacksmith" published in the *Knickerbocker*, XVI, 419 (Nov., 1840).

8. Frank Luther Mott, *A History of American Magazines*, New York, 1930, 510. This news item was published in the *New York Mirror*, to which Longfellow subscribed.

9. MS copy of "Midnight Mass for the Dying Year," with a marginal note to Clark, dated Sept. 18, 1839. Pennsylvania Historical Society.

10. MS, dated Jan. 2, 1840, CHP.

11. *Life*, I, 343.

12. *Complete Writings*, VIII, 86.

13. MS journal entry for Dec. 4, 1838, CHP.

14. MS, dated Feb. 3, 1840. CHP.

15. MS, dated Jan. 7, 1840, CHP. Compressed in the *Life*, I, 344.

16. See page 162.

17. See page 162 and note.

18. See pages 188–89.

19. See pages 241, 251.

20. MS, dated May 28, 1840, CHP.

21. MS, journal entry, dated March 26, 1838, CHP.

22. MS, dated March 28, 1838, CHP.

23. MS, dated June 2, 1838, CHP.

24. MS, dated June 15, 1842, CHP. Eventually, Felton was able to sing part way through his "*nunc dimittis*," for S. G. Howe married Julia Ward.

25. This brief attempt at love is mentioned in his journal. It is also a familiar tale, told with delightful additions, among members of the Ward-Howe family, even today. For one version, see Maud Howe Elliott, *Uncle Sam Ward and His Circle*, New York, 1938, p. 375. Two journal references are:

"May 5, 1840. A dull day, clouds threatening rain. But I shall see perhaps the light of Sumner's countenance, and of my dear Anna, light as a daughter of the air." (She was expected to arrive in Boston from New York, with her brother Sam.)

"May 18, 1840. Sam Ward came out, and we had a long chat. After lecture went to town to dine with him; and see him start for N. York. Sent Swiss basket to my dear little Annie. . . . Sat by the open window till midnight, weaving fond, foolish dreams of one who is far away, and not dreaming of me." (MSS, CHP.)

The last sentence seems to fit a young lady in New York better than another young lady who was not dreaming of him in Boston.

26. A complete account of this return trip is given in the *Life*, I, 347–48.

27. Quoted in the *Autograph* (New York), I, 122 (1912); also described in the catalogue of sale, *Anderson Galleries*, for March 27, 1916, lot No. 277.

CHAPTER XXVII: INNER CONFLICT

These last two chapters intend to make clear that as the inner conflict continued, the struggle became more of a burden than Longfellow was able to handle, mentally, nervously, physically. To understand this sympathetically is to appreciate that the third trip to
Europe was actually made because Longfellow had failed to solve his
many-sided unhappiness.

1. MS journal entry, dated Dec. 11, 1839, CHP.

2. MS journal entry, dated Oct. 4, 1839, CHP.

3. MS, dated June 20, 1840, CHP. Another letter from Ward
refers to Longfellow's fastidious taste in dress and makes fun of it:
"I never before heard of a man's being afraid to come & see a friend
for fear of being seduced to run up a bill at his Tailor's. To my eye
there is little of the Delilah about Franer's & his wares for a Sampson
like you. I mean to send you a waistcoat however & some wine. I
have an 'Endymion Waistcoat'—too gay for me but well suited to
your temper. You can put it on when you go to see Miriam again
for I learn that Sears' servant hussey positively took us for ruffians."
(MS, dated Sept. 17, 1841, CHP.)

4. *Life*, I, 353. Information drawn from MS journal entry, dated
May 2, 1840. The Longfellow family has refused me permission to
quote the original. In the *Life*, Samuel Longfellow has performed
another one of those successful operations in which the passage dies.

5. MS, dated Aug. 3, 1840, CHP.

6. MS journal entry for June 4, 1846, CHP.

7. MS journal entry, dated March 28, 1840.

8. MS, dated July 8, 1840, CHP.

9. *Complete Writings*, I, 122, 123.

10. *Life*, I, 365.

11. MS, dated Oct. 4, 1840, CHP.

12. Quoted in MS, Longfellow to his father, dated Dec. 20, 1840,
CHP.

13. MS, dated Philadelphia, Jan. 29, 1841. Sumner Correspondence, Harvard College Library.

14. MS, dated New York, Feb. 3, 1841, CHP.

15. MS journal entries, for March 7, 11, 12, 13, 1840, CHP.

16. MS, Longfellow to his father, dated March 21, 1841, CHP.

17. Even Ward, who knew all of his troubles, did not think of
him as a gloomy friend, as is shown by the teasing letter Ward wrote
him on August 13, 1841:
" 'Is not Mr. Longfellow a tall thin man, quite emaciated, & has he
not great, dark melancholy eyes with a *deep* expression?' said a lady
to me the other day—'No Ma'am, he is as round as a barrel and as rosy
cheeked as yourself & his eyes

" 'Oh they resemble
Blue Water Lilies &c &c'

" 'Dear me, is it possible? But isn't he often very unhappy?'

" 'Are you?' 'Yes, no, not exactly, you know one has blue moments sometimes—heigho! but that isn't what I mean. Does he not sit abstractedly with his eyes fixed—musing mournfully to the Tune of the Psalm of Life?' 'Not that I ever saw Ma'am. He is generally merry & cheerful—a good deal more so than myself—likes a smiling chat & good glass of wine with a friend or ½ a dozen.' 'Dear me.' 'You must know,' continued I, 'that the Psalm of Life was composed as an exorcism against all bad spirits, blue devils & others— It was sung to cheer on the unhappy and not to chime in with their wailing.' "

In answer, Longfellow wrote on Aug. 21, 1841:

"How could you deceive that lady so, by saying I was *not* 'a tall thin man, quite emaciated'? I will never forgive you for telling her I am 'round as a barrel'; and I will tell the next woman, who inquires about you, that you are only five feet, three; with a white swelling on your knee, and the erysipelas in your face; and if she does not say 'Dear me!' to that, then *dear-mes* have risen.

"Nevertheless, I am melancholy. . . ." (MSS, CHP.)

18. Henry Marion Hall, "Longfellow's Letters to Samuel Ward," *Putnam's Monthly Magazine*, III, 42 (Oct., 1907).

19. MS, dated Sept. 1, 1841, CHP.

20. MS, dated Sept. 17, 1841, CHP.

21. MS, dated May 28, 1840, CHP.

22. MS, dated Oct. 24, 1841, CHP.

23. Henry Marion Hall, 171.

24. Henry Marion Hall, 302.

25. MS, dated Feb. 1, 1842, CHP.

26. MS, dated Feb. 17, 1842, CHP.

27. MS, dated Feb. 25, 1842, CHP.

28. George E. Woodberry, "Lowell's Letters to Poe," *Scribner's Magazine*, XVI, 172 (Aug., 1894).

29. MS, dated Jan. 2, 1840, CHP.

30. Quoted in my more detailed study, "Longfellow Sells *The Spanish Student*," *American Literature*, 6, 141–50 (May, 1934). The $150 was paid promptly.

CHAPTER XXVIII: PEACE

So thoroughly has Professor Hatfield recorded the essential facts concerning Longfellow's third visit to Germany that it is unnecessary to cover the ground again. I have continued to concentrate particularly on his inner, rather than outer, problems. I have touched very lightly on Longfellow's friendship with Dickens because that has already been treated with sufficient clarity in the *Life* and in Payne's *Dickens Days in Boston*, mentioned below.

1. MS, Longfellow to his sister Anne, dated May 21, 1843, CHP.

2. MS, dated March 9, 1842, CHP.

3. MS, dated April 23, 1842, CHP. See *Life*, I, 401.

4. MS, dated Marienberg, July 20, 1842, CHP.

5. *Life*, I, 407. The letter is a long one. Another letter to Mrs. Norton from Marienberg is quoted in the *Life*, I, 413.

6. *Life*, I, 417.

7. Hatfield, 91.

8. Hatfield, 91, 96.

9. An account of this visit is given in Edward F. Payne, *Dickens Days in Boston*, Boston and New York, 1927, 122–26. A page of a letter, Longfellow to Greene, dated May 28, 1840, is reproduced in this book, facing p. 124, because it shows Longfellow's drawing of the plans of his rooms at the Craigie House. See also the *Life*, I, 397–98.

10. *Life*, I, 398.

11. *Life*, I, 418.

12. *Life*, I, 433.

13. J. T. Hatfield, "The Longfellow-Freiligrath Correspondence," *PMLA*, XLVIII, 1244 (Dec., 1933).

14. See p. 202 and note.

15. *Life*, I, 431.

16. I have quoted the review entire! *The Dial*, Vol. III, No. 3, p. 415 (Jan., 1843).

17. *Life*, I, 430.

Although many of the abolitionists did not feel that Longfellow had spoken with force and courage enough, Elihu Burritt was satisfied. One of his letters offers a good instance of the bitter hatred vented by the worst of the abolitionists:

"I have just learned with pious indignation, that your beautiful *Poems on Slavery*, which deserve to be republished & read in heaven —have been almost entirely suppressed from circulation by that pusillanimous, niggardly, dough-faced servility to Southern sentiment, which has enslaved the North with a meaner bondage than negros suffer at the South. I have no doubt that you will understand & appreciate the reason why even your beautiful apostrophe to *Channing* could hardly secure 300 readers of your *Slave's Dream*, through the whole country, when a thousand copies of the work ought to be sold in Cambridge. It is with the persuasion that you feel with us unwilling that this snaky, blear-eyed prejudice, like the serpent around Laocoon, shall crush within its pestiferous convolutions every liberty-breathing genius of this free land—that I venture to ask if you will not give us that little volume of poems, after you have ceased to realize or expect any profit from it." (MS, dated Worcester, Nov. 6, 1843; CHP.) Seven of the poems were reprinted by the New England Anti-Slavery Tract Association, in pamphlet form.

18. MS, Alleyne Otis to J. F. Fisher, dated Boston, March 20, 1840, CHP.

19. MS, dated Rome, May 5, 1840, CHP.

Catharine Maria Sedgwick, author of *Redwood* and *Hope Leslie*, published *Letters from Abroad to Kindred at Home* (New York, 1841) after her return from Europe. A native of Stockbridge, Mass., Miss Sedgwick was intimately acquainted with the Appleton family.

20. MS, Frances Appleton to her cousin, J. A. Jewett, dated Boston, Nov. 4, 1839, CHP.

21. Charles Sumner, who knew the Appleton sisters well, thought Fanny too offish in quite another sense. On July 15, 1842 (while Longfellow was in Europe) Sumner wrote to Hillard:

"I drove the Lyells out in a barouche to see Fanny Appleton & Miss Austin. These maidens were at Miss Appleton's, & we drove there. Fanny was engaged in archery—a game at which she has played too much." (MS, Harvard College Library.)

Nevertheless, Frances Appleton wrote to her aunt, Miss Martha Gold, in announcing her engagement to Longfellow, under date of May 16, 1843:

"My heart has always been of tenderer stuff than any body believed and it needed not many propitious circumstances to set it visibly flowing." (MS, CHP.)

22. MS journal entry, dated April 13, 1844—the first anniversary of the event. The Longfellow family has refused me permission to quote the original entry, but it may be found in fragmentary form in Hatfield, 70.

23. MS, CHP. The date of the postmark on the envelope containing this letter is "April 19"; but according to the calendar for 1843, Monday of that week fell on April 17—the date I have supplied. If Frances Appleton held this letter for two days before mailing it, there is room for interesting speculation as to her hesitancy.

24. MS, CHP. This lovely little note makes a perfect climax to the seven years which Longfellow had endured. For that reason, I am particularly sorry that the Longfellow family has refused me permission to quote it.

25. MS journal entry, dated May 10, 1844—another first anniversary recollection. The entire entry reads thus:

"The Tenth of May! Day to be recorded with sunbeams! Day of light and love! The day of our engagement; when in the bright morning—one year ago—I received Fanny's note, and walked to town,

amid the blossoms and sunshine and song of birds, with my heart full
of gladness and my eyes full of tears! I walked with the speed of
an arrow—too restless to sit in a carriage—too impatient and fearful of encountering anyone!—Oh Day forever blessed; that ushered
in this *Vita Nova* of happiness!—How full the year has been!"
(CHP.)

26. MS, dated May 11, 1843, CHP.

27. MS, to J. A. Jewett, dated Boston, May 23, 1843, CHP.
Frances Appleton's additions, at the end of the letter (but not
quoted here), are less rhapsodic—possibly because she remembered
writing to this same cousin concerning Longfellow and describing
him as "a certain impertinent friend of mine." See the passage documented in note 20 of this chapter.

28. Higginson, 172.

29. MS, undated, CHP.

30. MS, Anne Longfellow Pierce to Elizabeth Poor, dated Portland, Aug. 15, 1843, CHP. All the details of the wedding as given
here are drawn from Anne's long and minute description.

31. Edward L. Pierce, *Memoir and Letters of Charles Sumner*,
Boston, 1881, 2 vols., II, 263. Letter to Francis Lieber, with whom
Sumner had been waging a very heated epistolary war, over the
merits of Longfellow's poems.

Lieber also spoke his mind on Longfellow and *Hyperion*. In a
letter to Sumner, dated Feb. 27, 1842, Lieber answered Sumner's
reference to *Hyperion*:

"As to the 'stern-chaser' I thought so too when I read it, and him
that made, at least published it, none the better for it. It is neither
delicate nor fair to make a girl talked of, especially as she has been
talked of in connexion with Hyperion. Enough in all conscience. It
is the old story: 'Beware of mad dogs and poets'; they make free with
every thing and every one."

(MS, Huntington Library, California. I am indebted to Professor
Theodore Hornberger for calling Lieber's letters in the Huntington
Library to my attention.)

32. Roger Wolcott, *The Correspondence of William Hickling
Prescott*, Boston and New York, 1925, 369. Letter from a former
Boston resident, Mrs. Fanny Calderon de la Barca, to Prescott, dated
Edinburgh, June 16, 1843.

33. MS, CHP.

34. Frances Appleton's original sketch book is in the Craigie
House.

The reader will recall that Paul Flemming, in *Hyperion*, finds essays
as well as sketches in this book of Mary Ashburton, and proceeds to
read one or two. In the original manuscript draft of *Hyperion*, an
unpublished passage (perhaps one of those pruned by the cautious

Felton) reveals that Longfellow had intended to let Flemming say, upon finishing his perusal of Mary Ashburton's sketch book:

"I know not what others may think, but in my opinion a young lady of twenty, who can sketch thus, should not show her sketches to a young man of thirty, who has a reverence for intellect, unless she means he shall fall in love with her!"

INDEX

Although no separate bibliography is given, all book-sources directly used are listed in the index under author or short title. Reference to full documentation of a short title is placed first in the sequence of page numbers which follow the short title.